FOOTBALL CAPTAINS

The All-Ireland Winners

▼ 1943   FOOTBALL CAPTAINS   1993 ▲

FOOTBALL CAPTAINS

The All-Ireland Winners

BRIAN CARTHY

WOLFHOUND PRESS

Dedication

To my wife Trish and our son John Brian

First published 1993
WOLFHOUND PRESS Ltd,
68 Mountjoy Square,
Dublin 1.

British Library Cataloguing in Publication Data
Carthy, Brian
    Football Captains:All-Ireland Winners
    I. Title
    796.334092

    ISBN 0-86327-394-7

Photographs ©
We are grateful to the following for supplying us with photographs:
JIM CONNOLLY, Dublin, for photographs on pages 17, 19, 22, 25, 28, 33, 36, 39, 45, 47, 50, 53, 55, 59, 61, 64, 68, 70, 73, 76, 79, 83, 85, 91, 93, 96, 98, 100, 104 (bottom), 110, 112, 114, 116 (bottom), 118, 124, 127, 130, 133, 138, 142, 147, 151, 152, 155, 157, 163, 164, 173, 178, 180 (bottom), 191 (bottom), 194, 196 (top), 200, 206, 209 (bottom left), 212, 218, 223, 231 (also inset), 277, 292.
LENSMAN, Dublin, for photographs on pages 104 (top), 107, 116 (top), 172, 177, 182, 191 (top), 192, 196 (centre and bottom), 201, 203, 204 (top), 209 (top and bottom right), 226, 234, 236, 237, 243 (top and bottom), 250, 251, 252, 256, 260, 261, 263.
OLIVER McVEIGH, Sportsfile: page 10
INPHO, Dublin, for the front cover photographs, page 2 (top), p.25 (bottom), and all the colour photographs except the following: page i bottom Karen Scott; p.iii bottom *The Donegal Democrat*; p.xvi bottom The Mercier Press

We also gratefully acknowledge the individual captains who supplied photographs (pages 20, 159, 165, 167, 169, 180 (top), 185, 188, 215, 253, 258, 266, 280, 301, 305, 309).
Our thanks to individuals and institutions who assisted in locating material, including Eamonn Mongey, Peter Brady of Cavan, Paddy Carolan, Kevin Beahan, Liam O'Connor, Tom Lyons; The Irish Nationwide Building Society, The National Library of Ireland, Dublin Public Libraries, RTE, *The Irish Press*, *The Irish Independent*, *The Donegal Democrat*, *The Cork Examiner*, *The Kerryman*, *The Anglo-Celt*, *The Western People*. Every effort has been made to identify and contact owners of copyright material. In instances where this has not been possible, we request that the owners contact the publishers.

Photographs on page 2: *Top:* Henry Downey, Derry captain, 1993 All-Ireland. *Bottom left to right:* Jim Quigley (6) and Eddie Boyle, Louth, Jimmy Murray (captain) and Phelim Murray, Roscommon

Cover design: Jan de Fouw
Typesetting: Wolfhound Press and Books Ireland
Printed by: Colour Books, Dublin

Contents

JOE LENNON	Down	1968	*166*
PETER DARBY	Meath	1967	*174*
ENDA COLLERAN	Galway	1965, 1966	*181*
JOHN DONNELLAN	Galway	1964	*190*
DES FOLEY	Dublin	1963	*193*
SEÁN ÓG SHEEHY	Kerry	1962	*199*
PADDY DOHERTY	Down	1961	*205*
KEVIN MUSSEN	Down	1960	*211*
MICK O'CONNELL	Kerry	1959	*217*
KEVIN HEFFERNAN	Dublin	1958	*225*
DERMOT O'BRIEN	Louth	1957	*233*
JACK MANGAN	Galway	1956	*240*
JOHN DOWLING	Kerry	1955	*245*
PETER McDERMOTT	Meath	1954	*252*
JAS MURPHY	Kerry	1953	*259*
MICK HIGGINS	Cavan	1952	*265*
SEÁN FLANAGAN	Mayo	1950, 1951	*271*
BRIAN SMYTH	Meath	1949	*279*
JOHN JOE O'REILLY	Cavan	1947, 1948	*284*
PADDY KENNEDY	Kerry	1946	*289*
TADHGO CROWLEY	Cork	1945	*294*
JIMMY MURRAY	Roscommon	1943, 1944	*298*
JOE FITZGERALD	Dublin	1942	*306*
BILL DILLON	Kerry	1941	*311*
DAN SPRING	Kerry	1940	*315*

Preface

What better way to know about the most popular game in Ireland than through the eyes of the special players who captained their counties to victory on All-Ireland final day? That was the thought that occurred to me in September 1992 as I sat in the RTE commentary box in the Hogan Stand and listened to Anthony Molloy's impassioned speech before thousands of green and gold-clad supporters swarming over the pitch moments after Donegal had won their first All-Ireland senior title.

There and then, I made up my mind to find out more about those men — the Anthony Molloys and Paddy O'Rourkes and all their distinguished predecessors — men who had surely turned their dream into reality. I was thinking then in particular of my home county: Roscommon's Jimmy Murray was one of only six to raise the Sam Maguire Cup twice. So I began with Jimmy Murray in 1943, a convenient half century, but later decided to complete the decade. The book, therefore, runs from 1993 back to 1940.

Little did I realise then the size of the task I was about to venture! Soon, I was travelling the highways and boreens from Valentia Island to Killybegs, from Dublin to Galway and all points in between. Thousands of miles but also thousands of memories.

Heartfelt thanks to the captains for enriching my life with story and anecdote. My research became a rediscovery of the hospitality and the art of conversation that we hear repeatedly noted by visitors but often fail to notice ourselves. It was fascinating to listen to these modest sportsmen reminisce and philosophise about teammates, opponents, tactics, organisation, motivation and the great characters on and off the field. It was extra special to see them relive moments of high significance in their lives when football was the centre of their world.

This book underlines the important role of the captain as a team player and as a leader. It is intriguing to discover the varied understandings of the role: a famous captain of the fifties told me: 'The performance of the team at its best is far greater than the sum of the individual abilities of fifteen players. I believe a captain can contribute. Some certainly have done so. Before the start of our All-Ireland winning year, I gathered the forwards together and told them that no team in Ireland would score more than ten points against us, giving them a scoring target minimum. We achieved it.'

Another speaks of the need to 'feel confident enough that other people have confidence in you'; the need to 'balance the people that you can encourage ... that you can criticise and that you leave alone' in order to bring out the best in each player.

These interviews showed me Gaelic games, vigorous, alive and enriching: one captain in his Sunday suit racing across Croke Park less than half an hour before the match; another strolling alone down O'Connell Street the night before the final, unrecognised by hordes of his own supporters; a captain being handed a miraculous

7

medal on his way into Croke Park and yet another collecting the Cup in his very first game of the year. There are hundreds of moments to savour: the captain tempted to ask his brother to take over the job just minutes before the game began; the winning and losing captains coming face to face under the Hogan Stand after the final; the captain who had his speech stored in his stocking and threw it away at half-time because the game was going against his team; another who compared himself to 'a frightened rabbit looking for somewhere to run'; in the early hours of Monday morning a captain kicking the hallowed Sam Maguire Cup back to his goalkeeper, commenting: 'that's what the blood, sweat and tears are all about. There it is now'!

Then there is the famous captain who, as he was leading his team onto Croke Park, spotted his neighbour and sat down beside him on the sideline for a chat; the captain who was back on his island home on Sunday night without the cup; the captain who looked up at Micheál Ó Hehir in the commentary box and determined to 'do or die for his own village'; the man who lost the famous cup; and the Kerry man who captained Dublin, and although spending almost his entire life in the Kingdom still shouts for the men in navy and blue.

In addition to deciding to interview each captain, and provide statistics on his career in the 'fact file' box, I have also included action photos from many finals and other games, the full line out of every team that won an All-Ireland since 1940 and the substitutes used on All-Ireland final day. I am deeply indebted to the many individuals and organisations who helped me to compile this information, and to locate and caption official team photographs and historic action shots.

Football has been part of my own life since I was a child growing up in the townland of Ballymore, at the foothills of Sliabh Bán near Strokestown in County Roscommon. The deeds of former Roscommon greats like Jimmy Murray and Gerry O'Malley were part of every football discussion. Soon, I not only listened but began to read at every opportunity about the famous players of the day — Mickey Kearns, Mattie McDonagh, Joe Lennon, Paddy Doherty, Mick O'Connell, Enda Colleran and of course Dermot Earley who wore the primrose and blue with such pride and distinction for so many years. Those household names, together with hundreds of other footballing greats created my own dream. The great Micheál Ó Hehir was then the voice of sport, and those vibrant living commentaries combined with the games I watched and the talk I heard to inspire my childhood ambitions. Suddenly, I was out in the fields near home kicking a football and doing imaginary commentaries on imaginary games. Like most youngsters I dreamed of representing my county in an All-Ireland final.

Every All-Ireland winning captain is a hero not only in his own county but wherever football aficionados congregate to talk of the great games and the great players. My aim has been to create a unique portrait of fifty years of Gaelic football, and a fitting tribute to these heroes. Meeting those men, so generous with their time and their memories, has indeed been an honour and a privilege.

Brian Carthy

Henry DOWNEY

Derry Captain 1993

'We decided not to give them a goal, absolutely no way. Under no account should Cork score a goal and Derry should have a good start. That was the plan. Derry made a terrible start and after me preaching and shouting that Cork shouldn't score a goal, my own man Joe Kavanagh scores a goal. Time to hide!'

HENRY DOWNEY was in a jubilant mood when I met up with him in Ryan's pub in Ballyronan a few miles outside Toome just three days after he became the first Derry man to raise the Sam Maguire Cup. He was still savouring the occasion and assured me it would continue for some time to come. The Lavey man, his voice feeling the rigours of overuse, was surrounded by teammates Johnny McGurk, Gary Coleman, Danny Quinn, Karl Diamond and Damien Cassidy.

Football is the cornerstone of the twenty-six-year-old schoolteacher's life. He first came to prominence on the county team as a hurler. There was no tradition of football in his immediate family but his father continually encouraged his sons to get involved. Henry attended many matches with his father and admits that the player he admired most as a youngster was Anthony McGurk, whose brother Johnny won the Man of the Match Award for his superb performance in the All-Ireland final.

If Anthony McGurk was his big hero, Henry is in doubt whatsoever but that it was Adrian McGuckian who exercised the single biggest influence on his football career. Adrian was a coach in St Pat's College, Maghera and according to Henry, quite a number of the other players that featured in the 1993 All-Ireland final against Cork also owe a debt of gratitude to their influential schoolteacher.

'I remember the first time I got drafted in to the St Pat's team for the McRory Cup and I couldn't wait to play. At the first training session there was a foot of snow on the ground. But Adrian McGuckian took every one of us out to play and I kept saying to myself, "This is crazy and absolute madness". I remember Adrian saying we were out playing in such dreadful conditions because nobody else would be training. Of all the training sessions I ever had, it is that particular one that sticks out most in my

---

FACT FILE

HOME PLACE: Lavey, County Derry

BORN: 27 December 1966   CLUB: Lavey

CLUB ACHIEVEMENTS: Three County Senior Football Championship medals 1988, 1990 and 1992; two Ulster Club Championship medals in 1990 and 1992; one All-Ireland Club Championship medal in 1991; two County Minor football Championship medal in 1983 and 1984; two McRory Cup medals with St Pat's, Maghera.

INTER-COUNTY ACHIEVEMENTS: One All-Ireland Senior Football medal in 1993; one Ulster Senior Football medal in 1993; one National League medal in 1992 and one Ulster Under-21 Championship medal in 1986.

mind. It was like a sandstorm in the desert and impossible to see anything.

Henry was on the two McRory Cup-winning teams of 1983 and 1984. However St Pat's were beaten at the All-Ireland semi-final stage in '83 and lost the final to St Jarlath's the following year.

'Mark Butler scored a point with the last kick of the game to beat us in the final. We were really disappointed. After that I went to Queen's University and it was great. We never actually played in a Sigerson Cup final but I had the distinction of marking my brother Séamus in the semi-final against St Mary's. It was a strange game. He even hit me before it began! The game was played at the Queen's University Grounds and all the supporters were right along the sideline. Before the match got underway Séamus walked up to me and hit me a punch on the back. The Queen's crowd didn't realise what was going on and they were trying desperately to attract the attention of the referee. It was a very funny incident.'

Henry considers himself very lucky to have grown up in Lavey at a time when a lot of his friends like the McGurks, Scullions and the Chivers were totally dedicated to Gaelic football. 'Paddy Chivers put a lot of effort into underage teams in Lavey and he is still manager of the Lavey football team. Our biggest breakthrough was probably winning two county minor championship titles in the early eighties and the bulk of that team went on to win the All-Ireland senior club football championship. We beat Salthill of Galway in the final in 1991.' Henry feels it important also to acknowledge the contribution of John Grant who was manager of the football team in St Bridget's Primary School in Mayogall.

Henry laughed when I asked him to trace his inter-county career making the point that it was very short. He never played as a county minor. 'Éamonn Coleman was over the minor team and he didn't pick me and he hasn't apologised since,' Henry says jokingly. 'I think I deserved to be selected but Éamonn didn't think so.' In 1987 Henry had the cruel misfortune to break his leg while playing against Donegal in the first round of the Ulster under-21 Championship. He was out of football for a year. 'I

Back, left to right: Joe Brolly, Dermot Heaney, Anthony Tohill, Damien McCusker, Séamus Downey, Tony Scullion, Damien Barton, Brian McGilligan.
Front, left to right: Enda Gormley, John McGurk, Henry Downey (captain), Kieran McKeever, Gary Coleman, Fergal McCusker, Damien Cassidy.

found it very frustrating and I was probably the most crabbed person that you would ever meet during that time. I couldn't even bear to go and see Lavey play in the club championship. I stayed away completely. In 1988 I was very lucky to be chosen as captain of the Lavey team. It was a great honour for one so young. I was only twenty-two and we won the championship that year for the first time since 1977.'

But Johnny McGurk was captain when Lavey won the All-Ireland club title in 1991. It was the best thing that ever happened to the area. 'I couldn't describe to you how much that meant to all of us. It was out of this world. Bellaghy had really cornered the market at that time and had won so many club titles including the All-Ireland club championship in 1972. Suddenly out of the blue along comes a neighbouring parish that never really had any tradition at that level and we win an All-Ireland title. That was just a real special night.'

But Lavey lost out to Dungiven in the quarter-final of the Derry county championship the following year and it was a real lowpoint. As he made his way off the pitch he was approached by Éamonn Coleman who told Henry he was considering making him captain of the Derry team. It meant nothing at the time. Henry believes it was an important step for Derry to win the League title in 1992. Éamonn Coleman continually stressed the importance of winning the competition. He felt it was necessary to become accustomed to winning in Croke Park.

'It was great to beat Meath in the semi-final and then Tyrone in the final. It meant a lot but later on that year we lost in the Ulster Championship.

'To train all year and to be so well prepared and to dethrone the All-Ireland champions Down in a spectacular game at Casement Park and then to go to Clones and perform like we did was a heart break. The next day we felt pathetic. Donegal were good but they beat the worst Derry team that probably ever played. We were terrible and showed no imagination. We were very poor and very tired looking. On the day when it mattered most we were at our worst. After beating Down we probably felt we were better than we were. We had never beaten an All-Ireland winning team before that and it probably went to our heads. We took Donegal for granted and we paid the price.'

The defeat by Donegal rankled. A meeting was called soon after and as Henry explains, 'There was a lot of truth spoken. We ironed out a few wrinkles and set about beating Down in the 1993 championship. That was all. We didn't think about winning an All-Ireland. No way. Our first objective was to get over Down and that was some game. It was the only game I enjoyed this year because every other one was very close and tight.

THE 1993 DERRY TEAM

Damien McCusker

Kieran McKeever	Tony Scullion	Fergal McCusker
John McGurk	Henry Downey (Captain)	Gary Coleman

Anthony Tohill   Brian McGilligan

Dermot Heaney	Damien Barton	Damien Cassidy
Joe Brolly	Séamus Downey	Enda Gormley

Substitutes: Dermot McNicholl for Damien Cassidy; Éamonn Burns for Séamus Downey

---

'We met Monaghan in the semi-final and that was the game I was most nervous about. I hated that game. We were far the better team and had everything to lose. It was hard to raise ourselves for that match and I was worried. But we won it.'

So Derry were back in the Ulster final and the opposition they so badly wanted was awaiting them. It mattered little that Donegal were defending All-Ireland champions. Derry were determined to win. The game was ruined because of the dreadful conditions, possibly the worst ever for a championship game.

'No question about it the game should have been called off. I didn't know the pitch was so bad until I stepped onto it. I said to Kieran McKeever, "this game shouldn't be played". And it shouldn't have been played! The pitch was treacherous. If those in authority had guts the game would have been called off. If the people who were in charge were put out onto that pitch to play a game of golf, do you think they'd play? A game of cricket? Would you imagine they'd run up and down it? Do you think they'd put their best shoes into it? Yet they made players who had trained all year turn around and play on a pitch like that. They were a disgrace to allow the game go ahead. And do you know what the worst disgrace of all is? Whatever about the players, it was unforgivable to expect supporters to stand out in such dreadful weather after paying hard-earned money. It was an insult to the supporters who are the most important people in Gaelic football. Those who are in charge have a lot to answer for in allowing that game go ahead. Without fear of contradiction I would say that if that was a club league match it would have been called off. The people in charge had no guts. They were scared of losing face.

> 'First of all I'm a player,
> secondly I'm a captain,
> not the other way around.
> If you think differently
> then you're in trouble, major trouble.
>
> My role as captain was small.
> I am probably the biggest
> worrier on this team.'

'There was more pressure on Derry. This was not the Donegal team that had won the All-Ireland. They were missing five or six players through injury. So if Derry could not have beaten a Donegal team minus five or six of their best players where were they going to go?'

It was a relief more than anything else to beat Donegal. Derry had to do it or live with the consequences. Henry believes it would not have meant the same to beat any other county. They enjoyed the after match celebrations but before the night was over thoughts had turned once again to football and the quest for Sam Maguire.

Dublin provided the opposition in the All-Ireland semi-final. They had lost to Donegal in the final the previous year and they like Derry had much to prove.

'We thought we were dangerous because we had lost an Ulster final but Dublin had lost the All-Ireland final and were therefore the most dangerous team of all. The Derry supporters went through every single emotion during that game. We had lost it, we had absolutely lost it at one stage. We were five points down going in at half-time and it looked like Dublin had taken control. The scribes had probably written it. Suddenly we were back in the game. It was all down to what Mickey Moran said at half time. The quiet man spoke. He is very quiet and rarely speaks. But he just lost his head completely at half time. He had played on the Derry team in 1975 and '76 so it meant an awful lot to him to get back to Croke Park again. Suddenly it looked like Derry had given up their best ever chance and he went mad. Éamonn Coleman couldn't get a word in. It was such a shock that the players reacted. We came out in the second half a different team. It was brilliant to beat Dublin but we knew it was no achievement to get to the final. Down and Donegal had won the previous years. So what if Derry got to the final! We had to win it!'

Henry recalls that the weeks leading up to the Ulster final and the All-Ireland semi-final flew by but that the weeks before the All-Ireland final seemed an eternity. The whole county was football crazy. Nobody contemplated defeat.

Was there more pressure because of his position as captain?

'First of all I'm a player, secondly I'm a captain, not the other way around. If you think differently then you're in trouble, major trouble. My role as captain was small. I am probably the biggest worrier on this team. A lot of players would probably feel exactly the same way but don't say it. The night before the match we were in our Dublin hotel and we watched "Up For The Match" on RTE television. It was touching to see Phil Coulter singing "The Town I Loved So Well" and Joe Brolly's parents singing the song about the Derry football team. There was barely a word spoken during the programme.'

Henry Downey hated the journey by coach to Croke Park. He was only happy when ensconced in the safety of the dressing-room. He remembers all the team being very relaxed. Almost too relaxed. He even began to worry that they were not as motivated as they should be.

It was very special to lead his Derry team into the cauldron. It was the first time since 1958 that Derry had made it and they were given a welcome rarely, if ever, witnessed at Croke Park. Derry flags enveloped the ground. He remembers the colours on The Hill as being very special. It took two photocalls before the parade was ready to begin.

Cork got a whirlwind start and led by 1-2 to no score after five minutes play. But soon after, Johnny McGurk opened the scoring for Derry and that settled the Ulster champions. Favoured by the breeze Derry went in front after fifteen minutes when Henry's brother Séamus fisted the ball past Cork goalkeeper John Kerins. An opportunist goal! Derry were now in dominant form and led by three points after eighteen minutes. That lead had been reduced to just one point when referee Tommy Howard booked Niall Cahalane who had flattened Derry corner-forward Enda Gormley. Two minutes later, Cork left-half-back Tony Davis was sent to the line for a foul on Dermot Heaney.

'Even when Cork were five points up I still had great belief in Derry. I never thought we were going to lose. The goal made a big difference. It was an important score and after being five points down we went in at half time three points in front. This Derry team never play well until they are behind. Niall Cahalane should have been sent off. No question about that. I would suggest Tony Davis should have been booked but not sent off. I don't think the referee, linesmen or umpires saw Cahalane striking Enda Gormley. If any of them had seen the incident Cahalane would have been sent off. Obviously the referee knew Cahalane was guilty but he didn't see him do it. That is why he booked him but he couldn't send him off. It is my opinion that nobody saw anything.'

Just ten minutes into the second half and Cork were back in front. John O'Driscoll collected a great pass from Don Davis and the full-forward beat Damien McCusker with a superb shot to the corner of the net. But incredibly Cork were not to score again in the remaining twenty-five minutes during which time Derry added four points courtesy of Johnny McGurk, Anthony Tohill and two from Enda Gormley.

'I think after being three points up and having an extra man we should have gone on and made ourselves comfortable long before we did. Even when Cork scored their second goal I never felt we were going to lose. It was a funny feeling. The second half just flew until the last five minutes which seemed to last forever. It seemed like everybody was standing on the Derry twenty-metre line defending the goal. I don't think Cork would have scored a goal at that stage. Never. They had scored two so I think we had given them enough for one match.'

As the minute hand on the big clock in Croke Park reached four fifty-seven on Sunday 19 September 1993, the final whistle sounded and Derry were All-Ireland champions. History was made and years of frustration were at an end. Thousands of Derry supporters raced onto the pitch to acclaim their heroes who had beaten the All-Ireland champions of 1990, '91 and '92 as well as the League Champions of 1993 on their way to claiming the Sam Maguire.

Henry Downey was very conscious of his role when he stepped up to collect the Sam Maguire Cup to round off the perfect day. A day that will never be forgotten as long as football is kicked around the Sperrin Mountains.

'It was a great feeling but it passes too quickly. When I lifted that cup there were thousands of Derry footballers who lifted it along with me. It meant the same to them as it did to me. It's not that I deserved to lift the Sam Maguire Cup more than any other Derry player, I was just representing all the fellows who played football for Derry. There have been some great Derry footballers and I am honoured to be the man chosen to collect the cup.'

More than ten hours after their journey began in Dublin, the Derry team arrived in Maghera early on Tuesday morning and tens of thousand of supporters waited to greet them. The team was given a civic reception in Drogheda and everywhere along the route, groups converged to greet the new football champions of Ireland.

As far as Henry is concerned, 'Sam Maguire' was never going anywhere else but to the Oak Leaf county in 1993. Over the years some great Derry teams failed to realise their true potential. What was it that made this squad into match winners?

'It's hard to know. Some of the teams of the seventies would have beaten this Derry team. No question about it. Maybe organisation would be the big thing. Maybe attitude. We were lucky this year that we had both. We started back training in January and it was non-stop until we won the All-Ireland. It was organised, it was professional and the players were totally committed.'

But is not almost every team putting in the same effort nowadays?

'Losing to Donegal in last year's Ulster Final in 1992 had a tremendous impact on this team. We were very disappointed the night of the match and we were cross with ourselves when we met the night after the match. We were cross! We totally hated ourselves. We just couldn't understand how we could be so pathetic on the day that mattered so much. We were very angry with ourselves. We believed that we could win an All-Ireland in 1992 but it didn't work out that way. We were determined to make amends. And we did.'

Anthony MOLLOY

Donegal Captain 1992

WHEN MIGHTY MIDFIELDER Anthony Molloy took hold of the Sam Maguire Cup on the Hogan Stand on 20 September 1992 his actions sparked off unprecedented scenes of jubilation at home and abroad. The long wait was over and history was made. The Sam Maguire Cup was at last on its way to the hills of Donegal. Croke Park has witnessed many emotional scenes down through the years but few compared to those which greeted the final whistle at the end of the 1992 final. This was Donegal's big moment all right, but their victory took on even greater significance than the players themselves imagined. By virtue of their 0-18 to 0-14 victory over favourites Dublin, this skilful Donegal side had struck a blow for the weaker counties.

Anthony Molloy grew up in the little townland of Leamagowra, situated at the top of Glengesh Pass, one of the most scenic spots in the whole of Donegal. There are now just four houses left in Leamagowra: two are closed and the other two occupied by Anthony's parents and another family of Molloys. Most of his family have long since emigrated to America. He recalls days before emigration took its toll when there could be anything up to twenty youngsters playing football.

There was no history of the game in either of his parents' families but his older brothers were a great influence. Indeed Connie and Lanty represented the county at senior level before taking off for America in the early eighties. It was Connie who brought eleven-year-old Anthony to the Ardara club, where he soon made his mark and was chosen at centre-half-back in his first game for the under-14 team.

'My mother and father reared twelve children, and to see half of them forced to emigrate in just one year was heartbreaking. Even though I was only young I missed them all terribly. The sad thing about emigration is that as sure as six go off, six more will follow soon after. It destroys a community. I mind the time when there would be anything up to twenty-four people playing cards in our home on a winter's night.

FACT FILE

HOME PLACE: Leamagowra, Ardara, County Donegal

BORN: 28 May 1962   CLUB: Ardara; Donegal/New York

CLUB ACHIEVEMENTS: Under 14 County Football Championship medal in 1976; two County Under-21 Football Championship medals in 1980 and 1982; one County Senior Football Championship medal in 1981; one Senior League medal in 1989; two Shield medals in 1979 and 1980; Donegal Player of the Year in 1988 and 1990; three New York Championship medals with Donegal in 1986, 1991 and 1992.

INTER-COUNTY ACHIEVEMENTS: One All-Ireland Senior Football Championship medal in 1992; one All-Ireland Under-21 medal in 1982; three Ulster Championship medals in 1983, 1990 and 1992; one Railway Cup medal in 1989; Dr McKenna Cup medal in 1991; All-Star Award in 1992.

You wouldn't get two there now. I am very proud of where I come from, it means everything to me. We had some great nights in Leamagowra when I brought the Sam Maguire Cup home.'

Donegal had to play six games to win the title but not even their most loyal and dedicated follower could have held out much hope after the team's narrow escape in the first round of the Ulster championship. On that May day at Breffni Park Donegal were fortunate to earn a draw against Cavan.

'We hadn't prepared all that well and I don't think we trained as much as we should have for the game. I think we took Cavan for granted and almost paid the price. Cavan played out of their skins the first day. I remember looking over at Martin McHugh as much as to say, "We're gone here, another first round exit". I didn't need to say anything, the way I looked at him said it all. In all fairness to Martin that day, he kept his composure and stuck over some important frees to keep us in the match. We beat Cavan fairly well in the replay at Ballybofey.'

The second round against Fermanagh at Healy Park, Omagh, marked Anthony Molloy's one-hundredth appearance in a Donegal jersey at senior competitive level. It was a runaway victory, sixteen points separating the sides at the finish.

'The Fermanagh game was the turning point for us that year. After the game a few of us had a meeting and came to the conclusion that the training was not hard enough. As a result we asked our trainer Anthony Harkin and manager Brian McEniff to step up our training. It was the sorriest thing we ever did but it worked wonders. We started training in preparation for the Ulster final the following Tuesday night. It was the hardest training I had ever done. It was sheer physical work for two nights a week with only a little football on one night. It was complete stamina work and it definitely did pay off. We went in to the Ulster final against Derry in great shape.

'Even though we had the assistance of the breeze in the first half we didn't play all that well. We used the long ball into Tony Boyle in the first half and it didn't work

Back, left to right: Matt Gallagher, John Joe Doherty, Noel Hegarty, Gary Walsh, Brian Murray, Barry McGowan, Declan Bonner, Donal Reid.
Front, left to right: Martin McHugh, Joyce McMullen, Manus Boyle, Tony Boyle, Anthony Molloy (captain), Martin Gavigan, James McHugh.

out so we changed our game plan and used the short ball to great effect in the second half. We ran at Derry and it certainly worked for us. It inspired us when John Cunningham was sent off, as it was a harsh decision. It was a great win for us.'

Fourteen-man Donegal saw off the Derry challenge, winning in the end by 0-14 to 1-9. It was a particularly satisfying outcome for Anthony, who could hardly believe his good fortune. He had announced his retirement the previous year and now here he was captain of the Ulster champions and looking forward to a return to Croke Park. 'I had an operation on my knee in 1991 and found it hard to get into shape. I also had a problem with my back and wasn't getting a regular place on the team. I was disappointed at not being selected for the Ulster final in 1991, and the week after the game I decided it was time to hang up the boots. In my heart I didn't want to retire but I thought maybe it was best because of the knee injury. I found the enjoyment had gone out of playing football and I wasn't getting the same satisfaction any longer. I didn't play any football at all until I went to New York in October and while there I got back playing and even won a championship medal. Then in the new year Brian McEniff asked me if I would consider playing again and I can tell you he didn't have to ask me twice. It's funny how things worked out, and I never had any problems with the knee or the back that year.'

Donegal faced Mayo in the All-Ireland semi-final. 'There was a lot of pressure on us that day to do well and reach a first All-Ireland final. Physically we were okay but the mental barrier of us maybe flopping on the big occasion was very real.'

But Donegal triumphed 0-13 to 0-9 and the county became a sea of colour and alive with excitement and anticipation. Second best would no longer suffice.

According to Anthony, Brian McEniff emphasised the importance of not getting carried away with all the hysteria. 'There was a great buzz in every single village and town throughout the county. The talk was of football, football, football. This made us more determined than ever to achieve something for the people of the county.'

On the eve of the final Anthony placed a small bet at his local bookie's office in Killybegs and the horse romped home at odds of ten to one. The omens were good.

'We left Donegal town by coach about one o'clock on Saturday afternoon and the place was packed. They gave us a great send off and you felt you just had to bring home the Sam Maguire Cup. We owed it to the people of Donegal. The management had their homework well done and we were properly prepared. I think maybe that's where Dublin fell down. I don't think they had their homework done and just thought they were going to win. We had our man at all their training sessions. He was dressed up so as not to be recognised. That's what preparation is all about.'

As was the custom before games, Anthony and a few of the team members played

---

THE 1992 DONEGAL TEAM

Gary Walsh

| Barry McGowan | Matt Gallagher | Noel Hegarty |
| Dónal Reid | Martin Gavigan | John Joe Doherty |

Anthony Molloy (Captain) Brian Murray

| James McHugh | Martin McHugh | Joyce McMullan |
| Declan Bonner | Tony Boyle | Manus Boyle |

Substitute: Barry Cunningham for Brian Murray

17

poker until about one thirty in the morning. Other players attended the big greyhound race meeting at Shelbourne Park.

As the day of the final dawned, all was not well in the Donegal camp. News filtered through that Naomh Ultán defender Martin Shovlin was a doubtful starter. 'He had aggravated a neck injury the previous Thursday night in training but we didn't know it was so serious. As long as I live I'll never forget the way he cried when he heard he couldn't play. It was a bitter disappointment for Martin and it made us even more determined to win for his sake. Martin is a man of steel and probably the hardest man on the whole team. He is a wholehearted player, would never pull out of a tackle and would give you everything on the day. He is a great example to younger players and is always in great condition.'

At very short notice John Joe Doherty took over at left-half-back and soon it was time for the knock on the door. It was now or never. It took Donegal some time to settle down as Dublin began to find their range and pick off points. Anthony admits he was more than a little worried even at that early stage. 'We weren't playing well at all. I was right beside Martin McHugh at one stage and I said something like: "Come on, Martin, we'd better do something. It's not going to happen all over again, is it?" Funny enough, after I said that, Charlie Redmond missed the penalty and things started to happen for us. We played some great football in the closing twenty minutes of the first half. I knew at that stage we could win.

> *'I think maybe that's where Dublin fell down. I don't think they had their homework done and just thought they were going to win. We had our man at all their training sessions. He was dressed up so as not to be recognised. That's what preparation is all about.'*

'Midway through the second half I noticed the Dublin players were panicking and getting edgy towards one another. It was obvious things were not going all that well for them. I remember Brian running out to the middle of the field and saying to me, "Keep the pressure on for the last fifteen minutes". At that stage fines didn't matter.

'Dublin came back at us towards the end and it was very worrying when they came to within three points of us. There was always the fear that Vinny Murphy might stick the ball in the net. But we were so well prepared and Brian had it instilled in us to watch the big clock to see how much time was left. I remember looking up and seeing that there was only a minute or so left. Then Declan scored the point and I knew we had it. But you're never sure until the final whistle.'

Donegal won in the end by 0-18 to 0-14 and Manus Boyle won the Man of the Match award for his outstanding contribution of nine points.

'I had a speech prepared but I came away from home without it. It was only when I found myself on the steps that I began to think of what to say. It's not an easy thing do with the sheer excitement of the occasion. Things worked out all right. I'll never forget lifting the cup. It was the proudest day of my life.

'I eventually made my way to the dressing-room and it was bedlam. There were twelve of my family in Croke Park that day, including my mother and father. It was my father's first time in Croke Park. He always wanted to go there and his wish finally came true at the age of seventy-five. And no better day.'

President Mary Robinson speaks with Anthony Molloy before the final. Left is GAA president Peter Quinn, and Donegal's Manus and Tony Boyle on right.

After a short visit to the dressing-room and the meeting with family and friends, Anthony was called away to do some radio and television interviews, and by the time he arrived back the dressing-room was almost empty. His home address was printed in bold letters on a big Donegal banner in Croke Park and consequently he received up to a thousand congratulatory letters and cards from people all over Ireland. The homecoming to Donegal was as emotional as it was exciting. Thousands greeted their heroes in Sligo and in Brian McEniff's home town, Bundoran, where Anthony and the manager walked across the Drowse River carrying the cup between them. There were massive crowds too in Ballyshannon, and Donegal town was wild with upwards of fifteen thousand there to greet them. After visiting many other towns and villages the following day, Anthony arrived in his home town of Ardara on Tuesday night. There was no let up in his schedule over the next days and weeks as the Sam Maguire Cup was paraded in every village and town.

Before Christmas Anthony and Martin McHugh travelled to America, and one of

Anthony Molloy near his home in Ardara.

the high points was when he took the Cup to 'The Sam Maguire' pub in New York, which is jointly owned by his brother and his uncle James McGonigle.

To round off a wonderful year, Anthony was one of seven Donegal players to receive All-Star Awards. The others honoured were Gary Walsh, Matt Gallagher, Martin Gavigan, brothers Martin and James McHugh and Tony Boyle.

All good things come to an end and Donegal were beaten by Derry in the 1993 Ulster final in the mud and rain at Clones. Atrocious weather conditions made it impossible for the players to display their skills. 'The final should never have been played. It rained most of the week leading up to the game and there was a downpour shortly before the start. It was a disgrace to ask players to try to play football in such conditions. It was dangerous and I think Derry would have been happy enough to get it called off. It was a terrible way to lose your crown because we never got an opportunity to defend it in style. But having said all that, Derry deserved their win.'

He pays tribute to his own club, Ardara, to Brian Sheridan, his teacher in Glenties Comprehensive School, and the great Donegal players of the past, especially Kieran Keeney who was an influential member of the county team when Anthony made the breakthrough. He is loud in his praise of manager Brian McEniff and all the back-room team for their roles in guiding Donegal to All-Ireland success.

Anthony Molloy is acutely aware of his unique position in the annals of Gaelic games: 'I consider myself the luckiest man in the world to be the first man to bring the Sam Maguire Cup to Donegal. Football is the main topic of conversation everywhere we go now and without it I don't know what we'd talk about.'

Paddy O'ROURKE

Down Captain 1991

IT WAS THE DAY the focus of attention centred on the two O'Rourkes. It ended in sheer delight for one and sadness for the other. Before Down captain Paddy collected the Sam Maguire Cup, his namesake from Meath, Colm, who had been unable to take his place in the starting line-up because of a chest infection, turned the game around with a superlative display when introduced into the fray early in the second half. Whether the outcome would have been any different had the Skryne star been on from the start is a matter of conjecture. In years to come, records will show only that Paddy O'Rourke's men won by 1-16 to 1-14.

Down had scored just two points to Meath's 1-8 in the closing twenty minutes but the hard work had already been done and Down deserved their fourth All-Ireland success. When, on the second Sunday in June, the footballers of Down came face to face with arch-rivals Armagh, no-one, with the possible exception of those close to the team, had any reason to believe that 1991 was going to be different from any of the previous twenty-three years.

'It was a very, very poor match and I remember the players being very relieved to get it over with as we had failed on a number of occasions to get past the first round.'

Derry provided the opposition in the second round and looking back, Paddy O'Rourke believes he can pinpoint the exact time his team succeeded in shaking off the shackles of mediocrity.

'Derry pulled back a seven-point lead and went ahead by one point. We drew level but when Derry went ahead again in the closing minutes we looked to be in trouble. It took a marvellous free from Ross Carr with the last kick of the game to bring the game to a replay. We came back from the dead and I felt this was a Down team that didn't want to be beaten. Other years we'd have thrown in the towel but this team adopted the attitude that we'd got beaten often enough and it was time for

---

FACT FILE

HOME PLACE: Burren, Warrenpoint, County Down

BORN: 14 January 1960   CLUB: Burren

CLUB ACHIEVEMENTS: Eight Senior Football Championship medals in 1981, 1983, 1984, 1985, 1986, 1987, 1988 and 1992; two All-Ireland Club Championships in 1986 and 1988; five Ulster Club Football Championship medals in 1983, 1984, 1985, 1987 and 1988; ten all County Senior Football League medals.

INTER-COUNTY ACHIEVEMENTS: One All-Ireland Senior Football medal in 1991; three Ulster Senior Football Championship medals in 1978, 1981 and 1991; one All-Ireland Minor medal in 1977; one All-Ireland Under-21 medal in 1979; three Ulster Under-21 medals in 1977, 1978 and 1979; Ulster Minor League and Championship in 1977; one National Football League medal in 1983; two Railway Cup medals in 1983, 1984; two McKenna Cup medals.

things to change. We came into the Ulster final starved of success and we played exceptionally well and had a comfortable victory over Donegal.

'It was a fantastic feeling to lift the Anglo-Celt Cup as I had thought of retiring a few times before that. We had been beaten in the Ulster semi-final by Armagh the previous year and I didn't think we'd recover from it. But as the summer went on the pain went away, and I realised I didn't want to finish up on a losing note. Then when we won the Ulster final in 1991 I remember thinking "This is not enough: we can go on a step further". I told the players it was only a stepping stone and I knew it was a great opportunity to at least get into an All-Ireland final.

'The players were very easy to motivate after our Ulster final victory and the whole county was behind the team. We trained exceptionally hard for the semi-final and stepped up a gear in fitness. The players did everything that was asked of them and were only interested in doing things right. We had Kerry in the semi-final who had never beaten us so we went into the game with a fair amount of confidence but very well prepared. We had massive support in Croke Park and we won fairly comfortably in the end. The hardest thing to handle was when the final whistle blew and suddenly realising that I was about to play in an All-Ireland final. I became very emotional and when I went up to the RTE radio commentary box I saw Peter Rooney and it made me even worse. I had trouble controlling my emotions for a while.'

The county was alive with excitement in the build-up to their first All-Ireland appearance in twenty-three years. But in the midst of this carnival atmosphere Paddy O'Rourke was very conscious of not allowing his team lose sight of what had to be done. Meath were favourites but Paddy was confident that it would be Down's year.

'Once we had beaten Kerry we believed we were going to win the final. Personally I was convinced and if we had lost I would have been unbelievably shocked. I should have had doubts but I had none and I know a lot of the other players felt the same way. I stayed at home in Burren on the night before the game and didn't go to the phone that much. We went to evening Mass in Warrenpoint. I can remember the

Back, left to right: Éamon Burns, Paul Higgins, Conor Deegan, Neil Collins, Barry Breen, Greg Blaney.
Front, left to right: Ross Carr, James McCartan, Gary Mason, Brendan McKiernan, Mickey Linden, Paddy O'Rourke (captain), D.J. Kane, Peter Withnall, John Kelly.

British army stopping us on the way and they had the Down flag on the jeep. I remember thinking "This is something special." The priest who said Mass was Father Powell, a brother of Larry who came on as a substitute in the 1968 All-Ireland final. He mentioned the match and wished us well. I came back home and had a walk around the fields and focused on the game. I was determined not to let the occasion pass without enjoying it to the full. I went to bed around eleven o'clock and woke up the next morning at seven and thought to myself, "Today I'm going to play in an All-Ireland final". I met the rest of the team at Newry and we had a very enjoyable trip to Dublin by coach.'

At Croke Park the team made a quick dash for the changing-rooms, avoiding the throng of Down supporters. Before taking the field Paddy said to his players, 'It's an All-Ireland final and the stakes are high. Liam Hayes has his hand on one arm of the Sam Maguire and I have my hand on the other. Who is going to hold on the tightest?'

It was a wonderful feeling to lead the team out but Paddy felt fine and admits he was more nervous against Armagh in the first round of the Ulster championship earlier that year. 'Meath got a good start with two points in two minutes so I was a wee bit worried at that stage but when Down settled we pegged back the scores and I felt comfortable enough then. We led by four points at half time and I was still confident we would win.

'When Colm O'Rourke came on we were six points ahead but we stretched that to eleven points so I thought there was no way back for Meath. I probably started getting worried when Liam Hayes scored the goal to cut our lead to five points. There was still about ten minutes left to play. Another thing that sticks in my mind is Mickey Linden racing through with only the goalkeeper to beat and he blasted the ball wide. We kept plugging away and I continually asked the referee what time was left in the game. I was quite calm when it was all over, not nearly as emotional or uptight as I was after beating Kerry in the semi-final. It was tremendous to hold the cup and to look down at the mass of red and black. I was also conscious that many Down supporters would be watching on television. I was dragged all over the field with the cup and that was the least enjoyable part of it all. I was relieved to make it into the changing-rooms.

'The supporters' club was having a function in Portmarnock so we brought the Cup there and the place was packed. It was hectic. I spent about two hours in a corner signing autographs and shaking hands with everyone. It wasn't until I got back to the Burlington Hotel that I was able to sit down, relax and have a cup of coffee. It was absolute heaven after such a hectic day.

'On the journey home, I suddenly realised that there were only three other men —

THE 1991 DOWN TEAM

Neil Collins

Brendan McKiernan	Conor Deegan	Paul Higgins
John Kelly	Paddy O'Rourke (Captain)	D.J. Kane

Barry Breen Éamon Burns

Ross Carr	Greg Blaney	Gary Mason
Mickey Linden	Peter Withnall	James McCartan

Substitutes: Liam Austin for Barry Breen; Ambrose Rodgers for Peter Withnall

---

Kevin Mussen, Paddy Doherty and Joe Lennon — who ever brought the cup across the border and I was very proud walking across the platform bridging the border between North and South.'

There was no tradition of Gaelic football in the O'Rourke family and Paddy's earliest memory of the game was listening to Mícheál O'Hehir's commentaries on the Ulster finals in which Down were involved. From the age of ten he used to tag along with his older brother, Tommy, to the local pitch and he got his first taste of the game that was to change his life. The arrival of a new headmaster, Patsy McArdle, to Burren Primary School coincided with the formation of a school team that took part in organised competitions.

'I remember coming home pestering my mother to buy me boots so that I could play. There's fifteen in our family, nine girls and six boys, and although she had more important commitments she still bought me the boots. I played midfield in my very first game for the school and although we lost I can still remember the sheer enjoyment I got out of playing. I had looked forward to the match for weeks and weeks beforehand and I can tell you I wasn't disappointed. Children play a lot younger nowadays but back then most youngsters would not start playing until they had left primary school. There was always someone to play with and we spent most of our time outdoors in the fields and the woods. My father was a small farmer and also worked in Newry creamery.'

> '*I looked across the room and saw the Sam Maguire Cup sitting on the floor and I suddenly realised I was the only man waking up in Ireland and seeing that cup. It was special, I can tell you.*'

Soon after that initial introduction to organised football, Paddy was selected as goalkeeper on the under-13 team that won the local league. When he went to secondary school at St Mark's in Warrenpoint he was thrilled to find that the PE teacher there was none other than the great Down midfielder Colm McAlarney. 'I remember one day Colm was talking through an open window of a classroom to a few of the older students and some of us sneaked up close to hear what he was saying. He was explaining why Down had lost the All-Ireland semi-final to Galway. He was a superstar then. I played on all the school teams and Colm was probably the first man to play me in defence. He was only there for a few years and when he left to go to another school Barney McAleenan took over and he was another very dedicated teacher who helped me enormously.'

Paddy is in no doubt that Seán Murdock had the biggest influence on his own football career as well as influencing many others in the picturesque Burren area.

'Seán was in charge of all under-age teams and even used his own transport to bring us to games. He encouraged us to train and always gave of his time and energies. Nothing was ever too much for him to do. He was unbelievably dedicated. I can remember Seán from the very first time I went to the football field. He often said to me, "If you keep looking after yourself and keep working at it, you'll play for Down some day". That was a big incentive — for someone like him to say that.'

Paddy was only sixteen when he first played senior football with Burren.

'I came into a fairly physically strong and secure senior team although they hadn't

won a senior title since 1966. The losing trend continued for some time until 1981 when we won the first of eight championships in the eighties. We beat Cathal Digney's club, Saval, in a replay and I'll never forget the sheer excitement of that first senior county championship victory. The whole of Burren came to a stop and no one went to work on the Monday. Everyone was walking on air.'

Paddy O'Rourke arrived back with the Sam Maguire Cup to Burren football field early on the Wednesday morning following the All-Ireland, and later attended a function in the Social Club until 6.30 am. He walked back home through the fields where he had played as a child. When he got to the top of the hill he turned back, looked down at the football field and lifted the cup over his head once more ... 'It was a fabulous feeling, just me and the rabbits.'

Paddy's talent as a footballer was recognised early by the county selectors and at the age of sixteen he was chosen on the Down minor team. The following year he played at right-half-back on the Down team that defeated Meath to win the All-Ireland minor title. He was captain of the minors in 1978 but they lost to Tyrone in the Ulster championship. Shortly afterwards Paddy made the county senior panel. That year Down won the Ulster title and Paddy came on as a sub and marked Anton O'Toole as Dublin won handsomely by eleven points. He was on the Down team that won the All-Ireland Under-21 championship in 1979 and two years later he played in his second senior All-Ireland semi-final, this time losing out to Offaly.

If someone had told Paddy O'Rourke at the time that it would be another ten years before Down would again make it back to Croke Park in the All-Ireland championship he would have dismissed it out of hand. He had become accustomed to winning at under-age level. But as the county stumbled from one failure to another doubts grew bigger with each passing year. 'There was a change of manager every few years and of course they were unfairly blamed for the decline. The County Board was piling too much club football onto players and the county team was not getting enough time to prepare for championship matches. As well as that, team managers were not getting the necessary support required and there always seemed to be disagreements between the County Board and managers. It was disheartening and sickening. Every year we'd train and train and have high hopes of doing well and next thing we'd be knocked out of the championship. The same old story. When Danny Murphy was appointed chairman in 1991 he played a big part in getting the whole county behind the Down team.'

Then, according to Paddy, two things happened that led to the transformation that sparked off such scenes of joy around the mountains of Mourne in September 1991.

'The attitude of players changed. They became more dedicated and single-minded in their approach to winning something for Down. Then players like James McCartan and Conor Deegan came through from the All-Ireland winning minor team of 1987 and, much like myself in the late seventies, they fully believed they were going to do well. Our manager Peter McGrath was very dedicated and set very high standards for the players and turned things around.'

Paddy O'Rourke has another abiding memory of All-Ireland weekend, 1991.

'I remember waking up in the Burlington Hotel at a quarter to seven on the Monday morning after less than two-and-a-half-hours sleep. I looked across the room and saw the Sam Maguire Cup sitting on the floor and I suddenly realised I was the only man waking up in Ireland and seeing that cup. It was special, I can tell you.'

Paddy is married to Una and they have three children, Orla, Ciara and Pauric.

Paddy O'Rourke tackled by Meath's P.J. Gillic gets the ball in the All-Ireland final 1991.

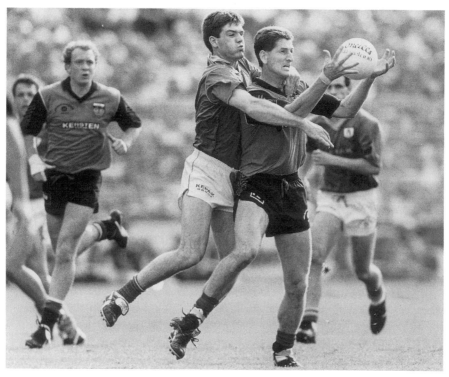

Larry TOMPKINS

Cork Captain 1990

NO GREATER OR MORE LOYAL player than Larry Tompkins ever wore the all-white of Kildare, and it was a heartbreaking decision for him to part company with the Lilywhites after falling out with the County Board over the purchase of an airline ticket. At the time it seemed nothing more than a storm in a teacup but sadly Larry Tompkins has never since lined out for the county of his birth. Those who know him from the time he was but a whip of a lad will tell you that all he ever wanted was to play football for his club and county. He himself confesses that the day he pulled on the Kildare jersey was one of the greatest thrills of his life. So where did it all go wrong? What was it that made Larry Tompkins eventually decide to throw in his lot with Cork?

Admittedly he has seen good times since swapping the all-white jersey for the red-and-white. He played a key part in Cork's All-Ireland successes of 1989 and 1990. Better still, he was captain in 1990 when his adopted county conquered Meath in the final after losing to the same opposition at the same stage in 1987 and again in 1988.

'My heart was always with the Kildare team and I don't think I ever missed a training session with them. I remember when I was serving my time in Kilcullen I used to thumb in the fourteen miles for work at eight in the morning. I had to work hard on the buildings until six in the evening and then had to try and get a lift in to Naas, where the county team was training. At that time there would only be twelve or thirteen players turning up for training and there was no great interest and it was hard to get things going. After about two hours' training at ten o'clock I had to thumb my way home another seven miles. I was the only player from the club and there was no one going out my direction. I wouldn't get home most nights until half

---

FACT FILE

HOME PLACE: Greenmount, Rathmore, Naas, County Kildare

BORN: 13 June 1963

CLUBS: Eadestown, County Kildare; Castlehaven, County Cork; Donegal Club in New York.

ACHIEVEMENTS IN CLUB COMPETITIONS: With Eadestown: won a Kildare Intermediate Football Championship medal in 1983; one Junior A Championship medal in 1982 and one Junior B Championship medal in 1981. With Castlehaven: won a County Senior Football Championship medal in 1989; one Munster Championship medal in 1989/90.

INTER-COUNTY ACHIEVEMENTS: With Kildare: Under-21 Leinster Championship medal in 1983; O'Byrne Cup medal. With Cork: Won two All-Ireland Senior Football medals in 1989 and 1990; five Munster Championship medals in 1987, 1988, 1989, 1990 and 1993; one National League medal in 1989.

Won Railway Cup medal with Leinster in 1985.

---

past eleven and would then have my dinner. It was hard going, three nights a week for two years. John Crofton and Paddy O'Donoghue were two men I always had great time for and they gave great service to Kildare. They will tell you that I never missed a training session, and they never missed one either. At that time Kildare County Board was badly organised and players were not being looked after properly. It was an ordeal for players even to get expenses for travelling. It was a messy situation.'

Larry finished his apprenticeship in early 1985 but he then found himself out of work for seven or eight weeks. Former Offaly footballer Mick Wright asked him if he would like to travel to New York to play football with Donegal and he agreed. He had been approached on a number of occasions before then but always declined the invitations.

'I was always a total home bird. I enjoyed playing with Eadestown and with Kildare. I didn't want to leave home at the time. I had to make a decision, as the building trade was not going too well at the time, so I decided to go for a few weeks to see what it was like. I went over in April for a week and played one game for Donegal, which we won. I gave them a commitment to spend the summer in America if Kildare were beaten in the championship. I played against Wicklow in the first round of the championship in early May. I was chosen as captain and it was a very proud honour. After that I travelled to the States as a replacement on the All Star trip and while over there I got full-time employment as a carpenter. Éamon O'Donoghue was over the Kildare team at the time and I told him that I would like to come home to play for Kildare in the next round if the County Board would look after the cost of the flight. And he said that would be no problem. I told them that I still had a return ticket from the All Star trip and, as that ticket was valid for one journey, all I would need was a one-way ticket. We were playing Meath in the Leinster semi-final and I could only come home for the weekend as I had to be back working on the Tuesday. I would have liked to be home for a week beforehand but unfortunately it wasn't

Back, left to right: Michael Slocum, Teddy McCarthy, Barry Coffey, Danny Culloty, Shay Fahy, John Kerins, Conor Counihan, Colm O'Neill.
Front, left to right: Paul McGrath, Stephen O'Brien, Niall Cahalane, Larry Tompkins (Captain), Dave Barry, Tony Nation, Mick McCarthy.

possible. We were beaten by Meath, and that's when the problem arose.

'They had told me two weeks earlier that everything had been arranged and that the ticket would be there. But they came to me after the game and told me that there was a problem with the ticket. When I went to the hotel afterwards Séamus Aldridge and Pat Dunny approached me and told me that the ticket they had purchased was costing them £740 and it was only right that I should pay half the fare, as they wouldn't be wanting me any more. I'll never forget the way they said it to me. I thought it was totally unfair and I asked them how a flight to America could cost so much. They told me it was the only ticket that was available. It was a business ticket and it did cost that price. I found it hard to understand why they couldn't have got a cheaper ticket.

'They gave me the cheque to pay for the ticket under promise that I would pay back half the money when I had it. As it happened, before I left New York I had suspicions that something would be amiss so I told a very, very good friend of mine, Dónal Gallagher, about my fears. He was over the Donegal team in New York and was very anxious that I would return to play in the New York championship, which they were determined to win.

'When I went to the airport the morning after the Meath game I found there was a double reservation. I suddenly realised it was Dónal in New York who had made the reservation to make sure there would be no hiccups. The ticket he had booked only cost around £400, and the County Board got their money. I felt I was totally used and I was angry. Maybe if it was a player who had been on the scene for a very short time one might think the County Board had a case, but I was with them for seven or eight years and had given total commitment to the county team.

'There was only one thing on my mind, and that was to play football and be good at it. And I knew the only way to do that was to train well and be part of a county team. It is a great thrill for anyone to wear a county jersey and that's the way I approached things. When I thought about what had happened I realised I was used and it was a terrible feeling. As far as the County Board was concerned, all my service to Kildare was worth nothing. I made no decision at the time. I was really enjoying my football in New York as the standard was very high. I captained Donegal on two occasions to win the championship and it was a great honour.'

The game against Meath marked the last appearance of Larry Tompkins in a Kildare jersey. To know the man is to know that it was one of the most difficult decisions of his career. He holds no animosity towards anybody but it is still evident that the whole episode has left a scar. This brilliant yet modest sportsman is fiercely

---

THE 1990 CORK TEAM

John Kerins

Tony Nation   Stephen O'Brien   Niall Cahalane

Michael Slocum   Conor Counihan   Barry Coffey

Shay Fahy   Danny Culloty

Dave Barry   Larry Tompkins (captain)   Teddy McCarthy

Paul McGrath   Colm O'Neill   Mick McCarthy

Substitutes: John O'Driscoll for Mick McCarthy; Paddy Hayes for Dave Barry; John Cleary for Paul McGrath.

proud of the county of his birth. Despite all the speculation, Larry Tompkins is now resigned to the fact that he will never again play football for Kildare. That is a reality. As far as he is concerned that matter is now put to rest.

According to Larry, the Donegal team of the mid to late eighties in New York would have proved a match for any county team in Ireland. And in a roundabout way that is the reason he eventually found himself playing inter-county football with Cork. The Donegal team was playing such good football in New York that Dónal Gallagher felt it would be a shame if those at home were not allowed an opportunity to see them. Donegal toured Ireland for three weeks, winning all four games against Cork, Laois, Mayo and Donegal. While playing with Donegal, Larry had become great friends with team members Anthony and Vincie Collins, Martin Connolly and Martin Mahoney. All four came from Castlehaven in Cork and had one ambition, and that was one day to see Castlehaven win the county senior championship.

'I had never heard of the place before I met the lads but after a while I found that the one thing that always cropped up in our conversations was Castlehaven. I found out later it is only a small country place, even a lot smaller than Eadestown. They kept telling me what it would mean to people in Castlehaven to win the county championship. It's like a second religion. They eventually convinced me to transfer to the club, and I signed on the dotted line in January 1987. As I was living in the county it gave me the right to play for Cork.'

And that he did with outstanding success. His transfer came through on 13 June 1987, his birthday. He played for Cork later that day in a challenge against Dublin in Parnell Park. Larry admits it felt strange being in a Cork jersey for the first few games, but he soon got used to it and was delighted to get support from players and supporters alike. It was also an advantage having another Kildare man, Shay Fahy, alongside him on the Cork team.

Larry has tremendous regard and affection for the people of Castlehaven. He will never forget the hospitality he received from the whole community. He singles out Nora Maguire as someone who typifies the spirit of Castlehaven and makes it such a wonderful place to live. That is why he rates Castlehaven's defeat by Muskerry in the quarter-final of the Cork championship in 1987 as his greatest sporting disappointment.

'I had scored eleven points against Galway in the All-Ireland semi-final and could do nothing wrong that day in Croke Park. Although I played well in general play for Castlehaven, I missed a lot of frees. It was just one of those nights when nothing went right with my frees.'

Cork qualified for the All-Ireland final against Meath that year. Larry scored the equalising point against Kerry in the Munster final and against Galway in the All-Ireland semi-final. Cork won both the replays fairly comfortably but lost to Meath in the All-Ireland final.

Larry went back to New York after the final but returned home in May 1988 and was on the Cork team that retained the Munster final with a one-point win over Kerry.

Cork accounted for Monaghan in the All-Ireland semi-final before again losing to Meath in the final after a replay. Cork made amends the following year when they beat Mayo in the All-Ireland final and New York in the league final. Larry was now captain of Castlehaven, and to crown a perfect year they won the county championship and the Munster championship. That was also the year he purchased his pub in Lower Glanmire Road in Cork city. A year to remember, all right!

Many people feel that Cork would never have won an All-Ireland football title were it not for Larry Tompkins. What does the man himself think?

'No individual will win a game, but I do think there are individuals that can inspire other players to play above themselves. I was always a very forceful and fit type of player who trained very hard. If there was anything that Cork lacked it was maybe a little bit of drive on the training fields, and I probably helped in that way. Because of the training we were that much tougher. If you train hard enough, you'll be tough enough.'

Larry Tompkins injured his back in the league semi-final defeat against Meath in 1990. He believes that loss to Meath made them even more determined than ever to win the All-Ireland. He was out of football for some time and there was a genuine doubt about his participation in the Munster championship final. But he played, and Kerry were well beaten for the fourth time in a row. Cork defeated Roscommon in the All-Ireland semi-final, and the way the deck of cards fell meant it would be Meath who would provide the opposition in the final.

> *'No individual will win a game but I do think there are individuals that can inspire other players to play above themselves.'*

'Naturally enough, people were saying that this team wouldn't be proven until we had beaten Meath. We had a fierce drive and an incentive to beat Meath and that was the only thing on our minds. The hurlers had already won and everyone was hoping for a double. You always hear in Cork: "The hurlers can do it but the footballers will always let you down with a bang".'

Larry Tompkins was struggling with a calf muscle injury leading up to the game and he was considered a doubtful starter. He had two pain-killing injections before the game began and another two at half time. Cork won a tense game by eleven points to nine and that despite the fact that their full-forward, Colm O'Neill, was sent off just before half time.

Larry Tompkins picked up another injury during the last quarter of the game when he severely damaged the cruciate ligament in his knee. According to medical opinion, it would be nearly impossible to play with such an injury.

'It was an accidental tackle and I nearly severed the ligament in my knee. My medial ligament was totally severed. Playing against Meath and being captain was the motivation to continue. It was very painful and my knee was totally unstable. I was barely able to jog on it. It was going from underneath me. I knew well I was in serious trouble but I couldn't let go. At the time I didn't care whether it was my last game once we won.'

That was the day he overcame all odds to prove his total commitment to Cork. It was well into the following year before he kicked a ball again. Despite his severe injuries, Larry made a valuable contribution to Cork's sixth All-Ireland victory that day, kicking four points.

31

'It was not a free-flowing game. There was great tension and friction between the players and probably at the time we didn't get on that well. I know for a fact that both sets of players remember the good battles and are now friends. Both sides respect each other. Meath are good warriors and will always hit hard but fair. I would never condemn them for that. There was great satisfaction to beat a great team.'

It was special for Larry to captain Cork and for that honour he is extremely grateful to his Castlehaven club. It was a proud, proud moment when he raised the Sam Maguire Cup for the people of Cork.

On the day itself, Larry was delighted to meet many of the faithful followers who supported Cork through good times and bad. He has tremendous admiration for the genuine followers who are there on wet and wintry days to lend support. Those people mean everything to Larry Tompkins. He got more satisfaction from handing the Sam Maguire Cup to those supporters than anything else that happened to him over the weekend.

Apart from the injury in the All-Ireland final, which kept him out of football for the best part of a year, Larry has since suffered a number of other setbacks. He was out for about nine months in 1991, then had a cartilage operation on his right knee in early 1993 and just when it seemed it was all behind him he picked up a severe knee injury that ended his hopes of playing in the 1993 All-Ireland final. He will be out of action for about another nine months, and yet he remains optimistic. He is already looking forward to resuming playing for Castlehaven and for Cork. This is no ordinary man.

Coming from a rural area, there was not much else to occupy the mind of a youngster in the early sixties but kick football, and this Larry Tompkins did to his heart's content with his near neighbours, the Sargeants and Fitzpatricks.

His father, Martin, a native of the Red Bog in Clonmore, and his mother, Annie Wright from Castlemitchel near Athy, encouraged all their offspring to play sport. Football was more on his mother's side of the family. She was related to the Donnellys of Castlemitchel, a famous footballing family. At one stage, seven of the Donnelly brothers played for the local team. Her first cousins, the Wrights, played for Kildare, and there was also a link with the Delaneys from Laois, a family with a rich sporting tradition. Larry's father played hurling and football in his time and he too had a major influence on his son's career.

From as far back as he can recall, Larry, the youngest in a family of seven, was brought along to games to see his older brothers playing. It was a great thrill.

'They were all a great help to me from the time I began kicking football in the back yard at home. My brothers were all good footballers, particularly Joe, who played senior with Kildare. Martin also played minor and under-21 with the county. My father loved the game and he helped me in so many ways. He would never criticise me but at times he would tell me that I could have done better. He was not the kind of man who would praise you to the heights, and this ensured you wouldn't start getting any ideas. I don't think I am that type of fellow anyway. I go out to enjoy every game and do my best at all times to play well and win. I am just one of fifteen players and I'm always very aware that it is a team effort.'

Football was the main sport in the community and it was at Rathmore National School that Larry got to know and love the game of which he was later to become

Larry Tompkins with Colm Coyle in pursuit.

such an outstanding exponent. 'The love of the game was instilled in us at a very early age and it continued on from school matches to eventually playing with the county. It was very exciting and I just took to it. You find that most players who are successful at the game usually became attached to it at a very early age. It becomes the cornerstone of your life.'

Larry later attended Blessington Secondary School in Co Wicklow, and it was there he spent some of the best days of his life, with football at the very core of it. Rathmore is part of the parish of Blessington, no more than half a mile from the Wicklow border. Under the tutelage of the principal, Mr Dempsey, and teachers like

Paddy and Bill Hendrick, Larry continued to hone his skills and enjoyed considerable success with the school team.

'It brought home to me the importance of the game from the point of view of enjoyment and the friendships on and off the field. I was very enthusiastic and from a young age I was determined to make it at the top level. I admired players like the great Mick O'Connell in the early days and later Jack O'Shea and Brian Mullins, and hoped that some day I would possibly be there and be as good as them. I really enjoyed going to Blessington School and I still get cards and letters from past pupils and teachers wishing me well. Even since I moved to Cork, people from the school continue to write to wish me luck. They haven't forgotten me and I certainly haven't forgotten them and the good days we had.'

Larry was captain of the Wicklow Vocational Schools team that won the Leinster championship but lost to Derry in the All-Ireland final in 1980. He also loved hurling and was on the county Vocational team around the same time. At the age of sixteen he played minor, under-21 and senior for Kildare. He was on the minor team for three years, had a five-year spell on the under-21 team, and made his senior championship debut against Roscommon in Hyde Park in 1979. In the space of one week in 1980 he featured on two losing teams in Leinster finals: Meath beat Kildare by three points in the minor final and then Dublin got the better of the Lilywhites in the under-21 provincial decider after a replay.

Larry Tompkins felt it would be only a matter of time before Kildare would win a senior provincial title. But it was not to be and he never won a Leinster senior medal. Incredible as it may seem for a county with a rich footballing tradition, Kildare are still searching for their first senior provincial title since 1956.

However, Larry did win a Leinster under-21 souvenir in 1983, when Kildare beat Louth in the final. Unfortunately he missed the All-Ireland semi-final after suffering a hairline fracture of the skull while playing for Eadestown in the Intermediate county final. This kept him out of football for nearly a year and he was advised to quit the game. He was under the care of Gerry McEntee, and it was ironic that they were both later to meet in three All-Ireland finals.

Larry was back with the county for the 1984 championship, but defeat was Kildare's lot against Laois in the opening round. But if things were bad that year the worst was still to come. The following year started brightly when he was part of the Leinster team that won the Railway Cup for the first time since 1974. He was captain of the Kildare team that defeated Wicklow in the first round of the Leinster championship and travelled home from America for the Leinster semi-final. It was yet another defeat for Kildare, this time at the hands of Meath. But that was only the beginning of a story that would rock Kildare football and rumbles to this day. Perhaps Larry Tompkins' move between counties is a sign of things to come.

Dinny ALLEN

Cork Captain 1989

CORK HAS PRODUCED SOME of the truly outstanding forwards of Gaelic football, and among that exalted company has to be listed the name Dinny Allen. The multi-talented Nemo man collected the one souvenir to have eluded him when he won an All-Ireland medal in 1989, and to make it all the better he was captain the day Cork defeated Mayo in the final.

The first sport Dinny Allen got involved in was soccer at the age of six or seven. The game was played on the road in Maiville Terrace. 'We organised games between ourselves and I remember the captains at the time, who were some years older than the rest of us, would have a bet of threepence or sixpence on the outcome. As a result the captains would be putting a little bit of pressure on us to play well so that they could make a few bob. I suppose one of the reasons we played soccer was because the street was so narrow and it was an easier game to play in the circumstances. There was also a tradition of soccer in the area, as Turner's Cross was the home of Cork Celtic and everyone on the road would have supported them.

'A famous Cork Celtic player by the name of Gerry O'Brien was living in Maiville Terrace, and just up the road from us was Maggie "Blueshirt" who used to wash the jerseys. I remember Cork City had shiny orange-colour jerseys and green shorts. We used to see them hanging up on the line and the colours were very prominent in my mind.

'I always had a leaning towards soccer but hurling and football were our first games. Because of the Ban I didn't play with a soccer team until the early seventies. All of my friends played with Nemo and Turner's Cross School and we never got

---

FACT FILE

HOME PLACE: Maiville Terrace, Evergreen Road, Turner's Cross, Cork

BORN: 9 August 1952

CLUB: Nemo Rangers

CLUB ACHIEVEMENTS: Eight County Senior Football Championship medals in 1972, 1975, 1977, 1978, 1981, 1983, 1987 and 1988; four All-Ireland Club Senior Football Championship medals in 1979, 1982, 1984 and 1989; six Munster Club Senior Football Championship medals in 1976, 1978, 1979, 1982, 1984 and 1989; one Minor Hurling Championship medal in 1970; one Minor Football Championship medal in 1970; one Intermediate Hurling medal in 1971.

INTER-COUNTY ACHIEVEMENTS: One All-Ireland Senior Football medal in 1989; three Munster Senior Football Championship medals in 1983, 1988 and 1989; one Munster Under-21 Football medal in 1971; one Munster Senior Hurling medal in 1975; two National Football League medals in 1980 and 1989; five Railway Cup medals in 1975, 1976, 1977, 1978 and 1982; one All Star Award in 1980.

involved with a soccer club. Tramore Athletic was the local soccer club but we didn't hang around with them and therefore we were never tempted to play with them.'

His father, Denis, was closely involved with Nemo and his older brother, Gerry, played for the club, which meant that young Dinny often watched the team training and his first task was to fetch the ball from behind the goal. One of his earliest memories of playing with Nemo was in an under-15 game in 1964, the day Preston and West Ham met in the English Cup Final. Nemo were short some players and Dinny was sitting on the wall outside Coláiste Chríost Rí when Frank Cogan came looking for him to play a game on the north side of the city. He had played a few times before then, but that is the game that stands out in his memory. One of his abiding memories of primary schooldays is being part of an under-13 winning team that swept all opposition before them. Dinny scored three goals and three points in the final against Sullivan's Quay.

Then it was on to secondary school and a place on the Coláiste Chríost Rí team that won a Munster title in 1967. He suffered a broken leg in 1969 which kept him out of sport until September. As a result he played just one year as a county minor, and that was in 1970, when Cork were easily beaten by arch-rivals Kerry. 'It was a very hot day in Killarney, and some time before the game we were having tea and sandwiches. Unfortunately someone spilled a cup of hot tea on John Corcoran's leg and he was badly burned. The Cork selectors made five positional switches to replace John at corner-back, which meant that the whole rhythm of the team was disrupted. Cork had won the previous four Munster finals and went on to win four more and yet I had to be on the only one that we lost in nine years.'

There was further disappointment a year later when Dinny, despite playing very well in the semi-final, was left out of the Cork team that won the All-Ireland under-21 title with victory over Fermanagh.

Dinny was right-half-forward on the Nemo team that defeated UCC in the final of the county senior club championship in 1972 and life seemed good again. Around

Back, left to right: Michael Slocum, Larry Tompkins, Teddy McCarthy, Barry Coffey, Shay Fahy, John Kerins, Conor Counihan, Stephen O'Brien.
Front, left to right: Paul McGrath, Niall Cahalane, Jimmy Kerrigan, Dinny Allen (Captain), Tony Davis, Dave Barry, John Cleary.

that time, too, Dinny began taking a keen interest in soccer, because of the success of Cork Hibernians, who had won a number of trophies, including the league in 1971 and the Cup in 1972.

'A few people from Cork Hibs approached me and eventually I met Dave Bacuzzi and joined the club in January 1973. Some of my friends gave me a lot of slagging because of not joining the local team, Cork Celtic, who were my first love. Dave Bacuzzi had played at the top level in England and his presence added glamour to the club, and that is probably why I joined them. I myself would have preferred to have played with Cork Celtic but my intention was to play with a good team with a view to getting a move across channel.'

Just four months after joining the club Dinny Allen collected a Cup medal when Cork Hibernians beat Shelbourne in a replay at Flower Lodge. Some of the players on that team were Dave Wiggington, Karl Humphries, Noel and Declan O'Mahony and John Lawson.

'There were upwards of 15,000 spectators at every match we played that year, whereas before that nearly all the Gaelic football matches I was involved in would have had just a handful of people watching. I loved every minute of my time with Hibs. The Cup Final was a bonus, but just to play with some of the great players like Wigginton was a great thrill.'

In every match Dinny played at that time he was closely watched by managers and scouts from top English clubs. Bobby Charlton, Brian Clough, Tommy Docherty and Dave Sexton were among those who sought his signature. Charlton made him an offer to play with Third Division Preston but Dinny declined, feeling it better to wait for a move to a higher division. After Dinny had transferred to Cork Celtic, Brian Clough made an offer of £25,000 for Dinny and £15,000 for a player called Christy Egan. That was in 1975. Clough pulled out of the part of the deal involving Dinny, feeling he would be a risky investment because of his involvement in Gaelic games, which might tempt him to return home.

Dinny was getting very little advice at the time from any source and he believes that he himself was a little naive. 'All my friends were GAA people and they had no idea how the transfer market worked.'

He regrets that he left it so late to take up soccer. He was twenty years of age before he played his first competitive game and feels he lost the basics of the game because of not starting earlier.

'I was considered a good dribbler but I don't think I was myself. I used my speed to get by an opponent and I was only developing close control when I was

---

THE 1989 CORK TEAM

John Kerins

Niall Cahalane   Stephen O'Brien   Jimmy Kerrigan

Michael Slocum   Conor Counihan   Tony Davis

Teddy McCarthy   Shay Fahy

Dave Barry   Larry Tompkins   Barry Coffey

Paul McGrath   Dinny Allen (Captain)   John Cleary

Substitutes: Danny Culloty for Shay Fahy; Mick McCarthy for John Cleary; John O'Driscoll for Barry Coffey.

---

twenty-four instead of doing it ten or twelve years before that. If you could get rid of the pulling and dragging out of Gaelic football, which I think at this stage you can't, then I would rate both Gaelic football and soccer equally. At the moment I enjoy a game of soccer more because it is all pure football with no pulling jerseys.'

After giving a commitment to soccer Dinny was no longer being selected by Nemo, although he himself could see no reason why he could not have played both codes. Neither was he accommodated on the county team. This lasted for two years, which meant he missed out on an All-Ireland medal in 1973 when Cork, under the captaincy of his good friend Billy Morgan, defeated Galway in the final.

Dinny returned to the Cork football colours in 1975 and there followed a stream of disappointments. He was a member of the Cork team that lost eight successive Munster senior finals to Kerry.

'One match was worse than the other. Cork were favourites in 1975 but we only scored seven points. The following year's Munster final put us back a lot. We were beaten in a replay. The first game marked the opening of Páirc Uí Chaoimh and it was a disaster from the point of view that spectators were in around the sideline. I scored the equalising point and the replay went ahead again at Páirc Uí Chaoimh. It was a hot sweltering day and we were beaten in extra time. It was supposed to be one of the best Munster finals of all time. Kerry scored 3-20 to our total of 2-19. That win definitely helped Kerry on their way to becoming a great team and it put us back years. Still, we were always optimistic each year that we would win.'

'Before the second half the referee, Mickey Kearns, brought the Dublin captain, Gerry Hargan, and myself together in everyone's view and told us to talk to our players and warn them of their behaviour in the second half. We huddled together and the lads asked me what the referee had said. I told them he had wished us the best of luck and had hoped the weather would get better.'

Cork eventually got the better of Kerry in the Munster final of 1983 thanks to a last-gasp goal from Tadhg Murphy, and they drew with Dublin in the All-Ireland semi-final at Croke Park. The replay went ahead at Páirc Uí Chaoimh.

'I remember discussing the change of venue with Kevin Kehilly and he was in favour of bringing the game to Cork but I was very much for playing the game in Croke Park. I felt it would put the pressure back on Dublin again. We were well beaten at the end of the day.'

Kerry regained the Munster final the following year and so began yet another heartbreaking chapter in Dinny Allen's sporting life. He was dropped by the selectors in 1985 although he himself felt he was still playing well enough to command a regular place on the team. He continued to play with his club, and when Billy Morgan returned from America things took a turn for the better.

'In 1987 Billy was appointed coach of the Cork team and I remember going to the All-Ireland semi-final, in which Cork were playing Galway. Larry Tompkins scored a point to level the game. The Cork forward line had played very badly that day, and as I was playing good football for my club a trial match was arranged between Nemo and the county team a week before the replay. It was felt if I played well that day I would be back on the Cork panel. There was a few thousand at the game and the

pressure was enormous. I played reasonably well but I didn't set the world alight. I met Billy the night after the trial match and he said, "I think you played your last match for Cork back in '84, as they're not in favour of selecting you on the team".'

Nonetheless, Billy asked Dinny in October 1987 to play in a League game against Monaghan.

'Although the thought crossed my mind that I would be leaving myself wide open for criticism again at the age of thirty-six I still agreed to give it a try. I was never afraid to put myself on the line. I played at right-corner-forward in the 1988 All-Ireland final and we lost to Meath in a replay.'

At the beginning of 1989 Cork's own supporters were asking whether the team had the mettle to win an All-Ireland. Cork had lost the previous two finals to Meath and those defeats rankled. Would 1989 be any different? It was!

'I remember the home final of the League against Dublin very well as I think it was one of the best Cork displays in which I was ever involved. We were in the Burlington Hotel in Dublin before the game and it was the time when there was a lot of talk about whether Dave Barry would play for Cork City against Bohemians in the FAI cup final or against New York in the League final if Cork should beat Dublin. Dan Hoare stood up and said, "I don't know what Dave Barry is going to do next Sunday but I wish him the best of luck whatever he does. All that matters is that we win against Dublin today." The team went out floating and we played brilliantly and beat Dublin. Dave played in the cup final the next Sunday and was back on the Cork team for the second leg of the League final at the Gaelic Grounds in New York.' Dinny was presented with the League cup by Ed Koch, the Mayor of New York.

Cork retained the Munster final in July with a three-points victory over Kerry. Dinny remembers there was extra pressure on the team as newly-crowned National League champions.

'We travelled to Killarney the night before and stayed in the Castlerosse Hotel. We had Mass in the open air that night. I also remember we had our team talk in the back garden of the hotel under an old oak tree. Even though we were on top for a long period we were hanging on for the last ten minutes of the game. Looking back, it was a good thing that we had a hard match and a fright. People in Cork were dissatisfied with our performance and we came in for a fair bit of criticism. After losing two All-Ireland finals in a row the satisfaction of beating Kerry wasn't immense. There was still a big job to be done.'

Dublin provided the opposition in the All-Ireland semi-final and it turned out to be a fiery encounter.

'I can remember the game vividly as I was involved in some skirmishes with Keith Barr and the weather was diabolical. Cork and Dublin always like playing against each other, and being two city teams, the rivalry is keen. Dublin won the toss and decided to play with the gale-force breeze in the first half. I was full-forward and I remember the ball never came up near me for a very long spell. Dublin built up a good lead but then we got two penalties, both of which John Cleary put away. Keith Barr was sent off for a late foul on me in the first half. We had been involved in a skirmish before that. There was a little argy-bargy, a few threats and pushing and shoving in the tunnel going in at half time.

'The Cork players squared up to the Dublin players outside their dressing-room but there were no punches thrown. I remember stewards and GAA officials running around trying to calm things down. Before the second half got under way the referee, Mickey Kearns, brought the Dublin captain, Gerry Hargan, and myself together in everyone's view and told us to talk to our players and warn them of their behaviour in the second half. We huddled together and the lads asked me what the referee had said. I told them he had wished us the best of luck and had hoped the weather would get better. When a situation is getting out of hand I see nothing wrong with the referee calling the captains aside to calm things down. The weather was completely changed in the second half, it was like a different season. The wind died down, the sun came out and it was hot. Again it was a situation of fourteen men putting it up to the team with the extra man and we were glad to come away with a four-points win.'

There was considerable tension in the build-up to the All-Ireland final. Cork had failed to deliver the goods the previous two years and the players were conscious of the consequences of defeat.

'We were very much aware that we would never be forgiven if we lost three All-Ireland finals in a row. That certainly put extra pressure on us and although we tried to pass it off lightly it was never far from our minds. It was a brilliant game, with both teams intent on playing good football. Mayo put it up to us to the end and tried to beat us by playing football, which is the way it should be.'

Before he was engulfed by the crowd that swarmed onto the pitch Dinny Allen had about ten seconds to savour the occasion. His feeling was one of total relief, nothing more, nothing less.

'I don't get emotional about matches because after all it's only sport and not the most important thing in the world. There was always the fear before the game that we would lose and have to live with it for the rest of our lives. It was a ridiculous situation but that's the hard facts. People would be saying, "that crowd there lost three in a row; they hadn't the bottle". We were almost getting paranoid about the situation.'

The homecoming was a never-to-be-forgotten experience. The team were not aware of what the win meant to Cork people until they arrived back in their home city on the Monday evening. Tens of thousands turned out to greet the newly-crowned champions and the city was festooned in red and white. The All-Ireland final was Dinny Allen's last game. He announced his retirement from inter-county football soon afterwards, although many were of the opinion that the 37-year-old had plenty to offer. Dinny has no regrets about his decision.

Dinny Allen was no mean performer as a hurler and won a Munster Senior Championship medal in 1975 when Cork trounced Limerick in what was the first seventy-minute final. He lined out at left-half-forward but suffered concussion during the game. He also played in the All-Ireland semi-final when Cork went down by two points to Galway.

Dinny Allen played football, hurling and soccer at the highest level. Those who played against him in any code will tell you he was outstanding at all three. But he himself is of the opinion that he lost out because of his versatility.

'I remember going into the King County Hotel in Midleton some years back and there were three photographs hanging on the wall of winning Cork teams of different years. One was the Cork football team, the second was the Cork hurling team, and the third the Cork Hibernian soccer team and, would you believe it, I was not included in any one of them. The particular years those teams featured in the photographs won, I happened to be involved with one of the other teams that failed to win anything. Definitely a case of being in the wrong place at the wrong time.'

But that was certainly not the situation in 1989, when Dinny became only the third Cork man to raise the Sam Maguire Cup. It was Cork's fifth All-Ireland title and Dinny Allen's first. A perfect end to the career of a man who must rate as one of the greatest all-rounders of his generation.

Joe CASSELLS

Meath Captain 1988

THE FIRST PLAYER to lift the new Sam Maguire Cup, presented in 1988, was Meath's Joe Cassells. It is very likely that Joe created even more history as the only man to captain an All-Ireland winning team having played just one game. That 1988 final went to a replay in which Meath defeated Cork by 0-13 to 0-12. Mick Lyons had been Meath captain in the drawn match but Joe was on the team for the replay and took over the role of captain, as his club, Navan O'Mahonys, were reigning county champions.

It was one of the most controversial All-Ireland finals of recent times, fuelled still further when hard-hitting comments and articles by players from both sides were published in newspapers after the game.

There is nearly always much more tension in a replay and this was certainly the case in 1988. The fact that Meath had defeated Cork in the 1987 final did not help relations either.

It is generally accepted that Meath were very fortunate to escape with a draw the first day, and their chances of victory looked even less remote in the replay when midfielder Gerry McEntee was sent to the line after only six minutes' play.

'It really put our backs to the wall and I remember thinking, "what are we going to do now?" Suddenly, I found myself just drifting into the midfield area and covering ground along with Liam Hayes. Colm O'Rourke also moved out from his corner-forward position and he began organising as well. We were talking and watching to see who would be the extra man at the kick-out. We were very much on top of the situation, even more so than if we had an equal number of players to Cork on the field. The fact that we felt we had extra work to do just motivated us that bit more. I have visions of Bernie Flynn going for a goal and we five points up or something like that and the goalkeeper, John Kerins, saving it. I remember saying to

---

FACT FILE

HOME PLACE: Athlumney, Navan, County Meath

BORN: 10 October 1954   CLUBS: Navan De La Salle; Navan O'Mahonys

ACHIEVEMENTS IN CLUB COMPETITIONS: Eight County Senior Football Championship medals 1973, 1979, 1981, 1985, 1987, 1988, 1989 and 1990; two County Senior Hurling Championship medals in 1985 and 1986; one County Junior Football Championship medal; numerous Feis Cup medals; won every under-age competition from Under-12 to Minor.

INTER-COUNTY ACHIEVEMENTS: Two All-Ireland Senior Football Championship medals in 1987 and 1988; four Leinster Senior Championship medals in 1986, 1987, 1988 and 1990; one Leinster Minor medal in 1972; three National Football League medals in 1975, 1988 and 1990; two Railway Cup Football medals in 1985 and 1986; captain of the Meath team that won the Centenary Cup in 1984.

---

myself "why did he not put that blinking ball over the bar?" Next thing Cork began to whittle down our lead and there was just a point in it at the end. I was running myself into the ground after anything that moved. I remember a couple of Meath backs getting the ball and not really looking where they were kicking it and there was this wall of Cork fellows just attacking our goal. They had us on the rack for a long time but just couldn't get the scores. They kept trying to walk the ball in, but our backs stood their ground and played very well.'

There was a strong feeling within the Meath camp that they had allowed Cork dictate matters and push them around somewhat in the drawn game. To a man the team was not prepared to allow it happen in the replay. Tensions ran high during and after the second game.

'The whole thing went a little overboard. There were too many comments made to the press. A lot of fellows suddenly became journalists and it didn't help the situation. Loads of things happen on a football field that are not personal, as anyone who ever played the game knows. You shouldn't seek to make incidents on the field personal, as they happen in an instant and should be forgotten about just as quickly. Trying to analyse things that occur during play doesn't lend itself to good relations between two teams.

> *'The year I was born Meath won the All-Ireland final and their captain, Peter McDermott, brought the Cup into the Lourdes Hospital in Drogheda as his daughter was born around the same period. My mother put me sitting in the Sam Maguire Cup in the hospital. It was uncanny how things worked out.'*

'Both teams were more relaxed in 1987 but no one wanted to give way in 1988. There was just too much at stake to lose. If people took time to compare the photograph prior to the 1988 final with the one taken in 1987 they would see a big difference between the two. The players were much more relaxed in 1987 but there was a fierce determination on all our faces for the replay in 1988.'

Joe Cassells will never forget the relief he felt when Kerry referee, Tommy Sugrue, blew the final whistle. Meath had survived against all the odds and what for Joe himself seemed like an impossibility earlier in the year was now a reality.

'I was absolutely exhausted. I was never as tired or as completely drained in my whole life. I had nothing left as I had run myself to a standstill. Séamus Clinch from Navan grabbed a hold of me in a big bear-hug and probably saved me from getting twenty lashes as everybody was back-slapping at that stage. Eventually I got up on to the podium but I found it hard to think for over a minute. I wanted a drink of water as my voice was gone. All I needed was something to clear my throat and give me a couple of minutes to regain my composure. There was nothing left in the lungs. I have looked at captains on the podium since then and there wouldn't be a bother on them but I was in a bad way. My mind was blank for a few seconds but suddenly the voice came back and everything worked out well.'

The homecoming was extra-special. An open-decked bus took the victorious team through Navan, much to the delight of thousands of delirious Meath supporters. 'One of the publicans in Trimgate Street threw a bottle of champagne onto the bus but I didn't see it in the dark and the bottle hit the side of the Cup and bounced back onto the street. It was the first dent to be put in the new Sam Maguire Cup.'

Many GAA followers in Meath feel that their team never got due recognition for their achievements in winning two All-Ireland titles.

'We didn't get the credit from the media and obviously because we were keeping Dublin down didn't help the situation either but it was reflected in other ways. It came home to me a few years ago when I met a fellow from Sligo and he said to me, "How times have changed. People in Sligo are no longer asking how is Kerry getting on but how did Meath get on today?" He had played club football in Meath at a time when football was very poor and not looked upon at all. He maintained that it was the greatest compliment our team could get when people from other counties were anxious to find out how Meath were performing.'

Luck was certainly on Joe Cassells' side in 1988. He had torn a muscle in his thigh before the League final of that year but decided to play with heavy strapping against Dublin. The match ended in a draw. Meath won the replay five weeks later. The same year Joe travelled with the All-Stars to America where he picked up yet another injury which forced him out of the entire Leinster Championship campaign. He was not selected for the All-Ireland semi-final or the drawn final but was chosen for the replay in place of Mattie McCabe. Colm Coyle and Terry Ferguson were also recalled at the expense of Kevin Foley and Pádraic Lyons.

'Once I got my place back on the team there was never any question in my mind but that I would be captain.

'It didn't make that much difference being captain. All right, it made the difference of leading the team out on the field and all that but not as regards team talks. Being one of the longest-serving members of the team I would still have contributed as much when not playing as I did when captain. We had got to the stage where it was no longer necessary to bang the table to motivate each other and instead we would be calculating and talking about what needed to be done. I certainly didn't go round telling everyone what to do; instead I concentrated very deeply on my own performance to make sure I got that right. I was always a great believer in leading by example on the field more so than talking about it. I think some things in life are destined for us. I often thought about it since and wondered how things could work out in such a manner so that I was given that chance. The year I was born Meath won the All-Ireland final and their captain, Peter McDermott, brought the Cup into the Lourdes Hospital in Drogheda as his daughter was born around the same period. My mother put me sitting in the Sam Maguire Cup in the hospital. It was uncanny how things worked out.'

Almost from the time he was able to walk Joe Cassells kicked ball with his three

---

THE 1988 MEATH TEAM

Michael McQuillan

| Bob O'Malley | Mick Lyons | Terry Ferguson |
| Colm Coyle | Liam Harnan | Martin O'Connell |

Liam Hayes   Gerry McEntee

| David Beggy | Joe Cassells (Captain) | P.J.Gillic |
| Colm O'Rourke | Brian Stafford | Bernard Flynn |

Substitute: Mattie McCabe for P.J. Gillic

---

brothers and other youngsters around the village.

His father, P.J., and mother, Mary, were a great source of encouragement, as was Paddy O'Brien who exercised a huge influence on Joe's early football career. He organised a whole series of street leagues which allowed youngsters display their skills. Joe also pays tribute to Brother Leo from the local De La Salle College.

'I was more interested in athletics at one stage in my school days. I won under-12 and under-14 county championships in athletics. I remember winning the under-14 Meath Championship but I never got to the Leinster Championships. I was waiting to be collected at our front wall but no one arrived. We had no car in the family at that time. It was my first big disappointment.'

Football took over after that and Joe came in contact with Dónal O'Grady who saw enough talent to persevere with the youngster. There were many times when Joe would forget to bring his boots but this never deterred his mentor. 'I remember searching the front of his Volkswagen for an old pair of boots. I can still see myself looking under the spare wheel searching for the boots, not wanting to play at all but being lugged along by Dónal. It is an awkward age for a lad and if someone guides you over those difficult years then everything works out. Remember, you are asking a youngster to go out and play against physically stronger men. At that time there was a third-man tackle and certain players would take no prisoners. I was on the Navan O'Mahonys team that won the Junior Championship in 1970 and made it onto the senior team the following year.'

As was the fashion of the early seventies, Joe wore his hair long but there was one day he wished he had not. 'Navan O'Mahonys played Ballivor that day. Bertie Cunningham was playing against us and I had this massive long hair way down my back. I remember going for this ball and Bertie grabbed me by the hair and lifted me about two feet off the ground and swung me around. All I can remember is my two feet going off the ground and finding myself in a heap!

'When I played my first senior match for Meath I was at left-half-forward against

Back, left to right: Colm O'Rourke, Mick Lyons, Gerry McEntee, Michael McQuillan, Martin O'Connell, Brian Stafford, Liam Hayes, David Beggy.
Front, left to right: P.J. Gillic, Colm Coyle, Terry Ferguson, Joe Cassells (captain), Bernard Flynn, Bob O'Malley, Liam Harnan.

Laois at Croke Park in 1974. My mother was down the country with the ICA and was listening to the match on the radio. She was getting a bit of a ribbing about her son playing when suddenly the commentator on the radio said, "I have seen long hair in Croke Park but this man Cassells has the longest hair I have ever seen."

'I had been picked out of the blue for the team as Oliver O'Brien was out through suspension. Oliver got his place back for the Leinster final against Dublin and I was named in the substitutes but came on during the game at midfield. Brian Mullins and Stephen Rooney were the Dublin midfielders that day. They beat us by five points and of course then went on to win the All-Ireland. We had a great win over Dublin in the League final in 1975 and that was a big day for me.'

It was to be eleven years after that League final before Meath won a provincial title, their first since 1970. In that time Joe Cassells never missed one championship game, making it all the more disappointing when an an injury forced him out of Meath's Leinster final wins over Dublin in 1987 and again in 1988. There were some good Meath teams during that period but they gave their supporters very little to cheer about in terms of winning silverware. Joe Cassells contemplated retirement only once in that time but was persuaded to change his mind.

Can he pinpoint the formula that transformed Meath from being constant losers to big-time winners?

'When Seán Boylan arrived he brought organisation into the camp. He got fellows to make sacrifices and there was no longer any excuse to miss training. Before that some players would have opted for club football rather than playing for the county team but Seán changed all that. If nothing else Seán knows people inside out and he knows how to treat people with respect. He allowed the players express themselves in team talks more so than trying to tell players what he wanted. In that way he actually pulled it together.'

Seán Boylan took over the Meath team in 1982 but it was the same old story in 1983 as the Royal County lost out to Dublin in the early rounds of the Leinster Championship. Things seemed to be taking shape when Meath won the Centenary Final in 1984 but it was back down to earth with a bang in 1985 when they suffered a humiliating defeat at the hands of Laois in the Leinster championship.

'Laois were inspired that day. It was certainly a low point for the Meath team. Seán cleared out a fair percentage of players after that defeat. He found six new players: Terry Ferguson, Kevin Foley, Liam Harnan, David Beggy, P.J. Gillic and Brian Stafford.

'We beat Dublin in the 1986 Leinster final and I was played at right-corner-back for a specific reason. It was the first time I ever remember a Meath selection committee planning a strategy. Brian Mullins had taken over Dublin and was playing Tommy Carr at full-forward. We could see from Dublin's previous matches that Tommy was starting in his selected position but he then proceeded to go all over the field bringing the full-back out. I was playing midfield at the time but the selectors decided to play me at right-corner-back and let me follow Carr. The idea would be for Tommy Carr to start at full-forward then roam out the field and Joe McNally would move into his position which would leave it very awkward for any player marking him. Mick Lyons would be the ideal man but if he was running all over the field that was no use. I played right-corner-back against Wicklow and it went very well. Kevin O'Brien was playing full-forward and their obvious ploy was to get the

ball into Kevin and try and take on Mick. An awful lot of teams had this perception that Mick was slow which wasn't the case at all. He was quick of mind and quick on the field and would make it very difficult for any man. The Leinster final started and, as we expected. Tommy Carr took off out the field and I said "good luck, Mick" and followed him and spent the whole match running around the field which suited me down to the ground.'

Meath won the game but they were now faced with the dilemma of where to play Joe Cassells in the All-Ireland semi-final. The team was beginning to take shape and although Joe was not a natural corner-back the selectors opted for the same line-out that had done so well in the Leinster final. That semi-final will be always be remembered above all else for Ger Power's freak goal.

'The fact that I was captain had put the selectors in an awkward position. Being a long-striding player, I was a more central type of footballer than a corner-back. But Liam Hayes and Gerry McEntee were playing very well at midfield so there was no place for me there. You need short steps and to be quick off the mark to be a corner-back. It's pure reaction stuff in there in those corners, more so than out in the middle. Then of course Ger Power was an opportunist and you'd have to watch him like a hawk.

'Ogie Moran kicked a high ball into space and Ger was beside me and took off and naturally enough with his short legs was going to get ahead of me. What was on my mind was to get goal-side of him. I remember reaching out trying to grab a bit of his jersey and suddenly being hit and the walls caved in. I got a woeful belt on the head and looked up to see what happened and saw Mick Lyons and Mickie McQuillan on the ground. The three of us had crashed into each other. I was gone for the rest of the match.

'I took a break for the 1987 League because of a combination of injuries. I got a bang on the shoulder from the "Bomber" Liston and it had a kind of whiplash affect. I often talked to him since and he doesn't ever remember the incident. It taught me a lesson and set me thinking, "here we are competing against the Kerry lads and they don't even know when they hit you". Nine times out of ten when you'd be playing on the field you'd say, "I gave that fellow a good souse there today". But when fellows are hitting you and hitting you so hard and don't even realise it then it's time to take note. I think we took a leaf out of their book. Over the next four or five years Meath fellows were hitting hard. It would be nothing personal, we'd just be going for that ball with all our might. And whoever was in the way didn't matter. We'd be going hell for leather!'

Joe was chosen at centre-half-forward for the 1987 Leinster Championship but unfortunately he missed the provincial decider against Dublin.

'Mattie McCabe came in and scored 1-2 and hit one gem of a goal from a volley. I remember saying, "there is not another Meath player would have done that". I got my place back for the semi-final and was on the team for the All-Ireland final in which we beat Cork. It was a great sense of achievement to win my first All-Ireland medal.'

Nowadays Joe runs his own electrical business in Navan. He is married to Louise and they have six children, William, Séamus, Stephen, Joanna, Fiona and Tracy.

Joe himself bowed out of inter-county football after Meath's defeat by Cork in the 1990 All-Ireland final. His entry into the the game fifteen minutes from the end was not enough to deprive Cork of their second All-Ireland title in a row. That last fling brought to an end the career of one of the greatest players to don a Meath jersey. Joe Cassells' sixteen years on the county team embraced three decades and he won a League title in each one of those.

Mick LYONS

Meath Captain 1987

THE COUNTY of Meath has long been renowned for producing outstanding full-backs and in that department none was better than that stout-hearted colossus Mick Lyons. The high-fielding Summerhill club man followed in the footsteps of those two other giants Paddy 'Hands' O'Brien and Jack Quinn. Like his predessors it can be said that Mick always led by example and was never known to shirk a challenge, no matter how daunting. He ruled his patch like few other defenders of his generation and such was his reputation that it was often said that the mere presence of Mick Lyons was worth a few points on the scoreboard to the Royal County even before a ball was kicked. This was especially so when the opposition was provided by Dublin whom Meath defeated in five Leinster finals between 1986 to 1991.

His early sporting influences came from his Mayo-born father, Patrick, who played county football with Kildare in the late forties and early fifties.

In 1967, then a starry-eyed nine-year-old, Mick was brought by his father to Croke Park to see his native county, Meath, captained by Peter Darby beat Cork in the All-Ireland Final, and when it was all over he was allowed into the dressing-room to meet his heroes.

Twenty years were to pass before Meath would be crowned champions again and when it happened in 1987 it was the same Mick Lyons, now grown to be one of the great full-backs of his generation, who held the Sam Maguire Cup aloft in triumph.

His father never pushed his sons into football but was glad to see them involved in sport.

'He would say to you, "if you want to go, then go". I remember one day I was going for a minor trial and he said to me. "you're not good enough". That was it. I still had another year left as a minor. I thought a lot about what he said, as he was never too far off the mark.

'And mention of those days involved with the Meath minor team I have to say a special thanks to Pádraig Cribben, who brought me to all the minor trials. I played

---

FACT FILE

HOME PLACE: Oldtown, County Meath

BORN: 22 February 1958   CLUB: Summerhill

ACHIEVEMENTS IN CLUB COMPETITIONS: Three County Senior Football Championship medals; two Feis Cup medals.

INTER-COUNTY ACHIEVEMENTS: Two All-Ireland Senior Football medals in 1987 and 1988; five Leinster Senior Football Championship medals in 1986, 1987, 1988, 1990 and 1991; two National Football League medals in 1988 and 1990; two Railway Cup Football medals; Centenary Cup medal in 1984; two All Star Awards in 1984 and 1986;

Played against Australia in the Compromise Rules Series.

full-back for one year with the county minor team but we had little success. I started off playing football at corner-back for Summerhill and then played for a while at full-back but nearly all my football with the club was at midfield.'

Although his name will always be linked with Summerhill, Mick Lyons grew up about six miles from the village in the small rural parish of Oldtown near the banks of the canal close to the Kildare border. He attended Coole National School, in the half parish of Summerhill, and, as he jokingly says, all the best footballers came from there.

Growing up nothing much else mattered to Mick and his two brothers, Terry and Pádraic, only playing football at every available opportunity. They also played tennis and rugby or whatever sport was getting most coverage on television at any time. The lawn in front of the house was where it all happened. It was there that games were won and lost and it was there too that he mastered the art of high catching from constantly jumping for a ball with his brothers.

After he finished at National School, Mick attended Trim Technical School but left to start his own plant hire business at the age of seventeen. He admits that he never liked school but he still continued to play with the school team for about six months after he left at the request of Mr Moran, the teacher in charge of football.

Mick acknowledges he was very fortunate to have come in contact early on with Mattie Kerrigan, whom he credits with shaping the football careers of many players in the Summerhill area. Mattie was centre-half-forward when Meath won the All-Ireland football title for the third time in 1967. Starting in the early seventies, Summerhill won five County Senior Senior Championships in a row.

'I was very young at the time and was very lucky to have been involved as a sub and to come on in the last year of that good senior team. I always thought that the club at that time was ahead of itself in its training methods and the way they organised everything. Mattie was a kind of a god around here. If he told lads to train six nights a week that was it, no bother. By persuasion and encouragement he got

Back, left to right: Colm O'Rourke, Mick Lyons (captain), Michael McQuillan, Gerry McEntee, Brian Stafford, Martin O'Connell, David Beggy, Joe Cassells.
Front, left to right: P.J. Gillic, Terry Ferguson, Bernard Flynn, Bob O'Malley, Liam Harnan, Kevin Foley, Liam Hayes.

more out of players than anyone else ever could. He made average players believe they were very good. There is no doubt but that the success of Summerhill club was due in no small way to Mattie, Fr Behan, Paddy Daly and Martin McDonald, who was the headmaster of Coole National School.'

Mick came onto the Meath team at centre-half-back for the 1979 Leinster Championship and was with them through many lean years. He remembers travelling to play Clare in a League game and, as he himself says, 'there wasn't ten people outside the wire watching us. Lads would be laughing at you playing for Meath then.'

The first time he realised Meath were capable of winning a major championship was about a year into Seán Boylan's tenure as manager.

'Seán was getting at least twenty-five fellows to train. Before that I remember you'd get six lads in one night and the next night there would be ten different fellows. Then the week before a big match the whole place would be packed with fellows. That all stopped when Seán took over. After a while he instilled in us the belief that we could win something. Remember, when he took over as manager no one wanted the job. We won the Centenary Cup in 1984 when we beat Monaghan and we seemed to be going places but then Laois demolished us in the Leinster Championship the following year. They absolutely tore us asunder. We prepared well for that match but we were annihilated. Lads were running everywhere and we not able to do anything. I'd say it was naievety, although at the end of the day I don't think we were good enough. Seán Boylan's position was under pressure too after that game. There was an awful lot of changes after that and Seán picked up some great new players like Liam Harnan, Bobby O'Malley, Brian Stafford and Bernie Flynn.

'We hadn't real confidence until we beat Dublin in the Leinster final of 1986. It was a very wet day and this time we won by two points, due mainly to the free-taking of Brian Stafford. I always reckoned that Brian would keep you in a match when you were going badly. He could always be relied on to get scores. That was an important win against Dublin. You can have yourself convinced that you have all the confidence in the world and think you're going to win but it's no use until you finally nail something. We didn't really believe we could beat Kerry in the All-Ireland semi-final until the match was half over. It was too late before we realised we had the beating of them.'

That was the day when Kerry star forward Ger Power scored one of the strangest goals even seen at Croke Park. Three Meath players, goalkeeper Michael McQuillan, corner-back Joe Cassells and Mick collided with each other going for a ball.

'I still can't believe it happened. A high ball came in and I went for it, which I

THE 1987 MEATH TEAM		
	Michael McQuillan	
Bob O'Malley	Mick Lyons (Captain)	Terry Ferguson
Kevin Foley	Liam Harnan	Martin O'Connell
Liam Hayes		Gerry McEntee
David Beggy	Joe Cassells	P.J. Gillic
Colm O'Rourke	Brian Stafford	Bernard Flynn
Substitutes: Colm Coyle for Joe Cassells; Pádraic Lyons for Martin O'Connell.		

think was the right thing to do although no one took responsibility afterwards for the mistake. I remember falling to the ground with a thud half dazed. Next thing I looked around and saw the ball hopping and Ger picking it up and kicking it into an empty net.

'I couldn't believe it was happening and I thought someone would surely tackle him but next thing, " bang" into the net. End of story. That's the way it goes. We were very disappointed to lose as time was running out for the likes of Gerry McEntee, Joe Cassells, Colm O'Rourke and myself.'

Mick considers the Meath team that won the All-Irelands of 1987 and 1988 to be exceptionally talented outfits. He believes that the Kerry team of 1978-1982 was the greatest of all but, after that, he reckons Meath were right up there with the best of them.

'We knew going into matches that we had the beating of teams, all we had to do was play. We had the power and we had the skill. We could mix it or we could play great football and had a lot to offer.'

Does he feel the Meath team got credit for what they achieved?

'I felt if we had won three All-Irelands we would have got plenty of credit. We wanted a third All-Ireland badly but we didn't get it.'

In 1988 Meath defeated Cork for the second year in a row in the All-Ireland final this time after a replay. Mick was captain the first day but Joe Cassells returned to the team for the replay and took over the captaincy. Mick was delighted to see his good friend get his just reward after such long service in the green and gold.

> *'I was a ruthless player but not dirty. I'd go full out for a ball and if I got a chance to give a fellow a good shoulder and a tackle then I'd do it. I often got into a tangle with a fellow but I would never turn around and hit a player off the ball. I never believed in that. I know it's not supposed to be nice in sport but I played to win.'*

Mick Lyons' greatest sporting disappointment was Meath's defeat by Down in the 1991 All-Ireland final. It was a shattering blow especially since they had to play four games before eventually beating Dublin in the Leinster Championship.

'At the start of that year, Meath were not a great team but we kept improving with each game. The move which brought the goal against Dublin was something we had done in training time and time again. It was great to do it in front of such a big crowd and to the "old enemy". No better time to do it! I could feel for the Dublin fellows as it's not nice to be whipped at the posts.

'After the way the year had gone a lot of people were hoping we would win the All-Ireland final but it was not to be and Down, with a great football tradition, came and did their stuff. It was heartbreaking.'

A significant chapter in Mick's career was his selection on the Ireland team that travelled to play Australia in 1986. He never considered there was a future in the game but he thoroughly enjoyed the experience, which gave him an insight into the life of a professional footballer. It also provided the opportunity to meet and befriend players from different counties. That was an aspect of the tour that he liked.

'If I had a choice I'd have played football professionally, no doubt in the world. The Ireland manager, Kevin Heffernan, was a very shrewd man and it was only

Mick Lyons airborne and in control.

when I saw him in action that I understood why Dublin were continually beating Meath in the years previously. I suddenly realised what it would take if Meath were ever to beat Dublin. My brother Pádraic and myself travelled to Australia the week after we won the club championship. Both of us had injuries from that game so we had to undergo physiotherapy before we were passed fit to travel. We won two out of the three Test games and were delighted to win the Series.'

Mick would go so far as to say that a Leinster final between Meath and Dublin is no different from an All-Ireland final. 'There is never any holding back and once the ball is thrown in it's through the trenches and away. There is never anything between the teams and it was no different in 1987 when we beat Dublin by just four points. We got fed up being beaten by Dublin up to 1986 and it went so deep you wouldn't know where to start dragging it out. I have always felt that the Meath and Dublin clashes are very special.'

Meath defeated Derry in the 1987 All-Ireland semi-final and advanced to meet Cork in the final. It was to be the first of many stormy meetings between the sides. 'We had fierce rivalry with Cork after that and it probably went overboard from constantly playing each other in big matches. It was a different rivalry to Dublin. You could have it out with Dublin on the field and that was it, but this went further. Probably too much talk to the media from both sides and as a result relations between the teams deteriorated. People would have been better off to have kept their mouths shut. The hype with Dublin was different. Once the match was over that was the end of the story.

'I remember two incidents in particular during that match; one was when I dived full length to block Jimmy Kerrigan's shot. I decided he was going to kick it and it worked out well for me. If he had toed it up it could have been different. The second incident was when Colm O'Rourke scored a goal. It was the turning point of the game and we went on to win it by six points.

'With a few minutes remaining I suddenly realised, this is it, barring a disaster. At that stage Cork were just kicking the ball in high anywhere at all and we were getting it. I always believed our midfielder Gerry McEntee was another defender. He was a special man on that team. Near the end of the game against Cork he was looping back into defence, helping out as usual.'

Seán Boylan had left no stone unturned in the effort to bring the Sam Maguire Cup back to the county and Mick believes without him it would never have come back. Every detail was thought out well in advance of the final. Even though the team was travelling to Dublin on the morning of the final and was only staying at a hotel in Malahide for a few hours before going to Croke Park, Seán still felt it necessary to bring his captain to the hotel some weeks beforehand to check the beach.

'We wanted to see what the beach was like and to make sure we could get to it without any difficulty. We had a grand walk and a chat on the beach the morning of the match and we kicked a ball around for a while. Seán had everything perfectly planned and he always had his "little lads" around him who were super. Everyone had their own job to do and there was no confusion. We used to meet in Dealgan Park and go to Mass every Saturday night before a match and then we'd go and have something to eat. My brother Pádraic, Liam Harnan and myself always travelled together to the games and it was the same on the day of the final. There was the usual sneering, codding and messing in the car that morning. It was all good fun.'

Mick always rated his brother as an outstanding corner back and he feels he 'got the hard end of the stick' during Meath's glory days. He came on as a sub in the All-Ireland final of 1987 and played in the drawn final of 1988 but was dropped for the replay. Even today it is plain to see that Mick feels for his young brother. Sport can be so cruel.

Because of his great composure under pressure, most people would be of the opinion that Mick Lyons did not have a nerve in his body. But he himself admits to being as nervous as the rest when his turn came to lead the Meath team onto Croke Park on final day.

'The first couple of minutes [...] legs would be heavy and you'd say [...] yourself, "what am I doing out her[...] and I not able to run". Then as soon as the game would start everything would be all right.'

Of his reputation as a hard man, Mick says: 'I was a ruthless player but not dirty. I'd go full out for a ball and if I got a chance to give a fellow a good shoulder and a tackle then I'd do it. I often got into a tangle with a fellow but I would never turn around and hit a player off the ball. I never believed in that. I know it's not supposed to be nice in sport but I played to win and that was it. I enjoyed the cut and thrust of playing full-back. I enjoyed having to make split-second decisions. I miss that part of the game, now that I've quit the inter-county scene. I got a high out of playing football.'

Mick was never a man into 'yahooing', as he puts it, and once he had been presented with the Sam Maguire Cup he passed it over to some of the other players to show to the supporters. Meanwhile he made his way to the dressing-room by the back of the Hogan Stand and was overjoyed when he came face to face with his great friend and mentor Mattie Kerrigan. 'You would think it was planned. The tears were flowing down his face. It was a very special moment. It was wonderful to meet my wife, Helen, and my mother and father after the game. The homecoming to Summerhill was a once-in-a-lifetime experience. It was unbelievable and I still think of it.'

Tommy DOYLE

Kerry Captain 1986

᠁ **1986,** Chicago-born Tommy Doyle was the last Kerry captain to collect the original Sam Maguire Cup. The following year that trophy was presented to Meath's Mick Lyons before it was retired and replaced by 'Sam Óg'.

Under Tommy Doyle's captaincy Kerry had become the first county in either code to win thirty All-Ireland Senior titles. But it was a far from easy win. The chances of a 'Kingdom' victory looked very remote when, early in the second half, they trailed Tyrone by seven points. And it could have been worse, had Tyrone right-half-back Kevin McCabe not blasted a penalty over the bar. It was the turning point of the game. The Ulster champions were to score just two further points as Kerry took complete control, adding two goals and eleven points. The final score was Kerry 2-15 Tyrone 1-10.

Recalling that 1986 final, Tommy Doyle admits he was a worried man going into the dressing-room at the interval.

'It didn't look too good for Kerry at that stage. But we kept our heads in the second half. I would say that the Tyrone players thought they had it won after Kevin McCabe's point from the penalty. Even though they didn't get the goal, I feel sure they still thought their lead was sufficient. But we kept playing and concentrated on

---

FACT FILE

HOME PLACE: Camp, Annascaul, County Kerry

BORN: 12 March 1956 in Chicago, Illinois.

CLUBS: Annascaul; West Kerry; Also played with John Mitchels in Tralee for one year in 1990

ACHIEVEMENTS IN CLUB COMPETITIONS: Four West Kerry Championship medals; four West Kerry League medals; one Kerry County Novice Championship medal; one County Junior Championship medal: three Intermediate County Championship medals; one Senior County Club Championship medal; two Senior County Championship medals with West Kerry; won all League Division medals in County Kerry with Annascaul; numerous Tournament medals.

INTER-COUNTY ACHIEVEMENTS: Seven All-Ireland Senior Football medals in 1978, 1979, 1980, 1981, 1984, 1985 and 1986. (Even though I didn't play in the Final in '78, I received an All-Ireland medal. I broke my arm in the semi-final against Roscommon. I was very sad to miss it, because it would have been my first All-Ireland Senior Final.); Two National League medals 1982 and 1984; three Under-21 All-Ireland medals in 1975, 1976 and 1977; three All Star Awards at right-half-back in 1984, 1985 and 1986; eight Munster Senior Championship medals 1978, 1979, 1980, 1981, 1982, 1984, 1985 and 1986; three Munster Under-21 Championship medals; two All-Ireland Vocational School medals.

the game. We got the breaks, took them and won. We went into the game with an awful lot of injuries, some very serious. Páidí Ó Sé, Sean Walsh and myself were genuinely injured. Jack O'Shea had a sore throat and temperature before the match and then Ambrose O'Donovan got injured very early in the game, but stayed on the field until half-time. His ankle was out like a balloon. I even think Ger Lynch was having a bit of injury trouble as well. The lads showed great courage, everybody stayed on and fought it out. Tyrone were very hungry and seemed to have won when they built up a seven-points lead five minutes into the second half. But we dug deep and through pain pulled off a fantastic victory. It's only now, when I think back and look at today's results and performances of teams in All-Ireland Finals, that I can fully appreciate it. I mean any team today that would go seven points up in the second half of an All-Ireland Final would win it. But, in 1986, Kerry had the resolve to keep going to the end.

'I remember going up for the Cup and thinking to myself, "a lot of good men have gone up here before me". I thought of some great Kerry captains, who never had the honour of walking up the steps of the Hogan Stand to receive the Sam Maguire Cup. It was then I realised just how lucky I was. It was a wonderful feeling. The Tyrone players were shattered after that final. I was talking to Damien O'Hagan sometime later when he called to see me in Tralee and he told me that they just could not believe what had happened.

> 'We would not have won half of the titles but for Micko and his backroom team. He was like a father-figure to us. He was always trying to get us to play the game both hard and fair, with a high degree of skill. At all times he wanted us to enjoy Gaelic football. His favourite saying was: "Practice makes perfect".'

The Tyrone lads were very gracious in defeat and thanked us for a good clean match. An All-Ireland final is a great experience. It can pass by quite quickly, but can be very nerve-wracking. Although we were there several times, the tension was the same each year. We learned to cope and to keep our concentration on the match at all times. Concentration can be the difference between winning and losing. We didn't rush kicks or do other silly things, we just concentrated on playing our usual game. We followed Micko's advice, which was to play ball at all times. Our experience was vital. If we had been in Croke Park for the first time, Tyrone would have beaten us that day.'

Five Kerry players collected their eighth All-Ireland All-Ireland senior medal in 1986. It was a remarkable achievement for Páidí Ó Sé, Pat Spillane, Mikey Sheehy, Ger Power and Denis 'Ogie' Moran, the only player to win eight All-Ireland football medals playing in the one position.

Tommy Doyle was nominated for the captaincy by Lispole, the West Kerry Champions in 1985. The selection process in Kerry ensures that the captain comes from the team that wins the County Championship and West Kerry retained their title in 1985.

'To captain Kerry is a massive honour, but to captain Kerry to All-Ireland victory is something one only dreams about. I knew if we were to win the All-Ireland title in 1986 it would take a supreme effort. It's never easy to win a national title but I felt 1986 was going to be exceptionally difficult. I felt that we only had about one more year, so I asked all the lads to put in one last effort. They didn't let me down and for that I'm deeply grateful. Pat Spillane turned in a "Man of the Match" performance, as did all the forwards. We had injury worries (Jack O'Shea only decided to play less than half an hour before the start), but even those players gave their all and at the end, we deserved our victory.'

Because of injury, Tommy's own training regime was very restricted and he was over a stone overweight taking the field for the Munster Final against Cork. Even more remarkably, both his ankles were encased in plaster just ten days before the All-Ireland final.

'I myself did not play well in the final, as I had been injured all year. I must thank Mick O'Dwyer for allowing me start matches when only half fit, but I always told him before the games that I wouldn't let him down and he trusted me. We in turn gave him our total trust and dedication and would do anything that he required of us. He believed our biggest obstacle to winning in 1986 would be avoiding injuries.'

Tommy himself struggled with injury throughout the whole year. He was continually undergoing physiotheraphy treatment and played on occasions with the help of cortisone injections. He admits he was extremely lucky to make it to the final.

'There were so many leaders in our team and this gave me great confidence. I got a nasty injury just above my eye after an accidental clash with Colm O'Rourke in the semi-final against Meath. The referee gave me his handkerchief to wipe the blood away. It was coming up to half time and I could hardly see with all the blood, so I had to get four stitches at the interval. At half-time, I asked Páidí Ó Sé to take over in the dressing-room. While I was still being treated, I heard the referee blowing the whistle and I said to the doctor: "quick, get it done, get it done". I just arrived back on the field for the start of the second half and played well enough.'

Tommy Doyle began playing competitive football with a small club named Derrymore. This little rural club owed its existence to Con O'Shea and Pat Healy, who saw to it that the young lads under their care were properly treated. Con and Pat also did the driving and sometimes as many as fifteen or sixteen youngsters would crowd into the two cars.

Tommy remembers buying his first pair of Blackthorn football boots for two pounds ten shillings from John Dowling, Kerry's All-Ireland winning captain in 1955. While at Aughacasla National School, Tommy came under the guidance of teacher Paddy Moriarty who encouraged his students to play football at all times.

'When I started secondary school at Tralee Technical College, my brother John and I joined the Annascaul Club. We would have been illegal to play with Derrymore. We played with Annascaul from Under 16 grade upwards. At that time, I also played

---

THE 1986 KERRY TEAM

Charlie Nelligan

Páidí Ó Sé	Seán Walsh	Mick Spillane
Tommy Doyle (Captain)	Tom Spillane	Ger Lynch
Jack O'Shea		Ambrose O'Donovan
Willie Maher	Denis 'Ogie' Moran	Pat Spillane
Mikey Sheehy	Eoin 'Bomber' Liston	Ger Power

Substitutes: Timmy O'Dowd for Ambrose O'Donovan

Under 16, Under 18 and Senior football with our Technical School, as well as playing with Annascaul senior team. I played senior county championship football at the age of seventeen. We were playing football seven days a week and training as well. Sometimes it makes me laugh when I hear people saying that present-day players are getting too much football. We lived for it, but I do also agree that times have changed. I captained the Kerry Vocational Schools team, along with playing for the Kerry minor and Under 21 teams. Our school, Tralee, won two Vocational Schools finals and they were great games. It was at this stage that I got to know a lot of the players that I later teamed up with on the Kerry team. We played against each other in under-age competitions. It was a great thrill to play with these fellows later on. Liam Sayers and Donie O'Sullivan gave us great help and encouragement at school.'

Tommy Doyle is fiercely proud of his club. Nothing gave him greater satisfaction than pulling on the all-blue Annascaul jersey.

'It was great to play in All-Ireland Finals at Croke Park, but training and playing with the lads in the club gave me fantastic enjoyment. Those lads used to try their hearts out every Sunday and for a small club we managed to win some major honours. We won every competition in Kerry GAA, except the Senior Football Championship. We played with West Kerry in that competition. I always got great pride from playing with my club. At times we used to find it hard to field a team, but we gave it everything. For years, Tommy McCarthy, Din Linehan (RIP), Tommy Ashe, Páidí Ó Sé (RIP), Batty Cronin, Mike, Seán and Thomas O'Shea, the O'Driscolls from Camp, Thomas Kennedy and our present team manager, John O'Donnell, kept the club going. They worked hard towards the development of our field and dressingrooms for our fine young and skilful team of today. I thank them all very much. Our followers are second to none and I'd like to pay tribute here to Pa Driscoll, one of our very best supporters. I used to concentrate on my fitness at all times. I was regarded a good natural athlete. I still play club football with Annascaul and I now find I am playing with the sons of fellows I started out with years ago.'

Back, left to right: Jack O'Shea, Tom Spillane, Mikey Sheehy, Charlie Nelligan, Ger Lynch, Willie Maher, Pat Spillane, Seán Walsh.
Front, left to right: Eoin 'Bomber' Liston, Tommy Doyle (captain), Páidí Ó Sé, Ambrose O'Donovan, Mick Spillane, Ger Power, Denis 'Ogie' Moran.

No mention of the Kerry team of the seventies and eighties would be complete without reference to the great Mick O'Dwyer, the most successful manager in the history of Gaelic games. Tommy Doyle is in no doubt whatsoever of the immense contribution of the man from Waterville. He was the key figure in Kerry's unprecedented run of success.

'There are times when I hear people in Kerry not giving Micko the credit he deserves and it annoys me. Some would say that the team trained and picked itself and that O'Dwyer and his selectors just sat back. If you ask any of the players involved they will tell you that we would not have won half of the titles but for Micko and his backroom team. He became involved when I started playing inter-county football. At all times he tried to instil in all of his players everything that was good in the game, both on and off the field. He was like a father-figure to us. He was always trying to get us to play the game both hard and fair, with a high degree of skill. At all times he wanted us to enjoy Gaelic football. His favourite saying was: "Practice makes perfect". His dedication and commitment were an example to all of us. His will to win was as strong as it was when he was playing. He used to train with us and play backs and forwards and he would always give as good as he got. He was the most influential figure I have been fortunate to be involved with and it was he, more than anyone else, that helped me develop as a player. Me and all my former football colleagues will forever be thankful to Mick O'Dwyer.

'Micko gathered us all together in 1984 and said we should have another go at winning an All-Ireland. I remember him telling us if Dublin could win an All-Ireland title with twelve men, then Kerry could certainly win one with fifteen. It was the first time we really trained for the League. We started training in October '83 and continued right up to the All-Ireland final in '84. I particularly remember a training session in the old Austin Stacks Park in Tralee one bitterly cold and wet wintry evening when every player was present. I had my blue Annascaul jersey on me and I was down on the ground, hands in the mud, doing press ups and the hailstones hopping off my back. I remember thinking to myself, "what am I doing here". But whatever way I looked up I saw Mick O'Dwyer also on the ground doing the push ups and this made me work harder. He showed us all he was not afraid to go through the hardship with us. But for Micko we would never have won anything in 1984!'

The only time Tommy had a falling out with Micko was when he disobeyed the manager's orders and lined out with Annascaul just a week before a Munster final. His club was in danger of being relegated and Tommy answered the call without a moment's hesitation. Annascaul surivived and so too did Kerry.

'We had an idea that Mick was going to go in 1989 after the Munster Final defeat by Cork. Everyone was very upset and there were tears streaming down Micko's face. He had become sick and tired of all the back stabbing, but even though I knew he was going it came as an awful shock when we heard it officially. The day after he resigned I rang him, as did all the other players, and begged him to stay on, but he had his mind made up and there was no way we could make him stay. It should also be remembered that the late Joe Keohane and Frank King were father-figures to myself and many others. They helped me no end and were great friends. I miss them very much and would like to tell their families, how lucky I was to have known them.'

Tommy has another good reason to remember the 1986 final as his wife, Joan, an avid Gaelic games follower, was in hospital giving birth to their first child Kevin. There were so many things happening, Tommy hardly had time to appreciate the importance of being an All-Ireland winning Kerry captain. That is, until he delivered the Cup to his home place Annascaul, where thousands had gathered for the celebrations.

Exactly forty years earlier, another Annascaul man, Paddy Kennedy, had brought the same Cup to the same place when Kerry defeated Roscommon in a replay. There was magic in the air as thousands turned out to honour Tommy Doyle, the local boy.

'I was at many of the homecomings but I never witnessed anything to compare with that night in Camp and Annascaul. It was wonderful the way everyone came out to welcome us home. It was a sign from the people that they appreciated what I had done. Kerry people will always show their appreciation if a person deserves it. The place was alive until eight o'clock the following morning.'

One of the characteristics of the Kerry teams of the seventies and eighties was their sportsmanship. They were as gracious in defeat as they were generous in victory. Nowhere was this trait better exemplified than in the aftermath of the 1982 All-Ireland final in which they had been deprived of a history-making five-in-a-row title by a controversial last-minute goal from Séamus Darby. There were no complaints to be heard from the Kerry team, only that they failed to take their scores which allowed Offaly take the initiative.

It was a particularly traumatic experience for Tommy Doyle who was in the thick of the action when he raced ahead of Séamus Darby to collect a high ball.

'I remember going for the ball, it was inside in our square. A lot of people would say if Jimmy Deenihan had been playing corner-back, Darby wouldn't have won that ball. But I wasn't playing at corner-back. I'm not shrugging off responsibility or anything like that, I'll stand up and be counted as good as the next guy, but I was playing as a half-back that day. I was being called back, because there was a forward inside in our square all alone and I just ran back to mark him. I went for the ball because I had a ninety per cent chance of winning it. And it's like the story: "what do you do when the ball is in the square, you must go for it". A back will not stand down and let a forward win the ball in the square. I went for the ball, because I was quite confident of getting it. I'd have gone for it anyway! I went for the ball to win possession and clear it and just as I went for it, I remember it whizzing past the top of my fingers. I was that close to it, I couldn't believe it. Now whether I was pushed or not, I'm not prepared to say. All I know is that at the end of the day the ball wound up in the back of the net and Offaly won the All-Ireland final. And good luck to them. The goal was a goal! It's as simple as that! I was very disappointed and I wished the ground could have opened up and swallowed me. I took it too much to heart. If it happened to me now, it wouldn't worry me as much and I feel I'd get over the disappointment much quicker, I blamed myself too much but Mick O'Dwyer and my club mates gave me great help and I got back playing again. I never talked until now about the '82 All-Ireland final or neither did the team. We took our beating and made no excuses.'

It says much about the character of Tommy Doyle and that Kerry team that they overcame that setback and a similar one in the Munster final the following year, when Tadhg Murphy scored a last gasp winning goal for Cork, to go on and win three more All-Ireland titles. We will not see their likes again!

Páidí Ó SÉ

Kerry Captain 1985

FOOTBALL IS A SECOND RELIGION in Kerry and life as a county footballer has never been easy. Much is demanded of those who wear the green and gold and comparisons with former greats are inevitable. In a county where players are judged by the number of All-Ireland medals in their possession Páidí O Sé has an honoured position. When Kerry defeated Tyrone in the 1986 final, Páidí, Mikey Sheehy, Pat Spillane, 'Ogie' Moran and Ger Power became the first players ever to win eight All-Ireland medals. Remarkable by any standards.

But because of the exceptionally high standards set by men such as Páidí it is now more difficult than ever before to earn respect as a Kerry player. This inspirational and wholehearted defender played a central role in the unrivalled success of the Kerry team from the mid-seventies to the mid-eighties.

The current crop of footballers are invariably compared to the likes of Páidí, Johnno, Mikey, 'Ogie', Pat, Ger, 'Bomber' and a dozen or more equally outstanding footballers who elevated the status of Kerry football to an all-time high.

There was no tradition of football in the Ó Sé side of the family but Páidí's father Tommy and mother Beatrice gave their youngest son every encouragement. He considers his mother to have been the driving force behind his football career and later on his wife Máire was ever supportive. According to Páidí his academic career was undistinguished due to the fact that football dominated his every waking hour.

'My mother wasn't too worried about how many A's I got in my Leaving or how many degrees I got above in UCD because I was never up there anyway. I came from the college of hard knocks. She was a happy woman to see me take my football degrees up to Croke Park; and I did. When Paddy Bawn Brosnan was asked to give

---

FACT FILE

HOME PLACE: Ard an Bhothair, Ventry, County Kerry.

BORN: 16 May 1955

CLUBS: An Ghaeltacht and West Kerry

ACHIEVEMENTS IN CLUB COMPETITIONS: Under-16 County League with team comprising players from An Ghaeltacht, Dingle and Lispole in 1971; one West Kerry Senior Championship medal with An Ghaeltacht in 1970; one West Kerry League in 1988; two County Senior Championship medals with West Kerry in 1984 and 1985.

ACHIEVEMENTS IN INTER-COUNTY COMPETITIONS: Eight All-Ireland Senior Football medals in 1975, 1978, 1979, 1980, 1981, 1984, 1985 and 1986; eleven Munster Senior Football Championship medals in 1975, 1976, 1977, 1978, 1979, 1980, 1981, 1982, 1984, 1985 and 1986; three All-Ireland Under-21 Football medals in 1973, 1975 and 1976; three Munster Under-21 Football medals in 1973, 1975 and 1976; five All-Star Awards in 1981, 1982, 1983, 1984 and 1985.

---

the principal parts of the Latin word vinio he said, "Sorry brother I'm only here for the football". It was the same with me and I have no regrets.'

Páidí attended Cill Mhic a' Domhnaigh National School and vividly remembers chipping in with the rest of his classmates to buy a football. His pays tribute to his teacher Mick Murphy who gave his students every help and encouragement. Mick himself was an outstanding footballer who played on the Kerry team that beat Dublin in the 1955 All-Ireland final, 'We used to kick ball in the school yard and we played our All-Irelands there. I used to go down to the strand on my own and imitate players. Now, Mick O'Connell was a God in my eyes. He was the player I most admired. One of the best thrills I ever got in my life was in August this year when Micko called in to the pub and we finished up in the churchyard kicking a ball at each other. He is a fantastic man and has been an inspiration to so many footballers since the fifties.

'I remember as a youngster my mother giving me money to go to a Munster final but I jumped over a wall and got in for free. I made my way into the dressing-room after the game and came face to face with Mick who was togging in. I was thrilled. I just couldn't believe that I could get so near to this great man. He told me to go out and get him a tub of ice cream. I remember buying five tubs for him thinking I would get great praise but instead Mick said, "I only told you to get one".

'Another big influence was Joe Keohane. When giving out the jerseys in Croke Park he would always say, "wear that jersey with dignity, we're carrying no prisoners today. That's a very dodgy jersey you're pulling over your shoulders. If you let the Kingdom of Kerry down you might be walking up the church to christen a child in twenty years time and there'll be a crowd at the back of the chapel and they'll say, he's the fellow who let the Kingdom down years ago. He's the windy fellow".'

On leaving national school Páidí spent one year in Dingle CBS before moving on to St Brendan's College in Killarney. 'I wasn't great at the books, I just wanted to play football. End of story. Things didn't work out and I was asked to leave St Brendan's

Back, left to right: Jack O'Shea, Johnny Mulvihill, Tom Spillane, Liam Kerins, Ger Lynch, Charlie Nelligan, Mikey Sheehy, John Keane, Dermot Hanafin, Pat Spillane, Seán Walsh, Gerry O'Sullivan, Diarmuid O'Donoghue.
Front, left to right: Seán Liston, Timmy O'Dowd, Eoin 'Bomber' Liston, Tommy Doyle, Páidí Ó Sé (captain), Ambrose O'Donovan, Mick Spillane, Ger Power, Denis 'Ogie' Moran, John Higgins, John Kennedy.

FOOTBALL IMAGES

Author with 'Sam Maguire' — and son John
Brian, a budding captain!
Top: Croke Park on final day

Henry Downey, Derry captain, All-Ireland final 1993

Brian Corcoran, Cork, and Derry's Joe Brolly in the 1993 final

Above: All-Ireland final 1993. Dermot Heaney, Derry, and Barry Coffey, Cork

Overleaf: Action tableaux — Donegal v. Dublin All-Ireland final 1992

and *facing page:* Anthony Molloy, Donegal captain, Brian Murray, Paul Bealin, Paul Clarke and Jack Sheedy, National League final 1993

Below: Dublin's Paul Bealin, Tommy Carr and Paul Clarke v. Donegal's Anthony Molloy, Martin Gavigan and Barry Cunningham

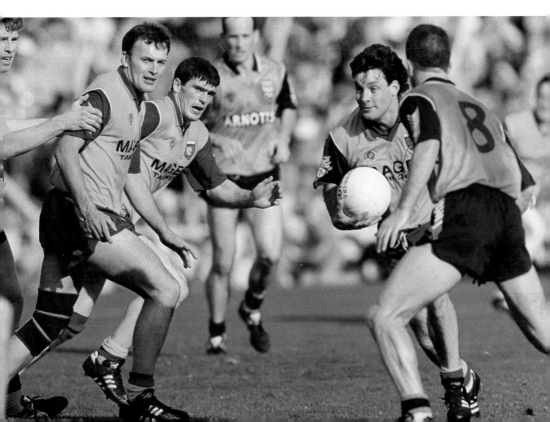

Above: Down fans scent victory, 1991 *Below:* Down captain Paddy O'Rourke and *right:* James McCartan, Down, and Kevin Foley, Meath, 1990 *Facing page:* High ball! Kerry captain Ambrose O'Donovan challenged by Cork's Shay Fahy and watched by Larry Tompkins in the 1991 Munster semi-final

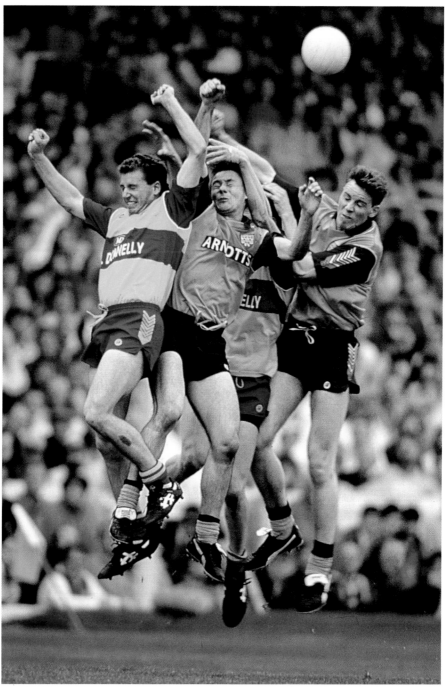

In 1992 Clare shook the football world with victory in Munster — a triumph for the weaker counties. *Above:* Clare and Dublin in the air — All-Ireland semi-final

and I went from there to St Michael's College in Listowel.

'One of the things that sticks out in my memory about my schooldays is winning the O'Sullivan Cup with St Michael's. The present Bishop of Kerry Diarmuid O'Suilleabhain was President of the College at the time. We won the Munster B Senior Colleges title and the O'Sullivan Cup when we beat St Brendan's in the Kerry Senior Colleges final. It took two draws and two periods of extra time to decide the issue. That was one of the major highlights.'

But the memory he treasures most is winning his first senior All-Ireland in 1975. It was the day a young Kerry team beat odds-on favourites Dublin in the final.

'I can remember every kick of the game. My abiding memory was John Egan's goal early on and then Dublin came at us. Pat McCarthy from Churchill was midfield that day and he made some great catches; Paudie Lynch had a great shoulder challenge on Brian Mullins in the second half. Indeed, I had a go at him myself. Brian is a very good friend of mine. I also remember Ger O'Driscoll's goal which put the final touches on a great victory. It was a fantastic feeling to hear the final whistle. It certainly was the biggest thrill of my sporting life. We were all young and bachelors. It went to our heads in 1976. We couldn't handle all the fuss and publicity. We allowed ourselves be carried away by it all and we paid the price. Then in 1977 we were beaten in the All-Ireland semi-final and that was a hard one to lose. We trained very, very hard for that. It was regarded as a great game but I would much prefer to win a bad game than to lose a good one.'

Páidí Ó Sé is fiercely proud of his West Kerry roots. Nothing in the world matters more to him than his family and friends in the close knit community around Ventry.

'If a man has any ambition in life it is to reach the top whether it be in politics, sport or whatever. It was more intimate with me because I am very proud of the area where I live. I am a very, very proud man and West Kerry means everything to me. They always say in Kerry, "To win an All-Ireland, you have to have West Kerry backs and Tralee forwards." The people of West Kerry demand a very, very high standard of their footballers. Over the years there were some wonderful players from the area like Pat "Aeroplane" O'Shea from Castlegregory; Paddy Kennedy from Annascaul; Billy Casey in Lispole; Bill Dillon from Dingle and here in the Gaeltacht great men like Bat Garvey, Mick Murphy my teacher and my first cousin Tom Long.'

From the time he was but four years of age Páidí Ó Sé kicked ball morning, noon and night. The gable end of the chapel wall near his home was the perfect place for a youngster to learn the basic skills but it had its drawbacks.

'I got into a bit of bother one time when I broke one of the windows in the chapel and my mother thought it was the end of the world. But we replaced the glass and

---

THE 1985 KERRY TEAM

Charlie Nelligan

Páidí O Sé (Captain)	Sean Walsh	Mick Spillane
Tommy Doyle	Tom Spillane	Ger Lynch

Jack O'Shea   Ambrose O'Donovan

Timmy O'Dowd	Denis 'Ogie' Moran	Pat Spillane
Mikey Sheehy	Eoin 'Bomber' Liston	Ger Power

Substitute: John Kennedy for Ger Power

everything was okay. The upshot of it all was the parish priest saying, "if he doesn't play for Kerry, nobody will play for Kerry." I never left the ball out of my hand.

I played senior football with An Ghaeltacht when I was fifteen years of age. Nothing else mattered to me only football. My main ambition in life was to play with Kerry and wear the green and gold. It meant everything to me. I played county minor for three years. I also played senior football for my club at fourteen and a half and that's how I came to be recognised by the county selectors. You were out there in the rough and tumble and I was able to hold my own.'

He believes that an awful lot can be done by oneself to improve skills and fitness. He himself was always noted as a player who prepared diligently for every game.

'I never believed in P.E. instructors. I did three hours training every day from 1974 right up until I got a little bit careless around 1982. It consisted mostly of running on soft sand dunes. In 1975 when we won the All-Ireland an awful lot of the players came from small clubs and this year when I trained the Kerry Under-21 team I went out into the small clubs of Kerry in search of young fellows with raw talent who wanted, not to represent Kerry, but to play for Kerry. Representation is no good to me, you've got to play. There's a big difference between the two. I got together a very good team and we very nearly pulled it off. We were beaten in the All-Ireland final. My only ambition left in sport is to train a team to win an All-Ireland.'

Páidí was named after a very famous Kerry footballer of the fifties and sixties. He was the youngest of the Ó Sé family and his two older brothers convinced their mother to call the new arrival after Paudie Sheehy who was one of the big names in Kerry football in 1955. Páidí Ó Sé played minor, senior and Under-21 for Kerry in 1973. He was part of the Kerry team beaten by Cork in the Munster Senior final in 1974. The following year he was a trainee Garda in Templemore and feels it only right to commend the Kerry County Board for their generosity. 'Things were so well organised by the County Board that I was allowed go up to the Templemore Arms Hotel and have a steak right through the championship. Kerry County Board always take care of their players provided they make the effort.

'It was all new to us. We had a great win over Cork in Killarney. I should have been sent off the same day. I think I lamped Dinny Allen. I pleaded with the referee that it was an accident. I'm a bit of a rogue that way and thankfully he didn't send me off. I had a great game after that. We played Sligo in the All-Ireland semi-final. It is my mother's county. I felt the highlight for Sligo that year was winning the Connacht title and I'd say they couldn't see beyond that.

'I always believe that the team going to play Dublin in Croke Park has a big advantage psychologically because it is very easy to psyche yourself up for a visit to the lions den. Croke Park was something else for me that day. Getting my togs dirty was a great thrill. I came home to my mother and said, "look, these are my dirty togs, I've played in Croke Park". That was the type of pride I had. It is a great honour to play in Croke Park.'

What Páidí remembers most about his first All-Ireland is what his Uncle Joe Ó Sé said to him after the game. 'Joe had travelled over from London specially for the final and he came over to me in the hotel afterwards and said, "God Páidí, I'm a proud man today. It's great to see you winning your All-Ireland medal and it's great to think we have it from the Ó Sé side of the family rather than the Longs." We had all been so proud of Tom Long's achievements and now we had an Ó Sé winning an

All-Ireland medal and it was great. Tom is a first cousin of mine.'

In 1984 Páidí was player manager of the West Kerry team that won the County Championship. This afforded him the opportunity of captaining the county team in the 1985 All-Ireland championship.

'I didn't approach the games any differently but there were areas that I had to tackle that captains normally wouldn't have anything to do with. I was involved with Frank King, (RIP) with the Bendix Washing Machine sponsorship deal. I was the spokesman for the players, and with the County Board I had to make sure that gear was organised.

'The other thing I was very, very conscious about was the fact that many players who captained teams in All-Ireland finals never played to their potential. I was determined to play well. The year I captained the team I didn't have a great All-Ireland even though I still pinned down my man and kept him scoreless.

'I don't agree with Man-of-the-Match awards but I do agree with a player being chosen for his performances throughout the course of the championship. No man can win a match on his own. On principle I wouldn't go to a man-of-the-match award function. Our first game of the 1985 championship was against Clare and then we beat Cork in the Munster final. We drew with Monaghan in the All-Ireland semi-final and they could nearly have beaten us. The "Bomber" was sent off early in the first half during the replay but we proved that "when the going gets tough, the tough get going". I played one of my best ever games for Kerry.

> *'I don't agree with Man-of-the-Match awards but I do agree with a player being chosen for his performances throughout the course of the championship. No man can win a match on his own. On principle I wouldn't go to a man-of-the-match award function.'*

'There was a strong wind in the first half and we were nine points ahead at half time but Joe McNally got two goals and they came within a point of us. Pat Spillane was having a relatively quiet game by his own high standards but just then he came up the field, caught a ball and bisected the crossbar. A great player.'

The captaincy did not bother Páidí unduly. He was determined not to allow the pressure of the captaincy affect his own game. 'I couldn't be concerned about anyone else the day of the game. You do your bit of work before the game and you don't worry about anyone on the day. It was wonderful to collect the Sam Maguire.' It was Kerry's twenty-ninth All-Ireland title.

Listed among his many accomplishments are five All-Star awards. Despite the fact that he played some of the best football of his career in the seventies, Páidí failed to win recognition until 1981. This baffled him more than a little at the time.

'I'd say some of the sports correspondents felt I was a dirty player. I thought I was the best wing back in the county in 1975 and 1976 but I wasn't selected as an All-Star on either occasion. I was playing midfield in the 1977 All-Ireland semi-final and in 1978 I was sent off in New York so I wasn't eligible for an award. Unfortunately, I was sent off in the All-Ireland final in 1979 and that was that as far as an All-Star award was concerned. It was a terrible experience. There is nothing worse can happen a footballer than to be sent off in an All-Ireland final. In 1980 I still figured I

was one of the best wing backs in the country but again no award. I won my first All-Star award in 1981 and was also selected for the following four years. It is a very big honour to win an All-Star award. What basically disappointed me totally about the All-Star system was the fact that I won an award in 1983 as a right-corner-back even though I only played once in that position. I played all my football in the course of the year as a wing back but conveniently they gave me an All-Star as a corner back. I don't know for what reason but I didn't deserve it that year as a corner-back.'

Páidí Ó Sé was resting on the Tuesday before the All-Ireland when Diarmuid Ó Súilleabháin called. He asked if Páidí had a speech prepared should Kerry win.

'I said that I would worry about what to say on the day if we won. But he said that I should have the speech ready in advance. He prepared it with me and I just glanced at it on my way up from Kerry thinking to myself, "it would be great if it worked out". Diarmuid was one of the very first that I met after the game and he handed me a note with five headings. Normally captains address the president and the hierarchy but I said, "A mhuintir Chiarraí agus a chairde go léir". It went down very well.'

Top heavyweight boxing contender Zorra Foley once said about Muhammad Ali, 'this guy has a style all his own. He could write the book on boxing and anyone that fights him should be made to read it.' When it comes to the sport of Gaelic games those same words could apply to Páidí Ó Sé who only conceded one point from play in eight All-Ireland finals.

Páidí now runs a very successful pub and grocery business in Ventry. He is married to school teacher Máire and they have two children Neasa and Siún.

Ambrose O'DONOVAN

Kerry Captain 1984

IT WAS THAT BIT extra special to be crowned All-Ireland champions in centenary year 1984 and it was Gneeveguilla's Ambrose O'Donovan who had the honour of receiving the Sam Maguire Cup from the President of the GAA, Paddy Buggy. Twenty-five years earlier another Kerry midfielder, the mighty Mick O'Connell, had captained Kerry to victory over Galway and the Valentia Island man and his team were given a rousing reception on being introduced to the crowd before the Centenary Final.

What made the occasion all the more noteworthy for Ambrose was the fact that it was his first year playing senior championship football with Kerry. He went on to win two more All-Ireland medals with Kerry, forming a hugely successful midfield partnership with Jack O'Shea.

Ambrose admits it was a great help that he knew all the players before he made the championship breakthrough as he had played with them during the League. However, he missed the first round of the championship against Tipperary because of a thumb injury.

'The week before the Munster final we were playing a challenge game in Fitzgerald Stadium and before the game Mick O'Dwyer called me aside and told me I was very "near" the team and a good display that evening would nearly guarantee my place.

'Things went reasonably well for me and the following Tuesday night I came in for training, which was really only a winding-down session, and Micko came to me and said: "as far as I am concerned you'll be on the team anyway, but we must have a meeting and see how it goes as there are four selectors". The team was to be announced on the Wednesday morning. I tuned into RTE Radio and the first thing the presenter said was: "Kerry selectors drop a bombshell". As soon as I heard that, I turned to Mary, my wife, and said: "I'm on the team anyway". The presenter then proceeded to name the team and I was delighted to hear my name called.'

Everyone Ambrose met that day offered their congratulations but he admits that the idea of captaincy never entered his mind. It was just wonderful to be on the team

---

FACT FILE

HOME PLACE: Gneeveguilla, County Kerry.

BORN: 11 June 1962   CLUB: Gneeveguilla

ACHIEVEMENTS IN CLUB COMPETITIONS: All East Kerry Championship medals from juvenile to senior; County (Rural) Under-12 and -16 medals; won three East Kerry Senior Championship medals; one Kerry County Senior Football Championship medal in 1980.

INTER-COUNTY ACHIEVEMENTS: three All-Ireland Senior Football Championship medals in 1984, 1985 and 1986; four Munster Senior Championship medals in 1984, 1985, 1986 and 1991.

---

for a Munster final. It was only when people started to look at the team sheet that they began to realise that the club champions, Killarney, were not represented.

Gneeveguilla had won the East Kerry Championship in 1983 and as Ambrose was the only player from the area on the county team, Killarney decided to nominate him for the captaincy. He heard the good news just three days before the Munster final.

'My initial reaction was fear and then a fierce sense of pride at the thought of playing the "old enemy". I always had great rivalry with Cork as I was born on the Cork-Kerry border just a stone's throw from the Blackwater. The rivalry is much more intense for someone living in a border village. Then I went through a phase where I began to doubt my own ability and my fitness but Micko had a chat with me the Saturday before the game and put me right. Whether you were or not, he always made you feel that you were a world beater and perfectly right for the position.

'I was given every encouragement from Micko and all the rest of the players I looked up to, like Ger Power, Mikey Sheehy, "Bomber", Ogie and Pat Spillane. They were brilliant and rowed in behind me and said things like "You'll be fine, you'll be fine, just concentrate on your game now and forget about the captaincy". Kerry were really hyped up for the Munster final as they had been beaten the year before by a last minute goal from Tadhg Murphy and the year previous to that, Offaly beat them in the All-Ireland final with a late goal from Séamus Darby. The players had been hit by two bitter disappointments and it wasn't going to happen a third time round and it definitely wasn't going to happen in our own back yard. The great saying at the time was "get the circus back on the road".

'No player needed motivation, we all had it and the fact that it was centenary year made us even more determined. Being captain of that team was irrelevant in that it was a team effort. That was always the password, there's no one man going to win any game.'

One of the things Ambrose remembers about the occasion was the humidity. He believes he never played on a warmer day. After being told by the referee that there

Back, left to right: Jack O'Shea, Tom Spillane, Ger Lynch, Charlie Nelligan, Denis 'Ogie' Moran, Pat Spillane, Seán Walsh.
Front, left to right: John Egan, Eoin 'Bomber' Liston, Tommy Doyle, Páidí Ó Sé, Ambrose O'Donovan (captain), Mick Spillane, Ger Power, John Kennedy.

was just three minutes remaining Ambrose recalls checking the scoreboard and making a mental note that his team were five points in front. He caught a ball with just about a minute or so remaining and felt like holding on to it. In the end, Kerry won by a margin of seven points and looked forward with confidence to being back in Croke Park once again.

There was great fun in the dressing-room with the players ribbing Ambrose about his speech. That night he visited Gneeveguilla with the Munster Cup and as bonfires blazed everywhere he recalls thinking to himself: "wouldn't it be great to come back here again with the Sam Maguire Cup".

His abiding memory of the All-Ireland semi-final was a point he scored early on after running on to a pass from Ger Lynch. It was the perfect 'settling down' score for a player appearing in Croke Park at senior level for the first time in such an important championship game. Galway failed to find their form on the day and Kerry had twelve points to spare at the final whistle.

In the O'Donovan household the phone was hopping but Ambrose and his team had been forewarned by Mick O'Dwyer not to get carried away with the press. This was no ordinary All-Ireland! It was centenary year and better still the Kingdom were facing the Dubs. No one could have asked for a more ideal pairing. Ambrose had a scare the week before the final when he picked up a hip injury in a challenge game. He had to undergo extensive physiotherapy and was very worried in case he might miss the game. Although the injury helped keep his mind off the game it was a fright he could have done without. It was the eve of the game before he fully recovered.

There was a great sense of fun as the players travelled to Dublin on the Saturday but at about ten o'clock that night after their pep talk on the Malahide strand, Ambrose noticed players who were 'a bundle of laughs' all day were now very tense. Ambrose himself slept little that night. The team attended Mass next morning and afterward the players had to tog out and pose for a team picture which would later be sold to finance a foreign trip. During the photo call Ambrose recalls Mick O'Dwyer saying: 'All this is for nothing, lads, if we lose'. The Tipperary minor team was staying in the same hotel and the Kerry players went out to wave them on their way to Croke Park. Soon it would be the turn of the Kerry men to set off.

The journey to 'Croker' was the one part of the whole build-up when Ambrose felt truly petrified. He was coping fairly well until the coach approached Jones's Road. It was only then he realised what the occasion was all about.

'I remember getting off the bus and going in through the gate and on over to our dressing-room. But passing the shop under the Hogan Stand this elderly lady with a Kerry hat came up to me and gave me a miraculous medal. She just put it into my

---

THE 1984 KERRY TEAM

Charlie Nelligan

Páidí Ó Sé   Seán Walsh   Mick Spillane

Tommy Doyle   Tom Spillane   Ger Lynch

Jack O'Shea   Ambrose O'Donovan (Captain)

John Kennedy   Denis 'Ogie' Moran   Pat Spillane

Ger Power   Eoin 'Bomber' Liston   John Egan

Substitute: Timmy O'Dowd for John Egan

hand and said: "God go with you, I hope we're lucky". I looked at it and thought to myself: "There's someone praying very hard for us". There was a television inside in the dressing-room and we watched a bit of the minor match, but it was a nerve-wracking time. I remember saying: "I don't care if we never again win a match, we have to win this one. This is what all the extra training and eight months hard work is all about". I'll never forget going through the tunnel and finding the gate shut as the steward wanted the two teams to come out together. I went up and caught the gate and insisted the steward open it. Dwyer then came up and we had a fierce job to get him to open the gate. It was a crazy situation as we were as high as kites. While we were waiting for the gate to be opened one of our players shouted from the back: "lads, if we go down, we'll go down as a team, if we win, we win as a team".

It turned out to be a comfortable enough victory for Kerry by 0-14 to 1-6 and Ambrose O'Donovan played his part with a fine performance. That was it for another one hundred years!

'Páidí Ó Sé came up to me after the game and reminded me not to forget to say a few words in Irish. I turned to him and said: "it's going to frighten me to talk in English never mind Irish". As it happens I have a good bit of Irish and the speech went fine. I could have floated up the steps of the Hogan Stand. On the way Pat Spillane said to me: "For God sake make it short and sweet." My back was sore for a solid week from all the clapping as I made

> *'Passing the shop under the Hogan Stand this elderly lady with a Kerry hat came up to me and gave me a miraculous medal. She just put it into my hand and said: "God go with you, I hope we're lucky". I looked at it and thought to myself: "There's someone praying very hard for us".'*

my way to the dressing-room. I was never hit as hard in any match.' Afterwards at the celebrations Ambrose, an accomplished singer, performed a version of the popular song, 'Sweet Forget Me Not'. It was a joyous occasion.

'There were two function rooms in the Grand Hotel in Malahide that night and both of them were packed with Kerry supporters and it was only when I had to bring the Cup to both places that it struck me what the win meant to everyone. People were shouting and roaring for the Cup and it was a wonderful proud feeling to stand in front of our supporters with the Sam Maguire. I remember thinking: "This is a day I'll never forget".

'The following Tuesday I visited my old national school, Tureencahill, and I saw old men cry as I was going in the door with the Cup. I also got a lovely presentation, and things like that will always stick in my mind and remind me of that day.'

From as far back as he can recall, Ambrose O'Donovan kicked football by himself, morning, noon and night. He had his own set of goalposts on the family's half acre under the shadow of the Pap mountains and in those games he was goalkeeper, defender, free-taker and scorer in chief. He remembers it was 'hell for leather' and all his imaginary games were close ones. Often as he left the field his next door neighbour, Dan Cronin, would say to the youngster: 'Well, Ambrose, who won this evening?'

'My mother and father never pushed me but I knew at the same time they were

both very happy that I was playing football and not hanging around the house. Our own club, Gneeveguilla, had very good men in charge at under-age level like Ambrose Donnelly, Séamus McCarthy and John Kelliher who kept us interested in football.

'In later years, I was very lucky to meet Donie O'Sullivan who trained the Kerry team that won an All-Ireland Vocational Schools title. We all knew of Donie's record and what he'd won as county player, and the fact that he was such a great player made us all listen more carefully to what he had to say. I was about fifteen which is a critical age in a footballer's career.'

Ambrose still reckons his most memorable moment on the field of play was scoring a goal against Cork in the 1980 Munster Minor Final in Fitzgerald Stadium. He hit a rocket of a shot from thirty yards and could see it screaming past Ger Cunningham into the net.

'I got a great kick out of that score. The goal came with the last kick of the game

73

and we drew with Cork and beat them in the replay at Páirc Uí Chaoimh. Tommy Dee gave me the pass and I knew I had to go for a goal. I never ever dreamed I'd get it but there was no choice at that stage. I'd say Ger Cunningham didn't forget it for a while either. He still mentions it to me.'

The Kerry minors eventually lost in the All-Ireland final that year, so before they resumed training for the following year's championship they were called to a meeting by Tom Prendergast, the team coach.

'I remember him saying: "Names mean nothing to me. Ambrose got a great goal last year, but that stands for nothing. That year is gone. He will have to start back again and fight his way on to the team". No player was allowed get a swelled head which was vitally important. A player knew what was expected of him and if he didn't deliver the goods he wasn't selected.

'Then of course I came under Mick O'Dwyer which was a totally new experience again, in terms of breaking the pain barrier. Dwyer was an exceptional trainer and he'd do a lot of the training himself. He would often say: 'It's no good in the world going training and leaving the pitch knowing you have more in the tank, but it's a great feeling coming off a field and knowing that you have given your all'. I think that was a big factor with a lot of his success. The players got it into their minds that if they weren't giving it one hundred per cent then the session was no good and they'd be in bad form leaving the pitch that night. Once you believed Mick O'Dwyer's philosophy then you wouldn't duck in training.'

Ambrose's own philosophy is worth noting: 'If you're going to win a ball in the middle of the field and you want to get it into your forward line, they want it first time because they're gone off their mark. They don't want you adoring the ball.

'What made the Kerry team was the fact that they were continually striving for perfection. Every one of them had a desperate competitive edge. Even in backs and forwards at training no one wanted to get beaten. All of them were great ambassadors for the game.'

His greatest sporting disappointment was the Munster Final defeat by Cork in Páirc Uí Chaoimh in 1990. It was a real low point. 'I wouldn't have minded being beaten but I thought we were way better than our performance suggested. We proved it twelve months later when we beat Cork. It was a disastrous day and everybody felt so low. We knew we hadn't done ourselves justice. None of us had done ourselves justice. It was a freak thing that everybody struck an all-time low on the day.'

He has strong views on the standard of refereeing which he regards as scandalous and getting worse every year. 'If you questioned the top five referees in the country you would find that there are rules within the game that each of them interpret differently. There's nothing more infuriating for a player than to see a referee make a silly mistake, particularly in a big match. 'And believe me they have done it. I think the GAA should take a much more professional approach with their referees: train them a lot better and pay them if needs be. Bad refereeing decisions also spoil games for spectators at both club and inter-county level.'

Ambrose O'Donovan cherishes the friendships he made through Gaelic games and will never forget the day he held the Sam Maguire Cup aloft on the Hogan Stand.

Tommy DRUMM

Dublin Captain 1983

TOMMY DRUMM was centre-half-back and 'Captain Magnificent' when Dublin won their twenty-first All-Ireland football title. In what must surely rate as one of the most dramatic and ill-tempered finals ever played, Antrim referee John Gough felt it necessary to send four players to the line as the 1983 Final stumbled from one unsavoury incident to another. Despite playing with only twelve men, Dublin had two points to spare at the finish over fourteen-man Galway on a 1-10 to 1-8 scoreline.

Whatever about the quality of football, which it must be said failed to do justice to either side, it was nevertheless a victory for sheer strength of character against all the odds by Tommy Drumm's men in atrocious weather conditions.

Midfielder Brian Mullins, hero of many a Dublin victory, was the first player to be sent for an early shower as the game threatened to go out of control. Before the first half had run its course Dublin left-full-back Ray Hazley and his direct opponent, Tomás Tierney, also received their marching orders and the dismissal of Ciarán Duff shortly after the interval brought the tally of sending-offs to four, the highest ever in an All-Ireland final.

Tommy Drumm believes that the never-say-die attitude of his team on that wintry September day proved vital, particularly in the second half when Galway with extra manpower and favoured by the strong breeze, bombarded the Dublin goal.

'The day itself was very unsuitable for football — very wet and very windy. The conditions were treacherous underfoot and we played with the wind in the first half. We needed to build up a reasonable lead for the second half but Galway had a stronger start than us. The turning point was when Barney Rock scored an opportunist goal after about ten minutes. I got great heart from this as I still remembered Mikey Sheehy's goal against us in 1978 and the effect it had on us. The real spur came when Brian Mullins was sent off. His contribution to the team since his accident had been inestimable. I did not agree with the handling of this incident nor with a number of other incidents. This one factor simply made the team more determined to win.

FACT FILE

HOME PLACE: Whitehall, Dublin

BORN: 22 March 1955   CLUB: Whitehall Colmcille, Dublin

ACHIEVEMENTS IN CLUB COMPETITIONS: Were not successful at club level in the sense that we did not win trophies but we did achieve promotion one year.

INTER-COUNTY ACHIEVEMENTS: three All-Ireland Senior Football medals in 1976, 1977 and 1983; six Leinster Senior Football medals in 1976, 1977, 1978, 1979, 1983 and 1984; four All Star Awards 1977, 1978, 1979 and 1983; one Leinster Under-21 medal in 1975; two National Football League medals in 1976 and 1978; Texaco Award 1983.

'The shortage of one man seems always to defy the law of probability. There are two reasons for this — one factor is the lack of any specific game plan or tactic pre-planned to handle this eventuality and the other invariably is the inability of one person to adapt to their changed role in the team strategy. Ray Hazley and Tomás Tierney were sidelined before half time and as it was not as clear to me what had happened in this instance it was therefore more difficult to judge at the time.

'We changed ends with six points in hand and against the odds we managed to score two points before reply at the beginning of the second half.

'Considering we won by two points, the psychological effect of those scores was crucial to the result. There were missed goal chances by both teams in the second half.

'When Ciarán Duff was sent off very early in the second half and we were playing into impossible conditions, it was then that the true mettle of the team came to the fore: they simply refused to give in. Every man left on the field knew that they had to do the work of two men and somehow close Galway down. That second half seemed like an eternity but when the final whistle went I felt a mixture of relief and elation. The performance that day by the Dublin team was remarkable.

'It was my first year as captain of Dublin and to be going up getting the Sam Maguire Cup was special. It's only years afterwards really that you can put the proper weight on the achievement. It happened so quickly and while waiting for the cup to be presented, I do remember those moments vividly, just standing there and soaking up the atmosphere of the win and looking at everybody around, capturing those few moments for ever.'

The 1983 All-Ireland final is also remembered for the tunnel incident involving Brian Mullins and Galway midfielder Brian Talty. The flare-up was over by the time Tommy Drumm arrived and it was never mentioned in the dressing-room.

'I came into the tunnel and there were a lot of people around and there was shouting going on between the tunnel into our dressing-room and the one into the

Back, left to right: Tommy Conroy, Barney Rock, John Caffrey, Gerry Hargan, Joe McNally, John O'Leary, Anton O'Toole, Mick Holden, Ciarán Duff.
Front, left to right: Brian Mullins, P.J. Buckley, Tommy Drumm, Pat Canavan, Ray Hazley, Jim Ronayne.

Galway dressing-room. I simply was not aware of what was happening. We got into the dressing-room and with ten minutes to discuss the first half, the only talk was how we were going to cope with facing the wind in the second half. Every player had to be aware of the fact that not alone had we to mark our own man when Galway were in possession but we also had to cover the space in between and be careful not to lose possession ourselves going forward. If we lost possession going forward it meant the back line would be exposed. If we were going to do one thing and one thing only we had to finish our moves, and if it meant putting the ball wide that was fine. It would give us a chance to regroup. We did that quite well.'

Tommy thoroughly enjoyed the celebrations and good-humoured banter at the Mansion House and the GPO the following day. 'Winning the All-Ireland generates such excitement throughout the city, it does tend to go on for quite some time. I felt very pleased to have been the one nominated to collect the Sam Maguire Cup and I enjoyed my time as captain. Neither of my parents were alive to witness it — I would have liked them to have been part of it. I was never advised why I was chosen as captain. I did ask!'

But the one incident above all others that remains etched in his mind of the 1983 final happened the Monday after the game when both teams gathered for lunch and the customary viewing of the previous day's final.

'There was a lot of ill-feeling between the two teams during the dinner in Jury's. Having lost in '78 and '79 I was well aware of how the Galway players must have been feeling and have often wondered about this get-together from the losers' perspective. Anyway, feelings were still strained when after lunch it was traditional for one player from each team to sing a song. Joe McNally got up and sang 'The Fields of Athenry' and I felt it went some way towards defusing the situation. It was a special moment.'

Dublin had begun their quest for the 1983 title with a draw against Meath in the second round of the Leinster Championship. The sides were again level at the end of normal time in the replay but a determined and rather lucky Dublin took the honours by two points in extra time. Dublin defeated Louth in the semi-final to set up a Leinster final meeting with favourites Offaly. It proved to be a very exciting high-scoring game as the young eager Dubs dethroned the All-Ireland champions by a margin of five points. Tommy and his teammates could look forward to an All-Ireland semi-final meeting with Cork who themselves had won the Munster Championship for the first time in ten years when they beat Kerry thanks to a last-gasp goal from Tadhg Murphy.

For most of the All-Ireland semi-final Cork looked certain of victory until Barney

---

THE 1983 DUBLIN TEAM

John O'Leary

Mick Holden	Gerry Hargan	Ray Hazley
Pat Canavan	Tommy Drumm (Captain)	P.J. Buckley

Jim Ronayne · Brian Mullins

Barney Rock	Tommy Conroy	Ciarán Duff
John Caffrey	Anton O'Toole	Joe McNally

Substitutes: John Kearns for Tommy Conroy; Kieran Maher for John Caffrey.

Rock levelled the game with a goal in the last seconds. After great deliberations it was eventually decided that the replay should go ahead at Páirc Uí Chaoimh in Cork, and this time Dublin won a high-scoring game handsomely by eleven points. Tommy Drumm feels that game worked wonders for the Dublin team. 'Our morale was sky-high after the thrilling win against Cork. We also had to go to a replay and extra time against Meath, and because of the additional games we had established an inner confidence which had been lacking in the two previous years. We worked hard not to become overconfident.'

He played some wonderful football that year and it was no surprise that he was honoured with an All-Star award to add to his three already won for outstanding performances at wing-back in the seventies.

Tommy Drumm is a true-blue Dub who grew up in Collins Avenue, Whitehall, and received his primary education at the local Larkhill Holy Child School. His father Jack was from Meath but died when Tommy was only thirteen years old. Tommy missed their banter, particularly during the Dublin/Meath clashes in which he played. He recalls that soccer was the game played on the streets at every available opportunity whereas Gaelic football was pursued mainly at school. His older brother, John, who still plays with Whitehall Colmcille, encouraged Tommy to take a keener interest in Gaelic football and as a result the youngster was selected on the club's Under 14 team.

'My first motivation to play Gaelic football seriously came from a remarkable man called Joe Lawless, who unfortunately died a few years ago. Joe was a larger-than-life figure who gave generously of his time and company. We had some very memorable games at minor level in Whitehall under Joe's management. Without Joe's influence my leaning would would have been towards soccer as I was training with the local St Kevin's soccer club at the same time as starting to play minor football. It was nothing to play three matches at the weekend!'

In 1968, Tommy moved on to the new local CBS, St Aidan's, less than five minutes from his home. 'We were very successful for such a new school, winning Under-15 and Under-17 Colleges titles. Semi-finals and finals were major occasions and I remember the whole school being transported in a fleet of double-decker buses, hired from CIE, to O'Toole Park and the like.'

Most memorable of all was the Under-17 Dublin Colleges final victory over Good Counsel in 1972. Future county teammate Kevin Moran was a member of the Good Counsel team. Tommy rates Kevin as his all-time favourite Irish sports star for 'his brilliance, his determination, his versatility, his humour, his skill as a motorcyclist and his choice of student attire!' St Aidan's lost to Gormanston, led brilliantly by Kerry's 'Ogie' Moran, in the Leinster colleges semi-final that year.

Tommy Drumm later played Gaelic football and soccer for six years with Trinity College and represented the Combined Universities in both codes.

He made his debut on the Dublin senior team in a Comhaltas Ceoltóirí Éireann Tournament game against Cork at Croke Park in mid-May 1976 at the age of twenty-one, and his first championship game was against Longford a few weeks later. That year he was to win his first All-Ireland medal when Dublin beat defending champions Kerry in the final by seven points and he was again at right-half-back when the Dubs retained the title with a convincing twelve-points win over Armagh. In the semi-final of that 1977 championship Dublin had beaten Kerry in what is

generally regarded as the greatest game of football ever played.

'There was great rivalry between Dublin and Kerry over the previous couple of years. We were at full strength and so were Kerry. It was a good day, conditions were ideal and what was remarkable about the game was the number of times that it swung backwards and forwards, from Kerry taking the lead to Dublin taking the lead. In the last twenty minutes either team could have won the game. The turning point from Dublin's point of view was when Dave Hickey got the goal.

'The ball went to Davey, I think it was a deflection off John O'Keeffe, and he put it in the net. What was interesting was that Dave religiously used to practise his kicking from twenty-one yards out every Tuesday, Thursday and Saturday at our training sessions. He could kick with both feet, was very strong and had a great ability to place the ball wherever he wanted. There used to be great banter in training sessions between Paddy Cullen and Dave who incessantly blasted the ball at him. If ever somebody's practice was to pay off it was Dave's when he won the ball on that occasion and he placed it in the corner of the net.

'Kerry came back straight away and stuck over a point and then Bernard Brogan scored a brilliant goal when Hanahoe laid the ball on to him as he was running in from midfield. Scoring goals at that stage was what really won it for us; Kerry were scoring the points from long range, whipping them over from all sorts of angles. The pace of the game was incredible. With about five minutes to go I remember feeling that Kerry believed they had won the game but I didn't believe we had lost. There's many a game that you're involved in when you believe you've lost before the final whistle blows, but not this one. I could see Kerry were starting to feel that they were in the final in those last five minutes and suddenly we took it from them.'

Tommy remembers Mick Holden as a great character of the eighties team. He had a great knack for enjoying life and made friends very easily, the joker in the pack. One Saturday morning Tommy and his teammates were training with Kevin Heffernan and were on the pitch about half an hour when Mick arrived in his car to the training ground.

'Kevin stormed off and went up to Mick and apparently said: "Holden, what's your story now, why are you late?" Mick said: "Kevin, I was coming across town this morning and was stopped by the police. There was a bank robbery yesterday and apparently I resembled one of the guys that was involved in the robbery". Heffernan was starting to get interested at this stage and said, "Is that right, Mick". Mick answered "No, but it sounds an awful lot better than saying I slept it out"!'

After their defeat by Kerry in the 1978 All-Ireland final, Dublin decided to change their whole regime for the following year.

'We moved up to Trinity's ground in Santry and everything, including the training methods and team talks, were changed. The day before the All-Ireland final we had a team talk for about an hour and a half after finishing our kick-around. At the end of the team talk Heffernan turned around and said: "Okay lads, if anyone is having any problems sleeping just put your hands up and we have a couple of sleeping pills here we can give you for tonight and you can get a good sleep and play an awful lot better tomorrow". Nobody was keen to put a hand up and admit having any problems sleeping. After a long delay one hand went up at the back and we all looked round and who was it only Holden. Now if anybody was going to have any problems sleeping it wasn't Holden. So Kevin looked a bit suprised but said, "Okay Mick, I'll see you outside before we head off". And again it turned out he was having him on. When Heffernan said, "Mick, of all the guys on the team you're the one guy I wouldn't expect to have any problems sleeping", Mick said, "they're not for me at all, Kevin, they're for my mother, she can't sleep before any of these big games".'

No mention of the Dublin team of the seventies and early eighties would be complete without paying tribute to Kevin Heffernan. Tommy Drumm saw a noticeable difference in 'Heffo's' approach in 1983 compared with his style of the mid-seventies. 'We were struggling with the formation of the team and style of play in the early eighties and were trying to find a formula that was going to prove successful. Heffo was involved with the great team of the seventies and then he had to go through a phase of rebuilding a team in the early eighties. He had a completely different batch of footballers to try and mould into a winning team. I noticed a visible difference in how he approached the team in the eighties. In the seventies Kevin would have taken very much a lead in all the talks, whereas in 1982 and 1983 he put more responsibilty back onto the team to try and get us to work out our own best way of approaching how we should play football.

'That was a very brave move from his point of view. He used to tell us to go off ourselves for an hour or two after training sessions and talk about the games we played and how we were going to prepare for the next game. He allowed us to dictate our own motivation. Brian Mullins, Mick Holden, Anton O'Toole and myself were, I suppose, seen to be important in how that was put together.

'Kevin Heffernan played at the highest level and therefore knew what it was all about. He is a remarkable personality in the sense he knows exactly what he wants. He has a very clear vision of what he wants to achieve and has a very good way of putting that across to the people around him. He is single-minded, decisive and put a great structure on the training sessions and preparation for football. Everybody turned up for training sessions right through the winter and summer and if you didn't turn up for training or a game you'd have to have a very good reason. It was a regime that worked on the basis of discipline. Once the discipline was in place you really felt comfortable. His ability to analyse a game and analyse every individual on the team and how they played in every game was amazing. Not everybody agreed with him and some people would strongly disagree with him and would have publicly stated that later on, but not at the time.

'There was a lot of ill-feeling between the two teams during the dinner in Jurys. Having lost in 1978 and 1979 I was well aware of how the Galway players must have been feeling. Anyway, feelings were still strained when after lunch Joe McNally got up and sang "The Fields Of Athenry" and I felt it went some way towards diffusing the situation.'

'We were a very close-knit unit and team at that time. But I personally felt that he was a tremendous leader, as indeed was Tony Hanahoe who took up the torch in 1977. Tony was manager, player and captain, all of which he did brilliantly. Heffernan put everything in place and I had the utmost respect for him. Once he felt you had the commitment, number one, he could work on the other aspects of your game. And that's what he had in Dublin, players who were committed to their objective, which was winning the All-Ireland.'

Tommy Drumm played his last competitive match when he captained the Dublin team that lost to Kerry in the Centenary All-Ireland in 1984. His final inter-county game was against Meath in a challenge game in September 1984. It marked the end of a brilliant career. He was presented with golf clubs and luggage by the team and supporters before emigrating to Qatar in the Middle East.

He nominates Offaly's Matt Connor as his most difficult inter-county opponent: 'He was simply brilliant at all facets of forward play; fielding, sidestep, both feet, strong, fast and he has the ability to score from long range. Almost impossible to mark effectively.'

Nothing else in sport compared to captaining Dublin in 1983. Those opportunities are rare and Tommy Drumm is delighted to have stood on the Hogan Stand with Sam Maguire.

Richie CONNOR

Offaly Captain 1982

IT WAS ONE OF the most dramatic All-Ireland Football finals ever. How many times since have you heard someone say: 'wasn't that the year Séamus Darby scored the famous goal?' Indeed! A famous goal and an equally famous victory over a Kerry team, acknowledged by friend and foe alike as the greatest in the history of the game. Remember, the 'Kingdom' had notched up four on the trot and were now raging favourites to create history. Celebrations were planned; thousands of 'Five in a Row' songs had been released and the appropriate 'T-shirts' proclaiming the good news were selling like hot cakes. And then a man called Séamus Darby had to pop up and spoil it all! It was as unexpected as it was exciting for Offaly followers. Had they not seen Kerry beat their men by seven points in the final the previous year? Had they not seen that footballing genius from Walsh Island, Matt Connor, score 2-9 in the 1980 All-Ireland semi-final and still lose to Kerry by five points? There was nothing to suggest it would be different in the 1982 final. But it was. And captain Richie Connor became the third Offaly man to have the honour of collecting the Sam Maguire Cup.

If one moment transcended any other after the final, it was Richie meeting a very disappointed Kerry captain, John Egan, in the bowels of the Hogan Stand. A moment shared between victor and vanquished. Richie was returning to the dressing-room after a radio interview, and John Egan, already dressed, was on his way out of the ground. It brought home to Richie what he had always known: that there is no time for losers on All-Ireland day. He himself experienced the same sense of heartbreak after Offaly's defeat the year before.

'John was bitterly disappointed but very, very dignified. I think I said something like: "We stole it on you, Johnny". It did strike me how awful it was for such a great player to be making such a quiet exit: no one slapping his back; no one shaking his hand and no one even sympathising with him. He was just going off to have a pint.'

FACT FILE

HOME PLACE: Monevane, Walsh Island, County Offaly.

BORN: 25 October 1955

CLUBS: Éire Óg, Offaly; Erins Hope, (Dublin) and Walsh Island, Offaly.

ACHIEVEMENTS IN CLUB COMPETITIONS: Six County Senior Football Championships with Walsh Island from 1978, 1979, 1980, 1981, 1982, 1983; two Leinster Club Championship medals with Walsh Island in 1978 and 1979; UCD All-Ireland Seven-A-Side Championship medal in 1979; Under-21 Offaly Championship in 1975 with Walsh Island; two Under-21 Dublin Championships in 1974 and 1975 with Erin's Hope; numerous tournament and county League medals.

INTER-COUNTY ACHIEVEMENTS: One All-Ireland Senior Football Championship medal in 1982; three Leinster Senior Championship medals in 1980, 1981 and 1982.

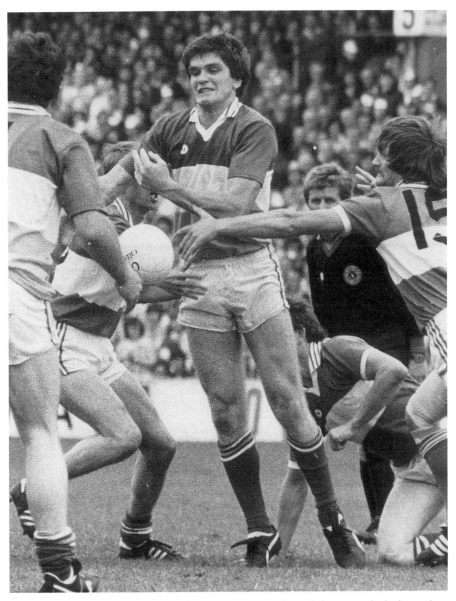

A few hours previously, the talk was of Kerry only and there was little fuss when the Offaly team arrived at Croke Park in the early afternoon.

'Nobody much recognised us, as we didn't have the smart jackets that teams seem to have nowadays. I remember a guy trying to sell us "Kerry Five in a Row" scarves and when he realised who we were, he said: "do you want one anyway?" I also recall hearing the "Five in a Row" song being played outside the ground. They even had "Five in a Row" team photos on display. If you needed something to motivate a team, it was all there.

'In our own minds, we had convinced ourselves that Kerry couldn't be getting any better, whereas we were improving all the time. We knew we couldn't be that far off them. They hadn't put us away the previous year — all right they beat us by seven points, but it was only a late goal by Jack O'Shea that had really put the game beyond doubt. The team had developed a certain amount of maturity and we were delighted not to have put our foot in it in pre-match comments. There was an air of composure and the team seemed to be purposeful as we waited in the dressing-room. Eugene McGee, who usually gave very defnite roles to players, spoke in general terms. He told us we had a great chance of winning and there would be no excuses. It was time to go out and do it or forget about it, he said.'

As far as Richie can recall, the only specific instructions the manager gave to any individual player was to Liam Currams. He told him to lay off the ball. It seems Liam had come too far forward in a number of challenge games before the final and kicked some wides. It was ironic that within a few minutes of the start, Currams came sallying up the field to kick one of the best points of the game.

At that precise moment, the Offaly team knew they had the winning of the game. History would have to wait another day.

'That score lifted the whole team and maybe Liam was telling Eugene something in his own way. It was just the start we needed. The message had been drummed into us that the first half wasn't that important, but we had to be careful not to get put away. The real match was going to be the second half. As it turned out, we played very well in the first half but Kerry proceeded to dominate the game in the second half. The rain came down and a few things went against us. Kerry were still in front when Mikey Sheehy's penalty kick was saved by Martin Furlong. If Mikey had scored from the penalty, it would have put us away, as a few breaks had gone against us just before that. The whole fortune changed after the penalty. We got a few breaks and Matt pointed two frees inside the last five minutes to bring us to within two points of Kerry.'

And then Séamus Darby's goal, perhaps the most controversial in Gaelic football. Few other scores have ever been so significant. It denied Kerry a place in the history books. But, was it a push in the back?

'I still think that any referee could have given the decision either way. It was a cute hip contact and if two people go for a ball, there's going to be some contact. I'm trying to be as honest as I can and if any referee gave a decision in that case, either way, he couldn't be faulted. Séamus Darby was a very skilful striker of a ball and it wouldn't be unusual for him in training to get a spectacular goal. It was a controversial goal only in so far as it deprived Kerry of their "Five In A Row". I don't think the way it came about was much different to many goals that were scored. It was just that the goal meant so much.'

THE 1982 OFFALY TEAM

Martin Furlong

Mick Lowry	Liam O'Connor	Mick Fitzgerald
Pat Fitzgerald	Sean Lowry	Liam Currams

Tomás O'Connor   Pádraig Dunne

John Guinan	Richie Connor (Captain)	Gerry Carroll
Johnny Mooney	Matt Connor	Brendan Lowry

Stephen Darby for Mick Lowry; Séamus Darby for John Guinan

Richie confesses that he did not enjoy the goal one bit. He was terrified in case Offaly would let it slip. His only worry was how much time was left. He was frantically trying to get his players back into their positions to mark up. As it was, Kerry had some chances to level scores, but failed to get on target.

'The minute the goal went in, I realised exactly what was after happening. We were a point ahead and we were within a couple of minutes of winning an All-Ireland. There was a fair few Offaly players going "mad", jumping up and down and I had to try and settle them. A few players over-reacted and we nearly blew it.'

He believes Eugene McGee and his management team made a tactical error in the closing minutes, which could have cost Offaly the game.

'Eugene has to be given an awful lot of credit for the win and for making several good positional changes during the game, but it was a mistake not to let Matt take a free under the Cusack Stand in the last minute. They let Gerry Carroll take it as a short free and there was a bit of messing around, but it eventually came back to Gerry and he kicked it wide. Matt would definitely have "killed" that ball, or scored a point. That was a foolish decision and could have cost us the game. As well as that, Gerry Carroll who was always one of Offaly's most influential players found himself in possession and probably over elaborated on the ball. I remember roaring for the ball and then, all of a sudden, I saw Páidí Ó Sé coming down the field. I could see a point coming from it. Páidí gave it to Tom Spillane and he probably would have been better advised to throw it off to the likes of Mikey or "Bomber", or fellows with old heads.

'But he did exactly what any good young determined player would have done in the same circumstances, he took it on himself to get the equalising score and lost possession. Mikey Sheehy had another chance, but missed it. Having been given the chance to win the All-Ireland, we very nearly blew it.

'If we had let it slip, we'd have had no one to blame but ourselves. It would have been a disaster. The team played with much more composure than in the 1981 final.

Back, left to right: Seán Lowry, Gerry Carroll, Padraig Dunne, Liam O'Connor, Liam Currams, Matt Connor, Tomás O'Connor.
Front, left to right: Mick Fitzgerald, Pat Fitzgerald, Martin Furlong, Richie Connor (captain), John Guinan, John Mooney, Brendan Lowry, Mick Lowry.

There wasn't the same amount of aimless kicking. I was moved out to centre field for the last quarter. It was a wonderful feeling to hear the final whistle.'

All the years of training and hard work had finally paid off. Richie had spent all his childhood days kicking football around the pasture and farm-yard in his Walsh Island home. The farm-yard had two ready-made 'goalposts': the 'horse house' door and the supporting walls for the diesel tank. Often times he got his knitted pullover tangled in the barbed wire as he made his way into the pasture with the leather ball.

There was no barbed wire that day in Croke Park but the problem was how to make his way to the Hogan Stand through hordes of green-and-gold-clad Offaly supporters. Croke Park was alive with excitement. And Richie Connor from Walsh Island was about to collect the Sam Maguire Cup.

'When the match was over I started angling my way towards the Hogan Stand steps as I realised I had a duty to perform: I had to get the Cup and say a few words. Although there was a lot of shaking hands, back-slapping and congratulations, I was very conscious about getting to the podium. As it turned out, I got there way ahead of all the other players. I was coaxed up the steps by the officials and was shaking hands with Charlie Haughey before any of the other Offaly players had even arrived at the bottom of the steps. The President of the GAA, Paddy Buggy, was wondering whether to go ahead with the presentation or to wait for the rest of the Offaly team to arrive. He eventually decided to start saying his few words. The Offaly supporters were going mad with excitement down on the field. The Cup was handed over to me and I lifted it up and started my speech. I said a few words in Irish and the usual "three-and-fourpence" but I don't think anyone heard it and I didn't give a damn! I'm sorry now that I wasn't clearer in my delivery, especially during the part where I thanked all those who made a contribution to our victory.'

Richie Connor believes that Offaly's win should be kept in perspective. It should be viewed as a wonderful team performance on the day, but no more than that. He just felt very lucky and privileged to be captain.

'I never had any illusions about our victory. I never thought that we were a better team than Kerry. We played well as a team and got the necessary breaks. Things went right on the day and we beat them. I realised that if we were playing Kerry the following Sunday, we might not have won. Even after winning that final I was still very much in awe of that team. I don't mind saying that at all. We were lucky to have a good manager at the time in Eugene McGee and lucky to get the breaks. I would have seen myself as one of three or four captains. I think most teams have dominant personalities throughout the field. Definitely, Martin Furlong was a natural leader and so too was Seán Lowry. I would have seen myself as just another player.'

They say every team needs a fair share of good luck to win a major championship. It was no different in Offaly's case. They had their narrow escapes as in the semi-final of the Leinster Championship against Laois.

'I was having problems with my knee at that stage and I didn't find it easy against Tom Prendergast, who was a very good player. We were very lucky to win and it took late goals from John Guinan and Gerry Carroll to turn the game around in Offaly's favour.'

Richie went into hospital to undergo an operation on his dodgy knee in the week leading up to the Leinster final showdown with Dublin. Martin Furlong took over the role of captain and Richie watched the match from the dug-out. Offaly had a comfortable win by nine points.

'It was the first time since I came on the team that I hadn't taken part in an important match for Offaly and I wasn't missed. It made me realise that I could be done without. Seán Lowry had played very well at centre-back, so I now had two problems: one was to get fit enough to play for Offaly and then I had to get my place back on the team. I was lucky to be on summer holidays from teaching and I put in a tremendous amount of work, building up my knee through extensive physiotherapy and cycling to make sure I was available for the semi-final. Right up to the time the team was selected I wasn't sure I'd be in the team for the game against Galway.'

In the event, he partnered Tomás Connor at mid-field and Offaly defeated the Connacht champions by a single point.

In the aftermath of the 1981 Final, Richie had many discussions with manager Eugene McGee about aspects of play and weaknesses in the Offaly team. They were agreed that a more confident approach was required if Kerry were to be defeated.

'The GAA puts itself forward as being democratic and on paper it is, in reality, the structure stagnates the whole process of decision making, because there are so many avenues to put down the people with energy and bright ideas.'

'In the 1981 Final a lot of ball was just belted down the field, without any sort of deliberation at all. Once the championship started in 1982, we worked hard on that aspect of play. We spent our usual couple of months doing hard stamina training in Rhode and it worked very well. We trained for most of the summer in Ballycommon. It's just a small club and they were very, very accommodating and looked after us very well. They made us feel very welcome. I was delighted for them as much as for anyone else that we won the All-Ireland Final in 1982.'

There was a bit of good-humoured banter in a Dublin pub in the aftermath of the 1982 All-Ireland final and someone made a comment about the 'great' Kerry team. A person from Offaly, of Richie's acquaintance, stood up and said, 'How could Kerry be any good, when a couple of families from the bog could beat them!' A slight exaggeration, perhaps, but the message was loud and clear. There were four Connors on that Offaly team, Matt and Richie are brothers and so are Liam and Tomás; Brendan, Mick and Seán Lowry are brothers and so are Mick and Pat Fitzgerald and Séamus and Stephen Darby. Truly a family affair.

No one played a more significant part in Offaly's success than Richie's younger brother, Matt, considered one of the most outstanding forwards ever. Sadly, Matt's career ended abruptly following a car accident which deprived the game of a wonderful sportsman and a footballing genius.

'We didn't see him as special until he came onto the Offaly senior team, although we should have, because he was getting the good scores and showing the classy touches at school level. But it wasn't something that hadn't been done by the rest of the family. I always played in the forwards in school competitions and was reasonably accurate; Willie had been a very good free-taker with Ballyfin, so it was no great deal to have a young brother coming up that seemed to be accurate enough at frees. He had way better balance than anyone else and in a very short space he was able to get in a mighty drive of a ball with either foot. He was able to get into a position to take a shot on either side very quickly. Even though I kick with both feet I know if I got into the very same position, I'd need to take an extra step to get the same balance as Matt.

'I once heard some one comparing other well known quality players to Matt and he put it like this: "Some top-class players do the expected brilliantly, but Matt Connor does the expected brilliantly and the unexpected even more brilliantly". He scored some great goals in important championship games, both for club and county, and was continually scoring marvellous goals in training sessions. It was no big deal to see him scoring great goals against top-quality opposition, because we saw him doing it time and time again in training sessions. He had a hunger for scores and it wasn't that he was over selfish. When there was a score on Matt seemed to have that extra drive to take it.'

His two points from frees in the All-Ireland final of 1982, which brought Offaly to within two points of Kerry, clearly demonstrated Matt Connor's temperament for the big occasion. Other, lesser players might have tried to conjure a goal, but not Matt. He believed in himself and in Offaly football and he knew they could still win the game. He was right!

Richie Connor began his playing career with Éire Óg, which was an amalgamation of Clonbologue, Bracknagh and Walsh Island. Although there was an abundance of talent in the three parishes, Richie believes they never realised their full potential. All they had to show for their endeavours was an appearance in the 1970 County Senior Final, which they lost to Gracefield.

'Éire Óg always promised well, but never really delivered. It was felt that there was too much favouritism by selectors to their own corner. I feel it's fair to say that. This favouritism also surfaced in close matches. If the Éire Óg team didn't win matches by a wide margin they were inclined to lose them in tight situations, due to bickering. It wasn't that obvious, but at the same time, for the amount of talent available, there should have been more success coming to the club. I've seen the same thing happen with other amalgamated teams.'

There was a meeting called at Christmas 1975 and it was decided that Walsh Island would form its own club and enter a team in the Senior Championship. In the very first year in operation, Walsh Island contested the county final. Richie was captain of the team and they lost in a replay to Ferbane, a team which included Tony McTague and the Lowry brothers. The following year, Walsh Island reached the semi-final of the championship but, although hotly tipped to advance to the final, they were beaten by Tullamore. It was a big disappointment as the club had already won the County League. But it all came right in 1978, when Walsh Island won the first of six consecutive Senior Football Championships.'

When asked to comment on the running of the sports organisation, Richie had strong and clear views and recommendations.

'It annoys me terribly that the GAA is so stagnant at senior levels, particularly County Boards. When I was teaching, I used the analogy that the GAA is very, very similar to the old ruling system that was in Russia, until quite recently. The GAA puts itself forward as being democratic and on paper it is, in so far as every post down to grass roots level is there to be contested. Every club has an AGM and anybody that wants has an opportunity of letting their voices be heard. But in reality, the structure stagnates the whole process of decision making, because there are so many avenues to put down the people with energy and bright ideas. A new idea can be ruled out of order at the Club AGM by a Chairman or Secretary, who have been involved for years and years and see this as a sort of threat to their "Open" policy. I think this is too common to be put aside. Even if someone does make it through, because they're respected at local level, and if his ideas seem anyway different or controversial, he'll find it very hard to get time at the County Board Convention. There can very easily be a clique against any sort of innovative idea that might cause hassle to the County Board.

'The way the system in Russia used to work was to have small Co-Ops that would run small farms. People were elected on to the small Co-Ops and usually it was the less progressive farmers that got involved in these type of things. Again, like certain elements in the GAA, it was people who liked bureaucracy. If they played their cards right then they'd get elected to the Regional Co-Op and eventually they might make the Kremlin. It's the very same in the GAA. If you say the "right" thing, do the "right" thing, talk to the "right" people and are happy with very, very slow progress then you'll find an office on the County Board and maybe eventually the Provincial Council and so on. That's the picture I have found and I think it's not good for the GAA that so many players and former players hold the same view.

'I have seen many people with energy and bright ideas who could do a lot to change the direction of the GAA at local and county level and they are disillusioned by sub-laws and other antiquated rules.

'I don't see why I should have to write my name in Irish to play a Gaelic football match. If I used an Irish name that would be fine. I respect the right of any person to use their own name, whether it's Irish, English or French. But for the GAA to insist on something that does nothing to promote Irish is not only a nuisance but is also wrong. It's confusing and small-minded.'

The memory Richie cherishes above all others is Offaly winning the All-Ireland Hurling final of 1981 for the first time. He knew most of the players and appreciated the small area from which the team came.

'Their pick would be less than some Cork clubs. It seemed to be a statement of defiance from Offaly. By right, demographically and geographically, there's no way Offaly should be winning All-Ireland hurling titles. There's just no way! These boys did it! They had fierce pride in the Offaly jersey. The players came from a small area of Offaly, just a few clubs and their pick was so small, yet they achieved the impossible.'

From as far back as Richie can remember, football has dominated his life. It took precedence over any major decision he had to make over the years. Football always came first. And the game in turn was kind to him. He knew of victory and of defeat but when memories of games won and lost fade away, he will still have the friendships — friendships nurtured through a long and very successful career.

Committed is a word that aptly describes the All-Ireland winning captain of 1982, Richie Connor.

Jimmy DEENIHAN

Kerry Captain 1981

JIMMY DEENIHAN will always have an honoured place in the annals of Kerry football as captain of the four-in-a-row team of 1981. It was a feat the Kingdom had previously achieved way back in 1932, under the captaincy of full-back Joe Barrett. The year 1981 also marked the occasion of Kerry's twenty-seventh All-Ireland Football title.

In leading his countymen to victory over the Richie Connor-led Offaly, the powerfully built corner-back from Finuge claimed the last of his five All-Ireland senior medals.

There is no doubt that Jimmy would have won many more honours with the Kingdom had not a bad injury effectively ended his inter-county career.

'I broke my leg at training in early summer 1982 and certainly it was a major disappointment. I felt I was at the peak of my football career both physically and mentally at the time. I had enjoyed a good season up to the time of my injury and had captained Kerry to beat Cork in the National League final and things were going very well for the team. We looked like we were all set for the five-in-a-row. The injury more or less marked the end of my football career at inter-county level. I lost eight months of training and in the meantime I had become involved in politics and I wasn't able to retain the level of fitness that I had prior to my injury.'

His last appearance in a Kerry jersey, at the opening of Tarbert GAA field in May 1983, signalled the end of a magnificent career that had begun over twenty years earlier in rather modest but familiar surroundings.

FACT FILE

HOME PLACE: Finuge, Lixnaw, County Kerry

BORN: 11 September 1952

CLUBS: Finuge; Feale Rangers (Divisional); Minor with Shannon Rangers (Divisional), Saint Senans and Listowel Emmet's; National College of Physical Education 1973-1975; Lixnaw Hurling Club.

ACHIEVEMENTS IN CLUB COMPETITIONS: Under-14 North Kerry Championship with Finuge in 1963; Under-16 North Kerry Championship with Listowel Emmetts in 1968; with Finuge won a North Kerry Senior League in 1970 and North Kerry Senior Championship in 1987; won Kerry County Senior Championships with Feale Rangers in 1978 and '80.

INTER-COUNTY ACHIEVEMENTS: Five All-Ireland Senior Football Championship medals in 1975, 1978, 1979, 1980 and 1981; three National Football League medals in 1973, 1977 and 1982; five Railway Cup Football medals in 1975, 1976, 1978, 1981 and 1982; All Star Award in 1981; seven Munster Senior Football Championships in 1975, 1976, 1977, 1978, 1979, 1980 and 1981; one All-Ireland Under-21 championship in 1973 and two Munster Under-21 medals in 1972 and 1973.

'The first toy I remember getting for Christmas was a football. I played my early football at Finuge Cross with the other lads in the village, as we had no football club or sports field in Finuge at the time. At the beginning of the 1960s, a local farmer called Paud O'Sullivan, who was himself a former Kerry footballer, allowed us use one of his fields. Finuge revived their club in 1961 and I played my first match with the Under-14 team in 1963. We won the North Kerry Under-14 Championship that year. I also played with Killocrim National School during this period up to 1966 in the School League in Listowel, although I attended Dromclough National School. From 1966 to 1971, I attended St Michael's College in Listowel, where my trainers were John O'Flaherty and John Molyneaux, both of whom I regard as two of the best I ever trained under. During the period from 1965 to 1971, I played Under 14, Under

16 and minor football with neighbouring clubs, St Senan's, and Listowel Emmetts. I played in the County Minor Championship with Shannon Rangers.'

Jimmy figured on the Kerry team beaten by Galway in the replay of the 1970 All-Ireland Minor final. That Kerry team was trained by Senator Dan Kiely who later became a political adversary. In the mid-seventies, he played football with the Divisional side, Feale Rangers, with whom he won two County Championship medals. His teammates included such stalwarts as Tim Kennelly, Johnny Mulvihill, Paddy Mulvihill, Tommy Bridgeman, John Bunyan, Robert Bunyan, John Wrenn, Gerald O'Sullivan, Patsy O'Connell, Gerald Leahy and Tom Connell, all of whom represented Kerry at some level.

Just sixteen when he lined out with Finuge senior team, Jimmy continued to play with the local club for over twenty years. In 1990 he finally decided to call it a day because of political and family commitments, which considerably restricted the time he could devote to training.

From 1973 to 1975, Jimmy was a member of that magnificent National College of Physical Education team which included the likes of Brian Mullins, Richie Bell, John Tobin, Tom Donnellan, Fran Ryder, Liam Fardy, Pat and Mick Spillane, Hugo Clerkin and Brendan Lillis. The team was coached by Dave Weldrick, a man Jimmy believes introduced a new approach and new thinking to the coaching of Gaelic football.

The years from 1975 to 1983 rank as the greatest period in his playing career. Under the leadership of Mick O'Dwyer, a man for whom Jimmy has great admiration, Kerry scaled new heights in Gaelic football. Their achievements are now history.

'It was a pleasure to be part of such an outstanding team. During that time, I was also a regular on the Munster team winning five Railway Cup medals. It was a great experience to play alongside Jimmy Barry Murphy, Dinny Allen, Declan Barron, Billy Morgan, Brian Murphy, Kevin Kehilly and Humphrey Kelleher among others'.

Jimmy Barry Murphy he regards as the most difficult opponent he encountered, a great 'goal poacher', very fast and difficult to mark. 'Occasionally, I had my differences with him on the field of play and in some cases, I would accept that I was the offender, but there were occasions when Jimmy himself was the culprit and that sometimes tended to be overlooked. There was always great expectation when Jimmy Barry took the field and I think Mícheál Ó Muircheartaigh summed it up precisely before one game when he said: "Ní fheadar cá bhfuil ina cheann aige inniu." You could never predict with any degree of certainty what his next move would be which meant that he demanded total concentration and attention for the entire duration of a game. He could be described as the Gary Lineker of Gaelic

---

THE 1981 KERRY TEAM

Charlie Nelligan

Jimmy Deenihan (Captain)	John O'Keeffe	Paud Lynch
Páidí Ó Sé	Tim Kennelly	Mick Spillane

Seán Walsh   Jack O'Shea

Ger Power	Denis 'Ogie' Moran	Tommy Doyle
Mikie Sheehy	Eoin 'Bomber' Liston	John Egan

Substitutes: Pat Spillane for John Egan; Ger O'Keeffe for Mick Spillane

football.' Dublin forward John McCarthy was another player Jimmy rated very highly. 'He was probably one of the most underrated forwards of the great Dublin team of the seventies. John was a tremendous competitor on the field and got some of the crucial scores for Dublin.'

Jimmy Deenihan loved the competitive element of Gaelic football and never wearied of playing games, wherever he was. He travelled extensively with the Kerry football team and played in London, New York, Boston, San Francisco, Los Angeles, Melbourne, Perth, Adelaide and Sydney. He played with the Kingdom club in London in the early seventies. He also found time to play for the Kerry club in New York, often travelling over for weekend games in the mid-seventies.

On one of his trips to America, with newly crowned county champions Feale Rangers, he was persuaded to take the Sam Maguire Cup although he himself had reservations.

'Because of previous experience of trips to America I was reluctant to take the Cup as I knew it would be a major responsibility. Normally when a club team goes over to America they do so to enjoy themselves. I took the Cup to a function in Gaelic Park in New York and as it was late when we were leaving I decided to leave it in the safe there rather than risk taking it back to our hotel in downtown New York at midnight. The next morning I had to go to hospital to visit one of our club members who was involved in a car accident the previous night. When I went back to Gaelic Park the Cup had disappeared, so we had to travel on to Pittsburgh without it. I had to come back to New York the following Thursday and remember going into the local police station in the Bronx only to be told that they had far more serious problems on their hands and didn't want to get involved in some ethnic Irish squabble about a cup. After the police saw some cuttings from Irish papers about the missing Sam Maguire Cup, they realised its importance and stepped up their enquiries. The Cup was dropped into Gaelic Park a few days later. Nobody knows how it disappeared and I wasn't too anxious to find out. I was just very happy to have it back. That was Easter

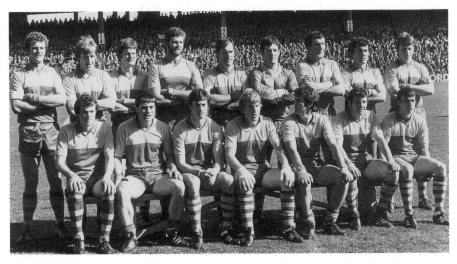

Back, left to right: Jack O'Shea, Pat Spillane, Paud Lynch, Eoin 'Bomber' Liston, John O'Keeffe, Charlie Nelligan, Tim Kennelly, Ger Power, Seán Walsh.
Front, left to right: Mikey Sheehy, Páidí Ó Sé, Tommy Doyle, Jimmy Deenihan (captain), Mick Spillane, John Egan, Denis 'Ogie' Moran.

1981 and it was ironic that I was to be the recipient of the Sam Maguire Cup the following September.'

The greatest thrill Jimmy experienced in his sporting career occurred off the field. It happened in 1980, the year he lost his place through injury on the county team.

'I was captain of the Kerry team, which lost to Cork in the National League Final in 1980. Following that, I was injured and, unfortunately, did not recover until a few days before the Munster final. By then the team had been decided on, so I was on the substitutes' bench. The team performed so well on that occasion that it remained unchanged for the All-Ireland semi-final against Offaly. At the time, I was probably playing the best football of my career, so naturally I was very disappointed not to be selected. I did come on as a substitute against Offaly in the All-Ireland semi-final and played reasonably well but, nevertheless, I felt that I hadn't done enough to secure a place in the team for the All-Ireland final. I trained very hard for the final, including training on my own every morning. What I really needed, to have any chance of getting on the team, was a good game in the final trial match, the Sunday before the All-Ireland final.

'I was marking John Egan on that occasion and before the ball was thrown in, I said to him, "I need a good game today, so please take it easy". John nodded in agreement but he had other ideas, judging by the way he played. In the second half, in particular, I remember he scored a goal and a point, which he rarely scored off me in any game before, be it in training or in trial games. So coming off the field that evening, I felt down and my head was hanging and the confidence had left my body, more or less. I came home that evening and went to Tarbert, where my divisional team, Feale Rangers, were playing a challenge game against a team from Clare. I was going to play in it but just in case I might get injured I decided I would give it a miss. Really, all I was looking for was some victim to go away and have a few pints with, but luckily for me, there was no one available. So I came home and was sitting by the fireside, very down and out, when the telephone rang and my friend John O'Keeffe told me I was on the team. I must say, I just couldn't believe it and it was the first time I ever felt I was floating on air. I was totally carried away for a few hours.

'I just couldn't believe I was on the team. I experienced several great occasions in football, I won an awful lot, but I must say, at that moment I experienced a sense of exhilaration I never felt before or since in sport. I suppose the message really of that whole experience is that you must never give up hope and there is a message there for young athletes, that sport is unpredictable: you can be down one day, but certainly the opportunities are there for you to be back on top the following day.'

In the build-up to the 1981 All-Ireland, Jimmy kept to himself as much as he could. He never liked to talk too much about football especially in the championship season. He realised what was most important was to keep fit, avoid injury and get sufficient sleep, rather than talk for hours about football.

'I never indulged in too much talk about football, but at the same time I always felt it was only proper to be courteous to people who were interested in the game. I felt it better to avoid long discussions as I felt it would break my concentration and introduce impediments into my thinking about an upcoming game. I liked to keep a clear mind and get my attitude right.'

Still no matter how hard he tried to close himself off from outside influences, Jimmy was very conscious that there was an air of expectation and excitement right around the county, especially in his home village of Finuge. And there were emotional scenes when he arrived back home with the Cup.

'It certainly meant a lot to the village and I got a very enthusiastic reception in Finuge. There was a massive crowd in the village and it was a great event for everyone, especially the older people. The 'Sam Maguire' to them was something like the Ardagh Chalice as they never thought they'd see it, much less touch it and lift it. Some of the older people had never even travelled to Dublin to see a match so it was their life's ambition to see the Sam Maguire Cup and study it. It certainly brought a lot of happiness to people in the latter days of their lives. That alone made it worthwhile.' He is deeply grateful to Offaly players Matt Connor, Gerry Carroll and Seán and Brendan Lowry for travelling to Finuge for the all-night celebrations.

The Kerry team was superbly prepared for the Munster final in 1981 and it reflected in their peformance against Cork, whom they beat by 1-11 to 0-3. There was another runaway victory in the All-Ireland semi-final when Mayo were handed a sixteen points hammering. 'It was a very good Mayo team and Willie Joe Padden dominated midfield in the first half and it took us some time before we took the lead. However, in the second half, Mayo totally collapsed and we played one of the greatest half hours of football our team ever played. We approached the All-Ireland against Offaly with a lot of confidence and there was a general feeling we had their measure. Mick O'Dwyer ensured that we would be well prepared and I think it reflected in our performance in the final. On the other hand it must be said that if Offaly had taken their chances it would have been much closer. They got inspiration from that particular game for the following year when they beat Kerry with a last minute goal from Séamus Darby. After analysing and studying the 1981 final, Offaly realised that there were opportunities which they missed.

> 'I was sitting by the fireside very down and out, when the telephone rang and my friend John O'Keeffe told me I was on the team. I just couldn't believe it and it was the first time I ever felt I was floating on air.'

'We emerged easy enough winners in the end and Jack O'Shea's goal in the last few minutes put an end to any hope that Offaly had of winning the game. That particular goal will always stand out in my memory as I had started the move right back on our own end line. It involved about seven passes from both the foot and hand and it was probably one of the best Gaelic football goals that was ever scored.'

After Jack O'Shea scored the goal, Jimmy began to concentrate on his acceptance speech, which he had well rehearsed beforehand. Unlike many of the other captains, the Finuge man was very happy with his few words after receiving the Cup. He found it hard to show a more emotional side as he was still keyed up and tense for some time after the game. He can remember his good friend and loyal Kerry supporter Joe Halpin coming up to him and shaking his hand with great vigour.

His strength and speed and his sheer commitment ensured that Jimmy was a very difficult defender to cope with, as many a forward will testify. He worked hard on his game and as well as perfecting the hand pass he could also kick with both left and right foot. If he has one regret about the way he played football at inter-county level

it is that he allowed himself to become too preoccupied with man-to-man marking.

'When you concentrate on close marking you can sacrifice your contribution to general play. Maybe I should have tried to express myself more on the field especially in league games when the stakes were not that high and when a mistake would not have been a disaster. I probably played too safe, but then again I played for the team and not for myself. I could have got more enjoyment out of the game if I had been more adventurous. But why should a back go up and try to score when we had the greatest forwards in the game? Mick O'Dwyer's philosophy was to get the ball up to the forwards as quickly as possible and let them do the business.'

Jimmy Deenihan feels strongly that there is need for a major improvement in the level of refereeing. He believes referees should be paid to officiate at games, in order to ensure high standards and fair play for participants. He thinks more emphasis should be placed on the rehabilitation and treatment of players. 'The careers of many players are shortened because of injury. The GAA, together with the other national sporting organisations, should establish a national rehabilitation centre for the treatment of sports injuries.'

He believes that the GAA should concern itself solely with the promotion of our national games. 'The GAA is there to promote and develop the national games and in doing that I think they are expressing one of the greatest and most positive forms of nationalism that this country could display and something that can stand on its own.'

And what did the playing of Gaelic football mean to Jimmy Deenihan?

'First of all I was very fortunate to be on that great Kerry team. I think any footballer in this century would have loved to be on the team. It enabled me to play with some of the finest individuals that anyone could ever choose to meet. It helped me through my formative years. It taught me a lot about discipline, motivation, punctuality and about one hundred per cent commitment in order to get results. It educated me in how to take defeat as well as victory and to realise that defeat is not the end of the world. It also enabled me to handle victory in a philosophical manner. No doubt my high profile as a footballer was the principal reason why I was asked to run for politics — I have never regretted this decision.'

Ger POWER

Kerry Captain 1980

VERSATILE, talented and good-humoured are words that spring to mind when describing Ger Power, one of only five players to have won eight All-Ireland senior football medals. He won six of those medals as a forward, one as a defender and another as substitute when he had the cruel misfortune to miss Kerry's win over Dublin in the 1979 All-Ireland final because of injury.

But records are for others to talk about; Ger Power is just happy to have been part of the greatest football machine in Gaelic football. Everything else is a bonus. Here is a man blessed with a tremendous attitude to sport. Sure he strove might and main to win and there was no more committed or determined player on the field but when the game was over that was it. His philosophy always was: 'if you win, you win; if you lose, well there's always the next time'!

Ger Power was just ten days old when his father, Jackie, who worked for CIE, was transferred to Tralee. A hurler of note, Jackie had won All-Ireland medals with Limerick in 1936 and 1940 and later played hurling with Kerry and Austin Stacks. Young Ger himself began his inter-county career with the Kerry Under 16 hurling team but as he jokingly says: 'I packed that in because it was too dangerous down in this county'.

He lined out with Kerry minor footballers for two years and was left-half-forward and captain when Kerry lost to Galway in the 1970 All-Ireland minor final. He later played for three years with the Kerry Under 21 team and was centre-half-back when the 'Kingdom' beat Mayo in the 1973 All-Ireland decider. That victorious Under 21 team formed the nucleus of the side that was to become the most successful in the history of Gaelic games. Among his colleagues on that 1973 Under 21 winning side were Paudie O'Mahony, Jimmy Deenihan, Ger O'Keefe, Paudie Lynch, Mickey O'Sullivan, Páidí Ó Sé, John Egan and Mikey Sheehy.

F A C T   F I L E

HOME PLACE: Tralee, County Kerry

BORN: 27 June 1952 in Annacotty, County Limerick

CLUB: Austin Stacks

ACHIEVEMENTS IN CLUB COMPETITIONS: Six County Senior Football Championship medals; one All-Ireland Senior Club Championship medal in 1977; Under-16 County Championship medal.

INTER-COUNTY ACHIEVEMENTS: Eight All-Ireland Senior medals in 1975, 1978, 1979, 1980, 1981, 1984, 1985 and 1986; eleven Munster Senior Championship medals in 1975, 1976, 1977, 1978, 1979, 1980, 1981, 1982, 1984, 1985 and 1986; one All-Ireland Under-21 medal in 1973; six Railway Cup medals in 1975, 1976, 1977, 1978, 1981, 1982; six All Star Awards in 1975, 1976, 1978, 1979, 1980, 1986; four National Football League medals in 1974, 1977, 1982 and 1984.

What is not generally known is that Ger Power was a sub on the Kerry team that lost in a replay to Offaly in the All-Ireland Senior final of 1972.

Three years later, Ger played at left-half-back on the young Kerry side that dethroned Dublin in the 1975 final. The brilliant Pat Spillane collected the Sam Maguire Cup as Mickey O'Sullivan, the Kerry captain on the day, was injured during the game and had been taken to hospital.

'We didn't expect to win because it was the first time in a senior final at Croke Park for most of the team except for John O'Keeffe, Paud Lynch and Brendan Lynch. Some people would say it was our greatest victory but looking back on it, I think 1986 was the best of all. What we did in 1986, coming from so far behind against Tyrone and winning by eight points, was a better victory than 1975. There were very few of the old team left in 1975 and we trained very hard. I had played with Mick O'Dwyer and Mick O'Connell but they were no longer on the team. Mick O'Dwyer was then manager. Every member of that 1975 team were brilliant as under-age players. We had a panel of twenty-one for that team and everyone was fighting for their positions.'

He readily agrees that Kerry could have won against Offaly in the 1982 final but he has never allowed it bother him unduly. Those associated with the team will tell you that Ger was his usual good-humoured self in the aftermath of that emotional game as he endeavoured to lift the spirits of his colleagues. He believes that their record of eight All-Ireland titles in eleven years will never be equalled.

'When you're playing for so long, you learn to accept that you win some and lose some. Losing may affect some people but it never affected me in any way.'

Ger Power got immense satisfaction from playing Railway Cup football as it provided him the opportunity to play with players like Dinny Allen, Jimmy Barry Murphy, Humphrey Kelleher, Dave McCarthy and goalkeeper Billy Morgan. It was different and it was enjoyable. And having a good time always appealed to the happy-go-lucky Ger Power. He won Railway Cup medals as a forward and defender.

Back, left to right: Jack O'Shea, Pat Spillane, John O'Keefe, Charlie Nelligan, Paudie Lynch, Tim Kennelly, Seán Walsh.
Front, left to right: Mikey Sheehy, Páidí Ó Sé, Tommy Doyle, Ger Power (captain), John Egan, Jimmy Deenihan, Ger O'Keefe, Denis 'Ogie' Moran.

He rates Mikey Sheehy as the most skilful footballer of them all. 'He was a total natural with the ball either on his right or left leg. I saw him getting some fabulous scores. He also played some unbelievable football with his club. John O'Keeffe was another great player for pure stamina and the way he could jump for a ball from a standing position.'

Ger Power got many important scores for both his club and county but nothing ever gave him more satisfaction than setting up a teammate with a good pass.

'In the 1986 final against Tyrone I remember Charlie Nelligan kicking out a long ball which was fielded by Plunkett Donaghy. I was hanging off him and fighting him for the ball until he dropped it. A lot of people said it was a foul but even to this present day I don't think it was a foul. It looked awful but then we always fought for everything. Whether it be a back coming out with the ball or a forward trying to score, he had to be harassed and put under pressure. When Plunkett dropped the ball I remember having one look up and spotting Mikey inside on his own and I hit it straight into his hands and he buried it!

'The type of training we did helped enormously. We fought for the ball all the time in training and the other way round we'd get hit hard when we had the ball. So you had to fight for the ball and then keep going because you'd get "killed" when you had the ball. I remember another occasion against Monaghan in the 1979 All-Ireland semi-final. Jimmy Deenihan passed the ball to John O'Keeffe and he in turn crossed it to me and I saw Mikey going on a run. I plonked it into his hands and he got a goal out of it. It was a great goal. You tend to always remember when everything just works out.

'People still come up to talk to me about the time the three Meath defenders banged their heads off each other and let me in for a simple goal in the 1986 All-Ireland semi-final. That was memorable. I met them afterwards and I said to them: "how are the head-bangers getting on?" We had missed a few chances beforehand and I remember "Ogie" kicked a high ball in and I tore in after it. There was no way it was my ball, it was a goalkeeper's ball. He came tearing out and I ducked because it was way up in the air for me and he had the advantage on the hop. All of a sudden I turned around and the boys were all knackered on the ground and I just picked up the ball and put it in the net. I was saying afterwards if I was caught in that bunch they'd be spreading my ashes over Croke Park.'

He believes that he was playing the best football of his career before he was injured in 1979. 'I scored 2-6 from play against Cork in the Munster final. I got a hamstring injury in a club match after the semi-final against Monaghan. The week after the All-Ireland final I played county championship football for Austin Stacks

---

THE 1980 KERRY TEAM

Charlie Nelligan

Jimmy Deenihan	John O'Keeffe	Paudie Lynch
Páidí Ó Sé	Tim Kennelly	Ger O'Keeffe

Jack O'Shea   Seán Walsh

Ger Power (Captain)	Denis 'Ogie' Moran	Pat Spillane
Mikey Sheehy	Tommy Doyle	John Egan

Substitute: Ger O'Driscoll for Ger Power

99

Ger Power wins the ball.

and the injury had disappeared. The way I look at it is that we were lucky to have so many great years. Everyone missed something as it was hard to keep it going.'

Naturally enough his father had a major influence on his sporting career and he recalls the many occasions people said something like: 'if you're half as good as your father and have as many medals, you'll be all right'. Ger vividly recalls bringing in neighbours and friends to show them his father's All-Ireland medals which were kept for safe-keeping in a drawer. This made him very proud. From an early age Ger travelled with his father and two older brothers, David and Jackie, to hurling and football matches.

100

He particularly remembers a rather dogged Munster Championship match between Cork and Kerry in the early sixties when tempers became a little frayed.

'Dave Geaney was playing for Kerry and the match was very tough and hard. A row broke out at one stage on the field and I remember jumping up in the crowd and shouting: "burst his nose, Dave".'

His father never pushed Ger into sport. The one piece of advice he always gave was: 'when you hit the ground, always bounce back up again'.

Ger was a key player on the Austin Stacks team that bridged a thirty-seven year gap to win the Kerry county senior football championship in 1973. Austin Stacks won the title again in 1975 and retained it the following year. They won their fourth championship of the decade in 1979 which meant that Ger Power was given the honour of captaining Kerry in 1980. Kerry had a bye to the Munster final where they easily accounted for Cork. Ger remembers little of the game or what he said to the players beforehand. All he knows is that he brought with him a bottle of holy water and passed it on to the members of the team to bless themselves before they went out on the pitch.

> 'People still come up to talk to me about the time the three Meath defenders banged their heads off each other and let me in for a simple goal in the 1986 All-Ireland semi-final.
>
> I met them afterwards and I said to them: "how are the head-bangers getting on?"'

Kerry went on to beat Offaly in the All-Ireland semi-final in what was a very high-scoring game. It was the day that the footballing genius from Walsh Island, Matt Connor, scored 2-9 for the Leinster champions, but still Kerry won by five points.

Ger Power had to retire early in the 1980 final. He knew beforehand that he would not possibly last the full game. 'My hamstring was gone and I was not supposed to be playing in the final. I had been receiving treatment in Cork from Dr Con Murphy for the whole fortnight before the game. The hamstring was very bad. I remember Con and myself discussing it and Con said: "the main thing now is that you lead the team out on the pitch as captain." We had more or less decided that. That was between Con and myself; nobody else knew that! I had to get the hamstring injected as near as possible before the start of the game. But a lot of time had elapsed from being given the injection to when the game started. By the time the referee threw in the ball the effects of the injection had almost worn off.'

But should Ger have played? Surely he was taking a big gamble? 'I remember training in Killarney on the Saturday previous to the game. I had to do sprints to prove my fitness. I felt I was fit but the problem was that the leg was going to give up and that's what happened. I just couldn't go any more on the day of the final and Ger O'Driscoll came on in my place.'

Ger spent the rest of the game in the dug-out and found it harder than if he was playing. 'I would say I'm a better player than a spectator. I'm a useless specatator. I would defnitely say that the difference between the two teams was that Kerry didn't foul and Roscommon kept fouling and they paid the price because Mikey was in great scoring form. They had us on the rack in the first twenty minutes. It was a bad mistake to change their style of football. I think Roscommon were the architects of their own downfall. The frees won it in the end for Kerry but I thought Roscommon should have won that game. Any team that went physically against us that time always lost; if we were going to be beaten it would take a team to match us playing football.'

He admits he was tearful before he received the Sam Maguire Cup. It was an emotional occasion and he was a happy man. He has no recollection of who presented the Cup but he does remember that his local TD, Tom McEllistrim, made his way up to the front row to be near him.

'The homecoming was very special and it was wonderful to bring the Cup up Rock Street and into the local pubs. Being captain meant more afterwards than it did at the time.'

Some players dream of captaining an All-Ireland winning team; not so Ger Power. He played football for sheer enjoyment and best of all were the friendships which have endured down through the years.

'I always say that sport helps a person cope with the disappointments in life. It helps you to take the good with the bad. It was great to play backs and forwards on a summer evening and it was a place to express your football ability. We might be a bit more cagey in an important game but the practice pitch allowed great freedom.'

According to Ger there was always a distance between Mick O'Dwyer and the players. 'It was hard to define but there was just a little 'distance' that a coach should have with his players. I would call it "an inch". I would say it went for the rest of the selectors as well. Nothing ever came out of selectors' meetings in my time. What helped Micko along the way was the fact that he had a superb panel of players. In our backs and forwards training, we had the best back line marking the best forward line. That's how we found it so easy. In training we marked each other very, very close all the time, then went out against opposition who weren't able to match the fellows we were used to marking in training.'

Ger admits he was hardly the best man in the world for training during the winter season. He liked to ease up a little and take time off to enjoy the other things in life. He believed there was a time to take things easy and a time when an all-out effort was necessary. His record would suggest he got it exactly right.

Nowadays Ger works in the Employment Exchange in Tralee. He is married to Patricia and they have two children, Jane and Gary.

Ger Power was a real driving force on that magnificent Kerry team and was truly outstanding both as a back and forward.

Tim KENNELLY

Kerry Captain 1979

Tim Kennelly had already won two All-Ireland Senior medals before he achieved the honour of captaining Kerry to All-Ireland success over Dublin in 1979. Kerry won by double scores, 3-13 to 1-8, and thus Tim Kennelly became the first Listowel player to take the Sam Maguire.

There was a great tradition of Gaelic football in his home place, Coolaclarig, part of the parish of Listowel, when Tim was growing up in the late fifties. One of his abiding childhood memories is of travelling to Croke Park with his father and uncle for the 1962 All-Ireland Final in which Kerry defeated Roscommon. He was just eight and it was his first train journey. Tim remembers little of the match, except that a Listowel man, Gary McMahon scored a goal very early on for Kerry. Tim was a football fanatic from an early age and even had a ball with him when bringing home the cows every morning and evening.

'I loved playing football so much that I often neglected to do the chores about the farm. My father would sometimes say, "Have you nothing to do. Why don't you put away that ball for a while". He would kick ball with me most evenings and had a tremendous influence on my career. That is why he got so much enjoyment later on when I began wearing the Kerry jersey.'

Every Kerry player will tell you that nothing compares to wearing the green-and-gold' jersey. 'It would fill your veins with pride the minute you put it on. No trainer or manager would need to say anything. You'd be hopping to get out on the field. In our time, there was great pride in the jersey on our backs. We were conscious of the fact that we were following some mighty footballers.

FACT FILE

HOME PLACE: Coolaclarig, Listowel, County Kerry

BORN: 6 July 1954   CLUBS: Listowel Emmets and Feale Rangers

ACHIEVEMENTS IN CLUB COMPETITIONS: Two North Kerry Senior Championship medals with Listowel Emmets in 1972 and 1976; two County Senior Football Championships with Feale Rangers in 1978 and 1980; one County Junior Club Championship with Listowel Emmets in 1972; two North Kerry League medals with Listowel Emmets in 1972 and 1978; numerous under-age League and Championship medals;

INTER-COUNTY ACHIEVEMENTS: Five All-Ireland Senior Football medals in 1975, 1978, 1979, 1980 and 1981; two National Football League medals in 1977 and 1982; four Railway Cup medals 1977, 1978, 1981 and 1982; nine Munster Championships in 1975, 1976, 1977, 1978, 1979, 1980, 1981, 1982 and 1984; two All-Star Awards 1979 and 1980; two B & I Personality of the Month Awards 1980 and 1981; one Man of the Match Award in the 1980 All-Ireland final against Roscommon; All-Ireland Under-21 medals in 1973 and 1975.

Action in the 1979 All-Ireland final. Kerry's Mikey Sheehy and Pat Spillane beaten by Dublin's Dave Foran.

'Football has a very important part in family life in Kerry and we were honoured to be carrying on that great tradition.'

There was no football pitch in Coolaclarig so Tim had to cycle five miles to play in Listowel. He was teased for being a 'country boy' but learned to cope.

'I think years ago a lot of young players from the country were lost to the game because they were reluctant to move into an area where the "townie" was a step ahead. It is not anything like as prevalent now as it was thirty or forty years ago.'

One of Tim Kennelly's greatest attributes as player was his strength on the ball and this, coupled with his ability to read a game, marked him as one of the very best centre-half-backs. He rarely moved futher than fifty metres from his goal and was renowned for his positional sense and dependability. Nothing motivated him quite

Back, left to right: Jack O'Shea, Paudie Lynch, Pat Spillane, Eoin 'Bomber' Liston, John O'Keefe, Charlie Nelligan, Seán Walsh.
Front, left to right: Jimmy Deenihan, Mikey Sheehy, John Egan, Tommy Doyle, Páidí Ó Sé, Tim Kennelly (captain), Mick Spillane, Denis 'Ogie' Moran.

like being under constant pressure. It was then the mighty Tim revealed his brilliant best. He loved being in the thick of the action and earned two All-Star awards for consistently outstanding displays.

Tim Kennelly is very proud of the fact that he was never once sent off. His philosophy was to play hard, but always fair. 'It's a hard man's game and if you do come across players who get nasty that is when they are beaten. If a player turns around and hits you a poke in the jaw you can be certain he is a beaten man. His actions are only upsetting himself.'

His year as captain began in style as Kerry trounced Clare in the first round of the Munster Championship in Milltown Malbay. Clare were unlucky in that many of the Kerry players were fighting for their places on the team and were anxious to consolidate their positions for the Munster Final in which Kerry beat Cork by ten points. Monaghan were also taught a football lesson in the All-Ireland semi-final as Kerry registered five goals and fourteen points to the Ulster champions' tally of just seven points.

The Kerry team was extremely confident if just a little apprehensive facing Dublin in the final. After all, Kerry had won the All-Ireland in 1975, but the Dubs reversed the result the following year. Then Kerry accounted for Dublin in 1978, so was it to be the Leinster Champion's turn in 1979?

Usually before a big game, Tim would withdraw into himself and he began to go through that phase from the Thursday before the Final. 'I was lucky my wife, Nuala, knew how to cope with it and she just steered clear and allowed me all the space I needed. I would always concentrate on who I was marking and the way he played the game. I remember thinking: "'Ogie' was successful in '78, so am I going to let Kerry down in '79"? People say there is no extra pressure on captains, but judging from my own experience I have to disagree with that assertion.'

On the Saturday before the Final, Tim visited his grandmother, Hannah Kennelly, in Coolaclarig as she was unable to attend the game. She wished him the best of luck and as he was leaving the house she caught a shoe and threw it at his legs for good luck. It was an old custom and Tim has never forgotten that little incident.

As he prepared to leave his home in Listowel for the greatest day of his life, Tim was surrounded by a huge number of well-wishers. He admits there were tears in his eyes and he became emotional, as he vowed not to let them down. On then to Killarney for a quick kick-around with the rest of the team. Afterwards they had dinner in the Park Place in Killarney, before eventually setting off by train to Dublin. On arrival in Dublin, the players and officials were taken by coach to the Grand Hotel in Malahide. There was time to relax and take it easy for a few hours before the

---

THE 1979 KERRY TEAM

Charlie Nelligan

Jimmy Deenihan	John O'Keeffe	Mick Spillane
Páidí Ó Sé	Tim Kennelly (Captain)	Paudie Lynch

Jack O'Shea   Seán Walsh

Tommy Doyle	Denis 'Ogie' Moran	Pat Spillane
Mikie Sheehy	Eoin 'Bomber' Liston	John Egan

Substitute: Vincent O'Connor for John O'Keeffe

---

whole team went down to the beach at about ten o'clock that night and sat on the wall for their customary team talk.

They had an early breakfast on the morning of the Final and then attended Mass in the hotel. They were not allowed to read any papers. There was great tension on the bus journey to Croke Park on the morning of the final and Tim recalls there being a shower of rain just as they alighted from the coach. They watched the minor match and then it was time to head for the dressing-room and focus the mind. And does he remember what he said to his players before leading them on to Croke Park?

'I told them that we had put in an awful lot of hard nights and hard training in Killarney and not to forget that when the going got tough out on the field. I finished by saying: "let's get out there, let's enjoy ourselves, don't let ourselves down, and above all else don't let that man over in the corner down".' That man was of course Mick O'Dwyer. Kerry were convincing winners by eleven points.

'It was a tremendous honour to bring the Sam Maguire back to Listowel. I remember Mícheál O'Hehir saying that it would make for a mighty week at Listowel Races. We arrived in Listowel on the Tuesday night and it was the biggest crowd I ever saw in the town. There must have been more than twenty-five thousand people there that night. It was electrifying and I'll never forget it.'

But it could all have been so different as Tim very nearly missed out on being captain. 'Jimmy Deenihan and myself were playing with Feale

> *'It's a hard man's game and if you do come across players who get nasty that is when they are beaten.*
>
> *If a player turns around and hits you a poke in the jaw you can be certain he is a beaten man. His actions are only upsetting himself.'*

Rangers at the time and we had decided that whoever won the game between Listowel and Finuge would become captain of the Kerry team. We beat Finuge by a point, but it was then suggested we toss for the captaincy. The toss was made at a Feale Rangers meeting on Good Friday night and I was lucky enough to win it. Jimmy was very gracious and wished me luck and I just said to him, "I won't let you down, we'll win the championship again".

'The following year we were beaten in the county semi-final and in 1980 I broke my collar bone about midway through the first half against Austin Stacks. We were trailing by two points and I had to go off to get an injection. Jimmy came over to me and said: "if you go off now, we're gone. The team will fall apart". So I stayed on and we beat Austin Stacks by three points. I was out of football for a long time after that, but Jimmy said to me later that I didn't let him down.' So Jimmy Deenihan in his turn, captained the four-in-a-row team to All-Ireland victory.

Nothing gives Tim Kennelly greater pleasure than to stroll down the streets of Listowel and meet some old friends. He loves the homely feeling of the north Kerry town. He worked hard at his game and had great times and great trips with Kerry.

'None of the players ever got big-headed, you could always have a conversation with them and go for pint or two. You're only going to be playing at the top for about ten to fifteen years if lucky, so there is more to life than football. It's nice to meet people and be pleasant with them.'

Kerry's 'Bomber' Liston in the air as Dublin's Paddy Cullen protects his goal in the 1979 All-Ireland final.

It meant everything to Tim that the people of Coolaclarig and Clounmacon were proud of his achievements and got great enjoyment from his year as Kerry captain.

Tim Kennelly is certain of one thing: Mick O'Dwyer exercised the most important influence on that Kerry team. 'Micko's contribution was unbelieveable and we would never have won as much without him. He was a bit of a rogue and a cute rogue at that, but he knew his stuff and was able to put us through our paces. We caught everyone by surprise and won a great All-Ireland in '75 and Mick had very little experience of us then. We went into the All-Ireland in '76 and we thought we were world-beaters. We weren't used to meeting people and personalities and the whole thing of back-slapping got to the players. I don't believe the players were mentally ready for the final in '76 as we were as good a team as Dublin that year.

'We went into the final with a couple of injured players and I believe they should not have played. The 1977 semi-final against Dublin was one of the greatest games that I ever played in and it was there for the taking. It was a fantastic game of football and I'd say the majority of the Kerry players were in tears in the dressingroom afterwards. We put in an awful effort to win the All-Ireland and yet we lost to Dublin again. Most of us were thinking: "will we ever beat Dublin again?" Everything worked out well for us after that.'

That it most certainly did and Tim Kennelly played a key role in making the Kerry four-in-a-row team the most feared and respected in the history of Gaelic football.

Then came the major disappointment of losing the 1982 final to Offaly and defeat by Cork in the 1983 Munster final.

'It was a major disappointment to lose 1982 final in the last few minutes and it's something I'll never forget. We had plenty of chances to win the game but we became too defensive when we went four points up and this allowed Offaly back into the game. I have often talked about the famous goal with Séamus Darby and how it came about, but if it was Kerry that got the goal, we'd be very happy with it. I think our supporters were more shattered than we were after the game. I think Kerry was the better team on the day but that's not much consolation as it's the scoreboard that counts. Defeat must be accepted with good grace. It's all part of the game. Great winners and bad losers make for poor sportsmen.'

Tim Kennelly's decision to retire in 1984 was a difficult one.

'Mick O'Dwyer came over to me in the dressing-room after a game and put his arms around me and said, "well done". I was also a selector at the time. A few days later we met at training and I told him of my intentions to bow out of inter-county football because of talk around north Kerry that I was selecting myself on the team. I felt it was time to retire from the county team, as I didn't want any controversy regarding the selection process. I told Mick the situation and he accepted it. I had regrets afterwards, but I felt the pressure was getting to me and it was the best decision at the time. I spent three good years as selector and we won three All-Irelands. I was proud to be with them and it was a great feeling.'

He thinks not enough of the players who represented their county very well get involved in Gaelic games when their playing days are over and wonders why. 'Is it that the players can see what's going on? Are they disappointed with the game? Are they wary of the people who are running the organisation? I would like to see a seminar arranged where former players would be given the opportunity to explain why they are not keen to get involved with the GAA.'

Denis 'Ogie' MORAN

Kerry Captain 1978

Denis 'Ogie' Moran stands apart as the only player to win eight All-Ireland senior medals playing in the one position. It is a phenomenal record that is never likely to be equalled. Furthermore, he was the only member of the Kerry team to have played every single minute in those eight victorious All-Ireland finals.

'Ogie' made the centre-half-forward position his own during Kerry's golden era when the Kingdom won the Sam Maguire Cup eight times in eleven years. Another rare distinction for 'Ogie' is that, as a six-year-old, he was the Kerry mascot at the 1962 All-Ireland Final when Seán Óg Sheehy's men defeated the Gerry O'Malley-led Roscommon team by six points. Sixteen years later 'Ogie' was back in Croke Park captaining his native county to victory over a hotly fancied Dublin side. From winning mascot to winning captain. A fairy-tale come true!

'My dad was born in Ballinskelligs and was a fanatical Kerry supporter. He brought me to a game every Sunday. He never missed a game when Kerry was playing. It was just a way of life for us all. He worked six days a week and Sunday was set aside for Mass and football. Sadly my dad died when I was nine, but I was fortunate that my cousin Mick, who lived with us all his life, took a special interest in me and took me to all the games and always gave me great support.'

'Ogie' was chosen to captain Kerry in 1978 because his club, Shannon Rangers, won the county championship the previous year.

'It is a fantastic honour to captain a Kerry team. The responsibilty of captain is not as onerous as possibly other sports. In Gaelic games captaincy is an honorary role

---

FACT FILE

HOME PLACE: Ballybunion, County Kerry

BORN: 16 January 1956 in Limerick

CLUBS: Beale; Ballybunion; Shannon Rangers

ACHIEVEMENTS IN CLUB COMPETITIONS: Two County Senior Championship medals with Shannon Rangers; seven North Kerry Championship medals with Beale; three All-Ireland Seven-a-Side medals with Shannon Rangers; numerous under-age medals with Beale and Shannon Rangers; one County Minor and one County Senior Hurling Championship medal with Ballyduff.

INTER-COUNTY ACHIEVEMENTS: Eight All-Ireland Senior Football medals in 1975, 1978, 1979, 1980, 1981, 1984, 1985 and 1986; eleven Munster Senior Championship medals in 1975, 1976, 1977, 1978, 1979, 1980, 1981, 1982, 1984, 1985 and 1986; three All-Ireland Under-21 medals in 1975, 1976 and 1977; three National League medals in 1977, 1982 and 1984; five Railway Cup medals in 1976, 1977, 1978, 1981 and 1982; one All-Ireland Special Hurling Medal with Kerry; one All-Ireland Colleges Football medal with Franciscan College, Gormanston.

and doesn't necessarily play a huge part in the success or failure of a team.

'The captain of the Kerry team is determined by the county championship. If a player happens to be on the county team and his club wins the county championship then he becomes captain. In 1977, Shannon Rangers won the county championship and that left me captain of the county for the following year. We had two members on the Kerry team, Eoin Liston and myself, and as I was the senior member, having played with Kerry since 1975, I automatically became captain. It is a great honour to captain Kerry. I'd say it's any young Kerry lad's dream. It is good for your own club that the Sam Maguire Cup resides in your parish for a year and it's good for an area to have an All-Ireland winning captain. It's also nice for your family, your friends and your club.'

The 1978 final is remembered above all else for Mikey Sheehy's magnificent first-half goal against Paddy Cullen, a goal which has since become one of the most talked-about scores in the history of Gaelic games.

'In many ways it was a worrying day to be captain as Dublin were very hot favourites to win three in a row. We were very much the underdogs. Dublin started off at a blistering pace and went six points to one in front. I remember Brian Mullins getting a great score early on and things seemed to be going all wrong for us. We were playing into the Hill 16 end and I could see the scoreboard and I remember thinking, "My God, this is going to be a disaster". Then John Egan got a goal and Mikey Sheehy scored the famous goal when he chipped Paddy Cullen and I think we went in at half-time a point up. The second half seemed to go so fast. Eoin Liston cut loose and scored three goals and it was a tremendous feeling. We were never in danger after that and with seven minutes remaining, I knew we were going to win it. I remember looking at the big clock in Croke Park and thinking "it's nearly over". Then I began thinking what I was going to say when accepting the Sam Maguire Cup. It was a wonderful thrill, because I think it's a relief to win a game when your favourites, but to win when you're underdogs is a great thrill.'

Back, left to right: Jack O'Shea, Eoin 'Bomber' Liston, John O'Keefe, Charlie Nelligan, Tim Kennelly, Seán Walsh, Pat Spillane,
Front, left to right: Mikey Sheehy, Páidí Ó Sé, Paudie Lynch, Denis 'Ogie' Moran (captain), John Egan, Ger Power, Mick Spillane, Jimmy Deenihan.

The final ended, Kerry 5-11, Dublin 0-9, and Ballybunion's Denis 'Ogie' Moran became the twenty-fourth player to captain the 'Kingdom' to All-Ireland football success.

The Dublin-Kerry clashes of the Seventies produced some of the greatest football ever seen at Croke Park. What was it like to be a player during that period when Kerry and Dublin dominated the game? 'It was fantastic. Whenever we played Dublin, it seemed the whole country was alive with excitement. It placed the whole urban-rural thing on the agenda. It was much different to playing any other county. There was a great rapport between the teams and the players respected each other on and off the field. At the same time, both teams had an almost obsessive determination to win. It was tough, hard and competitive on the field, but always very sporting. As well as that, there were great characters on both teams. Dublin had the likes of Paddy Cullen, Brian Mullins, Jimmy Keaveney and Kevin Moran. Special people and great sportsmen.'

'Ogie' has a particular grá for his Dublin namesake. 'I admired Kevin greatly as a footballer. I have known him for a long time, as I came up against him in Colleges hurling, whenever Gormanston played Drimnagh Castle. We also did a commerce degreee together in UCD and then we marked each other in an All-Ireland final. I still take a great interest in his career and always check the Sunday papers to get an update on his progress and to see how well he is playing. He is a tremendous competitior and has a great attitude.'

'I was always a great admirer of Jimmy Barry Murphy and had the pleasure of playing against him in Gaelic football and watching him play hurling. I always thought he was a superb artist in hurling and a great finisher in football. I admired him tremendously and liked his style. He was a smashing guy to meet off the field. He had a great attitude to the game and was very competitive and very sporting.'

In the 1978 Championship, Kerry notched up a massive eleven goals and thirty-six points between the Munster final, All-Ireland semi-final and the final, a huge average of twenty-three points a game. 'Ogie' recalls very little of the All-Ireland semi-final and only that he was marking Dinny Allen in the Munster final. He got immense enjoyment from playing with Kerry, but promptly forgot about the games as soon as the final whistle sounded. Then it was time to concentrate on the next game.

It is now generally accepted that the Kerry team of that era was the greatest in Gaelic games history. Eight All-Ireland titles between 1975 and 1986 bears testimony to their sheer brilliance. Mick O'Dwyer's footballing machine won respect and admiration in every county for their natural skills and team work. A class apart.

'We had a tremendous group of very talented players during that time. Mikey

---

THE 1978 KERRY TEAM

Charlie Nelligan

Jimmy Deenihan	John O'Keeffe	Mick Spillane
Páidí Ó Sé	Tim Kennelly	Paudie Lynch

Jack O'Shea　　　　　　　　　　Sean Walsh

Ger Power	Denis 'Ogie' Moran (Captain)	Pat Spillane
Mikey Sheehy	Eoin 'Bomber' Liston	John Egan

Substitute: Paudie O'Mahony for Jimmy Deenihan

Sheehy, Pat Spillane, Jack O'Shea, Eoin Liston, Ger Power and John Egan were all superb footballers in their own right. Then we had tremendous backs, like Páidí Ó Sé, Tim Kennelly, Paudie Lynch, John O'Keefe. They were a wonderful bunch of players and there was no obvious weak link on the team. Then there was the Mick O'Dwyer factor, which can never be underestimated. It takes a good man to get a team to the top, but it takes a better man to keep them there. He was tremendous at managing people and kept players with six All-Ireland medals as hungry for their seventh as for their first. And that is a tremendous skill. It was he who kept that team going. No one fell out with him and that was remarkable over such a long period. He had a great understanding of players and was ruthless in a very human way. Apart from having a very, very good team and a tremendous manager and selectors, Kerry also had an excellent County Board with the likes of Ger McKenna and Frank King. Ger had the vision to pick Mick O'Dwyer in the first place and then let him get on with the job. Frank played a huge rule in our success, very much the unsung hero. He was tremendous in the sense that he gave Mick O'Dwyer all the support he needed.'

> 'It is a fantastic honour to captain a Kerry team. The responsibility of captain is not as onerous as possibly other sports. In Gaelic games captaincy is an honorary role and doesn't necessarily play a huge part in the success or failure of a team.'

'Ogie' Moran would like to see the GAA do more to promote its image and its games. They are now competing more and more with other sporting organisations for young players.

'The GAA was very lucky in the past that the primary school teachers provided a tremendous pool of unpaid labour. There is far less Gaelic football being played in primary schools nowadays, mainly due to the growth of the school bus system and because there is now a lower porportion of men entering national teaching. Let me hasten to add there are plenty of women teachers who are well capable of coaching Gaelic football.

'As a youngster, all I ever played was Gaelic football and hurling, but that is no longer the case and youngsters, nowadays, have so much to choose from like basketball, swimming, gymnastics, speech and drama and many more worthwhile pastimes. Therefore, there is a need to be very conscious of promoting our games much more in an attempt to enhance the image of the GAA. This needs to be done at every available opportunity.

'The GAA has to sell its product and make sure the games are attractive and well run. I think the authorities are aware of this and are working hard to make it more appealing to youngsters.

'It is often a much-maligned organisation and may be seen as living in the past, but I feel they are conscious of what needs to be done. It's just that I would like to see them moving a little faster in certain areas of development.'

Not many know that 'Ogie' was a fine hurler and won a 'Special All-Ireland' hurling medal for weaker counties in 1974 when Kerry defeated Westmeath in the final. 'Ogie' now works with Shannon Development in Tralee as Development Manager for North Kerry.

He succeeded Mickey O'Sullivan as manager of the Kerry Senior football team and is thoroughly enjoying the challenging role. He played a key part in coaxing his former teammate and best friend Eoin 'Bomber' Liston back to the Kerry team for the 1993 championship. But the defeat by Cork in the Munster semi-final was a big setback.

'People in Kerry are used to success in Gaelic games and now almost demand it. It's the same in Welsh and New Zealand rugby. People in Kerry are not interested in a five-year plan. Now other teams are putting in the effort that Kerry did years ago. The Clare football team is an example of that. They are well organised and their whole status in football has been raised. Invariably, there are going to be cycles, the same counties can't go on forever winning All-Irelands.'

Record-breaker, captain, manager, but, above all else, a superbly skilful footballer, Denis 'Ogie' Moran is an outstanding ambassador for Kerry and for Gaelic games. His place in the history books is secure.

Tony HANAHOE

Dublin Captain 1976 & 1977

TONY HANAHOE was a central figure in the Dublin team of the seventies that played a major role in changing the face and the image of the GAA. He played in six All-Ireland finals and captained the back-to-back winning teams of 1976 and 1977, the only Leinster man to achieve such an honour.

Looking back, he remembers those exciting times and how they changed the lives of his fellow 'Dubs'. 'One was aware of all that buzz. Nobody in the group had ever been subjected to that kind of attention. We were beginning to be recognised in public and the focus of a lot of media attention.'

There was no tradition of football in the Hanahoe family but his father, a Donegal man, encouraged his four boys to go out and participate in sport.

'One fortunate aspect was that I lived relatively close to Croke Park so I started to go there at about the age of eight or nine. I was so enthusiastic in those days that I would go down maybe two hours before the gates opened. There was one other little fellow that used to appear at the gate with me and we used to vie to see which of us would be there first. We watched one another but we never spoke. I remember him in his gabardine coat. That person was none other than Jimmy Keaveney! We were the only two there usually for an hour or two before the gates opened.'

Growing up, there was a family of McHughs living across from Tony's home in Hollybrook Road and they were big into football which greatly impressed the youngster and he vividly recalls those days when his job was to fetch the ball.

His first school was the Christian Brothers in Scoil Mhuire in Marino and it was there he came under the tutelage of Brother O'Neill whom Tony credits with having a major influence on his career. He also pays tribute to Brother Coughlan, Brother Mahony and Brother Collins who taught him the game of hurling. Then it was on to 'Joey's' in Fairview where Brother Geraghty and Brother Murphy had an influential indent in his career.

'The Brothers in both schools took sport very seriously and anybody that had an inclination was encouraged. Like all schools, whatever was the major sport was the one to be considered and you didn't have much of an option. It was put to you fairly

---

FACT FILE

HOME PLACE: Hollybrook Road, Clontarf, Dublin

BORN: 29 April 1945   CLUB: St Vincent's

ACHIEVEMENTS IN CLUB COMPETITIONS: Eleven County Senior Football Championship medals in 1964, 1966, 1967, 1970, 1971, 1972, 1975, 1976, 1977, 1981, 1984; All-Ireland Club Senior Football Championship medal in 1976; three County Senior Hurling Championship medals in 1964, 1967, 1975

INTER-COUNTY ACHIEVEMENTS: Three All-Ireland Senior Football medals in 1974, 1976 and 1977; National League medals in 1976 and 1978; All Star Award in 1976.

forcibly what the Brothers opinion was. Certainly there was an element of army training in it and you didn't buck the system. "On parade was on parade".'

He is deeply grateful to all those Christian Brothers and makes the valid point that the effect of their demise is only now beginning to manifest itself.

'The Christian Brothers were pure educationalists, totally dedicated, knew what they were at and produced hundreds and thousands of young men who were better for the education and the training.'

Tony played both minor football and hurling for Dublin and was a member of the football team that lost to Westmeath in the Leinster final in 1963. Later that year Tony

Back, left to right: Kevin Moran, Anton O'Toole, Seán Doherty, Jimmy Keaveney, Paddy Cullen, John McCarthy, Tommy Drumm, Bernard Brogan, Bobby Doyle.
Front, left to right: Brian Mullins, Robbie Kelleher, Pat O'Neill, Tony Hanahoe (captain), David Hickey, Gay O'Driscoll.

Back, left to right: Kevin Moran, Anton O'Toole, Seán Doherty, Jimmy Keaveney, Paddy Cullen, Tommy Drumm, John McCarthy, Bernard Brogan, Bobby Doyle.
Front, left to right: Brian Mullins, Pat O'Neill, Tony Hanahoe (captain), David Hickey, Robbie Kelleher, Gay O'Driscoll.

got trials with the senior team in both grades and secured a place on the senior football team in 1964.

While he was studying in Trinity College, Tony went out of the inter-county scene.

'Jimmy Keaveney always says that I retired first in 1965. I was out of county football for about five years and came back in 1970. Dublin had won the All-Ireland in 1963 but they never moved on from that position.

Then in 1970, Kevin Heffernan decided on a managerial platform to try to put a team together. We had a few unglamorous performances in the Leinster Championship culminating in a fairly bad defeat by Kildare in 1972. I was actually captain of the team at that time. Heffernan and nearly all the players were sacked after that defeat by Kildare and Phil Markey was appointed as the new manager in 1973. I didn't play in 1973 at all. Every manager makes his own decisions and they have their own foibles.'

Tony remembers being at a party one Sunday afternoon in 1973 listening on the radio to a football match in which Dublin was playing.

'There were a lot of people in the company who were not interested in the game but I was keen to listen. I genuinely felt then that it was the end of my football career. Jimmy Gray came into the picture as chairman of the Dublin County Board and he re-appointed Kevin Heffernan, Lorcan Redmond and Dónal Colfer. Things then began to happen. We began to get a team together and started to pick up wins in Division 2 which didn't come that easily either.'

Dublin beat Wexford in the first round of the Leinster Championship in 1974 but, with the possible exception of those closest to the team, no one expected them to reach the Leinster final much less win the All-Ireland title.

'The game against Wexford was like the Mickey Mouse Show before the main event. I'm sure a lot of people there must have been quite amused with the regularity of the mistakes that were made. Then individual players started to gain confidence

---

THE 1976 DUBLIN TEAM

Paddy Cullen

Gay O'Driscoll   Seán Doherty   Robbie Kelleher

Tommy Drumm   Kevin Moran   Pat O'Neill

Brian Mullins   Bernard Brogan

Anton O'Toole   Tony Hanahoe (Captain)   David Hickey

Bobby Doyle   Jimmy Keaveney   John McCarthy

Substitutes: Fran Ryder for Tony Hanahoe; Paddy Gogarty for Bobby Doyle

THE 1977 TEAM

Paddy Cullen

Gay O'Driscoll   Seán Doherty   Robbie Kelleher

Tommy Drumm   Kevin Moran   Pat O'Neill

Brian Mullins   Bernard Brogan

Anton O'Toole   Tony Hanahoe (Captain)   David Hickey

Bobby Doyle   Jimmy Keaveney   John McCarthy

Substitutes: Paddy Reilly for Pat O'Neill; Alan Larkin for Bernard Brogan; Jim Brogan for Robbie Kelleher

and play better. We developed a new format of training and there was a whole new physical, psychological and managerial approach to team building and team performances. There was a whole new organisation orchestrated by Kevin Heffernan and Jimmy Gray who allowed it to happen.'

Tony believes it was a major confidence booster to beat Louth in the second round at Navan. It was a different kind of challenge for a lot of the players. By then that master footballer and free-taker, Jimmy Keaveney, had come back into the fold.

'I can remember days before then when we had seventy per cent of possession and would still lose the game. We reversed that equation in later years when we could win games with thirty or forty per cent of possession. We now had a championship kicker. For people like myself who were used to getting a fair battering one way or another it meant at least when you were fouled the opposition was punished with a score, every time and not occasionally. Jimmy's record was very high in terms of scoring. Then we went to Croke Park and beat Offaly in a very tight scoring game.

Possibly we were lucky that Offaly really underestimated us and never thought we'd have the credentials to beat them. It was a tough game and very competitive. When that game was over we then began to think realistically that we'd a great chance of winning the Leinster final. That was a major step for nearly all the panel. We then defeated Kildare in the next round and Meath in the Leinster final.'

Those five games in Leinster were the beginning of the momentum of the Dublin 'magic' starting to happen. Support grew and grew and grew.

'Whether it was naivety or innocence, after those games a certain self-confidence had begun to come into the team. I never thought during any of those games that we were ever going to be beaten. We had established a pattern with group therapy and hard work and training of a certain self-confidence which had been missing for some years. It rekindled itself in the group and it was just something that went right and we began to gather momentum and we began to have confidence in ourselves.

'All that was cemented together by victory which is a crucial element in the cementation of something that's going to succeed. We had now won a major title that most of us had not been even involved in before.

> *'Sitting here now talking to you so many years later I still can't believe that it's over and gone so fast. I think any athlete will tell you that. The only thing I really miss about it all is the playing element and competing. I looked on adulation and that kind of thing as a bit of an imposter.'*

'Now we had all these supporters and in a way the adulation was nice but it was also beginning to become a total invasion of your privacy. To some people that didn't bother them but I would have been essentially a private kind of person.

'All these new elements came into it and we were now personalities, if you like. That presented new problems and new challenges the like of which some people can cope with and others never cope with. It impacts on everybody's life. That is part of the sacrifice of being dragged into this so-called stardom role. It's enjoyable while it happens but there's a high price sometimes to be paid for it at the end.

'Sitting here now talking to you so many years later I still can't believe that it's over and gone so fast. I think any athlete will tell you that. The only thing I really miss about it all is the playing element and competing. I looked on adulation and that kind of thing as a bit of an imposter. People were very kind and nice and enthusiastic and it would be a bit dishonest if one said it wasn't nice to be recognised. At the same time one had to be wary of a change in life-style and new elements and influences coming into your life that were fleeting.'

In the All-Ireland semi-final of 1974 Dublin came up against favourites Cork. According to Tony the whole team was very psyched up for the match against the reigning champions. None of the players had ever been involved at that level before.

'One of the Sunday newspapers was callous enough to put up the names and faces and say, "on an individual basis how could Dublin be expected to beat Cork?" It was just like a boxing match in that we went out and threw the first punch and never stopped until the end of the game. It was just like a boxing champion being tagged and couldn't bring himself around to clear his mind fast enough to assert the initiative. We never stopped running and playing that day and Cork were totally rocked on their heels. That was one of the major games for Dublin. I think even Heffernan and the selectors were gobsmacked at what had happened. To say that Cork were gobsmacked would be the understatement of the century. They had let an important occasion slip by and they never ever thought that Dublin would be in a position to beat them. We were young, vibrant, enthusiastic and psyched up and things ran for us that day.'

Dublin went on to defeat Galway in the All-Ireland final, though strangely, Tony got little personal satisfaction from the occasion. He remembers it as a dour game and was none too pleased with his own role which was to negative his direct opponent, Tommy Joe Gilmore. 'It was not the way I liked to play football. Part of our overall strength was that people did play to instructions. It was a bit sacrificial but it had to be done at the same time.'

Dublin reached the two major finals the following year but lost both of them. They were beaten by a young Kerry team in the All-Ireland decider and went down to Meath in the League final. 'We possibly overtrained for the game against Kerry and there was an air of underestimating the opposition. Again luck was with Kerry that time in that John Egan got a very fortunate goal very early on that steadied them. I have no doubt we were stronger than them, if you can ever say that a team is better or stronger. We have ourselves to blame but Kerry won it on the day and that's all there is to be said about it.'

The defeat by Kerry in 1975 rankled. Feeling they had blown it, Dublin started off 1976 very determined. Under Tony's captaincy and Kevin Heffernan's management they prepared for twelve months and the way the cards fell meant that the opposition they so badly wanted was there waiting for them in the All-Ireland final. Dublin replaced their whole half-back line in 1976 with Tommy Drumm, Kevin Moran and Pat O'Neill coming into the team.

'We had a very, very hard game against Meath in that year's Leinster final. Nothing in Leinster is ever easy and, like in the Ulster championship, you have to start earlier than the rest of the provinces. You are facing different teams each posing different problems and you have to be fit from March or April and last all the way up to September. We very nearly lost the 1976 Leinster final. It was a close one and we won it in the end by just two points. We played Galway in a very bad-tempered semi-final and again it was very close, just three points in it at the finish. It was Kerry in the final and that was "die dog or eat the hatchet".'

The sooner a game started the better as far as Tony Hanahoe was concerned. He was never much into parades and other such pageantry. Every player has his own way of coping with nervous energy before a game and Tony was no different.

'You had whistlers, you had talkers, you had non-talkers and you had yawners. I was a yawner and I'd say, "God I couldn't be tired". Then you had fellows who kept going to the bathroom and fellows that always felt they needed another rub on an ankle or leg. All demonstrations of nerves in different ways.

'We're in the era of television and anybody playing amateur games now is being judged by professional standards. To emerge into the cauldron of eighty-thousand people, one could make comparisons with the old Colosseum and the rules are the same. The shouting hits you like a bang and it's not even that you can hear for or against you. Then you mark out where your adversary is, and he and you wonder if it's going to be a good day and how soon you can get your hands on the ball. If you consider that statistics show that most players have the ball in their possession for less than two minutes in any game, you're talking seldom is wonderful and particularly in an All-Ireland final. If you haven't got the mental agility and constraint to do what you've been trained to do under any given circumstances then you can blow the whole thing, so there is a lot of responsibility.'

Tony himself liked to speak to each player individually. He believes that there is an element of tribalism in the whole thing and players have to be made to feel part of the overall strength of the group.

'One has to feel confident enough that other people have confidence in you to do your job and that you have their support. That is essential. Kevin Heffernan was the manager and he'd be doing the banging on the table before the game. Like in any large group certain people require certain types of training, and dealing with a team game you have to balance the people that you can encourage, the people that you can criticise and the people that you leave alone to bring out the best in them. If you have the wrong approach on the occasion you can upset the overall strength of the situation. It's a seek and find mission to try to discover what is the best formula and to try to stick to it.'

It was a high-scoring final in 1976 and Dublin won it by seven points, the exact same margin by which they had lost to Kerry the year before. The status quo was now firmly re-established and everyone looked forward to the rubber match. Tony Hanahoe's memory of the day is that the Dublin team had no problem with Kerry's 'invincibility'. The Dublin team was more mature in 1976 and so too was Kerry. There was an open style of football in all those games involving Dublin and Kerry but yet it was very competitive and very tense.

'As a forward I was ambitious enough never to do the same thing twice and hopefully keep my opponent in a total state of confusion. Tim Kennelly was a formidable player and was very strong and much faster and cleverer than people gave him credit for. He was part of the bedrock of that Kerry team that kept them standing up under fierce pressure on occasions.'

It came as a shock when Kevin Heffernan announced his retirement in the aftermath of the 1976 All-Ireland victory. It was felt at the time that Dublin could never recapture their form under any other manager. Kevin told the players he was going to quit at a meeting in the Gresham Hotel and they were all shocked.

'David Hickey stood in the middle of the room in some kind of a white suit like Scott Fitzgerald and said, "You're just going, is that it?" There were consultations within the County Board and I was shoved into taking over the position. I think they moved very fast when they realised what was happening because they felt there would have been a certain resentment to a new person coming in. We'll never know. It was a kind of fearful job to take over at that level but as captain I agreed to take over the managership. The biggest challenge was to keep up my own form to justify selection which was never too far away from my mind. We had a lot of very good players who were on the periphery of the team and I'm sure it crossed their minds that they weren't going to get thanked for banjaxing the manager in work-outs and training sessions. My opposite number in those work-outs was Kevin Moran and I can tell you it didn't seem to bother him too much.'

By then Tony was in practice as a lawyer and the manager's job brought additional pressures and commitments. There were three to four training sessions every week with a game on Sunday as well as interviews with radio, television and newspapers. There were many functions and meetings to attend, all of which added to the work load. Dublin lost by two points to Kerry in the 1977 League final but made amends by beating Meath in the Leinster final.

'We had to meet the Munster champions in the semi-final and that meant one thing. I remember a lot of bold statements were made at the time on either side. The present shadow Minister for Sport, Jimmy Deenihan, was corrected by Con Houlihan who reminded him that he should always remember the old South American proverb that you should "Never criticise the alligator's mother before you cross the river". There was a tremendous build-up to that match.'

The 1977 semi-final is remembered as one of the best games of Gaelic football ever played. Tony remembers it as very enjoyable and tough. 'There was never a lull in the game and it flowed past like a dream. Everybody was so busy and active and the game just took off. I remember the crucial stage where it was tit-for-tat and everything was happening and everybody was tense in case they'd make a mistake. The standard of the game was very high.

'I vividly remember David Hickey's face when he turned around after scoring the crucial goal. He didn't often show that kind of emotion but his eyes were rolling and he was high as a kite. The biggest job was to try and get him back in his place for the kick-out because Kerry were urgently trying to muster another attack. Hickey had a habit of standing so close to goal in training that Paddy Cullen's health was frequently in danger. Hickey always felt that anybody could get a point and that it took real talent to score a goal. Cullen always told him that he was never going to get that close in a game to have that shot but that's where it happened. Shortly after that Bernard Brogan got a great goal. He didn't often score let alone score goals in a match of that significance but he came from nowhere and took a shot over Charlie Nelligan's head into the net. The whole place erupted and Kerry were in trouble!'

As soon as the final whistle had sounded Tony knew he had a real task on his hands. He wondered how all the hysteria would affect players who still had to face an All-Ireland final. That was a major worry. 'I remember leaving Croke Park and going to Garristown to a quiet pub and I could see fellows looking down from the bar wondering was it me or somebody identical. I was ahead of some of the supporters. As I sat down an ex-colleague of mine, Paddy Wilson, came over and we had a few drinks. I decided on a strategy before going back for the rest of the celebrations. I'd spend the next four weeks hammering the players psychologically and physically into shape about the challenge they could expect in the final. It's only one game away from a title and one team loses and one team wins. I was very worried that they mightn't have the one hundred and ten per cent concentration that's needed.

'We were a little facilitated on the day by Jimmy Keaveney scoring a goal early on which did more to damage Armagh than it did anything for us. I remember going out that day and I was psychologically and physically exhausted. It had been a long year and the win in the semi-final had dealt a blow to a lot of things. I was worried in case we might underestimate the opposition. There's no point in being the best team unless you win. It ended well.'

For the record, Dublin beat Armagh in that 1977 final by twelve points on the score, Dublin 5-12, Armagh 3-6. Quite a day for manager, selector and captain, Tony Hanahoe, the only man to fill all three roles on an All-Ireland winning team.

Mickey O'SULLIVAN

Kerry Captain 1975

Mickey O'Sullivan is the only All-Ireland winning captain since the Sam Maguire Cup was first presented not to collect the famous trophy. The Kerry captain was knocked unconscious seventeen minutes into the first half of the 1975 final against favourites Dublin. It was a frightening experience, and what should have been the happiest day of his life turned into a nightmare for the Kenmare man, who ended up in a Dublin hospital.

'I was really on my game that day and couldn't get enough of the ball. I had no doubt we were going to win. I can remember John Egan getting a goal early on and I ran in to him and said, "We have it now". That's what we needed, an early goal, and after that I felt we were motoring. I can't remember much about the incident that put me out of the game. I can remember getting the ball into space for John Egan on a few occasions. Mick O'Dwyer had suggested that instead of taking too much out of the ball, which I was prone to do, I should bang it into the space in front of John. I remember getting a pass from Paudie Lynch and probably that was the beginning of the final run. I saw an opening and I went for it. I can remember getting a belt and then the lights went out. I remember opening my eyes and not being able to see. I could hear people saying, "stand back, leave him breathe". I couldn't breathe and I thought I was dying. My sight had gone and I couldn't get air into my lungs. That was the end. I have no recollection of anything else.

'The next time I woke up I was in hospital. It must have been four hours later. There were two nurses looking down at me smiling and I jumped up immediately. I couldn't understand why they were smiling, as we still had an All-Ireland to win. They told me that the match was over and it was a total let-down. Even though we had won it, I felt empty. There was no outlet for the enthusiasm that I still had. I was discharged from hospital the following day.'

Mickey O'Sullivan has always had a positive attitude and, after the initial shock,

---

FACT FILE

HOME PLACE: Kenmare, County Kerry

BORN: 14 April 1952

CLUBS: Kenmare and UCD

ACHIEVEMENTS IN CLUB COMPETITIONS: One Towns Cup in 1968; three Intermediate County Championships in 1968, 1970 and 1972; one Senior County League in 1972; two Senior County Championships in 1974 and 1987.

INTER-COUNTY ACHIEVEMENTS: Three All-Ireland Senior medals in 1975, 1978 and 1980; four National Football League medals in 1971, 1972, 1973 and 1974; five Munster Championship medals in 1972, 1975, 1976, 1978 and 1980; captained Kerry Under-21 team to All-Ireland success in 1973; two Railway Cup medals in 1975 and 1976. Was captain in 1976.

he was delighted to know that Kerry had won. It would have been a sweeter victory if he could have raised the Sam Maguire Cup, but he has never allowed it to bother him.

'Since I was a kid the symbol of winning an All-Ireland was collecting the Sam Maguire Cup, the ultimate symbol of success. I had achieved the ultimate without the symbol. I would have liked to crown it by receiving the cup, but we won and that's what mattered.'

Mickey has no hard feelings about the nasty foul that put him in hospital. 'If Tony Hanahoe was going through the Kerry defence the same way as I was going through the Dublin defence and if our backs allowed him go through I would have no time for those backs. That's basically the situation. You're out there, winning isn't everything, it's the only thing. You can talk about sportsmanship all your life but in the long run winning is all that matters. But let me say that I would never, ever condone dirty play or bad play.

'I don't think the Dublin backs set out to put me out of the game: they went out to stop me, and there is a difference. Dublin backs were tough and you expected that. It was unfortunate that they connected in some part of my head that was soft and it put me out of the game. I've met the players that were involved since then and although we've never discussed it, I know they didn't go out to injure me but to stop me.'

Ger O'Driscoll replaced the injured captain and the young Kerry team beat Dublin comprehensively by 2-12 to 0-11 in what was the first seventy-minute final. The joke after the game was that Dublin were lodging an objection because Kerry were under-age. Pat Spillane was given the honour of collecting the Sam Maguire Cup.

Mickey O'Sullivan was able to travel home to Kerry with the team on the Monday evening. When he visited his home town with the cup he recalls saying something like, 'It is occasions like this that sow the seeds for future successes'. 'Past generations did that for us. I felt it was a perpetuation of the tradition and that was what we were doing. It wouldn't mean anything to me in the ego sense, bringing a cup back, even

Back, left to right: Paudie Lynch, Paudie O'Mahony, Pat Spillane, Tim Kennelly, John O'Keeffe, John Egan, Brendan Lynch, Ger Power.
Front, left to right: Denis 'Ogie' Moran, Páidí Ó Sé, Mikey Sheehy, Jimmy Deenihan, Mickey O'Sullivan (captain), Pat McCarthy, Ger O'Keeffe, Leo Griffin (team attendant).

124

though I was the first Kenmare man ever to captain an All-Ireland winning Kerry team.'

Mickey O'Sullivan was appointed captain of Kerry in 1975 by virtue of the fact that Kenmare had won the county championship the previous year. It was the first time for the club to win the title.

'I was hell bent on Kerry winning the All-Ireland in 1975, as I felt I would never again get an opportunity of captaining an All-Ireland winning team. This made me very determined to get the best trainer possible. In Easter 1975 I rang Mick O'Dwyer and I asked him if he would like to come with me to a coaching course given by Joe Lennon in Gormanston. Mick was fairly reluctant to attend the course but eventually I persuaded him to travel. We stayed for three or four days, and on the way back down to Kerry I asked Mick if he would train the Kerry team. This isn't the perception of what happened. Around the same time I also mentioned it to the then chairman of the County Board, Gerald McKenna. Mick said he would think about it but didn't give any commitment. In the meantime Gerald McKenna approached Mick to get him to train the team; but I felt his weekend in Gormanston sowed the seeds for him to take it up. I remember the first night Mick said to me, "how was the training?" and I said, "not half hard enough". Then it became really hard and we became super-fit and it generated a great spirit.'

Mickey remembers that Kerry got nothing easy against Tipperary in the first round of the Munster championship that year. 'We were trailing at half time by a few points. During the course of the second half Kerry brought John Egan to centre-forward and he turned the game around. We won well in the end but it was a real scare.'

Consequently, Kerry were not given much chance of dethroning Cork in the Munster final. Cork had won the All-Ireland Championship in 1973 but had lost in the semi-final the following year. They were very keen to get another tilt at Dublin. But it was not to be. Kerry won comfortably by 1-14 to 0-7, the first of what was to be a run of eleven provincial titles in the space of twelve years.

'We got a break early on when we got a goal against the run of play. That was the turning point and we grew in confidence after that. We played Sligo in the All-Ireland semi-final. I'll always remember reading a comment by Con Houlihan in the *Evening Press* about Sligo the Monday after the game. Sligo players were waving up to the crowd during the parade and he made reference to the fact that if they were racehorses they'd have to be wearing blinkers. The occasion got to Sligo, because they were a good team. We looked good but at the same time we were up against Dublin in the final and they were on a high, having won the previous year. To be honest, I

THE 1975 KERRY TEAM

Paudie O'Mahony

Ger O'Keeffe   John O'Keeffe   Jimmy Deenihan

Páidí Ó Sé   Tim Kennelly   Ger Power

Paudie Lynch   Pat McCarthy

Brendan Lynch   Denis 'Ogie' Moran   Mickey O'Sullivan (Captain)

John Egan   Mikey Sheehy   Pat Spillane

Substitute: Ger O'Driscoll for Mickey O'Sullivan

think we caught them on the hop. We had trained exceptionally hard and we believed in ourselves. We were very young but there was an awful lot of talent, as subsequent years proved.'

Mickey himself admits he thrived in the role of captain. It was the incentive he needed to lift his game. He was confident of his own ability to get the very best out of each player. 'I felt the only way was to lead by example. I don't think I ever played a bad game as a captain. I was captain of the Munster team that won the Railway Cup in 1976. I liked responsibility. I tended to be a little laid back and would have needed that little bit of extra pressure to perform at my best. I had no doubt whatsoever in my mind but that we were going to win against Dublin in 1975. We all believed we were going to win, as we had worked so hard.'

He believes that a player has a totally different perspective on an All-Ireland final from anyone else. There is a job to be done and nothing should get in the way. 'You don't look at it like a journalist or supporter would do, because if you go down that line then you're finished. There is a completely different perception and approach. If a player gets tied up with the euphoria, pageantry and excitement he will not deliver on the day. You must focus in on the job to be done and have tunnel vision. Nothing else matters. You have to go through the wall or through the door in order to win. I gave the pep talk before going out on the field for the final and I remember telling the lads we were born for that moment. I believed it,

> *'If a player gets tied up with the euphoria, pageantry and excitement he will not deliver on the day. You must focus in on the job to be done and have tunnel vision. Nothing else matters.'*

everyone believed that we were destined to win, because we were from Kerry and had such a tradition to live up to. Through the hard training we had been totally conditioned to believe that we were actually better than what we were. We believed we were better than a Dublin team which was far superior, man for man, that year.'

On the day itself, Mickey observed how the pressure of the occasion affected different players in different ways.

'Páidí Ó Sé was jumping out of his skin, whereas John Egan was as cool as a breeze. Páidí was sitting next to John in the dressing-room, and he turned to him enthusiastically and said, "I suppose you'll stick a few today", and John turned around calmly and said quietly, "It would be nice, Páidí". John was so cool and Páidí so exuberant. I was convinced we were going to win and I had to convince each player. That was Mick's job, but I as captain felt this was my role as well. I had to get across that I believed we were going to win. I was totally focused and couldn't wait to get out on the field. My adrenalin was pumping and I didn't hear anybody when I ran out. You knew you were in the middle of a cauldron of excitement and tension but it was a very silent place between you and what you had to achieve. Marching behind the band and all the other things associated with the build-up mean nothing. I would have died just to win. I remember saying to the lads that we must be willing to die on the field in order to win. 'I believed it, and as it turned out I nearly did die. That's the point we got to, and Mick O'Dwyer it was who got us to that level. I can remember seeing Ger O'Keeffe crying during the national anthem with determination. That was probably the nearest thing I ever experienced to complete commitment.'

It is a widely held view that because of the trauma of 1975 Mickey O'Sullivan was never the same player again. He played in the 1976 All-Ireland final, when Kerry lost to Dublin, and then won two more All-Ireland medals as a substitute in 1978 and 1980. Mickey himself thinks that the bad experience in 1975 had nothing to do with the fact that he failed to win another All-Ireland medal as a player. 'After captaining Kerry to the All-Ireland I found it very hard to get to the same pitch of motivation again. I had achieved everything in 1975, so the same edge

wasn't there any longer. The morning after the All-Ireland semi-final I went to Europe on a holiday for four weeks. No matter what country I was in I still trained twice a day on my own. I remember going out training one morning in a place called Worms on the Rhine. We had put up our tent the night before in an open place like the Curragh. The minute it got bright I went away training and was doing sprints when this guy in a uniform came out of nowhere with a rifle and stopped me. It was an army training camp, and he brought me back to base. 'I spent a long time explaining that I was a tourist and was out training before I was released. I was up on the Alps on a few occasions and couldn't find level ground to do some sprinting so I drove for miles just to find a field.

'The following year I suffered as a result of fluid on my knee. I never told anyone, because if they knew I had an injury it would have been the bench. There were too many lads on the end of the bench trying to get back on the team, so you never said too much about your injuries. I never really played well in 1976 and I was marking Tom Creedon in the Munster final. Tom died as a result of an accident some years later and it was a real tragedy. He was a great player and great friend of mine. We were beaten by Dublin in the 1976 final. They were psyched up and that was it.'

Mickey took a break from the game at the end of 1976 because of a loss of form. He felt a break would do him good. Soon after, he settled down and moved with his wife, Marion, to America and remained there until the end of 1977. On returning home he went back to college and began playing Sigerson Cup football with UCD. By this time he was playing some top-class football and was back on the Kerry panel at the beginning of the '78 championship. He played just a few championship games after that. The team was showing such devastating form that Mickey was unable to hold down a regular place. The positions he was vying for were occupied by Ger Power, Pat Spillane, John Egan and Mikey Sheehy.

'I opted out in 1979, as I felt there was no way I would get my place on the team as they were playing so well. I returned the following year and won a medal as a substitute. It's frustrating when you know you're playing well and there's no way in. It's great when a player is on the way up, but it's amazingly frustrating when a player is on the way down, because he has been through it. He has gone over the top to a certain extent and the chances of him getting back aren't great. A player will live in hope and will hang in there for years. I sat on the bench for a few years, and that was enough. It was a place for a young lad.'

Mickey O'Sullivan was in charge of the Kerry senior team for three years and is of the opinion that a manager's role is to channel the ego of each player for the good of the team. 'The more you get to know each player, the more you recognise their needs and know how to satisfy their needs. But you've got to accept that a player will not put the good of the team in the long run ahead of themselves. I found as a manager that you never allowed a player make a decision about an injury. A manager should always make the decision with a doctor and physiotherapist. A player will tell you how he feels, but you have to take that with a pinch of salt. Even though it's a team game, an awful lot of players don't give a damn as long as they play well. I would listen sympathetically and accept what the player has to say, but I would have to take the overall decision for the good of the team.'

When Mick O'Dwyer stood down as Kerry manager, Mickey allowed his name to go forward and was delighted to be appointed his successor.

'It was a difficult first year, because it was the end of an era. I knew we wouldn't be winning All-Irelands immediately. In my first year in charge Cork hammered us by sixteen points in the 1990 Munster final. We were probably too inexperienced and naïve. I took up the position of manager of the senior team on condition that I would also take charge of the under-21 team. In my first year I brought in twenty-one under-21 players in a panel of twenty-eight. I knew we had to start somewhere. We won the All-Ireland under-21 title that year, reached the All-Ireland under-21 final the following year and the All-Ireland under-21 semi-final in 1992. It was a very good record because we hadn't won an under-21 All-Ireland since 1977. That is the basis now of your future Kerry team. It meant an awful lot of work, because I trained the senior and under-21 teams separately. I enjoyed every moment of it. In my three years as manager we beat Cork in five out of the six championship games we played at senior and under-21 level. Our defeat by Clare in the 1992 Munster final was the most disappointing involvement I had with any team either as a player or a trainer.'

Despite the general perception, the Kerry team of 1975 was not created overnight. Mickey O'Sullivan makes the valid point that success came only after four successive years of failure. He counts himself lucky to have been involved with the greatest Gaelic football team of all time.

'Each one of them had an internal driving force within them, and every one of them wanted to be the best. They were wonderful athletes, every one of them. The standard of these guys in terms of speed, flexibility, strength and skill was exceptional. It was amazing that they all came at the same time. I knew it from our days playing minor football that these guys were special.'

Mickey O'Sullivan still lives in Kenmare, where he owns a very successful restaurant, Mickey Ned's. Mickey is also a secondary school teacher in Scoil Gobnatan in Ballyvourney. He is married to Marion and they have two children, Bryan and Éamonn.

Above: Shooting the team — Kerry — before the All-Ireland final

Left: The throw-in, Dublin v. Meath, Leinster championship 1991. Paul Bealin, Dublin, and P.J. Gillic and Liam Hayes, Meath

Kildare v. Leitrim 1993

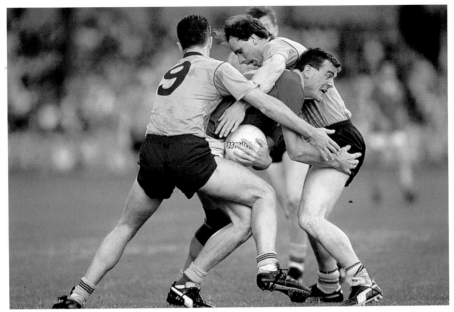

Above: Colm O'Rourke, Meath, wrapped up by Paul Clarke and Mick Kennedy, Dublin in the 1989 Leinster final. *Below:* Mayo v. Roscommon, Connacht final action. Tony McManus with the ball

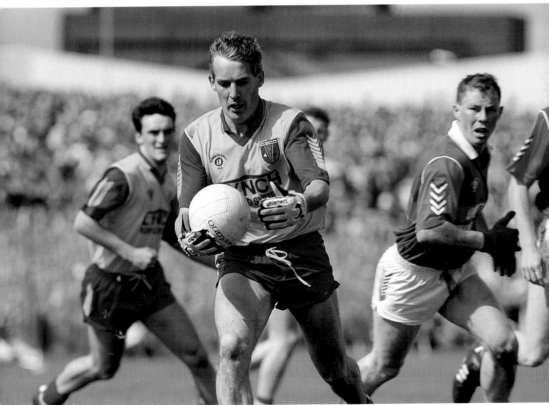

Above: Mikey Sheehy, Kerry
Left: Paídí Ó Sé and Sam Maguire, 1985

Facing page top: Antrim goalkeeper Liam Turbett with the ball, 1989
Bottom: Galway and Roscommon in action, 1990
Overleaf: The Cork v. Mayo final 1989 — Barry Coffey on high and Mayo's Michael Collins

Plunkett Donaghy, Tyrone with the ball tackled by Derry's John McGurk in the National League final 1992

Tumble action in the Connacht final between Roscommon and Galway

Above: Where's the cup? Dublin captain Tommy Drumm surrounded by Mick Holden, John Kearns, Ciarán Duff after the 1983 All-Ireland victory.

Below: Kerry's Mick O'Connell in typical high-fielding action. Front cover of his autobiography, published in 1974. Reproduced by permission of Mercier Press, Cork

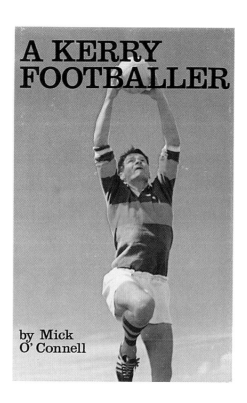

A KERRY
FOOTBALLER

by Mick
O'Connell

Seán DOHERTY

Dublin Captain 1974

DUBLIN were at a low ebb when the 1974 football championship season got under way. They had been relegated to Division 2 of the league the previous year and had not won the Leinster Championship since 1965. But all that was soon to change and by late September 1974, Wicklow-born Seán Doherty was being hailed by football followers everywhere as captain of 'Heffo's Heroes'. Before the seventies had run its course the no-hopers of 1974 had two more All-Irelands and six Leinster crowns to their credit.

Growing up in the remote area of Glenealy there was nothing much else for the young Seán Doherty in the way of recreation but football and hurling. Seán's father was very interested in sport and would join in the games the youngsters played whether they happened to be in the field, yard or on the road. Seán's uncle, Jack Doyle, was an accomplished footballer and played with the local Ashford club. He bought many a pair of football boots for his eager nephew.

Seán's love of both football and hurling was to be further nurtured in the CBS in Wicklow town where he came under the guiding influence of Brother Augustine and Brother Matthew. Seán remembers Brother Augustine as a great hurler who lined out with the local Glenealy club.

When the Doherty family moved from the heart of the country near the Devil's Glen to Ballsbridge in Dublin in the mid-fifties, Sean attended Oatlands College in Mount Merrion and was fortunate in that the same year the school formed their first hurling and football teams. Seán, the new boy, was chosen as captain of both.

Seán played minor football with Kilmacud, and although not living in the area, he later joined Ballyboden Wanderers, now known as Ballyboden St Enda's, because his cousin of the same age, Don Ferguson, lived in that locality.

'We were down at Hyland's shop one Sunday afternoon and the Parish Priest, Fr Ryan, happened to see us and suggested we would be better off playing football rather than hanging around doing nothing. One of the men running the team at the time was called Pearse Murray and after he had watched me playing a few games at

---

FACT FILE

HOME PLACE: Glenealy, Ashford, County Wicklow

BORN: 14 July 1946   CLUBS: Kilmacud; Ballyboden, St Enda's

ACHIEVEMENTS IN CLUB COMPETITIONS: One County Junior Football Championship medal; one County Junior Hurling Championship medal; one County Intermediate Football Championship medal and one County Intermediate Hurling Championshp medal.

INTER-COUNTY ACHIEVEMENTS: three All-Ireland Senior Football medals in 1974, 1976 and 1977; six Leinster Senior Football medals from 1974 to 1979; two National Football League medals in 1976 and 1978; one All Star award in 1974.

midfield, half-forward and all around the place he came to me one day and said, "there's only one place for you and that's full-back".'

He is still fiercely loyal to Ballyboden and rates captaining them to a county junior championship in 1968 as one of the high points of his career. It was the first time since 1928 that the club had won the title and there were huge celebrations when twenty-two-year-old Seán brought the cup back to Ballyboden, never dreaming that some six years later he would deliver the most sought after trophy of them all, the Sam Maguire.

Seán Doherty played inter-county football for his native county in the late sixties after being visited at his home in Ballsbridge by a Wicklow selector. 'I was astounded to be asked to play for Wicklow as I hadn't been selected at either minor or under-21 level for Dublin. I agreed to give it a shot and was chosen at full-forward in the first round of the Leinster Under-21 Championship in 1967. We were well beaten by a very good Kildare team in the final. As soon as the game was over I had to travel to the Phoenix Park to play with Ballyboden in a junior match. I hadn't even time to change my clothes in the dressing-room and remember walking to the car in my football gear and meeting the crowd coming in for the big match.'

Some months later he was contacted again and asked to make himself available to the senior team for a league match against Carlow. He played in the half-forward line on that occasion. His short career with the 'Garden County' ended in a falling-out.

'I had a car at the time and used to carry four players from Dublin to Aughrim for training sessions. I would leave work in the afternoon to be in Aughrim for training at 7.30 and wouldn't be home until well after midnight. I asked a member of the County Board if they could arrange for us to have something to eat and I also told him I couldn't afford the petrol money. Remember, I was only very young and had just started out in the plumbing business so money was scarce. His answer was, "if you don't do it for the love of football, you're no good to us". I said, "thank you very much".' Sean Doherty never returned.

Back, left to right: Stephen Rooney, Anton O'Toole, Robbie Kelleher, Jimmy Keaveney, Tony Hanahoe, Paddy Cullen, John McCarthy, Alan Larkin, Bobby Doyle.
Front, left to right: Brian Mullins, George Wilson, Paddy Reilly, Seán Doherty (captain), David Hickey, Gay O'Driscoll

Not long afterwards Seán was approached by Dublin County Board member, Arthur Nolan, to see if he would be interested in playing for Dublin juniors. He was selected at full-back and, true to form, was soon installed as captain. He was a sub on the senior team that made an early exit from the Leinster Championship in 1968 but by the end of the year he had taken over over as the regular full-back. He had to endure barren times as Dublin stumbled from one defeat to another. But nothing diminished the enthusiasm of the big defender.

'It was exciting for me to wear the jersey and to play for the county. We didn't know about success so we were never too disappointed when we lost which was a regular enough occurrence. It was more or less the end of the 1963 All-Ireland winning team. We had no regular training sessions and if you wanted to train you'd have to run around the park or kick the ball around.'

Kevin Heffernan's arrival on the scene changed all that. His main objective was to restore pride in the Dublin jersey.

'Kevin gathered a large group of players together in the Hollybrook Hotel in Clontarf and told us he was looking for players who were prepared to give their all for the cause of Dublin football. A number of players said they couldn't give total commitment for various reasons but there were plenty who were eager to give it a try. He soon brought in a whole new concept with regard to training, like an hour and a half of running, sprinting and exercising. Then he introduced exercises for warming up and cooling down. Before that our training sessions would have consisted of maybe ten laps of the pitch and then into the dressing-room. He was very forceful and could get his point across very well. He had played and won at the top level and had some very interesting ideas on how the game should be played. As each game approached he could tell us in advance how we would feel in front of bigger crowds. He told us how to deal with the press, radio and television as those were things we never encountered before. He was always one step ahead of the posse and he didn't allow us run into new areas without having us well prepared which was a great help.'

Kevin Heffernan was not long manager when the Dublin team met Kilkenny in a league match in late 1973. On arrival they found it extremely difficult to find parking space, such was the number of cars around the confines of Nowlan Park.

Says Seán, 'It was a cold damp Sunday afternoon and there was a hurling championship final in progress as we made our way into the ground. There was a huge crowd at the game and we watched it until half time when we went into the dressing-room to get changed. When I was leading the team out on to the field I thought for a moment that I had stepped onto the wrong park as the place was absolutely empty. We couldn't even get an umpire! The people had no interest in

---

THE 1974 DUBLIN TEAM

Paddy Cullen

Gay O'Driscoll	Seán Doherty (Captain)	Robbie Kelleher
Paddy Reilly	Alan Larkin	George Wilson

| Stephen Rooney | | Brian Mullins |

| Bobby Doyle | Tony Hanahoe | David Hickey |
| John McCarthy | Jimmy Keaveney | Anton O'Toole |

watching us play football and had gone home as soon as the hurling match was over.'

Croke Park on All-Ireland day still looked like the impossible dream in early 1974 when Clare beat Dublin in a league game.

'It was the only day I ever got injured playing inter-county football. I picked up a thigh injury that day and missed one club game and I was annoyed about that as it was the only time I ever missed a game through injury. But we qualified for the second division final which we lost to Kildare. We were very put out about missing a trip to London for the winners. At Easter that year we beat Tipperary in the Corn na Cásca tournament final and that was the first cup we won. I remember going up to collect the cup and Anton O'Toole said to me, "this is the first of many this year".' How right he was.

Seán feels it important to pay tribute not only to Kevin Heffernan but also to his co-selectors, Dónal Colfer and Lorcan Redmond. 'They were two super guys who had a great way of mixing with fellows. Some selectors can find it hard to communicate with players but Dónal and Lorcan were each just one of the lads and Heffernan was the same. I never remember Heffernan togging out while he was training us. He never put on a pair of boots, instead he always wore the pullover and the shoes. Even if it was teeming out of the heavens he still never togged out and would just pull on the anorak and out with him. But would he shout and roar and scream and lay the law down!'

> 'It was an incredible feeling to see all the cars and buses heading for Croke Park with flags flying. One of the flags in Westmoreland Street had written on it "Anton O'Toole, the Blue Panther". It sent a shiver up my spine and I knew then what it was all about. We had to go and win, these guys were coming to see us and expecting us to win.'

Seán's own game improved hugely due to the promptings and advice of Kevin Heffernan. He talked to his captain about marking a player tight and not allowing him room even to breathe. Seán had been playing football for enjoyment and had developed some bad habits and faults.

'I was a good man to win a ball in the air and was tall and reasonably strong. I had a problem with the low ball but from talking to Kevin I mastered that part of my game very quickly. I had good balance and wasn't one of these guys who fell all over the place. That's probably what Heffernan saw in me; big and raw but with potential. I presume he felt if he could tame me I would make a good full-back. He would pull you aside at a training session and talk to you for a few minutes. He had a super brain altogether.'

Dublin had to play five games in the 1974 Leinster championship before winning the provincial crown. Their first against Wexford was the curtain-raiser to the Roscommon-Kerry League final replay.

'It was a terrible game and we scrambled through but then again there are rarely good games between Dublin and Wexford. I always remember Wexford as big, strong, hard men. When you get the ball you'd be pulverised by them.'

Dublin went on to account for Louth, Offaly and Kildare on the way to a Leinster final meeting with Meath whom they defeated by five points.

So the Dubs were into the All-Ireland semi-final and pitted against the favourites and All-Ireland champions Cork. The build-up was something Seán had never

experienced. Unknown to him, his wife, Teresa, had given local priest Fr Lucey a Dublin jersey, shorts and socks and when he arrived at the church on the morning of the game he noticed his football gear was placed neatly on the altar. He also remembers getting a round of applause in the church. It was special. His good friend Johnny Griffin, brother of Pat who captained Kerry in the 1968 All-Ireland final loss to Down, called to Seán's house that morning with some silver for good luck.

'It was an incredible feeling to see all the cars and buses heading for Croke Park with flags flying. One of the flags in Westmoreland Street had written on it "Anton O'Toole, the Blue Panther". It sent a shiver up my spine and I knew then what it was all about. We had to go and win, these guys were coming to see us and expecting us to win. There was an air of excitement in the dressing-room rather than too much tension. I always found that whenever we were tense in the dressingroom we usually lost. If players were buzzing we knew we would win, if it was different something was wrong. One of the things I remember about the game was the fact that Cork made a substitution and had sixteen men on the field for a couple of minutes. We were screaming at the referee to halt the game and count the Cork men. There were forwards all around us.'

Seán recalls that there was not the same kind of atmosphere in the dressing-room before the All-Ireland final against Galway. Fear had crept in at that stage. 'More than anything else we were afraid to lose the game. The feeling was different against Cork and that allowed us express ourselves much more. We were scared of doing that against Galway. Paddy Cullen saved a penalty which helped us on the road to victory. I didn't play well, having fallen back into my old habits of defending by standing around the square. I was very conscious of defending, closing down the goal rather than going out in front to win the ball. I was afraid if Liam Sammon got too much of the ball we'd lose an All-Ireland. When you get in to a final you want to win it because the chances are you'll never get there again.'

There were wild and fantastic celebrations at the final whistle as Croke Park was transformed into a sea of blue. Ironically, the previous year Seán Doherty had been a steward on Hill 16 and had stood and watched Billy Morgan collect the Sam Maguire Cup. He recalls thinking he would give anything to be in Morgan's postion.

Kevin Heffernan had the dressing-room cleared by the time Seán arrived back with the Cup. He wanted time to congratulate his players for the hard work and effort during the year. When he had finished his speech he turned to the players and said, 'from this day on life will never be the same again'.

Although the team undertook a number of foreign trips during the following year they still qualified for the League final of 1975, going down to Meath. But the biggest disappointment of his sporting career as far as Seán Doherty is concerned was the All-Ireland loss to Kerry in 1975.

'We went in with an air of confidence and felt we would demolish this young Kerry side. Kevin Heffernan had warned us about over-confidence but we too were in-experienced in our own way. That defeat taught us a valuable lesson.'

By the time 'Heffo's Heroes' had captured their second All-Ireland in 1976 a new young giant had taken his place in their ranks, one Kevin Moran. Seán Doherty remembers his first encounter with the man who was to win international acclaim in the red of Manchester United and the green of Ireland.

'I marked Kevin a few weeks before he came onto the county panel. Kevin Heffernan knew we were playing Good Counsel and he came to me and said, "There's a fellow up there we're watching, Kevin Moran is his name; give him a few thumps and see how he takes to it. Knock him around a bit". He also asked me if there was any chance I'd move out to mark Moran wherever he happened to be playing. He played centre forward so I went out and played centre-back that particular day and it was like trying to get a skelp of the wind. Moran had never played county football at that stage but straight away I knew he was a good one. If you happened to hit him he'd bounce off you, land on his feet and be gone and there was no chance of getting at him again. He was training with us the following Tuesday. He was some player.'

Billy MORGAN

Cork Captain 1973

NO PLAYER OR MANAGER HAS MADE a more significant contribution to the cause of Cork football than Billy Morgan, who as goalkeeper and captain led the county to a seven-points victory over Galway in the 1973 All-Ireland final. Cork have won just six All-Ireland senior football titles in their history, and Billy Morgan played a very significant part in three of those victories. Apart from his role in the 1973 triumph, Billy was the influential manager some sixteen years later when Cork, under the captaincy of his close friend Dinny Allen, defeated Mayo in the All-Ireland final. Billy was again in charge in 1990 when Larry Tompkins captained Cork to victory over Meath by two points. It was the fourth time in as many years that Billy had steered Cork to an All-Ireland final. His team lost to Meath in both 1987 and 1988.

Billy Morgan never set out to be a goalkeeper. He played outfield most of his early life and lined out at centre-half-forward on the Cork minor team beaten in a replay in the Munster final in 1963 by eventual All-Ireland champions Kerry. The following year Billy had a falling out with a senior member of the Nemo club and as result played for a time with local soccer club Tramore Athletic. 'Being a Gaelic footballer, they decided to put me in goal, and that coincided with my first year in UCC. At the end of that year a good friend of mine, Paddy Brett, recommended me as a goalkeeper to Dave Geaney, who was the main man with UCC football team at the time. I won two Sigerson Cup medals with UCC in 1965 and 1966. At that stage I had no intention of staying on in goal. But things happened quickly. I was selected as goalkeeper on the Cork under-21 team and we were beaten by Kildare in the 1965 All-Ireland final. After that campaign I came on to the Cork senior panel. Things were happening for me, so it would have been folly not to stay on as a goalkeeper. I was a sub keeper with the Cork senior team for the League of 1965, and in the last

---

FACT FILE

HOME PLACE: Tonyville Terrace, High Street, Cork

BORN: 2 February 1945

CLUBS: Nemo Rangers; UCC

ACHIEVEMENTS IN CLUB COMPETITIONS: Eight County Senior Football Championship medals in 1972, 1974, 1975, 1977, 1978, 1981, 1987 and one medal as a substitute in 1988; two All-Ireland Club medals in 1973 and 1979; five Munster Club Championship medals in 1973, 1975, 1976, 1979 and one medal as a substitute in 1989; two Sigerson Cup medals with UCC in 1965 and 1966.

INTER-COUNTY ACHIEVEMENTS: One All-Ireland Senior Football medal in 1973; five Munster Senior Football medals in 1966, 1967, 1971, 1973 and 1974; one National League medal in 1980; five Railway Cup medals in 1972, 1975, 1977, 1978 and one medal as substitute in 1976.

game Cork played Kildare, and Brian Murphy, the goalie, at the time had a nightmare. The next game was a challenge against Offaly on Easter Sunday, and that was the day I made my debut on the senior team. Brian used to play outfield with his club and won his place back on the county team at corner-back, and I was delighted. He is a very good friend of mine.'

Cork beat Kerry in the Munster final of 1966 but lost to Galway by two points in the All-Ireland semi-final. They went one better the following year when they qualified for the All-Ireland final, only to lose by three points to Peter Darby's Meath. There was only one goal scored in the game, and a crucial one it was. 'Meath were awarded a fourteen-yards free in the second half and Tony Brennan took it and it went straight into Gerry Lucey's chest. Gerry cleared it out the field and everyone ran out, barring Terry Kearns, who stayed beside the posts. Mattie Kerrigan caught the ball and kicked it back in. I knew Kearns was there and I came to break the ball away, but at the last minute I changed my mind and tried to catch it and he stuck up his fist, got a touch to the ball and it went over my shoulder into the back of the net. I was very disappointed after the game, as I felt we should have won. After that defeat the selectors brought in many new players and broke up what was a very good team. Typical Cork. Chopping and changing the team was the one thing that used to frustrate me. Remember, we had a very good team in 1967. There seemed to be very little planning or thought put into the preparation of the team, with the exception of Donie O'Donovan. He was a great coach and trainer.'

Cork won their next Munster final in 1971 with a comprehensive eleven-points victory over Kerry, but defeat by Offaly was their lot in the All-Ireland semi-final. Billy believes it was that defeat that signalled the coming of the 1973 team. 'Cork had produced some great under-age team in the sixties, so I had no doubt that the talent was there to win an All-Ireland senior title. Nemo won the county championship in 1972 and Denny McDonnell became the chairman of the county selectors. He was also the man who was chiefly responsible for Nemo coming to the forefront in

Back, left to right: Donie O'Donovan (Trainer), Denis Long, Ray Cummins, Jimmy Barry-Murphy, John Coleman, Dave McCarthy, Declan Barron, Ned Kirby, Denis Coughlan.
Front, left to right: Jimmy Barrett, Con Hartnett, Kevin Jer O'Sullivan, Billy Morgan (Captain), Frank Cogan, Brian Murphy, Humphrey Kelleher.

football in the late sixties and early seventies. He had great organisational powers, and it wasn't long before he had a team doctor by the name of Dr Paddy Fitzgerald. He also arranged for John Kid Cronin to become the team masseur. For the first time since I began playing with Cork we had a very organised backroom set-up. If Donie O'Donovan wanted something, all he had to do was ask Dinny Mac and it was done. Donie was the greatest influence on my playing career. A wonderful man.'

In a high-scoring Munster final in 1973 Cork got the better of their arch-rivals Kerry by 5-12 to 1-15. 'Jimmy Barry Murphy was chosen at corner-forward and Ray Cummins was full-forward, but before the game the selectors decided to switch Jimmy Barry and Ray. Ray went out to the corner and Paud O'Donoghue followed him, and Jimmy Deenihan moved in to full-back to mark Jimmy Barry. It worked like a dream for us and we scored five goals in the first twenty-three minutes.'

In the dressing-room after the game, Billy remembers impressing upon his players not to get carried away with the victory, as it was only a Munster final. The All-Ireland was the prime objective. Cork put another five goals past Tyrone in the All-Ireland semi-final to set up a final meeting with Galway. Billy recalls the build-up to the final as calm but confident. 'There was a great atmosphere around the city and county and we were really looking forward to the game. Because of a clash of colours we had to play in white jerseys for the final, and Tyrone kindly sent us a set of their jerseys to use in training so that we could get used to the new colours.'

Billy Morgan has good reason to remember the morning of the All-Ireland final. He was rooming with teammate Frank Cogan in a Dublin hotel, and they were both relaxing and chatting when the phone rang and the chairman of the selectors, Denny McDonnell, ordered them to come down to a team meeting that had been planned in advance. 'We may have been a minute or two late but Denny blew us out of it for not making it on time. That was Denny's style. He was the kind of fellow who if you were up there he would knock you down a peg or two and if you were down he would make sure to bring you up. I'd say he wanted to show that there was no Nemo man getting any preferential treatment, because we were by no means the last to come in. We knew what he was doing and we had great respect for him.'

The Cork team had a kick-around in the grounds of St Patrick's Training College on the morning of the game, and Fr O'Sullivan, a brother of team member Kevin Jer, gave all the players his blessing. 'We all knelt on the ground, but when it came to Dónal Hunt's turn to get a blessing he raised his eyes to heaven, and everyone started laughing. It went a long way towards easing the tension. Dónal was not renowned for his religious fervour.'

THE 1973 CORK TEAM

Billy Morgan (Captain)

Frank Cogan	Humphrey Kelleher	Brian Murphy
Kevin Jer O'Sullivan	John Coleman	Con Hartnett
Denis Long		Denis Coughlan
Ned Kirby	Declan Barron	Dave McCarthy
Jimmy Barry Murphy	Ray Cummins	Jimmy Barrett

Substitutes: Séamus Coughlan for John Coleman; Dónal Hunt for Dave McCarthy; Mick Scannel for Humphrey Kelleher.

Billy remembers little of what was said in the dressing-room before he took the field at the head of his Cork team. He had received a letter from the wife of Weeshie Murphy, which contained the scapulars her late husband had worn in 1945. She asked Billy if he would wear the scapulars, and he was delighted to do so. Weeshie was chairman of the Munster Council and had died suddenly some weeks before that. He was also the father of Dr Con Murphy. Earlier, at the team meeting, Billy had read out the letter and had said to the players, 'let's win this one for Weeshie'.

As soon as he came on the field Billy gave the ball a hefty kick up in the air and it landed near the centre of the pitch. And therein lies a tale. 'We were then called to get photographs taken, and as you'll see, I'm looking to my right in every one of them.

That's because I was watching the ball. Galway then came out onto the pitch and came down to the Hill 16 end to kick around. As they passed down they picked up our ball. As soon as the photograph was taken I ran over and said to their captain, Liam Sammon, "Look, you have one of our footballs there". I felt he was all nerves. He seemed to be all choked up and gave me a ball without asking any questions. I remember then we went over under the Hogan Stand to line up to meet the President and I felt that the Galway players were shivering. As we were walking down I said to our players, "Take a look at them, they're very nervous".

'Galway got a point from a free in the first thirty seconds or so but Jimmy Barry Murphy scored a goal for us almost immediately. We played great football in the first half and were well ahead at half time. Early in the second half John Coleman suffered concussion and eventually had to go off. Galway came back at us in the second half, but Jimmy Barry Murphy scored another goal, and Jimmy Barrett got a third just before full time. We won by seven points and it was a great feeling.'

> 'It's necessary to have a good eye for the ball, quick reactions and good positional sense. Then you have to work really hard in terms of quick reaction training rather than long running. What I worked on a lot was weights, because I think strong legs are very important for a goalkeeper.'

When the game was over Billy turned around to get his cap and gloves but he was surrounded by well-wishers, among them one of his pupils, Johnny Bowen. He was delighted to see a familiar face. He remembers going through a sea of red and white to make it to the Hogan Stand to collect the cup. It was a hazardous journey back to the dressing-room, and he was tossed to and fro by the supporters.

Bringing the cup home was an unforgettable experience. Tens of thousands turned up in Cork to greet the football champions of Ireland. The reception in Beamish House, with lunch in the Blarney Hotel on the Tuesday after the final, were special occasions. That evening the Cork team travelled to Kinsale for Frank Cogan's stag night. Frank was getting married the following Friday.

The Cork team travelled to San Francisco the following March, and even then, some six months after winning the All-Ireland, many of the players were still in a partying mood. 'I remember at one stage Donie O'Donovan advised us to pack in the celebrations and asked us to start concentrating on playing football seriously again. Then when we were beaten by the All-Stars in San Francisco a second time, Donie came into the dressing-room and said, "Look, lads, this is the second and last time I'm going to say this to you; if you want to continue celebrating, fine, no problem, but you can do it without me". He was a man we had fierce time for but unfortunately we didn't heed his words, even then.'

Despite the celebrations Cork did retain their Munster crown in 1974, trouncing Kerry in the final by double scores. 'We were in the Victoria Hotel one evening after training about two weeks before the Munster final and we were sitting down with pints galore on the table. This commercial traveller who was staying in the hotel came over to us and said something like, "Are ye the Cork team? How come so much drinking just two weeks before the Munster final? The Kerry team are all in their beds by now". I remember one of the lads said, "They're in bed all right, but are they sleeping". There was a big laugh. We hammered Kerry and this added to our confidence. We were due to play Dublin in the semi-final. They had come from nowhere so we didn't regard them.

'Jimmy Keaveney was down in Cork the week before the All-Ireland semi-final and the Sam Maguire Cup was in Frank Cogan's house. Jimmy was leaving the house about lunchtime on the Monday, and Frank and myself ran in and came back with the cup and called Jimmy. He turned around and we said, "Take a good look at it, because it's the nearest you'll ever come to it". But unfortunately Jimmy went back and told Kevin Heffernan and he was able to use it to motivate the Dublin team. Dublin brought fitness in the GAA to a new level. I remember with about five minutes to go thinking, "if we're not careful here, we're going to lose it". I still felt we'd win it, even at that stage.'

Billy Morgan played until 1981 and had to endure the heartbreak of losing seven Munster finals on the trot to Kerry. It is a widely held belief that the Cork team of 1973 never realised their full potential. By the time Cork again won a Munster final Billy Morgan was in America, having gone to New York University in January 1982 to study for a master's degree in physical education. He remained in America until August 1985. Then in October 1986 he was asked to coach the Cork team, and this he has since done with unrivalled success. Under his guidance Cork have won two All-Ireland senior titles and five Munster senior championships and were runners-up in three All-Irelands. Remarkable by any standards, and testimony to Billy Morgan's brilliance as a team manager.

But it has not all been plain sailing. He has found his position of Cork manager very frustrating. He got the selectors he wanted in 1989 and 1990 and believes it is no coincidence that the Sam Maguire Cup came to Cork both those years. 'Why change something that's successful? In 1991 the County Board in their wisdom decided they would nominate the panel of selectors. That's the year they tried to get rid of me. It has been frustrating, and I have found it so because I am held responsible if the results are not favourable and Cork lose. You're bound to have different ideas, and that's grand, but if the coach or manager feels very, very strongly about something then that should be carried.'

Billy Morgan grew up in a hurling household. From his earliest days his ambition was to play hurling for Cork. His parents, Tom and Sheila, came from Galway, and there was a hurling tradition in both their families.

'I was more interested in hurling at an early age. There was a patch of waste ground in front of the terrace of houses where we lived and we played hurling, football and soccer there all the time. I began to play more football when I joined our local club, Nemo Rangers, which was more a hurling club in the early days but it gradually moved towards football. As well as that the school I was attending, Scoil Chríost Rí, leaned more towards football, which meant it was the game I played most often from then on.'

According to Billy, to make it at a high level as goalkeeper 'It's necessary to have a good eye for the ball, quick reactions and good positional sense. Then you have to work really hard in terms of quick reaction training rather than long running. What I worked on a lot was weights, because I think strong legs are very important for a goalkeeper.' Whatever it took, Billy Morgan certainly had it in abundance.

Tony McTAGUE

Offaly Captain 1972

WHO WAS THE BEST free-taker ever in Gaelic football? One of those questions impossible to answer but it is safe to say that Ferbane's Tony McTague had few peers in that department. Indeed, Tony set a number of national scoring records in the course of an outstanding career. Those were the years Offaly footballers ruled the roost and it was due in no small measure to the deadly accuracy both from play and frees of one Tony Mc Tague.

Who could ever forget him? That familiar stance as he registered yet another score for Offaly from the dead ball position. He was consistency personified. Defenders came to fear the man with the number 12 on his green, white and gold jersey. He was also one of the cleverest exponents of the solo run, very deceptive and almost impossible to dispossess.

So how did he come to master the art of free-taking?

'It's all down to practice. If you don't practise an awful lot, your mind will let you down on the day of a game. But, if you have it built-in by having the number of hours practised, it won't ever let you down, because it'll be part of you. If you don't work at it, and practise, your kicking will let you down, because your mind will let you down. It's really a mental thing. I know you have to have the kicking action as well, but in lots of cases you'll get that, if you practise often enough. I'd say there are hundreds of players in every county who could be good place kickers if they put enough time and effort into it. It's a discipline.'

'You have to be a perfectionist to be disciplined enough to be a good free-taker, because you'd get very browned off if you weren't. You also have to set goals for yourself. In my case, I used to have young lads kicking back the ball. That would be the hardest part of it. You'd get very browned off if you were kicking in the ball and then you had to go in and retrieve the ball and bring it back out and place it again, whereas if you could have someone kicking the ball out to where you are, first of all you'd be able to kick an awful lot more. And I used to have that kind of service down

---

FACT FILE

HOME PLACE: Ferbane, County Offaly

BORN: 29 January 1946 in Clonakilty, County Cork   CLUB: Ferbane

ACHIEVEMENTS IN CLUB COMPETITIONS: Three Offaly Senior Football Championship medals, 1971, 1974 and 1976; two Offaly Minor Football Championship medals 1963 and 1964 and one Offaly Junior Football Championship medal in 1964.

INTER-COUNTY ACHIEVEMENTS: Two All-Ireland Senior Football Championship medals in 1971 and 1972; one All-Ireland Minor Football Championship medal in 1964; four Leinster Senior Football Championship medals in 1969, 1971, 1972 and 1973; two Leinster Minor Football Championships in 1962 and 1964; two All-Star Awards 1971 and 1972.

in the field in Ferbane. I often met those lads since and they'd say to me "Do you remember the time I was down there with you" and I'd say "of course, and you were a great help to me". If your subconscious is right and you've done it often enough and practised it, and practised it, and practised it, you'll convince yourself you can't miss, no matter who is there, or who isn't there, even if people were standing on their heads in front of you. But then, the real test for anybody is when they miss a couple of frees. Then you start losing confidence in yourself, it's like putting in golf. You then have to relax and cool down and get back to the things you know worked in the past. It should be a very simple thing to do, but it becomes a lot harder when the pressure comes on. And the pressure is on only when you're missing. There is no pressure on a fellow when he's hitting them. That's no problem. But it's the day you're missing them, that becomes a very, very big problem.'

During those winning days for Offaly, Tony McTague put a tremendous amount of effort into the free-kick aspect of his game. He never practised frees at a training session with the county team, because that would be a physical session, mostly playing and running. But Tony would always have a couple of footballs at home and would very often go down to the field and kick frees from different positions.

'If I were to give advice to somebody, who wanted to be a good place kicker, I'd tell them to take three kicks at goal and set themselves the target of scoring with all three. It's no good hitting one, it's no good hitting two, hit three. It's the third in the series that becomes difficult. Anyone can hit one, anyone can hit two, but when you hit three, one after another, it's the third one that becomes a mountain. And you'll mentally have to put that ball over. That's the hard one. Some day try a fourteen yards free in front of the goal, and have three shots at it and see if you can put the three over. You'll put over one and two, no trouble, but it's the third one that becomes difficult. That's the ideal training for anybody taking free kicks. That's how you become good. Just say to yourself: "this is first of three, 'pump'; this is the second of three, 'pump'. You have two over now, so this is the last of three. Are you able to

Back, left to right: Paddy McCormack, Larry Coughlan, Seán Lowry, Martin Furlong, Seán Evans, John Smith, Mick Ryan, Kevin Kilmurray.
Front, left to right: John Cooney, Willie Bryan, Paddy Fenning, Tony McTague (captain), Martin Heavey, Eugene Mulligan, Séamus Darby.

do the three?" It's no good, if you did only two out of the three, then you're out. You have to hit the third. Now the third one becomes very hard. The pressure is on, but that's the kind of conditioning you have to give yourself. If you wanted to carry it further you could make it the best of five. If you're getting good at three, then you can always get better. If you can put down five, the first four will be no trouble, but the pressure will again be on you to kick the fifth one over.

'You have to say to yourself: "I'm not satisfied until I'm hitting all three and then all five over the bar." And the day you're hitting five over, with any kind of consistency, you're going to be deadly, you're going to be an awful hard man to beat. It's common sense, and you get the match reality by having to kick the third one, or the fifth one over, as the case may be. It smokes them out.'

Although he was a natural right-footer, Tony McTague had a great advantage in that he could also kick very well with his left foot, as many defenders can testify to their cost. 'I'd kick a ball with my left from a very narrow angle, because I'd have a draw with my right. I could kick a ball grand out of my hand with my left, so I then started kicking off the ground. My left foot was not anything like as good, but I'd knock over a fourteen yards free to the right of my post with my left. I wouldn't put the house on it, but I could do it nevertheless.'

His biggest fear as a place kicker was not the wind or rain, but whether the ball was at the right air pressure. 'If the ball was over-inflated, it would be impossible to control when kicking. This is the reason why players like to feel the ball before the start of an important game. I am sure that a lot of very important games were decided by the ball pressure.'

While growing up, there wasn't much else for Tony to do around Ferbane but go to the football field. And that he did, and loved every minute of it. He soon developed a great love for the game, continually trying to improve his skills. It was not long before he came to the attention of local selectors and became an automatic choice on under-age teams. Like most youngsters in the county, Tony was influenced to a certain extent by the successes of the Offaly Senior team of 1960 and 1961. The Offaly 1961 team, captained by goalkeeper Willie Nolan, lost to Down by just one point in the All-Ireland Final.

Says Tony, 'As a young fellow, the only matches you'd really be going to would be excursions by train from the local railway station to Portlaoise, Newbridge or some of the country venues. That would be your annual holidays. The more games you had, the more days out you had. My father, who had no interest in football, would bring my brother, who also had no interest, and myself to the games. I had an

---

THE 1972 OFFALY TEAM

Martin Furlong

Mick Ryan	Paddy McCormack	Larry Coughlan
Eugene Mulligan	Seán Lowry	Martin Heavey

Willie Bryan   Sean Evans

John Cooney	Kevin Kilmurray	Tony McTague (Captain)
Séamus Darby	John Smith	Paddy Fenning

Substitutes: Murt Connor for John Cooney; Nicholas Clavin for Eugene Mulligan;
Mick Wright for Larry Coughlan

all-consuming interest. I'd be totally engrossed and enjoying the game. It would be remiss of me if I were not to mention my own club and the wonderful times I had playing football in the local field. Little did I realise, when I started playing under 12 football in 1956, that one day I would be captain of an All-Ireland winning team. I certainly dreamed the dream often enough, but to have achieved it is wonderful. All the evenings we played football in Fleming's garden or in St Cynoc's Terrace, these were All-Ireland finals without the Sam Maguire Cup. I would like to pay tribute to Paddy O'Byrne, Jimmy Dolan [both now deceased] and John Cunningham for all the effort they put into under-age football during those formative years.

'As a young boy, I went to all the local games with Garda Dan O'Driscoll. It was he who also brought me to Croke Park for the first time to see the Railway Cup Final of 1957. We travelled in Tim Egan's car. Dan loved sport and would always get a lift for me to the local games with himself.'

Tony McTague's call up to the Offaly colours came sooner than expected.

He had a good year in the juvenile championship of 1962 and when one of the minor players was injured, Tony was drafted on against Meath and retained his place the whole year through, until the All-Ireland Semi-Final, which Offaly lost to Kerry. He was only sixteen at the time and was on the team that won the All-Ireland Minor Final in 1964. That victory still remains the highlight of his footballing career.

'I remember our bus was delayed going to the game and we only arrived in the dressing-room a few minutes before we were due on the field. The fact that we arrived late helped absorb our attention and therefore we weren't as nervous as we might have been. We were leading well at half time, but Cork came back in the second half and we only won it in the end by a point. I think success breeds success and I've no doubt that the minor victory was the makings of the 1971 and 1972 All-Ireland winning Senior teams. 'Six of that minor winning team played in the 1972 final: Martin Furlong, John Smith, Mick Ryan, Eugene Mulligan, Willie Bryan and myself. Seán Evans was a sub in 1964 and he was midfield on the senior team in 1972. Jody Gunning played in the 1964 minor final and was right-corner-forward when we beat Galway in the 1971 final. Mick O'Rourke came on as a sub in 1964 and he played at left-full-back in 1971, but missed the '72 final through injury.'

> 'Being captain did not suit me. Being the place kicker was more than enough team responsibility. A captain ought to be picked for his leadership and rallying skills. Preferably, a defender should be captain, in my opinion.'

Just eight years after the minor All-Ireland, Tony McTague led Offaly to All-Ireland senior success.

'We played Meath in the Leinster semi-final that year and the thing that stands out from that game was the superb display of Nicholas Clavin. We won easily against Kildare in the Leinster final, but struggled against Donegal in the All-Ireland semi-final. I was marking Brian McEniff, who was a very good player. We were lucky to get a draw against Kerry in the final and all I can remember from the drawn game is that I kicked an awful lot of wides.'

Interestingly, Tony can recall very little of the game itself or what it was like leading the team onto Croke Park. He also admits he would have great difficulty remembering anything about the 1972 replay either, were it not for the fact that he now has a video of the game. Disappointed with his own performance in the drawn game, Tony does, however, remember taking considerably more frees than usual in the build-up to the replay.

'It was to build my confidence back up, because when your confidence goes like that, it doesn't automatically come back, you have to work at it. You have to build up the credits again inside the mind with the lad that counts, the real hero. I did an awful spate of frees. It was hard work, but it worked out perfectly in the replay.'

As in 1971, the team travelled by train to Dublin on the morning of the game. But again, the Ferbane man remembers little of the build-up to that match or much of what happened afterwards. It's just that frills like parades never meant that much to him. It was the playing of the game that really mattered. He cannot recall what, if anything, he said to the players in the dressing-room before the game.

Offaly won the replay in style and Tony pays tribute to the dedication of his team.

'It was a team effort, it wasn't the individual. Everybody worked hard and didn't give in and supported each other. I certainly don't remember anything very much about the occasion, but I do remember that I was delighted when it was over and we had won. The replay was not as tense as the first game. The thing which stands out for me regarding the replay was, even with a few injured players, the will and determination of the team to overcome anything.

'I think a replay win is an anti-climax, as far as winning an All-Ireland is concerned. I don't think it's the same as winning first time; a replay takes a certain amount of the glitter from it to a certain extent. If it was a straight win, you'd probably remember everthing that happened, but not so much with the replay.

'The homecoming was the highlight of the weekend. We were beaten in the 1969 final, so we knew the difference. What a difference!'

A great student of the game, Tony feels blessed to have been so lucky in his football career. To captain an All-Ireland winning team is unquestionably one the greatest honours in the game, but not, so it seems, for Tony McTague. He would have preferred if someone else had the captaincy in 1972.

'Being captain did not suit me. Being the place kicker was more than enough team responsibility. A captain ought to be picked for his leadership and rallying skills. Preferably a defender should be captain, in my opinion. I was chosen to be captain because Ferbane won the 1971 Offaly Senior Football Championship — not the ideal reason. I would like to pay a tribute to our club captain in 1971, Michael Grogan. It was his leadership and drive which culminated in our victory. He had all the attributes of a natural leader with everybody holding him in very high esteem. It is absolutely vital in any team to have leadership on the field of play. There are natural leaders, who have great belief in themselves to the extent in particular that they never lose heart. By their actions, they get across to the rest of the team during training and games, the philosophy of never giving up regardless of how hopeless the case may appear. This type of person ought to be captain of the team. During our successful All-Ireland campaigns, Paddy McCormack gave us this leadership. He had the confidence in himself and would never despair. He always believed we were going to win and would never give up. We certainly owe him a debt of gratitude for this leadership.

'I can think of players who gave this leadership in the recent past, even though they were not the captains. Colm O'Rourke of Meath and Brian Mullins of Dublin in particular gave this leadership. When a team has to be rallied, the natural leader comes to the fore and all the other players automically row in.'

Tony likes nothing better than to watch the game played cleanly with a certain amount of physical contact. He deplores the use of the elbows to stop a player. He himself was the subject of such cowardly actions more than once in his playing days.

'I have noticed a number of those type of tackles in the last five years. They are very dangerous and the culprit should be sent off immediately and suspended for one year. I remember Mickey Linden of Down being taken out of the game in this way in the 1991 All-Ireland Final and the culprit escaped with just his name taken.

After such a tackle you'd be sick for a week and maybe worse. I do not see much harm when two players are involved in a few punches. Though it looks bad, there is never much damage.'

He believes that winning helps more than anything else to create friendships. 'If we weren't winners, we wouldn't be as friendly. I was part of many teams that didn't win and you wouldn't have the same friendships. You'd be bound together by the win, that would be the binder. Teams owe a great deal to the manager in particular and also to the selectors, coaches and masseurs, who give time and expertise to try to win the All-Irelands and county championships.

'I would like to pay tribute to Fr Gilloley, our manager in 1971 and 1972. He put a fantastic effort into our cause, always punctual and caring. He also treated our wives and girl-friends as part of the overall team. He saw the team as one big family and showed concern and respect for all. He often put his hand in his pocket to solve team problems. He could have been supported from those in authority far better than he was. Our selectors, Seán Brererton and Alo Kelly, were always confidential and fair as well as knowledgeable. They were former players who knew the game. Ossie Bennett was our masseur and was brilliant at the job. He lived in Portlaoise at the time and whenever you called to him, he would facilitate you. He represented all that is best in the GAA. To have a successful team the "camaraderie" between players, team management, wives and girl-friends as a group is very important as it helps to build a team attitude. A happy camp has to be fostered. It is a major function for the team manager. Our management successfully accomplished this.'

Tony is a great advocate of the Supporters' Clubs, firmly believing they give a vital service to the team.

'They help to procure jobs, finance holidays and generally act in the interests of the team. County committees are very poor in this regard and create problem after problem for different reasons, which destroys the morale of a team. When a thorny issue arises, a division is created between delegates, which is made public by local newspapers or by word of mouth from meetings. A Supporters' Club is far more helpful and confidential and solves the problem with the minimum of fuss.'

Tony McTague makes the valid point that Offaly's win in 1971 and 1972 helped to pave the way for the success of the county hurlers in the eighties.

'If you can look across the ditch at someone up the road with an All-Ireland medal you'd say, "I know him well, you don't have to be special to win an All-Ireland medal", which you don't.'

Tony works as a shift supervisor with the ESB in Shannonbridge. His hobbies are golf and coaching local minor football teams. He lives with his wife, Bernadette, and three children in Ferbane. He will always be remembered as a player and free-kicker supreme. An example to all aspiring footballers.

Willie BRYAN

Offaly Captain 1971

WILLIE BRYAN was a classic midfielder. His high-fielding, clever use of the ball and vision of what was unfolding on the field of play paved the way for many an Offaly victory, none so important as when he led his county to their first All-Ireland Senior victory in 1971. The Walsh Island man was just twenty-three years of age at the time. Seven years previously, Willie had lined out at right-half-forward on the Offaly team that won their first All-Ireland minor title.

Willie was nominated Offaly captain for the 1971 championship campaign even though his club, Éire Óg were not the reigning county champions. And whenever he reflects on a wonderful career, he is thankful that his long-range free kick in the closing seconds of an important club championship game found its target. Éire Óg were playing Rhode in the county semi-final at O'Connor Park in Tullamore. Rhode looked certain of victory when they led by four points with just a few minutes remaining, until Éire Óg scored a goal to close the gap to one point.

Éire Óg were then awarded a 60 yards free and with the last kick of the game, Willie brought the game to a replay.

'I just happened to catch it on the button and we won the replay. We lost to Gracefield in the final, but as they had no representative on the county team, this allowed me become captain. If Éire Óg had not won the semi-final, I would never have got the captaincy that year as Rhode had a number of players on the Offaly team.'

Willie Bryan's memory of the greatest day of his sporting life is clouded with a regret that is still very much with him well over twenty years after he lifted the Sam Maguire Cup to the acclaim of Offaly people everywhere. He was working in Dublin at the time and had opted to stay in the city on the eve of the Final in order to avoid

---

FACT FILE

HOME PLACE: Walsh Island, County Offaly

BORN: 2 November 1947 in Portlaoise   CLUBS: Walsh Island and Éire Óg

ACHIEVEMENTS IN CLUB COMPETITONS: Two County Senior Football Championship medals with Walsh Island in 1978 and 1979; one Leinster Club Football Championship medal in 1978.

INTER-COUNTY ACHIEVEMENTS: Two All-Ireland Senior Football Championship medals in 1971 and 1972; one All-Ireland Minor medal in 1964; All-Ireland Senior runners-up in 1969; All-Ireland Under-21 runners-up in 1968; four Leinster Senior medals in 1969, 1971, 1972 and 1973; one Leinster Under-21 medal in 1968; two Leinster Minor medals in 1964 and 1965; one Railway Cup medal in 1974; two All Star Awards in 1971 and 1972; Second Division League in 1978; three Grounds Tournament medals in 1971, 1972 and 1973; Texaco Sports Star of the Year, Gaelic Football 1972.

all the emotion and hysteria. Even to this day he is a quiet, almost shy man, never more at ease than when far away from the 'madding' crowd. He loves meeting people, but can also be direct and to the point if he feels people are going overboard with 'compliments'.

'I wanted to get away from all the hype and the "experts" clapping me on the back telling me how Offaly was going to win the All-Ireland. On the Saturday evening, my mother rang me at my flat worrying whether I had clean socks and togs. When I explained to her that we were getting new socks and new togs she said to me: "who is going to polish your boots?" and I said to her: "Mother, I can polish my own boots".

'I didn't realise it at the time, but all she really wanted was to have me home on that night. I couldn't see this and stayed in Dublin. I always regret not going home that Saturday night. My mother was a great support and was obviously very proud of me. Only recently, I was watching a video of the game and happened to see my mother in the crowd and to be honest I found it very emotional.'

> 'On the Saturday evening, my mother rang me at my flat worrying whether I had clean socks and togs. When I explained to her that we were getting new socks and new togs she said to me: "who is going to polish your boots?" I didn't realise it at the time, but all she really wanted was to have me home on that night.'

Willie had a flat in Pembroke Street and later that Saturday night, he strolled down O'Connell Street, unrecognised by the hordes of roaming football supporters. A man alone with his thoughts! He found it difficult to understand what all the fuss was about.

'Whenever I saw people with Offaly hats, I just pretended to look at the shop windows until they had moved on. I bought the Sunday papers at O'Connell Bridge and walked back on up to the corner of Leeson Street to Kirwan House on the corner of Stephen's Green. I drank a few pints and of course overheard the match being discussed. My name cropped up now and again, but I said nothing. No one realised who I was and I didn't make them any wiser. I listened to the banter and then went home at a reasonable hour. I read the Sunday papers and then had a good night's sleep.'

It was not unusual for Willie to have a few drinks on the eve of a big game and he never felt it affected his performance in any way. He loved his pint, but would never drink on the Friday night before a game.

He went to Mass in a little oratory in Leeson Street on the morning of the Final and then had breakfast in a small café in Baggot Street.

'After breakfast, I went back to the flat, grabbed the boots and got the bus to O'Connell Bridge. I waited for another bus to take me to Heuston Station and met the team off the train at about mid-day. One amazing thing was that someone had arranged for us to have a tour of Phoenix Park, which was a strange thing to plan on the morning of an All-Ireland. We used to train in Phoenix Park so it was something we could have done without as we were sick and tired of the place!'

He remembers little about the team's arrival in Croke Park, only that the Offaly dressing-room was a very tense place. 'We were all very quiet and reserved and each of us found our own little space and no one bothered us. Paddy McCormack was the driving force of the team, a man without a nerve in his body. He spoke forcefully and hit the table and got us all to focus on the game. Fr Gilhooly also spoke to us and I said a few words. As captain I was dragged away for a photograph as soon as we came on the pitch and I hardly got a touch of the ball before the game started. I felt there was too much pomp and pageantary before the match began. It would have been far better had we been able to run out and get stuck into the game immediately.'

When the game did get under way it was a less than savoury affair in the first quarter. It was a wet day and Galway and Offaly had met on a number of occasions that year and were perhaps over-familiar with each other.

'Although neither team was playing well, Galway were getting the better of the exchanges. The first ten minutes or so of the game was quite rough. The referee, Paul Kelly, called me aside and told me to go in and sort out the Offaly back line, where most of the action was taking place. I had hardly got a touch of the ball at this stage. I ran in waving my hands and trying to look authorative and there were players lying everywhere. I pulled Paddy McCormack aside and told him to take it easy. He told me in no uncertain manner to get out to my position, making the point that if I was catching the ball out in the centre of the field he wouldn't have it in the square. He was absolutely right of course as I had hardly touched the ball. After that, the game settled somewhat and Murt Connor got the crucial goal. Séamus Leyden scored two goals for Galway, but we won it in the end by 1-14 to 2-8.'

Willie was a little superstitious and made a conscious decision not to tempt fate by having a speech prepared. His philosophy was: 'if we win, we win and I'll think of something to say'. He survived the ordeal.

He was unaware of the significance of the captaincy at the time and viewed his position as nothing more than being the man chosen to call the toss. 'I never felt there was anything remarkable about being captain. It was a big deal from the supporters' point of view, but I was unaware of it at the time. I suppose I only came to appreciate the real significance of the achievement in later years. We were in the hotel after the match and I met a businessman, Pat Troy from Washington, in the toilet and he was standing up against a radiator trying to dry his clothes. He was leaving some of the dirt on his trousers as a keepsake. Many years later, I was in his house in America and the trousers, with plenty of dirt on them, were hanging up in a magnificent attic along with all kinds of other Gaelic games mementos!'

Amid all the hectic scenes in the dressingroom, Willie spotted life-long Offaly supporter Brendan Kelly from Edenderry sitting quietly on the bench unable to speak with emotion. Willie himself would have liked nothing better than to have found a quiet corner to savour the moment but it was impossible. Indeed, it would be many

---

THE 1971 OFFALY TEAM

Martin Furlong

Mick Ryan	Paddy McCormack	Mick O'Rourke
Eugene Mulligan	Nicholas Clavin	Martin Heavey
Willie Bryan (Captain)		Kieran Claffey
John Cooney	Kevin Kilmurray	Tony McTague
Jody Gunning	Seán Evans	Murt Connor

Substitutes: John Smith for Kieran Claffey; Paddy Fenning for Jody Gunning

months before he found the time and space to reflect on that historic day.

The victory gave a great lift to the whole county and close to thirty thousand greeted the Offaly team in Tullamore on the Monday night.

'The whole thing was an incredible happening. It's only now I realise how much it meant to the county to win our first All-Ireland. For any team to fully appreciate what winning an All-Ireland means, I think they'd have to understand what it's like to be a supporter first. I had been a player all my life and it wasn't until I retired that I came to understand the frustrations of being a supporter.

'This good friend of mine, Moss Buckley, would eat, drink and sleep the game for months beforehand and like everyone else would struggle to get a ticket. He sets off for a game hours before most people in order to get there in plenty of time. And yet after looking forward to the game so much, he just wants it to be over even before it starts. I think that Moss sums up the real supporter.'

When Willie Bryan's father, Har, took a job with Bord na Móna in the late forties, he moved his family from Portlaoise to Walsh Island. Willie was less than a year old. His was a happy childhood with football at the very core of it.

'The early years in Walsh Island were very tough as Bord na Móna was the only employer in the area. We all worked on the bog during the summer and the only source of social life was football. I played for a local school and have a lasting memory of losing an Under 12 Final by one point. Life seemed to end that day and to make matters worse I lost my first pair of new football boots. I left them outside a small shop in Tullamore and my mother was none too pleased when I arrived home without them. Thankfully, someone found them and I got them back a few days later.'

Before that Willie had to share the one pair of football boots with his older brother, Harry, who always wore the left boot. Another brother, Pat, played minor and under 21 for Offaly and was a sub for a time to the goalkeeper, Martin Furlong. He later decided to withdraw from the county panel. He was the Walsh Island goalkeeper

Back, left to right: Paddy McCormack, Mick O'Rourke, Murt Connor, Kieran Claffey, Nicholas Clavin, Seán Evans, Martin Furlong, Mick Ryan, Kevin Kilmurray.
Front, left to right: John Cooney, Tony McTague, Willie Bryan (captain), Eugene Mulligan, Martin Heavey, Jody Gunning.

during their six county championship victories.

Willie's eldest brother, Michael, who sadly died in a road accident when only twenty-five, was a very promising footballer in his younger days, but gave it all up to concentrate on music. He was a member of a number of well known bands and played for a time with Larry Cunningham. He wrote several songs, one of which was recorded by the Troggs. Willie himself was no mean performer on guitar, but unlike Michael he opted to concentrate his energies more on football.

'Michael was continually encouraging me to take up music full time, but football ruled in those days. God knows, I have often wondered if I was with him that fateful night would the accident have ever happened. He was killed travelling home after playing at a dance. He fell asleep at the wheel and hit a bridge just outside Tullamore. He left a lasting memory with us all.'

Willie Bryan was chosen at midfield on the first All-Star selection and was there again the following year when his wonderful display against the mighty Mick O'Connell helped to bring about Kerry's first defeat in an All-Ireland Final replay.

He understands clearly that life has changed utterly since his school days when he kicked football at every opportunity. He realises the GAA can no longer take for granted the loyalty of children to the national pastimes. Others sports, particularly soccer, have been making big inroads. His advice to youngsters is: 'Study the game as it should be played. There can be a lot of arrogance in the game, so respect those in authority at club and county level.'

He has been playing golf for a number of years and enjoys it immensely. In recent years, he won the 'Golfer of the Year' award in Tullamore and now plays off a handicap of five.

During his term as All-Ireland winning captain, Willie was invited as guest to many GAA functions. On one occasion he travelled with Paddy McCormack to a club in Birmingham to make a presentation of medals. He had the Sam Maguire Cup with him and Paddy and himself were wined and dined and made feel very important before the function got under way.

'We went to the dance to carry out our task and while we were standing on the stage the chairman of the club gave the "usual" speech that we were the best footballers in Ireland. He then introduced Paddy McCormack but couldn't think of my name. With the microphone still on, he turned to someone and said for all to hear: "what's the other chap's name".'

A similiar incident happened the following day. Willie and Paddy were both playing in the Railway Cup Final and were extremely lucky to make it to Croke Park on time.

'The flight was delayed and our taxi only arrived at Croke Park just a few minutes before the game was due to start. While I was paying the fare, Paddy ran ahead and the man at the gate knew him and let him through, advising him to hurry up. He then asked Paddy who the chap was coming behind him and Paddy jokingly said he did not know. Although I argued the point with the chap on the gate, he didn't believe I was a player and I ended up having to pay to get in to play. Not recognised twice in the one weekend. Enough to deflate a man's ego!'

Willie Bryan thinks it is time the GAA authorities got round to running the League and Championship together and give players an off season. He points out: 'A player can easily become drained if he is very successful at county level. The opposite applies if a player is with a poor county or club and has little or no competition. Soccer and rugby have a close season and they don't seem to lose out.

'There is also need for a better way of distributing All-Ireland tickets. There should be a points system where people who attend matches during the year are given preference on the big day. It is also important that the players who in the past helped to fill Croke Park on final day should not be forgotten, as now seems the case.'

Willie Bryan has deservedly guaranteed himself a special place in the annals of Gaelic football.

Donie O'SULLIVAN

Kerry Captain 1970

IT IS HARD to think of anyone who deserved the honour of captaining an All-Ireland winning team more than Kerry's 1970 captain, Donie O'Sullivan as this great defender was on the losing side in four All-Ireland senior finals.

In his prime Donie was noted as one of the longest dead-ball kickers in the game and a wonderful exponent of the drop kick, a feature that is now dying out in the game. To this day, teammates, opponents and supporters talk of his amazing ability to drive a free kick with uncanny accuracy further than any other player.

'It's hard to pinpoint what it came from. I think it was a matter of trial and error. It certainly wasn't coaching or being shown technique or methods. It was by practice and a bit of satisfaction as my kicking improved. At the age of about eighteen, I wasn't able to kick a ball off the ground further than thirty yards. Then as I began to kick the ball a few yards further, I became more confident and got more satisfaction out of it. The time I really thought about it was when I was put in at corner-back in order to be there to kick out the ball. I could kick it seventy to seventy-five yards when the co-ordination was right. It's a bit like a golf shot in that you always know what it's going to be like as soon as you make contact. There were times when things went wrong and I'd be always good for maybe one fluff kick-out, so I was aware that this could happen. As I got older and more experienced, I found that instead of trying to "lose" it, if I gave it ninety-five per cent the kicking was consistent and it helped to conserve energy. Strength was part of it but in the early days I thought the long

---

FACT FILE

HOME PLACE: Tiernaboul, Killarney, County Kerry.   BORN: 12 March 1940

CLUBS: Spa, Killarney; Dr Crokes, Killarney; Clanna Gael, Dublin; UCD; Kerry Club, New York and Clan na nGael, San Diego.

ACHIEVEMENTS IN CLUB COMPETITIONS: One All-Ireland Senior Club Football Championship with East Kerry in 1971. Beat Bryansford of Down in the final in Croke Park. It was the first official All-Ireland Club Championship; three Munster Club Championships with East Kerry in 1966, 1969 and 1971; four Kerry County Championships with East Kerry in 1965, 1968, 1969 and 1970; one Sigerson Cup medal with UCD in 1968; ten East Kerry Championship medals: seven with the Spa Club and three with Dr Crokes: one Kerry Intermediate Championship and one Senior League with Spa; two New York Championship medals with Kerry.

INTER-COUNTY ACHIEVEMENTS: Four All-Ireland Senior Football medals in 1962, 1969, 1970 and 1975; four runners-up All-Ireland shields in 1964, 1965, 1968 and 1972; seven National Football League medals in 1963, 1969, 1971, 1972, 1973 and 1974 and one with New York against Galway in 1967; one Railway Cup medal in 1972; two All Star Awards in 1971 and 1972; one Gaelic Sport All Star in 1965/66; captain of All Star team on US trip, 1973.

run-up was very important, but again with age I found that two steps were as good as twenty-two. It was more the position of the non-kicking foot and the follow through and, of course, the state of mind.'

In 1966 while studying in St John's University in New York, Donie came to the attention of the New York Jets football team who offered him a contract following a trial. But he declined and returned home to an outstanding football career with Kerry. He has no regrets. The lines of Hilaire Belloc are particularly apt: 'From our first beginnings to our undiscovered ends there is nothing worth the wear of winning but the laughter and love of good friends'. To Donie O'Sullivan, more important than any achievements have been the laughter and the love of good friends.

Donie has fond memories of playing with Spa in the 1966 East Kerry Championship. The club was founded in the late forties and was a mirror of the way the country was going at the time. Up to then, players from the Spa area played with either the Legion Club or Dr Crokes. The club did well until the early fifties when it ceased to function due to lack of members because of emigration. As a result of industrialisation around Killarney in the sixties there were more players around the locality and Spa decided to form a minor club.

'The first year the club entered senior competition after being re-formed was in 1966. In spite of being regarded as complete outsiders and no hopers in every game, we played very well and beat Kilcummin in the East Kerry Final. The amazing thing is that we didn't even have our own jerseys and had to use the blue-and-gold jersey worn by our club members back in 1948. The jerseys were so faded that they looked for all the world like what the Viet Cong wore during the Viet Nam War.

'The joke among ourselves was that the combined age of the Spa full-forward line was 126! It meant an awful lot for the older people of the area and many of them used to come down to the field to see us training. It wasn't much of a field at the time, but it became a place of identification. That championship win of 1966 assumed very quickly the character of myth at local level.'

Early in 1970 Kerry made a trip to Australia and Donie recalls a 'well tanned' Kerry team being well beaten by Mayo in a league game on their return from Down Under. It was not a good omen for the championship season ahead. Nevertheless they retained their Munster crown with a comfortable enough win over Cork.

'Playing Cork is always a toss-up, not only in recent years but back as long as I can remember. No matter how good Kerry were or how bad Cork were supposed to be, you'd still say: "if we win by a point, we're doing okay! So we were very pleased to beat them that year. We beat Derry in the semi-final, but they missed two penalties. If any team dominated the first half it was Derry, who were all over us. One of the

---

THE 1970 KERRY TEAM

Johnny Culloty

| Séamus Murphy | Paudie O'Donoghue | Donie O'Sullivan (Captain) |
| Tom Prendergast | John O'Keeffe | Mícheál Ó Sé |

Mick O'Connell   D.J. Crowley

| Brendan Lynch | Pat Griffin | Éamonn O'Donoghue |
| Mick Gleeson | Liam Higgins | Mick O'Dwyer |

Substitute: Séamus Mac Gearailt for Donie O'Sullivan

---

things I remember of that first half is Johnny Culloty saying to me as I was kicking out the ball, "if we prevent them getting a goal, we'll win it yet". As it happened they didn't score a goal, but they had many near misses. Mick O'Connell was off for part of the first half of that game after getting injured, so that was bound to have had an unsettling effect on the team. That was a fine Derry team and with a bit of luck would have won an All-Ireland and National League.'

It was Kerry versus Meath for the first eighty-minute final. The Leinster champions had accounted for a good Galway team in the semi-final.

'Meath were always Meath. It isn't only in recent years that Meath have got the reputation for commitment, determination and never being beaten. They had it always as far I can see. Certainly you'd always be afraid of Meath especially in a final and the most you'd ever hope for would be fifty-fifty and that the "breaks" would come our way. We hadn't that many injury scares, although Pat Griffin wasn't right after he picked up an injury during our trip to Australia in a famous place called Wagga Wagga. Pat never fully recovered from that injury. Then of course we had John O'Keeffe playing at centre-half-back on Matt Kerrigan, so there was a big question mark there about putting a nineteen-year-old in that position against a player of the ability of Matt. But John did very well and Tom Prendergast and Mícheál Ó Sé, the other half-backs, were outstanding. There were great individual contests between the likes of Brendan Lynch and Pat Reynolds, Éamonn O'Donoghue and Ollie Shanley and Liam Higgins and Jack Quinn, who was a magnificent full-back.'

When asked how he felt when the final whistle blew and he realised he was about to lift the Sam Maguire Cup, Donie paused, almost as if it was the first time he ever thought about its significance. Then: 'I have never felt relaxed or enjoyed big crowds. I could have got on fine without going up to receive the Sam Maguire Cup. I wouldn't have minded missing out on that. I had to go off injured after damaging a muscle in my leg during the game, so I suffered an awful lot when I was "carted"

Back, left to right: Mick Gleeson, Mick O'Connell, D.J. Crowley, Mícheál Ó Sé, Liam Higgins, Paudie O'Donoghue, John O'Keefe, Mick O'Dwyer.
Front, left to right: Tom Prendergast, Pat Griffin, Johnny Culloty, Donie O'Sullivan (captain), Brendan Lynch, Éamonn O'Donoghue, Séamus Murphy.

across the field with the Cup after the game.'

He remembers little about the scenes in the dressing-room or much about what happened afterwards. He is just not that type of man. The game was over, the cup was his and Kerry's. That is what mattered most of all. He does, however, remember the homecoming as being very special. It was a wonderful feeling after suffering so many disappointments. He was particularly pleased to be bringing the cup to his home club, Spa (the rural area of the parish of Killarney) and to share in the joy of the local community. 'After that I could appreciate why Muiris Ó Súilleabháin said that he wrote *Fiche Blian ag Fás* in order to give the old people of the Blaskets a few laughs.'

But the occasion at Croke Park he remembers best was much more recent. It was the 1990 National League Final between Down and Meath.

'I was just a spectator, but I've a very special reason for remembering that day as my son, Eoin, was able to come with me to the game. It was his first day back at a football game for over a year. The previous May, Eoin had been diagnosed with leukaemia and was very very ill. He went through a very extensive course of chemotherapy and barely survived on a few occasions. It was our first outing together for a long time. It was a beautiful sunny day at the end of April and it was like a rebirth. Spring was in the air and Eoin was back to health again.

> *'I have never felt relaxed or enjoyed big crowds. I could have got on fine without going up to receive the Sam Maguire Cup. I wouldn't have minded missing out on that. I had to go off injured during the game, so I suffered an awful lot when I was "carted" across the field with the cup after the game.'*

'It made me appreciate more the feelings of Patrick Kavanagh in his poem of celebration, "Canal Bank Walk". It is a poem of rebirth and renewal. I will never forget that day in Croke Park as long as memory remains. I had the miracle there beside me. A great day and a day to be thankful to God. Everything after that is a bonus. Any time I would have walked into Croke Park before that day, I'd have taken things for granted: "this is my right, nothing is going to happen to me". You don't dwell on those things. Certainly that put life in perspective and no comparison to All-Ireland or League finals, winning or losing. That day in Croke Park was the highlight.

His advice to those running the games is straightforward and to the point. He believes that the association's future vibrancy and vitality depends on the clubs and on the ordinary club members.

'Concentration on the skills, especially at under-age level, is more important than physical training and competition. County divisions, like Dublin city and county, will have to be examined. The GAA of the future cannot be divorced from a consideration of the Ireland of the future. A great challenge facing the GAA, I feel, is a danger of complacency.

'The history of the GAA shows that the association is very powerful while under threat and has a great resilience for surviving some very dangerous situations. It has now become a huge organisation with great material resources. There is a danger that the ordinary club member — the life blood of the GAA — might feel that the objectives have been achieved and as a result the promotion of the games among the young could suffer. The GAA was built on its games and it was the games that helped to achieve the other objectives. Success or failure depends on the games.

'The GAA of the twenty-first century cannot but be linked to the Ireland of the next century. Therefore the association will have to deal with the trends and resulting problems. Until recently, Ireland would have been considered a mainly rural society. Rapid and bewildering changes have taken place, particularly the growth of urban areas on the east coast. This has been at the expense of the remainder of the country. Throughout the rural decline, the GAA clubs continued to survive and ensured some type of local identity and focus. The dedication of officials and players was almost heroic and the rewards were never monetary. Now the GAA clubs in the new urban areas will have to create a sense of identity and help to provide civic pride and unity to those developing areas.

'These demographic changes mean that there has to be an examination of the inter-county competitions. More players in the urban areas such as Dublin and Cork must be given the opportunity of participating in the National League and championship. Other areas that are calling for attention and appraisal are unemployment, a young population, national identity and the growing emphasis on the acquisition of wealth. There is a limit to the sacrifices that are to be made in the quest for sporting glory. I think St Theresa of Avila put it best: "More tears are shed for answered prayers than unanswered ones". We in the GAA are in some respects over-democratic. We could be more selective and less elective. It might be more beneficial if officers at county committee in particular should serve for a limited period of time. Then, if their enthusiasm hasn't waned, they could devote their expertise and experience to the promotion of the games at under-age levels. Return to the Elysian fields for a while.

Donie O'Sullivan with Sam Maguire, 1970

Johnny CULLOTY

Kerry Captain 1969

JOHNNY CULLOTY is widely acclaimed as one of Gaelic football's greatest goalkeepers. But he was also a very accomplished outfield player and in 1955 at the tender age of nineteen, Johnny won the first of his five All-Ireland senior medals playing at right-corner-forward. Kerry defeated arch-rivals Dublin in that final.

'Dublin were hotly fancied as they had some great players like Kevin Heffernan, Ollie Freaney and Des Ferguson,' Johnny remembers. 'I couldn't understand how I was on the team at all and it was a great thrill to play alongside the likes of John Cronin, Micksie Palmer, John Dowling, Paudie Sheehy and Tadhgie Lyne. I was a little apprehensive in case I wouldn't be able to hold up my own end. There would have been fair old odds against Kerry winning the game, so of course that made us all the more determined. I played well enough on the day even though I didn't score.

'I was marking Mick Moylan who was well over six feet tall, a fine, clean player. We were very fit as we trained twice a day under Dr Éamonn O'Sullivan. I didn't need that much training myself at the time as I was only about ten stone four but at the same time the hard work stood to us in the final.'

Johnny Culloty spent most of his inter-county career between the posts, but it was a different matter altogether in club football where he nearly always played outfield. He ended up scorer-in-chief on many of the East Kerry championship winning teams. 'To tell you the truth, I had no notion whatsoever of playing in goal when I started out. I played in goal with Killarney minor hurlers when just thirteen because I was too small to play outfield. I was goalkeeper the following year with the Kerry minor team and was on that team for four years. I progressed to the senior team and played for a few years as a goalie. But I played all my club hurling and football outfield.'

Johnny suffered a cartilage injury while playing corner-forward in a Railway Cup match in 1956 and this interrupted his career for a considerable time.

FACT FILE

HOME PLACE: Lewis Road, Killarney, County Kerry

BORN: 9 July 1936   CLUBS: Legion and East Kerry

ACHIEVEMENTS IN CLUB COMPETITIONS: Four County Senior Football Championship medals and two Munster Club Senior Football medals with East Kerry; one County Senior Hurling Championship medal; three County Minor Hurling Championship medals; four County Intermediate Hurling Championship medals with Killarney.

INTER-COUNTY ACHIEVEMENTS: Five All-Ireland Senior Football medals in 1955, 1959, 1962, 1969 and 1970; twelve Munster Championship medals in 1955, 1958, 1959, 1960, 1961, 1962, 1963, 1964, 1965, 1968, 1969 and 1970; one All-Ireland Junior Football medal in 1954; one All-Ireland Junior Hurling medal in 1961; five National Football League Medals in 1959, 1961, 1963, 1969 and 1971; four National Hurling League Medals Division 2.

'I was picked as a sub on the Kerry team as a forward when we played Galway in a *Gaelic Weekly* semi-final in 1957. The goalkeeper, Marcus O'Neill, couldn't make it on the day and I played in goal. It was only just by chance. I remember well Seán Purcell scoring a penalty against us that day. I was still a sub when the League resumed and just played an odd game out the field. Then the same thing happened again in late 1958, no goalie turned up one day and I stepped into the breach and from then on played the rest of my inter-county football career as a goalkeeper.'

He confesses to never doing any special training for the goalkeeping position. He rarely if ever played in goal for his club. Other than the days he lined out for Kerry, the only occasions that Johnny Culloty stood between the posts was during training sessions with the county team in the build-up to the championship.

'I was good at organising backs because I reckon I knew from playing out the field what I'd be trying to do to score myself. I felt if I could marshal the full-back line I'd prevent a lot of scores. I was like a poacher turned goalkeeper.'

> *'I was like a poacher turned goalkeeper ... It was much more leisurely. Out the field you could say, "if I don't kick this one, I might kick the next one", whereas if you're inside in goal you certainly couldn't say, "if I don't catch this one, I'll catch the next one".'*

Johnny Culloty is certain of one thing: he much preferred playing outfield. He admits he never fully enjoyed a game in goal as he was always very keyed up.

'It was much more leisurely out the field and you could say, "if I don't kick this one, I might kick the next one", whereas if you're inside in goal you certainly couldn't say, "if I don't catch this one, I'll catch the next one". It's a different kind of a story altogether. I enjoyed playing in goal in hurling more than football. Possibly there wouldn't be as much to do in football where you could go for a quarter of an hour without getting a kick. All kinds of thoughts would be running through my mind: "I wonder is the ball wet?" or "would I want my gloves?" I often came off the pitch absolutely exhausted after a football match in which I would hardly have got two kicks. It's hard work trying to concentrate and getting onto fellows to mark their men and watch this and that. Then I could play two games out the field and not be tired at all. That's a fact! My aim as a goalkeeper was to keep down the number of mistakes I made. The mistake against Down in 1960 was the one that was highlighted the most. It was a dropping ball and it fell out of my hands and into the back of the net. I probably took my eye off the ball, maybe checking to see where I'd clear it and didn't concentrate enough on catching it. I was playing in goal with Kerry for about thirteen years and yet fellows would remark about that mistake much more than any good save I made. A goalkeeper certainly has a very responsible position.'

He preferred hurling to football and regrets that Kerry were never good enough to win an All-Ireland senior hurling title. He found it a cleaner game with not as much pulling and dragging as in football.

'Hurling is more skilful than football and I even enjoy it more as a spectacle. Fair enough, you might get "split" now and again, but with the advent of helmets those injuries are much less frequent nowadays. There are more knee and ankle injuries in football. I reckon a good hurling game is twice as good as a good football game!'

Johnny scored two goals from the corner-forward position when Kerry defeated Meath in the All-Ireland junior hurling home final at Croke Park in 1961. The Kingdom got the better of London in the Final.

Johnny relates an incident which happened the first year he played in goal for the Kerry minor hurling team. He was just fourteen at the time and Kerry were playing Limerick at the Gaelic Grounds in the Munster Championship. On that particular day the nets of the goal were being held up by railway line sleepers and he remembers a Limerick forward running through on a solo run and hitting a bullet of a shot from about twelve or fifteen yards.

'I went for the shot but it passed me and hit one of the sleepers at the back of the net and rebounded into play. The ball went out so quickly that another forward running in, tapped it over the bar. And what did the umpire do, only put the flag up for a point. Of course most people thought I was after saving the shot that hit the sleeper. There were a few people behind the goal going on about the "goal" all right but there weren't that many at the match. I pucked the ball out while at the same time thinking to myself: "How did the umpire make that mistake?" After a while I got talking to the umpire and I said to him: "I wonder was that a goal or what?" I remember well the way he looked at me and then he said: "You know as well as I do that it was a goal, but I'm a Kerryman as well".' Kerry lost to Limerick by a very narrow margin that day.

Johnny remembers another time over twenty years ago in a Kerry county hurling championship game in Tralee when a referee awarded a penalty with a difference.

'I was playing at centre-half-back for Killarney that day and the referee gave a penalty against our team. He cleared the goal except for the goalkeeper! We tried to explain to him that there was no such thing as a penalty in hurling at that time, but he wouldn't listen to us. Because I was the Kerry goalkeeper at that time our team decided that I should stand in goal to face the penalty. The opposing team knew there should be no penalty so whether or not their free taker tried very hard or not, I don't know, but I saved the penalty. It wasn't a very hard shot to save.'

His abiding memory of the 1969 All-Ireland itself was his vital second half save from Offaly full-forward Seán Evans. On the day, Kerry won by just three points.

'The thing that troubles most winning captains after an All-Ireland is having to make a speech. It's a bit off-putting really. We had two players from the Gaeltacht, Séamus Mac Gearailt and Mícheál Ó Sé, and they got on to me about Irish being downgraded by most the winning captains that spoke at All-Ireland finals. They had figured out that there were just one or two words in Irish first and then the rest of it was in English. They advised me to say five or six sentences in Irish and say nothing

---

T H E   1 9 6 9   K E R R Y   T E A M

Johnny Culloty (Captain)

Séamus Murphy	Paudie O'Donoghue	Séamus Mac Gearailt
Tom Prendergast	Mick Morris	Mícheál O Sé
Mick O'Connell		D.J. Crowley
Brendan Lynch	Pat Griffin	Éamonn O'Donoghue
Mick Gleeson	Liam Higgins	Mick O'Dwyer

in English. And I'm nearly sure that's the way I did it on that day. They wrote out the sentences for me and I stuck them into my stocking before the game. At half-time the game was dicey, it was kind of going against us, so I said "to hell with those sentences" and threw them out in the dressing-room. There seemed to be a jinx on them. I thought it would be very bad if I couldn't think of a few sentences in Irish. As soon as the match was over I said to myself: "that speech again". '

Growing up, Johnny Culloty kicked ball with other youngsters in front of the family home on Lewis Road and often spent whole days playing football in Fitzgerald Park. The youngsters used to organise games between themselves and many occasions on Sunday mornings, Johnny remembers leaving the field to go to Mass and then coming back to finish the game. It was a saga.

'People talk about learning skills, but we'd often spend four or five hours a day during our holidays kicking a football, so we were bound to be fairly skilful.'

His primary school school days were spent with the Presentation Brothers and he pays tribute to Brother Mel who did great work organising class games. His coaching helped develop the football skills and natural talents of the youngsters.

When he retired from inter-county football, Johnny, who played in nine senior All-Ireland finals, took over as manager of the Kerry team, a position he held for three years. It was a major disappointment when in his first year in charge Kerry lost to Offaly in the replayed All-Ireland final of 1972.

'I thought we were good enough to win, but it didn't happen on the day. It's much different training a team than actually playing. You can do something about the game when you're playing, but when you're on the sideline the day of a game, there's little you can do. You've done your best in training so when the team takes the field your job is more or less finished. It's a frustrating job really. I felt we should have won the first day, but a few things went against us in the replay which made a big difference and we lost by nine points. There's more pressure on you as a manager than as a player. You're meeting people every day and they're asking you about the

Front, left to right: Pat Griffin, Mick Gleeson, Mícheál Ó Sé, Mick O'Connell, Paudie O'Donoghue, Liam Higgins, Mick O'Dwyer, Mick Morris.
Back, left to right: D.J. Crowley, Séamus Murphy, Tom Prendergast, Séamus Mac Gearailt, Johnny Culloty, Brendan Lynch, Éamonn O'Donoghue.

players' well-being. As a player you just get yourself fit and you're ready to play your own part and you don't have to worry about everyone else. When you're in charge of a team you have to take care of everyone involved with the team.'

Although Kerry lost the Munster finals of 1973 and 1974 there was some consolation for Johnny in that they won successive leagues in 1972, 1973 and 1974.

Johnny Culloty believes that there should be a tartan track and a decent gymnasium in all the major Gaelic games stadiums in Ireland. This would allow teams to get in training no matter how bad the weather.

'Even the Kerry team finds it hard to get a stadium for training in winter.

Johnny leads his team out for the Final — following him are Michael Ó Sé, D.J. Crowley, Mick O'Dwyer, Eamonn O'Donoghue, Brendan Lynch, Mick O'Connell ...

Whenever I pass any of the GAA grounds they seem to be closed. I know they are well utilised for matches but I'm talking about the off-season.'

While justifiably proud of having captained Kerry to win the the All-Ireland football final, Johnny looks back even more fondly on his days as a hurler. 'I played from 1951 until the early 1980s. The highpoint for us was winning the county hurling championship. To me that would be just as important as captaining Kerry to win an All-Ireland.'

Johnny Culloty's motto: 'Never wallow in victory, never get too depressed in defeat. It's still only a sport.'

165

Joe LENNON

Down Captain 1968

THE COUNTY of Armagh has never won an All-Ireland senior football title. Yet a man from the Orchard County held the Sam Maguire Cup aloft on All-Ireland final day. That man was Joe Lennon, but he was wearing the red and black of neighbouring Down as he climbed the steps of the Hogan Stand in 1968 to accept the Cup. It was a proud moment for Joe, who had been a member of the double All-Ireland winning sides of 1960 and 1961.

Joe Lennon was just eleven years of age when in 1945 his family moved the few miles from their home in Poyntzpass, County Armagh, to a farm in Lisnabrague, County Down. It was a move that was to change young Joe's life. His sporting career began in earnest when he attended St Colman's College in Newry where he acquitted himself admirably at both football and handball.

But Joe had always been very keen on football at primary school and can clearly remember calling in regularly to the local shoemaker, Mr. Kearns in Poyntzpass for wax-ends to mend his old football.

'At St Colman's College, I got my first real taste of organised football training and coaching. Fr John Treanor and Fr Herbert Connolly were great coaches and managers. My college days were not very successful at football but I did win the Ulster Colleges handball title playing with Dessie Reavy, whose brother Eddie would have won the English Grand National on Zahia in 1949 had he not taken the wrong turn at the run-in. Between college and club football, I was very busy in my teens and got on the Down minor team at a time when Down was winning little or nothing.'

On leaving St Colman's College, Joe spent six years as a meteorologist before becoming a student again at Padgate College in Lancashire, where he qualified as a

---

FACT FILE

HOME PLACE: Poyntzpass, County Armagh.   BORN: 24 September 1934

CLUBS: Aghaderg, County Down; Irvinestown, County Fermanagh; John Mitchell's, Birmingham; St Patrick's, Stamullen, County Meath.

ACHIEVEMENTS IN CLUB COMPETITIONS: Down Minor Championship with Aghaderg in 1951; (Aghaderg combined with Banbridge to win title); Warwickshire League and Championship with John Mitchells; County Meath Feis Cup plus numerous inter-club tournaments with St Patrick's, Stamullen.

INTER-COUNTY ACHIEVEMENTS: Three All-Ireland Senior Football Championships in 1960, 1961 and 1968; three National Football Leagues 1960, 1962 and 1968; seven Ulster Senior Football Championship medals in 1959, 1960, 1961, 1963, 1965, 1966 and 1968; four Railway Cups in 1960, 1964, 1966 and 1968; numerous Lagan Cups and Dr McKenna Cups; one St Brendan's Cup versus New York; three Wembley Tournaments; Ulster Colleges and Ulster Minor Handball titles in 1951.

secondary school teacher. While living in England, he flew home as often as thirty times a year to play for club and county. He became the first Irishman to obtain a First Class Honours Diploma in Physical Education at Loughborough Training College, where he presented 'Coaching Gaelic Football for Champions' as the thesis for his diploma. Later, Joe was the first Irishman to get an MSc in Recreation Management at Loughborough. Joe was also a founder member and first President of the Physical Education Association of Ireland.

Many people may not know that Joe Lennon played for a short spell with Fermanagh. This came about while he was working in the county and playing club football with Irvinestown. At the time, he was out of favour with the Down selectors, but after a scintillating display for Fermanagh against the great Jim McKeever of Derry, Joe was soon back where he belonged on the Down team. Shortly afterwards, his work as a meteorologist took him to the Persian Gulf and he spent two years in Bahrain.

'When I returned things had changed a lot, and I was inveigled back into the game one Sunday evening. At that time, I saw my future as a badminton player, having played a lot in Bahrain. I had played for Loughborough Training College and for a season in Liverpool and was selected to play for Worcestershire but the game clashed with a Railway Cup match and that was the end of my county badminton.'

While he was in the Gulf, Joe's mother, Anne, kept him informed on football matters at home by sending the *Armagh Observer* and numerous letters saying how badly Down was faring.

'I remember one letter I wrote to her saying, "I'll be home soon, back on the Down team and we will win the All-Ireland".' His mother kept the letter and presented it to Joe in late 1960 when, by then, his prophecy had come true.

'In 1968, I brought the Sam Maguire Cup to Poyntzpass for a few days and left it in Mickey Waddell's shop window. A fanatical Armagh supporter, who was also the local milkman, would not deliver milk to my relations, the Lennons of Poyntzpass, until I took the cup away again.'

His career as a Down player was not always plain sailing and Joe fell out of favour with the authorities on a number of occasions. One incident more than any other remains etched in his mind.

'Having been substituted in the semi-final against Offaly in 1960, I left Croke Park in a temper because I felt I was playing well. I said I would not wear the Down jersey again. However, common sense prevailed after a lot of meetings and we got the substitution problem sorted out. I often felt that that little incident was the cause of me not being made captain until I was about to retire.'

Throughout the spring of 1968, Joe was pressing the authorities in Croke Park to convene meetings and to plan further coaching courses. Eventually, a meeting was called for the morning of the National League final between Down and Kildare. Although the timing of the meeting was such that Joe was not expected to attend, he surprised them all by turning up. At the end of the long meeting, the then President, Séamus Ó Riain, thanked the members for attending and shook hands with everyone including Joe, who said 'I'll see you later.' As he turned away, Joe felt the President was not fully aware that what Joe meant was that he would see him when collecting the cup.

Strangely, Joe does not remember much about the All-Ireland final days in which

---

THE 1968 DOWN TEAM

	Danny Kelly	
Brendan Sloan	Dan McCartan	Tom O'Hare
Ray McConville	Willie Doyle	Joe Lennon (Captain)
Jim Milligan		Colm McAlarney
Mickey Cole	Paddy Doherty	John Murphy
Peter Rooney	Seán O'Neill	John Purdy

Substitutes: Larry Powell for Joe Lennon; George Glynn for Larry Powell.

he was involved. Nor does he remember much about any of the games.

'Apart from scoring a point in 1960, I recall very little of the game. I left Croke Park and went to the Airport with Maurice Hayes and was back in England at college at seven o'clock that evening.

'In 1961, only a few incidents stand out, particularly James McCartan's goal. This time, I did stay for the celebrations, but later wished I had not, as we did not reach Newcastle until four thirty in the morning.

'In 1968, I was living in Gormanston, rather than England, and hence was much more involved with the hype. However, I remember playing golf on the morning of the game, going down to the hotel in Belcamp, where we had a light lunch, and then the whole outfit lounged around watching the first half of the Minor final before getting into the cars and down to the pitch.

'The parade was just like the other parades, only this time I was leading the team, and ten minutes into the game we were seven or eight points up, I think. At half-time we had a fairly good cushion. However, I was injured just before half-time and during the break it was left to me to decide whether to chance it, or come off. I took myself off because Brendan Lynch would have been too quick for me as I'd damaged a medial ligament in my right knee. The second half of that final was the longest half hour of my life. Kerry kept threatening to whittle the lead away and in fact scored a goal from a 14 yards free to cut the lead to two points with only a few minutes remaining. Somehow we survived.'

He remembers being shepherded across Croke Park to the presentation. The scene was one of wild and fantastic celebrations. After receiving the Cup, Joe made his captain's speech and ended it by saying: 'it is the captain's privilege to be presented with the match ball but I wish to present the ball to be raffled in aid of the Biafra Famine Relief Fund'.

'Next day I got all Down and Kerry players to autograph the ball and I gave it in to Croke Park for the raffle. I was given a lot of donations, which I passed on to

Back, left to right: Tom O'Hare, John Murphy, Ray McConville, Willie Doyle, Danny Kelly, Seán O'Neill, Jim Milligan, Dan McCartan.
Front, left to right: Brendan Sloan, Peter Rooney, Mickey Cole, Joe Lennon (captain), Paddy Doherty, Colm McAlarney, John Purdy.

Croke Park and I gather that quite a lot of money was collected. However, I never met the lucky winner, or heard any more about the raffle, till I saw an article about it in the paper several months later. I would have liked to know who won that ball. All-Ireland winning days mean different things to different captains.'

At the 1991 Final, Joe was watching the parade of the Galway team of 1966 when a few thoughts occurred to him and he jotted them down on his match programme. 'I had been on such parades twice before. Once at the centenary parade of past captains in 1984 and again the following year on the twenty-fifth anniversary of Down's first All-Ireland success. When I got home, those thoughts kept nagging at me till, I got up early a few days later and wrote a poem called "Parade of Past Champions".'

> Roll call, and players of the past parade
> Sprightly, greying, smiling, waving where once they played
> with honour and distinction — so much so —
> That nationwide we cheer them, friend and foe.
>
> Some household names are called and they don't come
> But represented by a wife or son
> They stride across the park and take their place —
> A smiling wraith around their loved one's face.
>
> If doubt there is amongst the young folk there
> And wonder if those old men really were
> Champions of Ireland twenty-five years past —
> Called to ensure our memory of them lasts.
>
> Be they assured that mighty deeds were done
> By those men there and those that could not come.
> Remember friends their 'far fierce hour and sweet
> With shouts about their ears and palms beneath their feet'.
>
> And if one day, I'm called and I can't come —
> Just represented by my wife or son,
> I'll be the happy halo around their face,
> And pray for those who put this scheme in place.

Every team has its characters and Joe remembers goalkeeper Danny Kelly as being a particularly humourous individual.

'We were playing in Casement Park one Sunday and things were not going too well, as we had conceded a couple of goals and Danny was in need of a bit of sympathy. He stayed down a bit long after one goalmouth incident and Tom O'Hare, who felt he was not all that badly hurt, said: "Danny, Danny, quick, here's Patsy McAlinden coming" (the sub goalkeeper). Danny leaped up immediately and let out, "Where, where Tom, I'm all right now".'

Joe Lennon has made invaluable contributions to gaelic games through coaching, teaching and writing. His first book *Coaching Gaelic Football For Champions* in 1963 led to the organising and running of the first National Coaching Course in Gaelic

Football at Gormanston in 1964 and a second in 1965. Three years later in 1968, Joe's second book, *Fitness For Gaelic Football* was another huge success. In 1988, his *Skills of Gaelic Football*, a fifty-five minute video with a book of the same title, won the Irish Television Award for non-broadcast training videos and fared well in the World Television Finals in New Orleans. From 1976 to 1990, he spent considerable time and energy researching a method of presenting the playing rules of Gaelic football with clarity.

'The first of these I called *specification* which deals with sizes, numbers, time etc. The second *control* dealt with the powers and duties of the officials in charge of the game on the field. The central section of course would deal with the actual rules applicable to the play.

'It also became obvious to me that many definitions of key terms should be made and included as part of the playing rules to ensure uniformity of understanding, and put an end to debate on what for example constituted a "hand pass", a "throw" or a "tackle".

> *'In 1968, I brought the Sam Maguire Cup to Poyntzpass for a few days and left it in Mickey Waddell's shop window. A fanatical Armagh supporter, who was also the local milkman, would not deliver milk to my relations, the Lennons of Poyntzpass, until I took the cup away again.'*

'The new format showed that all playing rules dealt with either fair play or foul play, and that each of these two sections had each got three rules — making six playing rules in total.'

It was the first time that an individual had taken it upon himself to re-draft and re-write the entire set of rules.

'My research was first of all discarded with contempt, but gradually as I developed all the arguments for changing to my format, more people started to listen. It took fourteen years to finish the work. Brian Smyth, the 1949 All-Ireland winning Meath captain, who was Meath county chairman at the time and Liam O'Craobhain, the County Secretary, must take a lot of the credit for the success of this venture, for had they not been so understanding and encouraging, the work would have been discarded. The motions were passed at the Meath Convention but were rejected by the Congress vetting committee in 1985. Five years later, the motions again passed in Meath, but not without serious objections and even some ridicule from senior delegates. This time they got on the Congress Agenda and the rest is history. We now have a completely new format for presenting the rules of football and hurling and defined terms are now part of the rules. The committee comprised the President, Peter Quinn, Director-General, Liam Mulvihill, Cork County Secretary, Frank Murphy, Down's Central Council delegate, Dan McCartan, referee Paddy Collins of Westmeath and former Galway hurling captain, Joe Connolly. I will never forget the fantastic commitment and stamina, particularly of Frank Murphy, Dan McCartan and Paddy Collins. This led to final acceptance at a Special Congress in Croke Park in December 1990'.

Joe Lennon is in no doubt that his work on the GAA playing rules is the most important thing he has ever done or achieved in Gaelic games and, possibly, in any other field.

Seán O'Neill and John Purdy of Down challenging Mick O'Connell in the 1968 final. Referee Dr Michael Loftus watches.

His new book, *Gaelic Football Rules OK?* is the story of how he got the rules re-drafted. It also deals with the philosophy of legislation, the characteristics of rules, the principles of play and the function of the rules. The second side of the title deals with the arguments for keeping Gaelic football as part of our national culture and condemns the attempt to make it akin to Australian Rules. His soon-to-be-released video deals with how Gaelic games can be used as a class subject at school rather than just an after-school game. The ever-enthusiastic and forward-thinking Joe has lost count of the number of coaching courses he has worked on and articles penned on the merits of coaching. One paper that stands out in his memory was titled, 'Counsel for the Defence', which Joe read at the first and only coaching conference held in Croke Park.

'This paper drew attention to the fact that the tackle is perhaps the most important but most maligned skill in Gaelic football.'

Joe Lennon has strong views on how the GAA should run its affairs. For instance he advocates that a reasonable percentage of the association's income should be devoted to research and development of the games and to the coaching and management of players. Our universities, he suggests, should treat games as important sociological phenomena and, as such, should invite and direct students to study and research them as part of their academic work.

At primary school level, he would like to see much less emphasis on championship-style competition and much more on skill development and league competitions. At secondary school level, he urges that all our games, handball, football and hurling are each played in each term.

In fact he says that as our games 'are important parts of our national heritage, an important national asset', they should be treated with respect and care and that 'any official of the GAA who promotes the idea of changing Gaelic football into a hybrid game — part Australian Rules, part Gaelic football — is in my view guilty of a most serious cultural crime. Our national games should not be tampered with to facilitate internationalism.'

Joe thinks that the influence of television and radio on our games can be very beneficial, if commentators are honest and knowledgeable. Television, in particular, has the power to eliminate much if not most of any dirty play or misconduct by exposing it, he argues, and the media generally should take on the legitimate role of educating as well as entertaining their audiences.

Joe Lennon was the third man to bring the Sam Maguire Cup across the border and these days as a faithful Down follower, he would love to see it make many more visits to the Mourne county.

Peter DARBY

Meath Captain 1967

Pᴇᴛᴇʀ Dᴀʀʙʏ captained Meath when they won their third All-Ireland Senior Football title in 1967 even though his club, Trim, were not the reigning county champions. He was given the honour as the most senior member of the team.

'Gaeil Colm Cille of Kells won the County Championship that year and in Meath it was traditional that the champions supplied the captain if there was a member on the county team. Kells didn't have any player on the team, so I was elected and it really was a great honour.'

The following month, Peter was captain again when the Meath team played the visiting Australian Rules side in Croke Park. Well over twenty thousand attended the game which the men from 'Down Under' won handsomely. But, therein lies a tale!

'There was great talk about these wonderful athletes from Australia and that we Gaelic footballers would never stand up to them, but in actual fact we went easy enough on them in the first half of that game. They had played one or two practice matches and Peter McDermott wasn't at all impressed with them and advised us to "go handy on them". We went out and took things casually enough and even though the Australians led by about eight points at half time, we went out in the second half confident of beating them. But, we couldn't do it. They had their tails up and there was no way we could stop them. It taught us the lesson that you should never take anything for granted.'

Peter McDermott himself in his book *Gaels in the Sun* admits he understimated the challenge posed by the Aussies.

'Perhaps, I leaned over backwards in trying to help the Australians and perhaps it led me to making the greatest underestimation of my life when I advised the Meath team, before they trotted onto the Croke Park pitch to meet the visitors, that the Aussies were only moderate footballers, at least at Gaelic. My advice was that the

---

FACT FILE

HOME PLACE: Stonehall, Trim, County Meath

BORN: 22 September 1938

CLUB: Trim

ACHIEVEMENTS IN CLUB COMPETITIONS: One Senior Football Championship medal in 1962; five Senior Hurling Championship medals; two Minor Hurling Championship medals; one Minor Football Championship medal; numerous Feis Cup in hurling and one in football.

INTER-COUNTY ACHIEVEMENTS: One All-Ireland Senior Football medal in 1967; runners-up in the 1966 All-Ireland Championship; three Leinster Senior Football Championship medals in 1964, 1966 and 1967; one O'Byrne Cup medal in 1967; one National League Division 2 Hurling medal in 1962; won Wembley Football Tournament against Galway in 1965; chosen at left-full-back on Sárpheileadóir CLG in 1964 and 1966 (before All Stars)

Meath boys should take things easy and not pile it on too much. I particularly asked them not to adopt any strenuous tackling since the Australians were on a world tour and did not want their enjoyment spoiled by having to have medical treatment or even undergo a period of hospitalisation. Who would blame me blushing a brilliant red as the match progressed and I found that we had all been wrong-footed by the brilliance of the performance served up by the Australians, who took full advantage of our early complacency. At the end of a humiliating hour, the visitors emerged victorious by 3-16 to 0-10.'

But, as Peter Darby explains, that humiliating experience in Croke Park was not in vain and Meath were much better prepared when they toured Australia in 1968.

'We played five games in Australia and won them all. It was a wonderful occasion and something I'll never forget. Before we played our first match against Western Australia, we went to a pub in Perth and the barman introduced us as the Irish fellas, who are playing Western Australia. The men in the bar sized us up for a moment and then said: "they'll eat yez". Some of us were fairly small and most of the Aussies would be well over six feet. They played all-attacking football, rugby style, which meant that the whole team would charge down the field with the ball. We backed with them and whenever they slipped up, we immediately kicked the ball up to our loose man. It worked out very well.'

> 'It's as if teams of accountants are running the organisation at the moment. We're getting away from the original ideals of the GAA which were to foster the games. I think it's wrong that many former inter-county players can't get tickets for the All-Ireland finals.'

The now famous tour would have ended tragically in Singapore had it not been for the quick actions of a Danish tourist.

'Kevin McConnell got into some difficulty at the deep end of the swimming pool and shouted for assistance. There was a bit of commotion and people went down towards Kevin to help him out. Jimmy Walsh and Paddy Cromwell were at the shallow end of the pool and started to walk towards Kevin to see what was happening, but they slipped in the part where the pool began to get deep and landed on their backs at the bottom. Luckily, a man from Denmark saw what happened and dived in and brought them to the surface. I was walking from the hotel over to the pool at the time and I saw this fellow dragging the two boys from the pool. At first, I thought they were messing, until I saw that Jimmy Walsh's face was completely black. I remember pulling the two boys up and the man from Denmark turned Paddy over and told me to start "pumping" him. I had never done anything like that before and I remember pushing Paddy and all the water started to gush out. He was working on Jimmy at the same time. It was a desperately close call and even to this day Jimmy will tell you that he heard the music.'

Peter Darby was captain during that historic trip to Australia. He was amazed at the importance placed on his role by the hosts.

'It doesn't really mean that much to be captain of a football team in Ireland in the sense that one is rarely called upon to do extra duties. But out in Australia, they treated me the same as if I was a rugby captain and had all the say. There was a reception at every airport and Peter McDermott, Fr Tully and myself had to talk to everyone. They made a big thing out of the captaincy which was something I never put any emphasis on. The games went very well and it was the best and most enjoyable trip of my life.'

No matter where Peter goes, people still come up to him to chat about football and the deeds of the 'Red' Collier, Jack Quinn, Ollie Shanley and all the others who wore the green and gold of Meath with such pride and distinction in the Sixties.

Meath lost the 1966 All-Ireland by six points to the Galway three-in-a-row team and were given such a wonderful reception by their followers in defeat that, to a man, they vowed to sacrifice all to win the 1967 All-Ireland.

Meath began their campaign with comprehensive victories over Louth and Westmeath, before struggling to beat Offaly in the Leinster final by two points.

'It was easily the hardest game I played in that series and would have to be one of the most difficult I ever played. Offaly threw everything at us in the last fifteen minutes and it was the only time I ever felt such constant pressure. I was just hoping it would ease off, but it didn't happen as they continually kept kicking in the ball and put enormous pressure on our back line.'

Victory over Mayo in the All-Ireland semi-final by six points and Meath were back in Croke Park on All-Ireland day for the second year in succession. Big crowds turned up to all their training sessions in the run-up to the final, an aspect Peter enjoyed. It always surprised him to see so many in Páirc Tailteann just to watch the players training. He was one of the lucky ones in that he never suffered any pre-match nerves. He never looked at a newspaper before a match and would have been hard pressed to know the name of his direct opponent.

'It was probably too casual an approach, but that is the way I was. We travelled up to Dublin the morning of the final and stayed in Barry's Hotel. We walked down to the pitch and it was a nice feeling just to mingle with the crowds. It was great to hear their comments about the game and the various players. From the very beginning of the year, I felt we could win the championship, having been there before. It was a great honour to be captain but it didn't affect my game or my thinking in any way. I remember telling the players before the game to give it everything as we might never have the same chance again.'

Meath playing against a stiff breeze scored just one point in the first half and trailed by three points at the interval. Cork had the better of the exchanges but missed a number of good scoring chances.

'Although I would be the kind of fellow who would have always maintained: "you haven't got it won, until the final whistle blows", funnily enough that day, I felt at half time that if we were any good we'd win. We picked off some good scores in

---

THE 1967 MEATH TEAM

Seán McCormack

Mick White	Jack Quinn	Peter Darby (Captain)
'Red' Pat Collier	Bertie Cunningham	Pat Reynolds
Peter Moore		Terry Kearns
Tony Brennan	Matt Kerrigan	Mick Mellett
Paddy Mulvaney	Noel Curran	Ollie Shanley

the second half and Terry Kearns got the only goal of the game. We won it by 1-9 to 0-9.'

With just three minutes of the game remaining, Peter twisted his knee and felt sure he would have to go off. But the pain disappeared very quickly and in the time it would take to say, 'Sam Maguire', Trim's Peter Darby had become an All-Ireland winning captain. He was one of the last of the Meath players to make it to the Hogan Stand, as thousands rushed onto Croke Park to offer their congratulations. The journey home was a memorable one with tens of thousands lining the route.

'Everybody wanted to fill the Cup and I remember leaving Clonee with it overflowing with whiskey. I thought it was a terrible waste as you had to dump it out before arriving in the next town.'

But the man who rarely lost possession on the field almost created history as the man who lost the Cup. Peter Darby will never forget the night the 'Sam' went missing.

'There was a victory dance in Trim and the Cup was on display during the night. After the dance, I was on my way out the door when some young fellow asked if he could hold the Cup. He hardly had a hold of it when a much bigger fellow ran in and snatched it from him and ran away with the Cup on his head. He ran out of the hall and down the street. At this stage I didn't pass much heed on things as everyone was in good spirits, but after about five minutes I began to worry a little. Then someone came running back to the hall and said that someone was after throwing the Cup into the river Boyne. When it failed to surface I rang the guards to notify them. I waited around for about two hours, but had to drive back to Dublin without the Cup.

'What happened was that someone from a neighbouring club wanted to have their share of the celebrations and decided to bring the "Sam" home to their little village. It was all done in jest and by all accounts everyone enjoyed themselves. The cup was retrieved the next day. Somebody rang the papers the night it went missing and the next morning the headlines in the newspaper read, "Sam Maguire Cup Stolen".'

Back, left to right: Bertie Cunningham, Paddy Mulvaney, Noel Curran, Peter Moore, Jack Quinn, Matt Kerrigan, Ollie Shanley, Pat Reynolds.
Front, left to right: Tony Brennan, Terry Kearns, Peter Darby (captain), Seán McCormack, Mick White, 'Red' Pat Collier, Mick Mellett.

Peter Darby recalls the excitement in the county when his boyhood heroes, Brian Smyth's 'fortyniners', won the All-Ireland title. One of his abiding memories is watching his father climb up on a large tree to place a Meath flag on top of it. His father had a great influence on his career.

'He was a very fair-minded man and would never condone rough or tough play and if I ever retaliated he would always say: "you shouldn't do that". One of the things I'm most proud of is the fact that in ten years playing inter-county football and hurling I was never sent off. I had my name taken once only and that was for dissent. I had the habit of tapping the ball down to lift it and on one occasion Brian Smyth, the referee, reckoned I picked it off the ground. I disagreed and he put my name in the book.'

Nowadays Peter Darby is very involved in golf, which he took up in 1967. He plays whenever he gets time and is an eight handicapper.

'I joined the Royal Tara in 1967 and moved to Trim Golf Club when it was formed in 1969. I became Honorary Treasurer of the club in 1976 for three years. I was captain in 1979 and have held the position of Honorary Secretary since 1981. I am also a Trustee. Apart from my involvement with golf, I play badminton during the winter. I am interested in all sports and attend all inter-county games. I like to go to the odd race meeting and watch most sports on television. I have never been to a soccer or rugby match in my life, for no particular reason other than I never seemed to have time. I'll go yet.'

He thinks there is too much emphasis on making money in the GAA

'It's as if teams of accountants are running the organisation at the moment. We're getting away from the original ideals of the GAA which was to foster the games. I think it's wrong that many former inter-county players can't get tickets for the All-Ireland Finals. I was on the Hogan Stand for the 1992 final and there was no atmosphere at all. You certainly wouldn't think you were at an All-Ireland Final as most of them were dignitaries of one kind or another. There was a mass of flags and colours right around the rest of the ground, but that type of atmosphere was missing in the best position in Croke Park.'

All-Ireland action on the goal line, 1965

Enda Colleran strikes

Enda COLLERAN

Galway Captain 1965 and 1966

O**F ALL THE GREAT PLAYERS**, many of them household names, who have played in the right corner back position in Gaelic football, Enda Colleran from the north County Galway village of Moylough was the one chosen to don the number two jersey on the 'Team of the Century'.

A most intelligent and skilful right-full-back, Enda played elsewhere when called upon and turned in many memorable displays at centre-half-back for Galway and at midfield for his club.

From his earliest days, Enda Colleran was football crazy and never remembers a time when he wasn't kicking a ball. Second youngest in a family of six — his father was a farmer and his mother a National School teacher — Enda from a very young age began showing the promise that would eventually bring him to the very top in his chosen sport.

Enda has very fond memories of his days growing up on the family farm in Moylough and recalls bringing the football to practise solo running when he was herding cattle. Some time after he had won an All-Ireland Minor medal in 1960, Enda was at his brother's wedding and met his football hero, Seán Purcell. He told Enda that he had the ability to become a good inter-county footballer, provided he was prepared to train hard and work at his game. It was just the encouragement Enda needed and for the next nine months he trained every day on his own in a big field near his home.

'I ran laps of the field first and would then do sprints up a hill and down again which meant I was very fit by the time spring came. I played really well in two trials for Galway junior football team, but when the team to play Sligo in the first round of the championship was selected, I was only a substitute. I was bitterly disappointed.'

FACT FILE

HOME PLACE: Moylough in the parish of Mountbellew, County Galway

BORN: 2 May 1942　　　　　　　　CLUBS: Mountbellew; UCG; Renmore.

ACHIEVEMENTS IN CLUB COMPETITIONS: Two County Senior Championship medals with Mountbellew in 1964 and 1965; one Connacht Senior Club Championship medal in 1965; won a County Juvenile League and Championship medal in 1956; one County Junior Championship medal in 1964; won a Connacht Junior medal with St Jarlath's, Tuam in 1959; one Connacht Senior Colleges medal in 1960; one All-Ireland Colleges medal in 1960; two Sigerson Cup medals with UCG and one County League medal; played for the Combined Universities against the Rest of Ireland and against Galway.

INTER-COUNTY ACHIEVEMENTS: Won three All-Ireland Senior medals in 1964, 1965, 1966; one All-Ireland Minor medal in 1960; one National League medal in 1965; one Railway Cup medal with Connacht in 1967.

He remembers getting a message from John Dunne, who was then the 'Supreme Authority' in Galway football, requesting him to be ready at his home in Moylough at noon on the day of the game.

'When he arrived to collect me, I told him I was not going to the match, as I thought that I should have been selected on the team. He was very annoyed. Galway beat Sligo that day and when the team to play Mayo in the Connacht Final was announced I was named at right-full-back. We went on to beat Mayo and were narrowly defeated in the All-Ireland Final by Louth. I believe John Dunne respected me for the stance I took and I think the proof of it was when he selected me on the

Back, left to right: Séamus Leyden, Noel Tierney, John Bosco McDermott, Tom Sands, Seán Meade, Mattie McDonagh, Mick Garrett, Mick Reynolds, Jimmy Glynn, Frank Canavan.
Front, left to right: Greg Higgins, Martin Newell, John Donnellan, Seán Cleary, Cyril Dunne, Christy Tyrrell, Enda Colleran, Brian Geraghty, Tommy Keenan, Johnny Geraghty, Pat Donnellan.

Back, left to right: Séamus Leyden, Noel Tierney, Mick Reynolds, Mattie McDonagh, Seán Meade, Liam Sammon, John Keenan, Frank McLoughlin, Tom Sands, John Bosco McDermott.
Front, left to right: Seán Cleary, Colie McDonagh, Cyril Dunne, Martin Newell, Enda Colleran, Jimmy Duggan, Pat Donnellan, John Donnellan, Christy Tyrrell, Johnny Geraghty

team to play Mayo. When my older brothers heard that I had refused to travel for the Sligo game, they thought I would never be selected for Galway again.'

There was always a great sporting tradition in the Colleran family and Enda emulated his older brothers, Gerry, Séamus and Fr Gabriel by making the county senior team in 1961. He commanded a regular place until he retired nine years later at the relatively young age of twenty-eight.

Football fortunes west of the Shannon have taken a nose-dive since Enda Colleran held the Sam Maguire Cup aloft on the Hogan Stand in 1966. He is not just the last Galway player, but also the last Connacht man to captain an All-Ireland winning football team. Since the glorious sixties, Galway teams have suffered one setback after another in search of an All-Ireland title. Why?

'It's difficult to pinpoint really, but as far as my own county is concerned they got to a few All-Ireland Finals in the seventies and the eighties and lost them. I think the big mistake was that after we had won three All-Irelands Galway people in general thought the All-Irelands would keep coming. I think this philosophy seeped through to the players as well. I really think the players underestimated the work that has to go into winning an All-Ireland. After losing one or two finals, the loser's mentality crept in and when things were going against them, instead of saying: "if we pull ourselves together, we can win this one", they were inclined to say: "look it's the same old thing again, another hard luck story".'

Enda Colleran knows better than most about that effort. When his club, Mountbellew, won the Galway Championship in 1965 he was chosen to captain the Galway side. There was an unwritten rule in Galway that the captain should come from the county champions.

'I remember at the start of the year thinking of the huge responsibility I was taking on and wondering how it was going to affect my game. Am I going to be too nervous, taking on too much and play badly, or is this going to encourage me and make me play better? I really thought about it and was worried about how the captaincy was

---

THE 1965 GALWAY TEAM

Johnny Geraghty

| Enda Colleran (Captain) | Noel Tierney | John Bosco McDermott |
| John Donnellan | Seán Meade | Martin Newell |

Pat Donnellan   Mick Garrett

| Cyril Dunne | Mattie McDonagh | Séamus Leyden |
| Christy Tyrrell | Seán Cleary | John Keenan |

Substitute: Mick Reynolds for John Keenan

THE 1966 TEAM

Johnny Geraghty

| Enda Colleran (Captain) | Noel Tierney | John Bosco McDermott |
| Colie McDonagh | Seán Meade | Martin Newell |

Jimmy Duggan   Pat Donnellan

| Cyril Dunne | Mattie McDonagh | Séamus Leyden |
| Liam Sammon | Seán Cleary | John Keenan |

Substitute: John Donnellan for Seán Meade

---

going to affect me. I was taking over from John Donnellan, a really great captain, there's no doubt about that. He was an inspiration and led by example. I remember thinking that there were other people on that team who should be captain before me. I looked to Mattie McDonagh, because he was a father-figure, who had won an All-Ireland medal in 1956 and said to myself: "he really should be captain and if I don't perform, I'm going to feel very badly about it". I analysed my performances after a few games and came to the conclusion that I had performed better when I was captain than before I took over the role. That gave me confidence and I was happy with the job after that.'

He remembers the 1965 Championship very well and admits that Galway were extremely fortunate not to have lost their Connacht crown.

'We should have been beaten twice — by Sligo and by Mayo. They had it on both occasions if they kept their heads. They really had. I remember playing against Mayo and they were a point up with a few minutes to go when they got a fifty. Three Mayo players wanted to take the kick. Between them, they couldn't agree and one player went to take it hurriedly and kicked it straight to one of our half-backs! He kicked it up the field and we got the equalising point. And then we got the winning point just after that. Mayo should have won that game, they were all over us. It's amazing how a small little incident like that can decide the destination of the All-Ireland.

'Sligo got two early goals and we really were in terrible trouble and we just came back to win it by three points. They looked like two games that we should have lost. But I always believe, if you are to win an All-Ireland, you have to get through one or two games playing badly.'

Losing in a major championship can be a bad experience and Enda recalls his feelings after Galway's loss to Dublin in the 1963 Final.

'There's no place for losers and when the final whistle blows, the supporters of the winning team, in their elation, just run through the beaten team. For that reason, I believe that the losing team should also be brought to the rostrum and honoured in some way.'

One special moment during the 1965 All-Ireland Semi-Final against Down stands out particularly in Enda's mind.

'Seán O'Neill had the ball around midfield and Paddy Doherty, completely unmarked, came at speed to the full-forward position. I had two options: one was to stay on my own man and the other was that Seán O'Neill would pass the ball to Paddy Doherty. I took the chance and ran for Paddy Doherty and Seán O'Neill passed the ball to him and I actually remember coming behind Paddy trying not to make any noise, so that he wouldn't hear me coming towards him and at the last second I nipped in front of him and got possession. I felt he had a certain goal, only for that. It's amazing with sixty thousand people present, that I still thought my approach had to be as quiet as possible!'

Nearly every player at some time or other has a game when everything seems to go just right. Enda had that kind of game against Down in '65. He himself believes it was the best game he ever played.

'I had a terrible start to that game. I was marking Brian Johnson and he scored two points off me in the first six minutes. I said to myself: "if I don't do something he's going to be the man of the match and he's going to have scored about twelve points by the time this game has ended." So I reassessed the situation and changed my

tactics. Down were storming our goal for all of the second half and I found that no matter where I went, the ball seemed to fall into my hands. I seemed to be in the right place all the time and made all the right decisions. Often I took terrible chances and went forward and left my man and still the ball came to me. I was so thankful that a thing like that did happen to me in an All-Ireland semi-final in Croke Park rather than in some isolated place. I was very, very lucky that a thing like that happened to me on an important day.'

As soon as any team wins an All-Ireland semi-final the county becomes alive with excitement. It was no different in Galway. Hopes were high of completing the double and the team was confident that victory would be achieved.

'Kerry had a fine team, but their forward line contained four players who had previously played in defence and we reckoned that they couldn't be a very slick forward line because of that. They had a very strong team of good footballers but I think they made the mistake of trying to put square pegs in round holes, in the sense that they picked probably their best footballers, but you had four of them in the forward line, playing out of position. I can remember quite a bit about the game. It was very tough as Kerry had a very strong physical team, as well as being good footballers, and they went out with a very positive attitude, determined to win the game at all costs. They tried very, very hard and hit us with everything and, in fact, Mattie McDonagh was concussed during the game, but he played on. They really hit us very hard, but they hit us fair and were very, very difficult opponents. Indeed, J.J.

Barrett, whom I was marking, had an excellent chance of a goal in the second half, but Johnny Geraghty brought off a marvellous save and deflected it around the post.'

The build-up to the 1965 All-Ireland final made more of an impression on Enda than the game itself. The team travelled to Dublin on the day before the final and stayed in a hotel in Malahide.

'It was an anxious time, worrying whether you'd sleep or not, worrying would you wake up in the morning sick, and not be able to play, or something like that, after all the preparation. Then you get up in the morning and you think about what you are going to eat and all that kind of thing. Everything is of vital importance to you. Then all of a sudden, it's time to get on the bus to go into the All-Ireland. That's when the butterflies really hit you. You get on this bus and you're travelling and you see all the traffic going to the match. And then you arrive in Croke Park. We used to come in the back way by Hill 16 and the minor match would already be on and you'd hear the cheering and you would be absolutely terrified. The feeling is frightening. You'd say to yourself: "I won't be able to handle all this". You'd go to the dressingroom then and you'd take out the togs and the boots, which would be beautifully polished and you'd put on those in two minutes, as if your life depended on it. All of a sudden, you'd find yourself with an awful lot of time on your hands and you're wondering: "how do the feet feel in the boots? are they comfortable?" Every little thing is of the utmost importance and you're there with everything ready and nobody to talk to, because you don't feel like talking anyway. You're just looking around and you see everybody else just as nervous, if not more nervous, than yourself.

'As the time approaches a steward would come and knock on the dressing-room door and shout "five minutes" or "ten minutes". Then the team manager would start revving up the team and at that stage there was a lot of shouting, because John Dunne, our team manager, liked to shout. Then the most frightening aspect of the whole lot is coming out the dark tunnel. All of a sudden you hit reality and the cheer goes up and that is enough to frighten the wits out of you. I would compare myself to a frightened rabbit looking for somewhere to run. In fact, I remember the terrible thought striking me: "I wonder did anyone ever collapse in a parade". My knees were shaking during the National Anthem, but I looked at my opponent and I also saw that his knees were shaking. So that was enough for me. I was satisfied then.

'But it is a most terrifying experience. You run around and you say: "I feel great", but when you're nervous, you never feel great. There's always a question mark hanging over you in that sense. Then the photographs and then the parade, which is a terrible thing, really. The parade is awful. I mean, it's a nice spectacle and everything like that, but for players to be subjected to it, it's very demanding. It really is. You're all geared up for action straight away and then you have to do this. The nice thing about the parade is that you know where your family are in the stand and you would always see them. That's a nice thing about it.'

At the sound of the final whistle there is a wonderful realisation that you are All-Ireland Champions. But it also has its drawbacks.

'It's a very, very happy occasion, but you are really man-handled and it's a little bit frightening, as you're lifted a lot. There are people pulling the Cup in all directions, as everybody wants to get hold of it and touch it, and maybe have it for themselves for a moment. It is a tough ordeal, no doubt about it, but anyone would be willing to suffer it.'

Enda is of the opinion that everybody has a speech prepared beforehand. On the second occasion as captain, Enda had just completed his BA and decided to make a conscious effort to have a good part of the speech in Irish to impress his Professor! There was mayhem in the dressing-room in 1965 when Enda finally arrived with the cup. And if one moment transcended all others for the captain it was the sight of life-long Galway supporter, Grellan Deeley crying his heart out.

'Grellan came to all our matches and he'd always be in the dressing-room afterwards because he was a friend of John Dunne. If we won the important matches he was crying with joy, and if we lost, he was crying with sadness. He cried bitterly after the 1963 loss to Dublin and there were tears of joy after we won in 1964, '65 and '66. He was a marvellous guy and great friends with everyone. His heart was in it.'

The homecoming 'West of the Shannon' made a big impresion on the team. Bonfires blazed everywhere and even though the players were tired after their exertions, they enjoyed the experience immensely. Enda left the coach in Moylough and remembers attending a carnival dance in Newbridge, County Galway, where the entertainer for the night was well-known accordionist and singer Dermot O'Brien, the 1957 All-Ireland winning Louth captain.

> 'The most frightening aspect of the whole lot is coming out the dark tunnel. All of a sudden you hit reality and the cheer goes up and that is enough to frighten the wits out of you. I would compare myself to a frightened rabbit looking for somewhere to run.'

A year later, Enda was captain again when Galway beat Meath.

'I think the big thing for 1966 was our great experience. Meath won their semi-final against Down by a margin of ten points and they looked firm favourites for the Final, but we knew in our hearts that they weren't. Anywhere a Meath forward took a shot from in the semi-final, it went over the bar. They gave a magnificent display of long-range point scoring. We knew they couldn't strike that form the very next time and also we were forewarned. Our back-line knew we would have a fierce task to hold their forwards. We approached it with such determination and such zeal that they didn't get their opening point until the twenty-second minute of the game. We were very determined to close them down and not to give them any shot at goal and we were even very disappointed when they did get the opening point.'

In the build-up to the final itself, Enda felt under more pressure than at any other time in his football career, as he was due to mark Ollie Shanley, then Garda one-hundred metres champion. Ollie was a tremendous athlete and he had had a magnificent game in the semi-final.

'Everybody in Galway was saying to me: "you've an awful job in the final to mark him, you'll never mark him". Martin Newell and I went out to the Aran Islands for a few days, just before we started training for the All-Ireland final and were sleeping in the one room; he was on one side and I on the other. He woke up at one stage of the night and I was standing over him. I was sleep walking! He told me the next day that I said: "By Jesus, if I can keep up with Shanley, I'll mark him". It just shows you the effect it had on me!'

On the day he was very happy with his own performance, but admits that the

Enda Colleran (right), challenged by J.J. Barrett and Mick O'Dwyer

1965 final was the sweeter victory as it had been his first as captain.

In the middle of our conversation Enda suddenly remembers something: it was the day Galway played Dublin at Wembley.

'There was a little bit of rivalry between the teams at that time and as the game was being televised in England, Seán Ó'Síocháin came into both dressing-rooms and said something like: "The honour and glory of the GAA is at stake on this particular day and everyone should behave themselves and be very sporting as it is going to be a shop window for our game". So we all went out with the best of intentions, but the game got rather heated and at one stage, our centre-half-back, Sean Meade accidentally collided with Lar Foley. And, I mean colliding with Lar was like colliding with a mountain. Lar immediately pulled himself together and got to grips with Sean Meade and was about to exert pressure on him when Seán quick as flash said: "The cameras are on you, the cameras are on you". And Lar dropped his hands by his side and walked away!'

A delicate moment in an otherwise serious game.

After he had officially retired from the game, Enda was instrumental in founding the Renmore club. His former Galway team mates, Martin Newell and Christy Tyrell also played with Renmore.

What were the qualities that made the three-in-a-row Galway team of the sixties so very special?

'One thing that made them All-Ireland winners is that individually they were all great players and most of them could play in nearly any position on a team. In fact, they all played midfield for their clubs and I think if you can play at midfield, then you can play in any other position. They were very talented and established a great relationship between themselves.

'We won an awful lot of games by coming from behind in the last minute or two and I think that the team possessed something special. When it comes to a close finish, a good team will say to itself: "look, if we can step up a gear, this game is there for the winning". Our fellows did that, whereas other teams would say: "Oh God, we're in trouble and we mightn't just make it". Lots of matches, that we should have lost, we won, and I think that it was our approach. It came from the unity of the team to a great extent. And the most amazing thing about it is that the friendship is still there. We all meet and play golf together, some twenty-five years afterwards.'

When his football career ended, Enda found another outlet for his energies. At the suggestion of Martin Newell, he began training with Corinthians Rugby Football Club as a way of keeping fit. At that stage, he had never even taken a rugby ball in his hands.

'I enjoyed the training immensely and after a while we were approached to play in the Thirds. The next week we were asked to play in the Seconds and a short time later, we made it to the First team. Our arrival coincided with a revival in the First team and we were lucky enough to be there when Corinthians won the Connacht League and Cup. We had the pleasure of playing against many international players and I got great satisfaction playing against Wanderers at Lansdowne Road and scoring twelve points. Kevin Flynn was at outhalf for Wanderers and Paul McNaughton was in the centre. I usually played at full-back and I found that the handling and kicking skills acquired from the Gaelic were invaluable. It is also much easier to kick a rugby ball off the ground than a Gaelic ball. The rugby ball sits up and you can really hit it. I was entrusted with the penalty kicks and I ended up top scorer for Corinthians. Rugby is a player's game and I did not realise that it was so enjoyable to play until I tried it.'

John DONNELLAN

Galway Captain 1964

JOHN DONNELLAN was an inspirational and confident captain when Galway captured their fifth All-Ireland title in 1964 with a five points win over Kerry. His greatest moment of triumph — hoisting the Sam Maguire Cup — was shortlived as moments later he was called aside to be told the tragic news that his father, Mick, had died in the Hogan Stand just before the start of the second half. Mick Donnellan, himself, had won an All-Ireland medal in 1925. That Galway team were declared champions after defeating Mayo in the Connacht final. He also captained Connacht to their first Railway Cup success with victory over Leinster in 1934 and was a very popular Dáil Deputy for many years. John was later to follow his father into politics becoming Minister of State from 1982-1987 in the Departments of Transport & Posts & Telegraphs, Health & Social Welfare and Forestry & Fisheries.

The 1964 final will also be remembered as the day another footballing great, Mick Higgins, captain of the Galway team that beat Dublin in the 1934 final, died while watching the game at his home in Galway.

John Donnellan was again back in Croke Park in 1965 when Galway, this time under the captaincy of Enda Colleran, once more saw off the challenge of Kerry thus becoming the only team to beat the Kingdom in two successive finals. But unfortunately ten minutes from the end following a flare up, the Dunmore man and his direct opponent Derry O'Shea were ordered to the line by referee Mick Loftus.

John Donnellan won his third All-Ireland medal in 1966 when he replaced Sean Meade in the closing stages of the final against Meath.

His name is synonymous with the most successful period ever in Galway football when the county won three All-Ireland titles in a row. A supremely confident wing back, John was marking the great Mick O'Connell in the 1964 decider and played more than a captain's part in Galway's first All-Ireland success in eight years. Mick O'Connell was moved to centrefield late in the first half as Kerry endeavoured to break the dominance of the Connacht champions. But it was not to be Kerry's day and Galway won with five points to spare.

FACT FILE

HOME PLACE: Dunmore, County Galway

BORN: 27 March 1937   CLUBS: Dunmore McHales; Carantryla

ACHIEVEMENTS IN CLUB COMPETITIONS: Five County Senior Football Championship medals 1961, 1963, 1966, 1968 and 1969; two County League medals in 1962 and 1966. three Connacht Club Championship medals in 1963, 1968 and 1969.

INTER-COUNTY ACHIEVEMENTS: Three All-Ireland Senior Football medals in 1964, 1965 and 1966; six Connacht Senior Football medals in 1960, 1963, 1964, 1965, 1966 and 1968; one All-Ireland Junior Football medal in 1958; one Railway Cup Football medal in 1967.

North Galway is the heartland of football in the county and backboned by inter-county stars John and Pat Donnellan, Tommy and John Keenan, Seamus Leyden and present Galway team manager John Bosco McDermott, the Dunmore McHales club won five senior county championships in the sixties. John usually played centre-half-back for the club.

His football began with the Carantryla Club which was the rural area in the parish of Dunmore. There was keen rivalry over the years between Carantryla and Dunmore before the two teams were forced to amalgamate due to emigration.

His contemporaries agree that John Donnellan never asked anything of his players on the field of play that he himself was not prepared to give many times over. He was a tenacious defender, very strong, fiercely committed and renowned for his long,

Front, left ot right: Martin Newell, Pat Donnellan, Christy Tyrell, Seán Cleary, John Donnellan (Captain), John Bosco McDermott, Johnny Geraghty, Cyril Dunne, Brian Geraghty, Tommy Kernan, Tom Sands.
Back, left to right: Séamus Leyden, Noel Tierney, Enda Colleran, Seán Meade, Mick Garrett, Mick Reynolds, Mick Coen, Mattie MacDonagh, Kieran O'Connor, John Keenan, Frank McLoughlin.

Goal action in the 1964 All-Ireland final.

well-directed clearances.

Social life in Dunmore in the forties, fifties and sixties centred around football and football only. It was from this background that John Donnellan emerged as one of the game's top defenders. I was greatly influenced by the Galway team of the sixties and recall as a youngster seeing them in action on numerous occasions. My own county, Roscommon, failed to win a Connacht championship from 1962 to 1972 and in that time Galway claimed three All-Ireland and seven provincial crowns. To every youngster like myself from opposing counties, that Galway team seemed always capable of coming from behind in the closing minutes to kick the winning score or snatch a draw. Impossible to overcome! Household names like John Bosco McDermott, Cyril Dunne, Seamus Leyden, Mattie McDonagh and other equally talented Galway footballers broke the hearts of Roscommon, Mayo, Sligo and Leitrim supporters on far too many occasions. However all of Connacht rallied behind the men in maroon and white once they had won their way to Croke Park. The West was fiercely proud and rightly so of the Galway three-in-a-row team.

For this book I have succeeded in interviewing every living captain from 1940 to 1993 — that is, except John Donnellan. It was disappointing for me not to secure an interview with him on this occasion. We'll have to settle for a draw this time round.

THE 1964 GALWAY TEAM

Johnny Geraghty

Enda Colleran	Noel Tierney	John Bosco McDermott
John Donnellan (captain)	Sean Meade	Martin Newell
Mick Garrett		Mick Reynolds
Cyril Dunne	Mattie McDonagh	Seamus Leyden
Christy Tyrell	Sean Cleary	John Keenan

Des FOLEY

Dublin Captain 1963

'My father was a soccer player and played for a time with Merville United. He later played with Bohemians. My eldest brother, Anthony, played League of Ireland with Dundalk and Bohemians. My mother had a great influence on us all and was continually worrying in case we'd get hurt. Imagine worrying whether Lar would get hurt! Everything had to be spotless and you always had to have new laces in your boots. She didn't go to many matches when we got older, but she listened carefully and was always interested in how we played. She would wait until one of us would be on our own and she'd say: "you were good today" and you'd have to say quietly: "well I wasn't that bad". And then she'd say "mind yourself". The interest was purely parental. My father was different. He didn't believe in losing. My memory of him is his intolerance of those who wouldn't make an effort. He made an effort himself always and expected others to do likewise. No matter what football had to be played, we always had to do the jobs about the house: feeding the hens and getting the sticks for the fire in the morning.'

A TRULY OUTSTANDING footballer and hurler, Des Foley was the first player to win Railway Cup medals in both codes on the same day. It was St Patrick's Day 1962 when Des lined out at midfield with fellow-Dubliner, Mick Kennedy, on the Leinster hurling team that beat Munster by two points and a short time later he held the same position, this time alongside Mick Carley of Westmeath, as Leinster defeated Ulster in the football decider.

It was one of the lucky things that happened to me during my career. People regard it as a fabulous achievement and perhaps it was, but at the time it didn't seem to be anything extraordinary. I could only do it because I had the fellows around me. I had a sore throat and a slight cold and I remember my mother giving me raw quinine and it was like eating seaweed. I never thought of the football game during

---

FACT FILE

HOME PLACE: Kinsealy, County Dublin

BORN: 12 Setember 1940   CLUB: St Vincent's, Dublin

ACHIEVEMENTS IN CLUB COMPETITIONS: Ten County Senior Championship Football medals in 1959, 1960, 1961, 1962, 1964, 1966, 1967, 1970, 1971 and 1972 and four County Senior Championship Hurling medals in 1960, 1962, 1964 and 1968; two County Minor Football and three Hurling medals.

INTER-COUNTY ACHIEVEMENTS: All-Ireland Senior Football Championship medal in 1963; two All-Ireland Minor Football medals in 1956 and 1958; one Railway Cup Football medal in 1962; three Railway Cup Hurling medals in 1962, 1964 and 1965; one National Football League 'Home Final' in 1964; selected on the Ireland hurling and football teams in 1962 and 1963.

---

the first match. Mick Kennedy had an absolute blinder that day. We had players with all the skills in the world. We were expected to win and we did. There was very little time between the hurling and the football so I had to race into the dressing-room for a quick wash. I then changed my togs and put on a new Leinster jersey and while I was doing all this the footballers were parading around the field. I didn't come onto the field until the game was ready to start. The first one to wish me luck was Seán O'Neill who was a marvellous intelligent footballer. There were some great footballers on that team, but no one paid much heed to me winning the two medals. The hurlers were delighted to win their medal and the footballers likewise. What happened in between was a bit insignificant as far as they were concerned.'

Des Foley was captain when Dublin minors won the All-Ireland football title in 1958 and five years later he achieved the same honour at senior grade, thus becoming the first player to captain minor and senior All-Ireland football teams.

'We were very lucky to win our first round game against Meath at Croke Park in 1963. We were a fairly good team and were expected to come through handily enough. The match was a draw. With very little time to go I caught a high ball in the middle of the field. I side-stepped a player and hopped the ball but was then tackled by two other players. When I got by them, I hopped the ball again and kicked it with my left foot from about fifty yards and it dropped over the bar. I hopped the ball twice and got away with it! We won the replay by a point. We played Kildare in the semi-final but I had to go off injured after only about a quarter of an hour of the game. I caught a high ball and fell over Mick Carolan and broke my wrist. I wasn't back for the Leinster Final and Lar [his brother] took over the captaincy. I was fit for the match against Down and that was the highlight of the championship. It was a great match and we played brilliantly. The final as a spectacle wasn't great. Galway were a little bit immature and we were a little bit lucky. But you need a bit of luck to win an All-Ireland. Galway struck the bar twice so we were very lucky. That was a very good Galway team, very well balanced.'

Back, left to right: John Timmons, Bill Casey, Mick Kissane, Lar Foley, Leo Hickey, Aiden Donnelly, Eamon Breslin, Paddy Downey, Sean Lee, Pascal Flynn, Christy Kane, Frank McPhillips, Brendan Quinn.
Front, left to right: Des McKane, Mickey Whelan, Paddy Holden, Noel Fox, Des Foley (captain), Gerry Davey, Brian McDonald, Simon Behan, Pat Synott, Des Ferguson, Sean Coen.

The championship season always coincided with the busiest time on the Foley family farm and Des remembers worrying in case he might injure himself pitching hay or doing other manual work. He now agrees that his preparation could not have been better. The fresh air and hard work combined to take his mind off the big game. He acknowledges the contribution of his neighbours and friends around Kinsealy in the build-up to the final.

'There was a tremendous atmosphere around the parish. At that time there was a group of fellows who would never miss a match no matter where we were playing. They were great football critics in the sense that they weren't very boisterous but if you listened to their opinions you'd find they were very solid. They were great judges of football and very loyal to Lar and myself. People would often joke about the "Dubs" being fed on chips and rashers but Kinsealy was more rural than some of wildest parts of Ireland. We didn't get electricity until the late-fifties and piped water wasn't installed until the sixties. Although we were adjacent to the city of Dublin we were still in the heart of the country. There's something very open and pleasant about a rural area and Kinsealy still has that.'

Des decided not to change his preparation for the biggest day of his sporting life. He always had the same routine for all games whether league or championship.

'I went to confession in Malahide on the Saturday evening and if I needed a haircut, I got one. I used to get my haircut nearly very week. My barber would say: "what do you want a hair cut for?", but I always felt these things had to be done before any match. I was always at home by a quarter past nine and usually went to bed around ten o'clock and would read for a while. I would cycle to eight o'clock Mass in Malahide on Sunday morning and then home for breakfast. Sometimes after eating I would go to bed and have a sleep. Before going to the game, I would wash myself in cold water. I did the exact same thing on the morning of the All-Ireland. I never changed my routine.'

He travelled in the family car to Croke Park and recalls Jones's Road teeming with Dublin followers. Even before the game, Des Foley never once doubted Dublin's ability to win. He just had a feeling that it was going to be the year of the 'Dubs'. How right he was! The Dublin team was accustomed to playing in Croke Park and Des recalls a 'nice atmosphere' in the dressing-room before the start.

'I sat inside the door on the left and Lar sat the other side of me. We all had our own places and if someone arrived late his position would never be taken. It was very important on All-Ireland day that everyone had their own special corner. Brendan Quinn gave the pep talk and everyone seemed in good form. There was a slight bit of nerves, but nothing serious.'

THE 1963 DUBLIN TEAM

	Pascal Flynn	
Leo Hickey	Lar Foley	Bill Casey
Des McKane	Paddy Holden	Mick Kissane
Des Foley (Captain)		John Timmons
Brian McDonald	Mickey Whelan	Gerry Davey
Simon Behan	Des Ferguson	Noel Fox
	Substitute: Paddy Downey for Paddy Holden	

Above: Des Foley parades his team behind the Artane Boys' Band, 1963

Above: Lar Foley in command against Galway 1963. *Below:* more action from the final.

In retrospect, Des felt that the whole atmosphere of the occasion went a little over his head. His only concern when he led Dublin onto the pitch was to get the game started as quickly as possible. It was all too intense and serious to really savour the occasion. Kevin Heffernan, then a selector, advised Des to take the advantage of the wind if he happened to win the toss. He knew the Galway team very well and felt Dublin had their measure. There were only two points between the sides and Des admits it was a very welcome relief to hear the sound of the final whistle.

'Galway were coming back at us at the end, and as we only had a slim lead it was always a case of every ball won being so important. I specifically remember winning a ball under the Hogan Stand with less than two minutes to go and looking for somebody and suddenly I saw Mickey Whelan running through about forty yards away. I remember giving it to him and thinking to myself: "Whelan, you've clinched this for us". I remember vividly Lar catching a "screecher" in the last few minutes. It was so important and those are the things that stand out most in my mind.'

> *'Suddenly I saw Mickey Whelan running through about forty yards away. I remember giving it to him and thinking to myself: "Whelan, you've clinched this for us".'*

While collecting the Sam Maguire Cup he began to pick out familiar faces in the sea of people down on the pitch. He saw a few of the players on the field and was worried in case some of them would not make the rostrum. He was greatly honoured to be captain but would have preferred if someone else had the task of receiving the Cup. When he eventually got down from the presentation area he was delighted to see a family friend, Wille Finn, who helped to get him back to the dressing-room through thousands of adoring Dublin supporters.

One of his abiding memories of the day was meeting his girl-friend, Rita Nugent, now his wife, outside Croke Park. Rita was there with life-long friends Mary Mullin, Mary Wright, Pauline Murphy and Maura Coll, all ardent Dublin followers who travelled all over Ireland to support the county team. He emphasises the importance of their loyalty and support in shaping a famous victory. Those friendships have lasted down through the years and for that he is deeply grateful.

He brought the Cup home to Kinsealy in the car, stopping to make short visits to the 'Refuge' in Donnycarney and Kyle's in Coolock. The Cup was on the sideboard at home by six o'clock that evening. Later that night he brought it to a celebration dinner dance. For weeks and months afterwards people came to the Foley home to take a look at the most famous of all Irish sporting trophies.

Des Foley found it much more pleasurable to play hurling than football and was continually honing his hurling skills and practising his frees using a knob on a door as a target. He regrets not winning an All-Ireland Hurling medal. He played at centre-field in the 1961 All-Ireland Final which Dublin lost by one point to Tipperary. It was bitterly disappointing.

Des enjoyed the sport and his memories include a clever trick during a league game against Laois. With just a few minutes remaining and trailing by two points, Dublin were awarded a fifty. 'John Timmons was playing in the middle of the field and he said he'd go into the square while I was lining up the kick. He told me to lob the ball in and I did just that but a Laois back caught it in the clouds. His way was blocked on the way out with the ball and John shouted and called him by name to pass the ball to him. And of course unknowingly the Laois back passed the ball to John and he stuck it in the net. John ran out and as he was passing by me he just tapped me and said: "you'd never have got away with that, you have to have a country accent"!

He believes that the GAA has its faults but prefers to offer advice rather than be too critical.

'There are enough people criticising the GAA from all quarters especially those outside it without me starting. They are not perfect. It is a tremendous organisation to survive as it does despite all the knockers. The system of refereeing needs to be cleared up. It's not that the referees are going out to be biased to one side or another. If you go to a Munster hurling final, the interpretation of the rules are different to that which pertains on All-Ireland day. It's a physical contact game and so long as it remains so, it should be played as such. It's getting to the situation now where the person who falls after a fair shoulder gets a free.

'I'm not altogether in favour of this new stadium. The GAA has fairly firm footings and should be happy to get seventy thousand at an All-Ireland Final in this present climate. I would prefer to spend the money on the promotion of the games among the clubs. There are many clubs struggling financially and yet they're catering for an enormous number of children and giving a great community service. We can build our big stadiums in our own time. I don't know in whose memory this stadium is going to be built, but if there is someone in Croke Park who wants to build a stadium in their own memory they should forget about it! Instead they should try to foster the game.'

Des Foley's greatest sporting disappointment was the All-Ireland Club Final of 1973 which St Vincent's lost in a replay to Nemo Rangers of Cork. Victory would have capped a magnificent career.

'I can remember both games very well. We were lucky to get a draw but we should have won the replay. It was a funny game. We were a better team than Nemo but we just didn't click on the day. Brian Mullins was playing at corner-forward and he was a big, long lanky young fellow. I remember on one particular occasion getting a ball about fifteen to twenty yards out and I turned and gave it to him real fast, but he fumbled it and we didn't get the goal we were looking for. He was only a "gasún", just after coming out of the minors. If it was five years later and I gave him that ball he would have put it in the back of the net, ball and goalkeeper. He went on to become one of the great midfielders of our time and a great Vincent's man. That particular Vincent's team of the "Heffo" era were all great club men which was a great tribute to them. They achieved everything and yet their home base, the club, was never forgotten.'

In truth of all the fine footballers and hurlers who wore the St Vincent's jersey, none was better that the great Des Foley himself.

Seán Óg SHEEHY

Kerry Captain 1962

WHEN Seán Óg Sheehy raised the Sam Maguire Cup aloft on the Hogan Stand in 1962 he was emulating his father, John Joe, who had captained Kerry to All-Ireland victory over Monaghan thirty-two years earlier.

The legendary John Joe was a double All-Ireland winning captain as he had previously led Kerry to victory over Kildare in 1926, two years before the Sam Maguire Cup was first presented.

The 1962 final was very much a Sheehy family affair. Seán Óg's two brothers, Niall and Paudie, were also on the Kerry team that defeated Gerry O'Malley's Roscommon by six points, 1-12 to 1-6 and their father was one of the selectors.

Nine years earlier the eldest of the Sheehy brothers, Paudie, began the the 1953 championship campaign as Kerry captain. He played brilliantly in the Munster final but failed to make an impression in the All-Ireland semi-final against Louth and was dropped. Jas Murphy took over the role of captain and Kerry defeated Armagh in the decider.

'I remember Paudie crying with disappointment at the function,' says Seán Óg. 'But he came back again and was captain in 1960 when Down beat Kerry. It was difficult for my father to be a selector. In a way I felt he probably did us a disservice because he wouldn't get involved in the selection of his sons. When they began discussing the idea of dropping Paudie in 1953, my father decided it would be unfair for him to get involved and left the meeting. If he had stayed, maybe Paudie could have been left on the team. His displays, apart from the semi-final, probably merited another chance.'

Brother Niall also captained Kerry in his time, but like Paudie, was on the losing side in the 1964 final when Galway won the first of three-in-a-row.

Seán Óg was disappointed with the 1962 All-Ireland final. He considers it to have been a very poor match. 'I remember getting into the car afterwards and my father was delighted that we won, but I found it difficult to get excited because the game had been so bad. Woeful is the only word for it.'

Seán Óg became captain because his club, John Mitchels, were county champions.

F A C T   F I L E

HOME PLACE: Cloonbeg Terrace, Tralee, County Kerry

BORN: 24 May 1939

CLUBS: John Mitchels, Tralee; UCC and UCD

ACHIEVEMENTS IN CLUB COMPETITIONS: Seven County Senior Football titles with John Mitchels, Tralee, including five-in-a-row from 1959 to 1963.

INTER-COUNTY ACHIEVEMENTS: One All-Ireland Senior Football medal in 1962; one National Football League medal in 1963; two Munster Senior Championship medals in 1962 and 1963; Munster Junior Football Championship medal in 1965.

They later became the only team in Kerry to win five senior club championships in a row.

After defeating Tipperary in the first round in 1962, Kerry easily accounted for Cork in the Munster final and saw off the challenge of Dublin in the All-Ireland semi-final. 'Mick O'Connell was brilliant. It was Micko's day. His fielding was only magnificent and his kicking with the left and right foot was absolutely superb. An unbelieveable performance. I consider Mick O'Connell to be the greatest exponent of Gaelic football. His fielding and kicking with left and right foot have not been surpassed.' It will also be remembered as the day Kerry midfielder Jimmy Lucey launched a high kick towards his own goal in the opening minute of the game!

Recalling the final itself, Seán Óg believes that Roscommon never recovered from an early goal which was scored by Gary McMahon. Then Gerry O'Malley got injured and that was a huge setback to Roscommon. The biggest day of his sporting life is tinged with regret.

'The game was very poor. It was a fierce come-down. I'd say a lot of the other players also felt disappointed. It was a pity really. Unfortunately, it was one of the worst All-Ireland finals ever. But those things happen. There is no such thing as an easy All-Ireland. Players go through an awful lot of pain to win an All-Ireland final. It was a terrible shame that Roscommon lost Gerry O'Malley so early on with injury. He was a great player.'

He recollects little of what happened after the game, only that he felt glad when he had received the Sam Maguire cup from GAA President Hugh Byrne. He felt somewhat happier when his acceptance speech was over.

I certainly enjoyed the homecoming with all the bonfires. It was great to see my friends and neighbours. That was very special.'

Football is a way of life in the Kingdom. It is the football capital of Ireland. So what did it mean to Seán Óg Sheehy to captain Kerry in an All-Ireland?

'It was a great honour and it was following the family tradition. Our family was

Back, left to right: Niall Sheehy, Noel Lucey, Mick O'Connell, Mick O'Dwyer, Paudie Sheehy, Jimmy Lucey, Tom Long, Dan McAuliffe.
Front, left to right: Jerry Ó Riordan, Séamus Murphy, Tim Lyons, Seán Óg Sheehy (captain), Timmy O'Sullivan, Gary McMahon, Johnny Culloty.

Throw-in: the game is on. All-Ireland final 1962

steeped in football tradition so that made it very special. I wasn't aware of the significance of being captain at the time. I was delighted to be captain, but would just as soon someone else had the task. I was tempted to ask Paudie to be captain on the day but as things had gone so wrong for him before, I felt it would be upsetting the whole thing. I was contemplating it going out on the field because he was standing beside me. Paudie died of a brain haemorrhage at the age of thirty-five. He was the star of the family, a very polished footballer. He had wonderful skill. He was very bright and even spent a year in Harvard University. He lived a great life and was very refined and gentlemanly. It was a terrible shock when he died.'

Seán Óg admits he was like a ghost coming out on the field and remembers thinking to himself: 'this is desperate'. 'Once I got a few kicks of the ball I settled down fine. 'I get more enjoyment out of being captain now than I did then. I'm very proud and happy to have been captain of Kerry.

'Unfortunately people who lose are never given much thought. I still follow Kerry and enjoy watching the team. The whole thing is discipline, the whole game is an exhibition of discipline. We lose discipline at times, but you have to be disciplined to play the game; you must abide by the rules and you have to take the ups and downs

---

THE 1962 KERRY TEAM

Johnny Culloty

Séamus Murphy	Niall Sheehy	Tim Lyons
Seán Óg Sheehy (Captain)	Noel Lucey	Mick O'Dwyer

Mick O'Connell   Jimmy Lucey

Dan McAuliffe	Timmy O'Sullivan	Jerry O'Riordan
Gary McMahon	Tom Long	Paudie Sheehy

Substitutes: Joe Joe Barrett for Tim Lyons; Kevin Coffey for Dan McAuliffe

in a sporting fashion.'

It would be hard to find a more modest and unassuming man than Seán Óg Sheehy. He is quick to play down his own considerable talents as a footballer and is much more at ease talking about the achievements of others.

Donie O'Sullivan the All-Ireland winning Kerry captain of 1970, rated Seán Óg very highly as a player.

'He was a very underestimated footballer. I think he was probably overshadowed by a great footballing family and a great footballing father. His father, John Joe, was a legend not only on the field but off the field as well. He was also involved as selector and was a dominant figure in Kerry. Then you had his three brothers, Paudie, Niall and Brian, who were outstanding footballers. Seán Óg wasn't a man to advance his own cause. He was an excellent footballer and was a great wing back in 1962. I really appreciated his talents when he was playing in front of me against Dublin in the semi-final. I think he would have made an excellent forward as well had he stuck with it. He had great speed and anticipation which few realised. He had a fantastic turn in a very small space. He could turn on a sixpence.

He was very quiet off the field but was a great man to encourage on the field. He might hide the light under the bushel off the field but on the field he was a great leader. He never went for glory or the front seats of the synagogue.'

Seán Óg regrets he never fully recovered his form after the All-Ireland

> 'It was a great honour and it was following the family tradition. Our family was steeped in football tradition so that made it very special. I wasn't aware of the significance of being captain at the time. I was delighted to be captain, but would just as soon someone else had the task.'

of 1962. From as far back as he can recall, football meant an awful lot to him. 'I often think maybe it was my physique; I was light and what I depended on was speed. I was a good man to read a game and watch where the breaks came. But my fielding or anything like that was poor. To get on the Kerry team and to stay on it for any length of time, a player must be very good and very dedicated. Things must also go well. I reckon if a player has three good games at the start then he is more or less guaranteed four or five more games but after that he must play well or be dropped.

'I'll never forget being dropped for the All-Ireland semi-final against Galway in 1963. I saw the team on the daily paper while travelling on the bus to Bray. I was named among the substitutes. It was between Bernie O'Callaghan and myself. In fairness to Bernie I had kept him off the team in a way. I always thought he was a wonderful footballer. I came on as a sub at half time and unfortunately I played badly.'

Seán Óg had a relatively short career with the Kerry senior team. He was first selected during the League in 1961 and played his final game when he came on as a sub against Mayo in early summer 1964.

'I wasn't striking great form at the time and was dropped from the team. Once you lost your place it was very difficult to get back on. You'd need a period where you'd have to be playing very well. John Mitchels had gone down as well at the time. We had gone over our peak with the five-in-a-row, so the club was only getting one

or two outings in the championship. I never made the Kerry senior panel after that. In fairness I don't think I was playing well enough to regain my place.

'I was going through a bad period in my life. Here I was doing accountancy for four years, caught in there and not wanting to be there. It was very difficult to make a change. I was very lucky in that I made up my mind once and for all to get out of accountancy.

'I had come to the end of my tether. I was at home for about a year driving a truck, which must have been difficult for my father. I had already done a degree in UCC, then spent four years studying accountancy and another year in a secretarial and teaching course. I eventually got a teaching job in Wicklow which I enjoyed very much. I had found my niche.'

One of his most memorable moments on the field of play was the day John Mitchels played South Kerry in a County Championship final in Tralee.

'We had a corner-back on the team called John Dalton, who was known as "The Guard". A fellow called Seán O'Shea came in on a solo run and I spotted his teammate Mick O'Dwyer around the full forward line. As I raced out towards Seán O'Shea I reckoned he would pass the ball to O'Dwyer, which he did. I made a decision and went for that option. He had passed me but I doubled inside and got the ball. We were beaten all ends up, but I took the gamble and it paid off. And John Dalton turned around to me and said: "you were brilliant". It was a great moment.'

Seán Óg talks fondly about his famous father and the extraordinary influence he exercised over his sons' football careers.

'Cars were very scarce when I was growing up and he would pack the family and some of the neighbours into the car and drive us out to the seaside at Kilelton. After our swim he'd organise a football match. And that was the start of it. He always encouraged us. We played football and hurling for hours every evening. I was a minor hurler with Kerry and much preferred the game to football. It is a fabulous game. A Brother O'Shea used to stay in our house regularly and would always bring a few hurleys with him. Niall, Paudie and Brian all played hurling as well.

'My dad came from Boherbue which is directly opposite Austin Stack Park. A lot of the families in that area were wiped out with TB. My father and his brother Jimmy survived. Jimmy went off to the British Army and died in the First World War. By all accounts he was a fabulous kind of man. He was also big and powerful.

'My father used to say that there was a crepe on the door for about twelve or thirteen years. Every year one of the family died from TB. It was very sad.

'I remember my father being taken to jail in the early forties. He was arrested on account of being a Republican. Even though I was only four or five, I can still recall the guards coming for him. I also remember when he came home. It was at Christmas time and we were all brought into the room to see who this man was. I thought it was my uncle Con. I'll never forget that.

'My mother died when I was about eight and that left it very difficult. We were looked after by housekeepers. My father became an inspector for the insurance company and was on the road from Monday to Friday which meant that we saw him mostly at weekends. He encouraged us all and brought us out on Saturdays and Sundays to play football.'

How well he succeeded. Between them Seán Óg, Paudie and Niall won seven All-Ireland senior medals and Brian a junior All-Ireland medal to go with the four senior medals John Joe himself acquired a generation earlier.

Rival captains' pre-match handshake 1962. Seán Óg Sheehy (Kerry) and Gerry O'Malley (Roscommon).

Previous page: John Joe Sheehy surrounded by his sons, Paudie, Niall, Brian and Sean Og.

Paddy DOHERTY

Down Captain 1961

PADDY DOHERTY from Ballykinlar ranks among the greatest forwards in Gaelic football. The left-footed sharpshooter's scoring talents were never more in evidence than in the historic 1960 All-Ireland final. Playing in his customary left-half-forward position Paddy contributed 1-5 of his side's total as Down defeated Kerry by double scores to take the Sam Maguire Cup across the border for the first time.

The following year Down successfully defended the title in front of over 90,500 spectators which still remains the largest gathering ever at a sporting event in Ireland. By then Paddy Doherty had assumed the mantle of captain and accepted the Sam Maguire Cup after Down edged out Offaly by one point.

It has been said that without the deadly accuracy both from play and frees of Paddy Doherty, Down would never have enjoyed such great success in the sixties. Here was a footballing genius who scored over nine hundred points in inter-county competition.

Joe Lennon, a teammate on the Down team that won three All-Ireland titles in the sixties, has no hesitation in nominating Paddy as his all-time favourite Gaelic footballer. 'He was an intuitive genius on the field. He had a feeling for the game which went far beyond his consummate skill. He had developed a philosophy on the game and players, including opponents, which gave him a unique insight into what Gaelic football is really all about.'

Enda Colleran of Galway admits that Paddy was the most difficult opponent he faced in inter-county football. 'He was more skilful than others. Even though he was only left-footed and everybody knew that, it was still impossible to block his kick. You felt that even if you were doing well on him he would always manage to get a few scores. He had a most unusual characteristic in that he talked to his opponent

---

FACT FILE

HOME PLACE: Marion Park, Ballykinlar, County Down

BORN: 28 March 1934   CLUBS: Ballykinlar; Loughinisland

ACHIEVEMENTS IN CLUB COMPETITIONS: One Junior Championship; two Senior League Division One medals; two Senior League Division two medals; numerous seven-a-side championships and tournaments.

INTER-COUNTY ACHIEVEMENTS: Three All-Ireland Senior Football Championship medals in 1960, 1961 and 1968; seven Ulster Championship medals in 1959, 1960, 1961, 1963, 1965, 1966 and 1968; three National Football League medals in 1960, 1962 and 1968; seven Railway Cup medals in 1956, 1960, 1963, 1964, 1965, 1966 and 1968; two Dr McKenna Cup medals; two Lagan Cup medals; four Wembley tournament medals; one Grounds tournament medal; played with Ireland on two occasions; won World Cup — two legs against New York in 1968.

during the game and when he did this to me I often found it hard to concentrate but I couldn't in my heart tell him to shut up. I remember in a League semi-final he turned to me and said, "the ball is very soft". He was after pointing two good frees at the time. I felt I should have said to him, "you're not doing too badly with the soft ball", but I was afraid I would boost his ego.'

Affectionately known as 'Paddy Mo' from the days when 'Little Mo', Maureen Connolly, ruled the tennis world, Paddy was very nearly lost to Gaelic football as professional soccer clubs in Ireland and England, among them Doncaster and Glentoran, vied for his signature. Eventually he signed for Lincoln City but left after eight weeks because of homesickness and joined Ballyclare Comrades. Playing at outside-left, Paddy scored thirty-three goals in just half a season with the Irish League club. This led to him being suspended by the GAA for twelve months. He served six months and was back playing in the Down colours soon afterwards.

'When I decided to quit soccer and return to Gaelic football I went to Ballyclare Comrades to collect my boots. They were anxious that I play one more game and I agreed but under the assumed name of Campbell. Everybody at home was talking about this new outside-left by the name of Campbell who scored three goals in his first game. It was reported in the paper on the Saturday night, 'Campbell scored two in the first half and raced through to complete his hat trick in the second half'! I couldn't bear watching Ballykinlar playing on a Sunday and not being able to take part, so that influenced my decision to quit soccer.

'Later when I met the Arsenal and Irish international player Billy McCullough he said I was a mug to have left soccer. But I have no regrets.'

A few years later, Paddy was approached by Ards, who offered him two hundred and fifty pounds to sign professionally with a salary of eight pounds a week.

'I couldn't make up my mind and my father eventually told them I wasn't going. Their manager told me that they would win the Irish League and get a trip to America. I remember saying to him that Down would win the All-Ireland and I'd get

Back, left to right: James McCartan, Tony Hadden, Joe Lennon, Leo Murphy, P.J. McElroy, John Smith, Dan McCartan, Pat Rice.
Front, left to right: Jarlath Carey, Brian Morgan, Seán O'Neill, Paddy Doherty (captain), George Lavery, Eamonn McKay, Patsy O'Hagan.

my trip that way.'

Gaelic football was in the blood. When Paddy was a youngster, seven Dohertys, including Paddy's father and his two uncles, played for Ballykinlar.

'Every Sunday when my grandfather got the dinner over he would put the coat on and bring us to watch them play. Ballykinlar had a right good team then.'

At school in Ballykinlar he was greatly influenced by his teacher, Master Walsh.

'The Magorrians used to bring a leather ball to school and I would kick it to my heart's content. Even when I had left at thirteen years of age I used to go up to the school and kick football at dinner time. When they opened a new park in Ballykinlar I used to spend seven nights a week there kicking ball. It was the only fun we had.'

Ballykinlar was proud of Paddy Doherty and he in turn never let them down. His scoring feats with the club over a period of twenty-five years are now part of folklore. He himself remembers one particular occasion when he was ill in Belfast and his brothers, Henry and Francie, arrived to bring him to play a match. 'I said to them, "I'm not fit to go", and Henry said, "we may as well not play then". I got out of bed and scored ten points.

'I remember once going on a holiday to Wexford and Henry asked me to be back the following Sunday to play for Ballykinlar against Warrenpoint. I set off from Wexford on the Sunday morning, got the train to Dublin and thumbed to Warrenpoint and was there for the start of the match. I met a few friends of mine in Dublin who were going to the All-Ireland hurling final and they wanted me to go to Croke Park with them.'

One particular incident from those days stands out in his mind.

'We were playing Castlewellan in Ballykinlar and after the match Francie Smith said to somebody, "carry that man off, for that is the greatest man in Ireland". Another time we were playing the Glen in Newcastle in the replayed final of the League. The Glen and Ballykinlar was always a tough match — the McCartans and the Dohertys. We were getting it tight and some spectator turned to one of our supporters, Joe Redmond, and said, "Dan McCartan has Paddy Mo in his pocket today". A few minutes later I slipped Dan and put the ball in the net and Joe said, "there must be a hole in Dan's pocket".'

Paddy Doherty's one regret is that he never won a senior club championship medal with Ballykinlar. He played for two years with the Down minor team but failed to win an Ulster title.

'We reached the Ulster minor final in 1952 but were beaten by Cavan in Clones. I played in the Junior Championship against Armagh in 1953 and the game ended in a draw. I scored five points that day. A bus load from Ballykinlar went to see me in the

	THE 1961 DOWN TEAM	
	Eamonn McKay	
George Lavery	Leo Murphy	Pat Rice
Patsy O'Hagan	Dan McCartan	John Smith
Jarlath Carey		Joe Lennon
Sean O'Neill	James McCartan	Paddy Doherty (Captain)
Tony Hadden	P.J. McElroy	Brian Morgan
	Substitutes: Kevin O'Neill for Pat Rice; Pat Rice for George Lavery	

replay but I never even got to the match. Arrangements had been made for someone to collect me but no one turned up and I missed the game. I felt rotten and was bitterly disappointed.'

Paddy played his first senior game for Down against Tyrone in a McKenna Cup game in 1954. Maurice Hayes used to collect Paddy for training in Banbridge. Paddy was a member of the Down team that won a first Ulster title in 1959 with a comprehensive victory over Cavan before losing to Galway in the All-Ireland semi-final. 'I got a kick in the knee after only about five minutes' play against Galway but the selectors kept me on for the whole match. I wasn't even fit to walk and didn't do myself justice at all.'

Down retained the Ulster title in 1960, again defeating Cavan in the final, to set up an All-Ireland semi-final meeting with Offaly.

By then the team was now more experienced and knitted together very well. Paddy believes it was his best performance in Croke Park for the red and black. The game ended level: Down 1-10, Offaly 2-7. But it had looked bleak at half time for the Ulster Champions when they trailed by seven points.

'I played well all day and had the winning of the game with the last kick but the ball hit the top of the upright and went wide. The team as a unit didn't play well at all and we'd have been out if somebody didn't play to form. I scored 1-7 that day including a goal from a penalty. The previous Thursday night in training it was decided that I would take penalties if the occasion arose. Our captain, Kevin Mussen, was away that evening and he didn't know of the arrangement. So when the penalty was awarded, Kevin came running up the field and instructed Seán O'Neill to take the kick. But Seán said, "Paddy's taking it". Any penalties that came our way after that I always took them.'

> 'We didn't realise the significance of our achievement until we saw the crowds on our journey home. It was powerful. We started off from Dublin on Monday afternoon and it was around four o'clock next morning before we reached the Slieve Donard Hotel in Newcastle.'

Although he kicked exclusively with his left Paddy Doherty did score one important point with his right foot that day.

'I cut in and chipped one over the bar with my right foot. Tony Hadden was coming through on a solo run and put the ball a yard too far ahead of him and I nipped in and put it over the bar. Tony gave me a look but never said anything once I scored.'

Down won the replay by two points to advance to their first All-Ireland final and a meeting with reigning champions Kerry.

'We stayed in our own homes the night before and got an escort to the border on the morning of the final. I was nervous in the dressing-room but once I got out on the field I was all right.'

As Paddy jokingly says, 'Maurice Hayes carried the strawberries to feed the butterflies'.

Down, led by Kevin Mussen, were first on the pitch and were greeted with a mass of red and black. 'We led by two points at half time but Kerry had their chances until

Above and right: action from the 1961 final. *Below left:* Paddy Doherty watches the ball

James McCartan's lobbing ball beat Johnny Culloty and we went to town after that. I scored a penalty shortly afterwards and we won in the end by eight points. We didn't realise the significance of our achievement until we saw the crowds on our journey home. It was powerful. We started off from Dublin on Monday afternoon and it was around four o'clock next morning before we reached the Slieve Donard Hotel in Newcastle.'

Paddy Doherty was not captain starting out the championship campaign in 1961. The 1960 captain, Kevin Mussen, continued in the role throughout the Ulster Championship but he lost his place for the All-Ireland semi-final, and Paddy took over. To this day Paddy has no idea why he was the one chosen to captain Down when Kevin was dropped.

He never asked why. He rated Kevin an excellent half-back and captain.

'Kevin would always say to me, "Come on now Mo, get a score". He was a great man to encourage a player. James McCartan didn't play in the first half of the Ulster final because of injury. Armagh were leading us by five points at the break and when we went into the dressing-room James was togged out ready to play. The first ball I dropped in the goalmouth James had it in the net. Armagh thought they had got the equalising goal near the end. They maintained the ball had crossed the line.'

The Paddy Doherty-led Down went on to overcome Kerry once more in the semi-final by six points, then had just one point to spare over goalkeeper Willie Nolan's Offaly in the final. He remembers Willie asking him for the match ball as he made his way up to collect the Sam Maguire Cup.

'I had given the ball to Paddy Fitzsimmons for safe keeping so I told Willie to get it off him. Willie found Paddy and got the ball. I was delighted to give the ball to Willie as he was a nice fellow. I don't think I have ever met Willie since that day. It was great being captain but I didn't like the idea of going up to collect the Cup. I must have given the shortest ever captain's speech. I just thanked the Offaly team and that was it.'

Apart from being banned for playing soccer in the early days, Paddy Doherty served two other terms of suspension in his career, once after incidents following a club championship game and again in 1967 for playing in the London Championship. But more than anything else those suspensions served to illustrate the determination of the great man and his love of football. Instead of quitting the game, as many in a similiar position would have done, Paddy picked up where he left off and along with Joe Lennon, Dan McCartan and Seán O'Neill of the 1960 and 1961 teams played a key role in helping Down win the All-Ireland final of 1968.

How would he describe himself as a footballer?

'All I ever wanted was the yard in front and they could never catch me. I never turned back,' he says with a hearty laugh. 'You don't turn back when you're clear. George Glynn who played with us in the 1968 All-Ireland final once said to Pat Rice, "Paddy's good in the clear". There's only one way to play football, clean and fair. Football will win ninety-nine times out of a hundred.'

A bricklayer by profession, Paddy has lived in Portaferry for a considerable time and was an SDLP councillor in the area for eight years. To GAA folk he is remembered as a natural genius who could always be relied on to rally a beaten team with a touch of sheer magic. A footballing superstar in every sense of the phrase.

Kevin MUSSEN

Down Captain 1960

'It was the life of people in county Down at the time. In the area I came from, Gaelic games was the sole diversion from work in the fifties and sixties. When I was growing up, I heard nothing else talked about but football and would have heard at the end of any conversation the pious hope that Down would win something, sometime.'

KEVIN MUSSEN will forever be remembered as the first man to bring the Sam Maguire Cup North of the Border. It was a momentous and historical occasion and earned the Clonduff player and his Down teammates a unique place in the annals of gaelic football. Thousands of cheering, flag waving Down supporters gathered at the border to witness that historic crossing.

'The English Customs were in place at the time and the question was: 'What were they going to do with 'Sam'. I remember the Customs man coming over to the bus and I presume a document was signed, but it certainly wasn't signed by me. We had to get out of the bus — this was by popular demand, not by Customs demand — and walk across the border with 'Sam'. I was carrying the Cup and on the other arm of the Cup, I remember, was our trainer, the late Danny Flynn. It was physically very demanding as there was an awful lot of jostling and pushing to get across the border. Newry was incredible, absolutely full of people. I'm sure we were a couple of hours getting through the town. There was an awful lot of Armagh people there also, as Newry straddles the river, with part of the town in Armagh.

'After the speeches had finished in Newry, we went on a limited tour of the county. Thank God at that stage! All we did was drive through my home village, Hilltown, then Castlewellan and finally Newcastle. There were more speeches when we arrived in Hilltown and my school manager, Canon Burke, was there to greet us and in his speech he said: "I can't give you a day off tomorrow as the Ministry don't allow that, but if no children come, there will be no school". So no children came to

---

FACT FILE

HOME PLACE: Hilltown, County Down

BORN: 8 October 1933   CLUBS: Clonduff; O'Donovan Rossa in Antrim

ACHIEVEMENTS IN CLUB COMPETITIONS: Two Senior Championship medals in 1952 and 1957; two Senior League medals in 1952 and 1963; Antrim County League and Championship with O'Donovan Rossa in 1956.

INTER-COUNTY ACHIEVEMENTS: Two All-Ireland Senior Football medals in 1960 and 1961; three Ulster Senior Championship medals in 1959, 1960 and 1961; two National League medals in 1960 and 1962; two Dr McKenna Cup medals; two Lagan Cup medals; one St Brendan's Cup medal versus New York (All-Ireland Champions, Down, defeated New York at Croke Park in 1960); two Railway Cup medals with Ulster in 1956 and 1960; two Interprovincial Colleges medals with Ulster in 1950 and 1951.

---

school next day!'

It was a proud, proud moment for Kevin Mussen as he raised the Sam Maguire Cup aloft in front of an ecstatic crowd in his home town, the realisation of the childhood dreams the young Kevin had dreamed in 'Mussen's Meadow' in Hilltown.

'When we got to Castlewellan there to greet us was the landlord of the area, Gerard Annsley, after whom an awful lot of the countryside is named. Then it was on to Newcastle, where I was living. We were to finish in Newcastle with supper and a céilí in St Mary's Hall, but it was long past the time for the céilí to end when we arrived in Newcastle. So there was no céilí, as it was impossible once we got into the hotel to get out of it again with the crowds on the street. We had to speak to the crowds from a window of the hotel and we also took phone calls of greeting from all over the country.'

For weeks afterwards, Kevin and his triumphant team travelled to different parts of the county with 'Sam'. Every member of the Down team had become a sporting hero. There was magic in the air around the Mourne Mountains and it would be a long time before the county got back to normal living. Life, post All-Ireland Final day 1960, would never be the same again for all the players, especially Kevin, who is still fiercely proud of his team's accomplishments and his own unique position.

'At the time it was hard work, very hard work. You had to be on your feet night after night and say the same things. Not being a man of words this presented me with great problems. Looking back on it now, I'm proud to have achieved what we did, as is the rest of the team. I think, mostly what it meant to me was the friendships created between twenty fellows. We still have lots of time for one another and when we meet we're still good friends. We've had a couple of reunions and they were very happy occasions.

Some players' recollections of events fade with time, but not so with Kevin Mussen. He vividly remembers the build-up to Down's appearance in Croke Park, the climax of twelve months of solid training.

Back, left to right: James McCartan, Joe Lennon, Jarlath Carey, Leo Murphy, Dan McCartan, Seán O'Neill, Kevin O'Neill, Pat Rice.
Front, left to right: Eamonn McKay, Patsy O'Hagan, Paddy Doherty, Kevin Mussen (captain), George Lavery, Tony Hadden, Brian Morgan.

'The last week is taken up mainly with dealing with the reporters and photographers, giving them everything they need for their weekend papers. The hard work is already done and it's only an exhibition of training really. Up to that point, we spent three to four nights a week training, which back in 1960, remember, was a bit revolutionary. Nowadays, teams train almost professionally, but then it would have been unknown for a team to train as much as Down did. We trained right through the winter, indoor training, circuit training and stamina work, finishing off then with ball work when the weather improved. So it was a full year's preparation for that All-Ireland Final.'

Down won the Ulster title in impressive fashion and were in no danger of losing any of their games. But it was a different matter altogether in the All-Ireland semi-final. 'We were taken to a replay by Offaly and were very lucky to draw the first match and lucky enough to win the replay. I think we underestimated Offaly, because they were an emerging team then. But we won the All-Ireland Final itself by double scores. It really wasn't our hardest game of the year. Offaly was the biggest barrier to the title.'

And what about the day of the final? Kevin's recollections are not of the match itself!

'My memories would be assembly that morning in Newry and a visit from Bishop O'Doherty to the hotel, where we had breakfast; the police escort to the border to avoid crowds, and a visit from the *Belfast Telegraph's* sports reporter. I also remember the sheer monotony of the wait for hours before the match started. We travelled by bus and lunched in a hotel in Iona Road, not far from Croke Park. We just hung around there bored, waiting for the match time to come around. The excitement didn't start hitting us until we moved closer to Croke Park and saw the fantastic crowd around the place. Our dressing-room, under the Cusack Stand, was next to the Galway minors and would you believe it, the last two people to wish us luck on the way out were Seán Purcell and Frank Stockwell, who were in charge of the winning Galway minor team.'

His most abiding memory of the final was the actual noise when Down came on the field. He remembers it was almost offensive to the ear until he became accustomed to it.

'It was the biggest crowd we had ever played in front of and it was also the noisiest. All those things were nerve-wracking, the parade, the introduction to the Archbishop of Cashel, the build-up seemed to last for ever. Once the match got going, it was just like any other match, you soon forgot the crowd and the occasion. It was just a match between Kerry and ourselves.'

THE 1960 DOWN TEAM

	Eamonn McKay	
George Lavery	Leo Murphy	Pat Rice
Kevin Mussen (Captain)	Dan McCartan	Kevin O'Neill
Joe Lennon		Jarlath Carey
Seán O'Neill	James McCartan	Paddy Doherty
Tony Hadden	Patsy O'Hagan	Brian Morgan

Substitute: Kieran Denvir for Joe Lennon

It was an absorbing final, but also very satisfying from a Down point of view, as they were always in control. 'Well into the second half, it became almost routine, as we were leading by four or five points. Even Paudie Sheehy, my immediate opponent, who was also the captain, said to me: "You have the All-Ireland now", even though there was ten minutes left in the game. I thought it was very, very big of him. The only other worrying thing about that All-Ireland was the crowds coming onto the pitch, anticipating the final whistle. With about a minute to go, they swarmed onto the pitch, but the referee made it plain that the match was not over. I panicked a little, afraid in case a replay might be ordered — and Kerry's reputation in replays was worrying. But again Paudie Sheehy said: "You needn't worry, you needn't worry, there's only seconds left". The crowd moved back to the sideline and a couple of kicks later "Sam" was ours!'

It was somewhat ironic that Down should beat Kerry in that final because Kevin remembers talking in 1956 to Paudie Sheehy's father, John Joe, who said to him: 'Isn't it sad to be playing for a county that will never win anything'. Four years after that conversation Down had won their first of three senior All-Irelands in the sixties. Proof if proof were needed of the unpredictable nature of sport!

The first person Kevin remembers talking to when the match was over was his father. A never-to-be-forgotten moment shared by father and son! During the pre-match parade he had spotted his father, who waved to him from his position in the new Hogan Stand. Kevin deliberately chose to look at the crowd and felt it had a calming affect on him.

> 'Being part of that winning team gave us all celebrity standing in the county and we'd still be greeted affectionately in any corner of the county. They were as fine a bunch of fellows as I ever ran across; they came from varying backgrounds, but they gelled completely and that was the secret of success.'

Kevin also recalls the desperate struggle he had to make it through the crowds to the presentation area in the Hogan Stand.

'I had been suffering before the game with a burnt elbow from heat treatment and, with people grabbing my arms, the wound had become very raw. I still bear the scar. It had nothing to do with the match at all, never got it touched during the match, but the crowd pulling and hauling aggravated it, and again coming across the border. Once the presentation was over, it was impossible to get back across the pitch to the dressing-room with the Cup, so I had to go down to the official area at the back of the Hogan Stand and, while there, I had a soft drink and was introduced to a few people. I waited for the best part of half an hour in the office area and then fought my way back across the pitch to join my colleagues.'

Strangely, it was a rather quiet and drained dressing-room which Kevin entered with the Sam Maguire Cup. There was no huge celebrations on the part of the players. Kevin found that the officials and supporters were much more excited than the team. 'The players revived again later on that night, but they were well drained immediately after the game. It took a terrible lot out of them.'

Speech-making can be a wearisome thing and Kevin recalls the reception that night as 'long and hard.' The next day was the fun day with a visit to Áras an

Dev watches Kevin Mussen's triumph

Uachtaráin for a meeting with President de Valera. Then the epic journey home.

Kevin Mussen played Gaelic football, simply because there was no other choice. Growing up in the village of Hilltown, there was one game and one game only, and that was Gaelic football in 'Mussen's Meadow', now known as Páirc Clondubh.

'I would have been eighteen or nineteen before I saw any other game. The talk was of football all the time. The school I attended, St Colman's College, played Gaelic football only, so there was no temptation to stray.'

Football was a long established tradition in the Mussen family. His father was a committee member of the local club all his life and his two uncles, George and Dan played for Down in the thirties; but his mother stayed in the background.

'Possibly the one and only match I saw my mother at was the 1960 All-Ireland final, but she always prepared my "skip"; washed my togs and cleaned my boots. She was very, very proud of me and was the one who pushed me out if I was reluctant on a bad day to go to a club match. "You have to go, you have to go", was my mother's motto. There is no escaping the encouragement my father gave me and I don't think I ever played a match that he wasn't there. My brother and I had a collection of programmes and rosettes from practically every county that ever played in an All-Ireland final. My favourite rosette was Mayo's. I still regard the red and green of Mayo as the nicest jersey in Ireland.'

Growing up in Hilltown, Kevin is thankful that Gaelic games, above all else, afforded him the opportunity to spread his wings.

'As a result of my football, I saw every corner of Ireland. I certainly wouldn't have done so if it hadn't been for football. I have friends in every corner of Ireland as a direct result of my involvement with Gaelic games and that is an aspect I take delight in. The friendships that Gaelic games create is something that should be seriously fostered. I think there should be more clubs where ex-players can go and meet and, in fact, I'm surprised there's no place around Croke Park where I could bump into players and say hello to them on All-Ireland day. It's only the elite that are catered for and while I don't begrudge them their place in Croke Park, the players should have something too. Possibly, with the new development, this will all happen and we'll have players' lounges and things like that.'

Kevin captained Down from the mid-fifties until 1961 when he lost his place after the Ulster final. He made a brief appearance against Kerry in the All-Ireland semi-final, but failed to regain his place for the final. 'It was disappointing, to be honest, to lose my place in 1961 and while I had been part of that year, I really missed playing in the All-Ireland final, but I bore no hard feelings. As events turned out, it proved a wise decision. I came back and played in the 1962 National League and was on and off the team then until I retired.'

As a player he had two vital ingredients, speed and judgement. He made up for his lack of height by keen anticipation. 'Some players run under the ball, or short of the ball, but I always got it at the maximum height, which was why I usually liked playing against a big man. I could put the taller man under the ball, whereas the small man was able to jostle me. I'd say I played constructively, although I was maybe not one of the greatest tacklers in the world.'

Kevin Mussen says that, while the 1960 All-Ireland final has to be the high point of his career, he cannot remember getting more satisfaction from any victory than from being on the Ulster team that won the Railway Cup final in 1956.

'We beat Munster in the final at Croke Park in front of a crowd in excess of fifty thousand. My most vivid recollection of the day was togging out in the dressingroom between Victor Sherlock and Phil "Gunner" Brady, two of the most famous footballers in Ireland at the time.'

He thinks the people at the top in the GAA should try to get a better standard of refereeing for matches. Inconsistency in refereeing standards and interpretation of rules is the biggest single problem facing players today, in his opinion. Kevin would also like to see less narrowness at the top level in the GAA. 'In a pluralist society, the GAA should learn to co-exist with other sporting bodies in Ireland. Our games need no protection and whan well presented will always have mass appeal at home.'

The views of a man who occupies a special place in the annals of the GAA And his final thoughts on that historic period when Down football came of age?

'Being part of that winning team gave us all celebrity standing in the county and we'd still be greeted affectionately in any corner of the county where Gaelic people are gathered. They were as fine a bunch of fellows as I ever ran across; they came from varying backgrounds, but they gelled completely and that was the secret of success. A lot of the credit for that camaraderie must go to our mentors, who saw to it that everyone was equal. It didn't matter whether some were rich, or some were poor, we were all equal and treated equally. There was a team spirit second to none in that group.'

Kevin never left his native county, and taught in Hilltown National School until 1992 when he took early retirement. His name will never be forgotten so long as fires remain burning around the Mournes.

Kevin Mussen the history maker.

Mick O'CONNELL

Kerry Captain 1959

ONCE IN A LIFETIME a player comes along who makes such a profound impact that all others before and since are forever being compared with him. Such a man was Mick O'Connell, the first 'superstar' of Gaelic football and the most admired and graceful midfielder the game has ever known.

It is no exaggeration to say that the strapping island man was the Pele of Gaelic football. Even those who knew little and cared even less about the game knew his name. He played football the way it was intended.

During a long and distinguished career in the green and gold of Kerry, Mick O'Connell made a lasting impression on everyone who saw him play. He was a footballing genius and the most talked-about player of his generation. In the course of my interviews with well over forty Gaelic football captains the names of Mick O'Connell and Seán Purcell cropped up most often in our discussions about all-time great players.

Tommy Doyle, Kerry's All-Ireland winning captain of 1986, puts it very well: 'Mick O'Connell was a fantastic footballer. He was untouchable in the air and was a very elegant player with a great delivery. He was also a great long range-kicker off the ground or out of his hands and off both feet. As youngsters we were weaned on the great Mick O'Connell. Micko in those days was every youngster's hero in Kerry and indeed throughout the country. We all wanted to play Gaelic football like him. Even when down the field kicking ball we would argue over who was going to be called Micko.'

Present-day Kerry manager 'Ogie' Moran, the only player to win eight All-Ireland medals playing in the one position, was greatly influenced by Mick O'Connell.

'He was my idol. He was in his prime when I was very young. I used to go to all the matches with my father and my cousin Mick.

'Mick O'Connell was really a folk hero and was the Georgie Best of football at that time. He still remains a great favourite. He caught my imagination as a youngster. He was very graceful and a magnificent fielder. My family were in the drapery business

---

FACT FILE

HOME PLACE: Valentia Island, County Kerry

BORN: 4 January 1937   CLUB: Young Islanders; Waterville; South Kerry

ACHIEVEMENTS IN CLUB COMPETITIONS: Seven South Kerry Senior Football Championship medals; three County Senior Football Championship medals with South Kerry.

INTER-COUNTY ACHIEVEMENTS: Four All-Ireland Senior Football medals in 1959, 1962, 1969 and 1970; twelve Munster Senior Championship medals in 1958, 1959, 1960, 1961, 1962, 1963, 1964, 1965, 1968, 1969, 1970 and 1972; six National Football League medals in 1959, 1961, 1963, 1969, 1971 and 1972; one Railway Cup Football medal in 1972; one All Star Award in 1972

---

in the Park Place in Killarney and I remember the day my father and cousin Mick measured Mick for a suit. It was a great occasion.'

Willie Bryan, who led Offaly to their first All-Ireland success in 1971 against Galway and marked the mighty Micko on final days in 1969 and '72, had another view of the maestro:

'He had everything as a player plus the fact that he was a total sportsman on the field. I can well remember being told I was marking Mick in the 1969 final and I was very worried. There was a question of his fitness before the game and right up to the time the Kerry team came on the pitch everyone was left wondering whether or not he would play. We were on the field first and I can remember looking towards the Kerry tunnel. Then there was a big cheer for the entrance of Kerry and then an even bigger cheer for Micko. I was genuinely weak at the knees. As luck would have it I caught the first ball and settled quickly. Over the years I think we may have just about broken even. He never put a hand near me and I think he got the same treatment in return. Remember, I was ten years younger than Mick, so I don't think I would have liked to come up against him if we were the same age. A great footballer and a nice man.'

All-Star defender Donie O'Sullivan, All-Ireland winning Kerry captain in 1970 and teammate of Mick O'Connell for many years, has this to say:

'I saw some outstanding footballers in my time but I would have to choose Mick O'Connell above them all. He had all the skills, particularly catching and kicking, amazing balance and vision and of course complete dedication. Playing with him, I feel, we often expected the impossible and he sometimes made it happen.'

Enda Colleran, two-in-a-row All-Ireland winning Galway captain of the sixties, says of the Valentia Island man:

'Mick O'Connell was the most stylish, graceful and sporting Gaelic footballer ever. He engaged in sport for sport's sake and believed everyone should enjoy the game. I believe a lot of the enjoyment has gone out of the present-day game because of the

Back row, left to right: Seán Murphy, Dan McAuliffe, Kevin Coffey, Jerome O'Sé, Mick O'Dwyer, Tom Long, Niall Sheehy, Tadhgie Lyne.
Front Row, left to right: Paddy Hussey Paudie Sheehy, Johnny Culloty, Mick O'Connell (captain), John Dowling, Séamus Murphy, Tim Lyons, Dave Geaney.

attitude to win at all costs.'

Seán Óg Sheehy, who steered Kerry to victory over Roscommon in the 1962 All-Ireland, saw the mighty midfielder scale the heights on many occasions. 'Mick O'Connell was an outstanding footballer and athlete with a wonderful physique. He was very graceful, a great kicker with left and right foot and there was no better fielder. I knew fellows who were great footballers, they could run the same way and jump the same way but O'Connell was different. He was the Arkle of footballers. A former Kerry selector, Bernie O'Connell, always referred to Mick O'Connell as the "Monarch". And we all knew who the Monarch was and is, the greatest!'

John Dowling, who played alongside Mick at midfield for Kerry and lined out against him at club level, rates the Valenitia man an exceptional player.

'We played against each other in the 1956 county championship final. He was just starting his career and there was talk of this good lad coming from south Kerry and he proved it on the day. He had style, was a great fielder, had a fantastic kick with either foot and could pinpoint a pass to any man on the run like a bullet out of a rifle forty yards or more. Against Dublin in the 1962 All-Ireland semi-final he put on the finest exhibition of football that I ever saw by any individual in Croke Park.'

Mick O'Connell's career with Kerry embraced three decades. He played his first game as a minor against Waterford in the 1955 Munster Championship and finished his inter-county career in the early 1970s.

'There was no such thing as spotting potential in our day. We just played away. My father bought a football for us and we used to kick near the house. You'd be fairly satisfied yourself that you were fairly useful at the game but there was no need to be pushed because it was different in those times. I was eighteen years of age before I got any break at all. I got my place on the county minor team but that was a low-profile thing.'

Kerry minors lost in a replay to Tipperary in the Munster Final that year. At that stage Micko had played just four games in the Kerry jersey and no one could have possibly envisaged the success that was to follow.

'I was part of a South Kerry team which won the County Senior Championship in 1955 and that sprung me to prominence. I played fairly well in that championship and got my place on the senior county team in 1956 as a result. After that I got the feeling of training and how good it felt to be fit and that's the thing that got me really involved in a fairly serious way.'

Micko's first outing with the seniors was in a tournament game against Cork at the Athletic Grounds in early May 1956. He never looked back. He lined out at

---

THE 1959 KERRY TEAM

Johnny Culloty

Jerome O'Shea	Niall Sheehy	Tim Lyons
Seán Murphy	Kevin Coffey	Mick O'Dwyer

Mick O'Connell (Captain)　　　　　　Séamus Murphy

Dan McAuliffe	Tom Long	Paudie Sheehy
Dave Geaney	John Dowling	Tadhgie Lyne

Substitutes: Jack Dowling for Tim Lyons; Moss O'Connell for Mick O'Connell;
Gary McMahon for Dave Geaney

---

midfield in his first Munster Senior final against Cork in 1956 and after fielding the very first ball that came his direction was unlucky enough to be accidentally floored by his partner John Dowling. It had an adverse affect on Mick's performance for the remainder of the game.

That game ended level but Cork won the replay by a point. The following year Kerry's championship aspirations came to an abrupt halt when Waterford knocked them out of the Munster Championship.

Mick O'Connell won his first championship medal in 1958 when Kerry easily defeated Cork in the Munster final. Derry provided the opposition for Mick's championship debut in Croke Park, and the Ulster champions, making their first appearance at All-Ireland semi-final stage, won by a point. Kerry got some consolation for that defeat when they beat Derry in the 1959 League final.

Later that year Kerry retained their Munster crown, beating old rivals Cork in a high-scoring game. Kerry accounted for Dublin in the semi-final, which meant that the Valentia Island man was about to take part part in his first All-Ireland final. And better still he was captain. Or was it? Did the captaincy mean that much to him at the time?

'No it didn't. It just happened that I was captain that year because South Kerry had won the County Championship the previous year and I was the only player from Valentia, the club champions of the region. It was just before the first game in the Munster Championship in 1959 that Jerome O'Shea turned to me and said "it's your turn to be captain today". That was a couple of minutes before the toss. There was no big discussion one way or the other who would be captain or who would not be captain and anyway in Gaelic games the captain is incidental and not important. He makes no decisions and is not involved in selection or anything else. He has no influence whatsoever and is not there even on merit because the least motivating player on the team could be captain as the system now stands and has stood in Kerry. I'm not complaining about it but it's just an honest reply. The captain is just there to accept the trophy from the President if the team wins.'

> 'If sport is to mean anything, first and foremost it must be to discipline yourself to play within the rules. That's the most important lesson or experience a person can get from the sport.'

After an outstanding year, Mick O'Connell was unfortunate in that he was injured very early on in the 1959 All-Ireland decider against Galway. He was bitterly disappointed. Kerry won easily in what has become known as the Seán Murphy final.

'I shouldn't have played at all as I had a fierce sore throat. I went for a few evenings' practice that week before the final and I got a lot of wettings. I got some tablets from Dr Éamonn O'Sullivan who was training the team and he told me to play. In the match itself I twisted my knee and had to go off. I had very few injuries but that was one of the days I was unlucky. I suppose that took some of the personal satisfaction out of it, but otherwise, especially for my teammates, it was very satisfying to see Kerry winning that All-Ireland. It was the first one I was involved in.'

Walking up the steps of the Hogan Stand to accept the Sam Maguire Cup meant little to Mick O'Connell. Medals or trophies were never important as far as he was concerned. He collected the Cup only because it was his duty. No more, no less. That is not to belittle the occasion on his part. Far from it. It is just that the Valentia man preferred to play football and everything else was secondary. After all that is the only reason he spent long hours in all kinds of weather practising his skills.

'It was just a job to be done on the day. There's nothing false about that. In fact the All-Ireland finals were the least enjoyable of the games I played. There was far too much emphasis on ritual and ceremony for me. What I would like to have seen is teams getting on the field, have a kick around and start the match. Often we'd be on the field for twenty or twenty-five minutes before the game got under way. Any person, keen to go on and play the game as an amateur as I was, would want the game first and all this other thing second. I just hated it!'

Mick O'Connell headed for Kerry by train shortly after the All-Ireland victory and

was back at home in Valentia Island that night without the Sam Maguire Cup. The team arrived on the island with the Cup some days later amid scenes of great celebrations. Micko was the first member of the Young Islanders Club to win an All-Ireland medal.

Mick O'Connell's father was a fisherman who supplemented his income by working the family's small farm. Nearly all of Mick's childhood memories centre around boats, fishing and doing the everyday jobs about the farm. There was a great football tradition on the island and the Valentia Young Islanders team competed locally.

'There was an army base on the island at the time and there was never any shortage of matches. We ourselves played in the school yard and generally the lads in my own age group had an interest in the game and it followed from there. But let me say there was no dreams or aspirations about being this, that or the other player, it was just playing the game for the sake of playing it. We developed an interest in techniques.

'From an early age I used to practise with the left and eventually my left kick was much stronger than my right. We weren't coached but between ourselves we discussed things and we tried them out. We didn't play any organised matches except among ourselves and that probably helped because there was no rush and bother. I think the push and pull of people running under-age teams nowadays is anti the development of a young sports player. Now and then it might be all right to have competitions but not too many of them. I'd say competitions should be held only very, very rarely, just enough to whet the appetite. What I see on the sideline is mentors and parents, who never played much themselves and have little or no knowledge, trying to get reflected glory or satisfaction through using youngsters and I think it is an abuse.'

Mick O'Connell had a reputation as a man who trained diligently to reach peak physical fitness. Nearly all this intense practice was done alone on Valentia Island and that was something he enjoyed immensely.

'It amuses me when people talk about training in Gaelic football. Gaelic players in the past, in the recent past and in the present time are far from super-fit. And I wasn't super-fit. I was as fit as any man in my time, but it was far from being super-fit. I have travelled the world and I have seen athletes who would slot into that category. I know the Gaelic players will tell you that they make a lot of sacrifices but I don't think they make half enough sacrifices to be super-fit. As regards training, I just did something to keep physically fit. There was no organised training because we were very scatttered. We won the League Final and the Munster Championship in 1959 without being together for one training session. We practised on our own. We didn't have any training session together until the month of August. That doesn't mean that we didn't practise and that we weren't physically fit but to be really fit people need to do a lot of training in competition with people who are going to extend them.'

Acknowledged as the greatest exponent of the high catch in Gaelic football, Mick plays down his mastery of what is now a dying art in the game.

'I would rate myself as a pretty good all-round footballer, good fielder, ability to kick equally well with both feet from hands and ground. Of course all these were cultivated skills. The only skill that I would rate a natural one is positional sense, that is to be well-positioned at any given time on the field to take advantage of the run of the play. However, I was far from being a master of the game although I did put a lot of effort and practice into it. There were so many handicaps which stood in the way of top quality practice which is the only road to near perfection. In all my playing years there were only rough sloping fields to practice in. There was no other county player in my club to do real intense training with although I was always grateful to my Valentia clubmates who would, during practice compete all out with me for the fifty-fifty ball. I remain convinced that only full-time professionalism provides the way to mastery of a sport.

'Personally, I would be slow to encourage any young lad to take up Gaelic football for the simple reason that now in 1993, Gaelic football is a certain game; in 1995 it could be a completely different game and by 1997 it could revert to the original game again. Thankfully, in my time between 1955 and 1972 there was no major change. The throw, that's what I call the hand pass, was not in vogue during those times. I wouldn't play Gaelic football again if I was a young lad starting off now! I wouldn't. That's an honest comment. It is too uncertain. You could practise for one set of skills and they could be completely changed in another couple of years. The people who are running the game are fiddling with the Australian Rules, a round ball code trying to cross breed with a code that plays with an oval ball. It is a crude game which is non-defined. Trying all sorts of schemes like that, I would say that it is too high-risk. I think it is a tragedy for a young man who has talent and finds at twenty years of age

he has developed certain talents to play a certain code and then through a decision made at administrative level that code can be changed drastically. The skills he has acquired and developed can become obsolete. Don't think I'm saying it was always great, it wasn't. In my time it had its deficiencies and it still has.

'One of the deficiencies it always had was the acceptance of a foul. That acceptance has become more and more prominent with the years. The foul in Gaelic football is an accepted part of the code and I think it should not be. If I foul in Gaelic football I think that's failure. It's not being able to play the game in accordance with the rules. People say that they love the game and they'd do anything for the game. I would doubt that. If they really did they wouldn't do anything to dishonour the game. I think that's the way I would look at it.'

He is appalled by the win-at-all-costs philosophy he discerns today: 'If winning is everything, then I can't understand why people will say that sport is good for you. You teach children to win and lose and take the ups and the downs. If sport is to mean anything, first and foremost it must be to discipline yourself to play within the rules. That's the most important lesson or experience a person can get from the sport. No doubt there will be high points and disappointments but if you haven't that basic respect for the rules and liking for the game then I think it's all in vain.'

Mick O'Connell is very glad to have played Gaelic football. It gave him the opportunity not only to play sport at the highest level possible as an amateur but also to travel and meet different people from all walks of life. No other Gaelic footballer generated so much interest inside or outside the sport.

'I met a lot of fine people and made many lasting friendships through my involvement in Gaelic fooball. While, naturally enough, they were mostly Irish residents I remember fondly people abroad especially those like John Kerry O'Donnell, Tommy Hennessy, Mickey Moynihan, John Cooper and Mickey O'Sullivan in New York. For myself personally, the game provided me a great opportunity to practise and experience a good healthy life when I was young and carefree. The fact that there was an All-Ireland at the end of the season meant there was an ultimate aim to train and to practise winter and summer. It gave me a great chance, as much as an amateur could do, to be really fit and feel good in oneself. I thank Gaelic football for that.'

The highpoint in Mick O'Connell's illustrious football career was not the winning of All-Irelands, Leagues or Railway Cups but the times, whether with club or county or at practise, he soared to the sky like an eagle and caught a really high ball.

'Any time I got a ball coming from a distance it was a challenge to oneself to field that and catch it inch perfect. I'm not talking about beating the other man, that's incidental to the whole thing, but the fact is that you judged the ball perfectly, got up and got it in full flight. That's the personal satisfaction that most stands out in my mind.'

Kevin HEFFERNAN

Dublin Captain 1958

KEVIN HEFFERNAN, the man who gave his name to an army, was responsible for restoring pride in Dublin football in the seventies. How he did it has become part of Gaelic games folklore. Introducing a style of play hitherto unknown, he transformed in the space of twelve months a team of no-hopers into perhaps the most dynamic and entertaining All-Ireland winning team ever seen at Croke Park before then.

That was September 1974 and a far cry from the position a little less than a year earlier, when the county's football fortunes were at an all-time low. But help was at hand in the shape of County Board chairman Jimmy Gray. Not prepared to let Dublin football drift into a wilderness, he persuaded Kevin Heffernan to take over the position of team manager.

'Jimmy guaranteed that there would be a smaller number of people involved in the selection of the team and we would have a reasonably free hand to get on with the job of preparing and selecting the team. I thought the five-man committees that were elected by the County Board before that were unwieldy, biased and unsatisfactory in many, many ways. Jimmy then appointed Donal Colfer and Lorcan Redmond, two able and astute football men, as fellow selectors.'

'All I set out to do was to try to get a team that could win. We had a poor record in the preceding years, and morale was at a very low ebb. What we wanted to do was simply start winning matches again. To start off we got a fairly large group of players together, many of whom we knew from earlier days and many of whom were recognised as very good footballers but had been unsuccessful at county level.'

Kevin's first objective was to produce the fittest team in Ireland.

FACT FILE

HOME PLACE: Marino, Dublin

BORN: 20 August 1929

CLUB: St Vincent's, Dublin.

MAJOR ACHIEVEMENTS IN CLUB COMPETITIONS: Fifteen County Senior Football Championship medals 1949, 1950, 1951, 1952, 1953, 1954, 1955, 1957, 1958, 1959, 1960, 1961, 1962, 1966 and 1967; six County Senior Hurling medals in 1953, 1954, 1955, 1957, 1959 and 1962.

MAJOR INTER-COUNTY ACHIEVEMENTS: One All-Ireland Senior Football medal in 1958; one All-Ireland Junior Football medal in 1948; three National League medals in 1953, 1955 and 1958; four Leinster Senior Football medals in 1955, 1958, 1959 and 1962; seven Railway Cup Football medals in 1952, 1953, 1954, 1955, 1959, 1961 and 1962; one Leinster Junior Football medal in 1948; one Leinster Minor Football medal in 1946 and one Leinster Minor Hurling medal in 1947; chosen at left-corner-forward on 'Team of the century'

'The idea behind that was to give some basis for optimism to the players. We decided that fitness would be the launching pad. We said to the players, "We'll be the fittest team in Ireland so that we'll outlast anyone we play". Having got them enthused with the idea we then started to plan what we were going to do tactically on the field.'

There were few enough new players on the team that eventually won the All-Ireland in 1974. They were virtually all experienced players. The younger players were Brian Mullins and Bernard Brogan, but the likes of Jimmy Keaveney, Tony Hanahoe, Sean Doherty, Robbie Kelleher and Anton O'Toole had been there for quite a while before that.

'I think we brought order and discipline into the business of training. The fact that the players all suffered together through the winter of 1973 brought an enthusiasm, a camaraderie and a team spirit which stood to them very well. On top of that, they were very intelligent footballers and it was easy to communicate with them and easy to get them to understand what was required of them on the field. It was easy to get them to respond and to react in the way we wanted them.'

Kevin believes it was a particular help to be playing in Division 2, because it allowed the players build up confidence based firstly on fitness. Dublin now had a team that could outlast any opposition.

'We always had the view that whether it took thirty minutes or fifty minutes, we'd be running when the rest were falling down. On that we were able to build confidence that we would win at the end of any game. Because we were playing teams that weren't as strong as the premier teams, we were able to develop tactics and see them work effectively. This gave us the confidence to apply those tactics when we met better teams later on in the championship.'

It was not all plain sailing. Dublin lost to Clare at Croke Park in early 1974, conceding a big score in the process.

'They beat us and deserved to beat us on the day. I was very disappointed to lose,

Back, left to right: Denis Mahony (Chairman County Board), Cathal O'Leary, Paddy O'Flaherty, John Timmons, Lar Foley, Johnny Joyce, Jim Crowley, Marcus Wilson, Seán Murray, Brendan Morris, Tony Gillen, Dermot McCann, Paddy Downey, Joe Brennan, Joe Timmons.
Front, left to right: Peter O'Reilly (trainer), Ollie Freaney, Johnny Boyle, Kevin Heffernan (captain), Paddy Farnan, Maurice Whelan, Christy Leany, Padraic (Jock) Haughey, Des Ferguson, Johnny Malone, Brendan Quinn.

and was very annoyed, as a matter of fact. But it's inevitable when you're on the road back that every now and again you'll have a setback. Everything can't be perfect. It was important to ensure that whatever it was went wrong on that particular day didn't go wrong again.'

Dublin had a less than convincing win over Wexford in the first round of the Leinster Championship in 1974.

'We were dreadful. The game was on before the League final, in which Kerry played Roscommon, and I remember thinking as I watched the League final that the difference between the two matches was the same as the difference between men and boys. But a few months changed all that. The biggest factor in the change was that Jimmy Keaveney returned to us, and he became many things to the team. He was the place kicker we needed so badly. In my view Jimmy was probably the greatest kicker ever. He was also a target man and a tremendous personality and influence with the other members of the team. He was a major difference from there on.'

Jimmy's return to the county colours came about in unusual circumstances. Travelling home after the Wexford game Kevin was decrying the fact that he had no place kicker. A youngster by the name of Terry Jennings was in the car and he suggested Jimmy Keaveney. Jimmy had retired from inter-county competition the previous year and had watched the first round Leinster championship game against Wexford from Hill 16. 'When I rang him to see if he was interested in returning, Jimmy in typical fashion made no compliment of it. He just said, "Heff, if you think I can be of any help, I'll be down there on Tuesday night". And down he came. He worked very hard to get fit, as he had to at the time, and became a major, major factor in winning that All-Ireland.'

So too did the contribution of Leslie Deegan, forgotten by some maybe but not by Kevin Heffernan. 'Every match was an adventure, because we didn't know where we were going to finish up. We played Offaly in a a nerve-tingling game in Croke Park, and won with virtually the last kick of the game. Les Deegan kicked a tremendous high ball which went into the stratosphere somewhere and landed on top of the net. It's amazing the way luck runs for you, because Les Deegan and perhaps Jimmy Keaveney were the only two who could have scored that point. They were the only two who had the particular kick. Les was being charged by three or four Offaly defenders and he kicked the ball up over them from about thirty yards. Because they came so close he had to kick the ball way up in the sky. We won by that point. I often wondered afterwards if that match had been a draw would the "Dubs" have developed in the way they did. But that's the way luck breaks. We had it that day

---

THE 1958 DUBLIN TEAM

Paddy O'Flaherty

Lar Foley	Marcus Wilson	Joe Timmons
Cathal O'Leary	Jim Crowley	Johnny Boyle

John Timmons   Seán 'Yank' Murray

Padraig (Jock) Haughey	Ollie Freaney	Des Ferguson
Paddy Farnan	Johnny Joyce	Kevin Heffernan (captain)

Substitutes: Maurice Whelan for Seán 'Yank' Murray, Paddy Downey for John Timmons.

---

and won.

'Les was a great player who was absolutely dogged with injury. He was so enthusiastic and so physically strong that he was always back playing quicker than any other individual would be with a similar injury. That day against Offaly he came on as a substitute mid way through the first half and scored an outstanding goal almost immediately and then scored the winning point. And he played an important part on various other occasions; but injury was his particular problem, because he was so courageous and so brave that he put himself in danger and sometimes paid the price for it.'

After a Leinster final victory over Meath, Kevin and his players began to think in terms of winning the All-Ireland. Reigning champions Cork provided the opposition in the All-Ireland semi-final.

The semi-final turned out to be a great game and Kevin believes that Dublin still had the element of surprise.

'I don't think Cork believed for one minute that we had the team to beat them. In fact we had a very, very good team. The fact that they were experienced players meant that once their confidence and team game improved, the jump to top class was much less than it would have been for any emerging team that didn't have an experienced background. There was a much more dramatic improvement in the standard of play in a short time than you could possibly expect from a team that was starting from scratch.

'Cork certainly didn't anticipate what we had waiting for them. The merit of the team expressed itself in the second half, when Cork got a goal when they had sixteen men on the field.

'There was argument over it, but immediately from the kick-out Dublin went straight up the field and put the ball in the Cork net. And that was the strength, confidence and belief that this team suddenly had in itself. From being nothing at the beginning of the championship we were a very potent force at that stage.'

Kevin remembers the final against Galway as a disappointing game and not nearly as enjoyable or memorable as the tussles with Offaly and Cork.

'I suppose because the prize at stake is so great, teams tend to be a little bit tentative and a bit negative in their approach to the opposition. My clearest memory at the end of the game was looking at my colleagues Dónal Colfer and Lorcan Redmond, in disbelief that we had achieved what we had been talking about from the Leinster final onwards. I can remember their faces quite distinctly, and I'm sure they remember mine — simple disbelief that it had come right. Generally these fairytales don't have the happiest of endings, but this one certainly had.'

Heffo's Army was on the march and he was number one with the Dublin public. Kevin was delighted to have played his part, but typically kept all the adulation in perspective. He was aware of the esteem in which he was held but was also conscious that one is only as good as one's last match, whether manager or player.

Dublin's defeat by a young Kerry team in the 1975 All-Ireland final ranks as one of Kevin Heffernan's greatest disappointments. But he is quick to dispel the notion that the 'Dubs' paid the price for complacency.

'There was no question of taking Kerry for granted. I still think the game turned on one little incident early on when John Egan toe-poked the ball into the net. It was the kind of score that, had it happened at the other end, we would have won the game. It settled them and gave them confidence. They were an exceptional team, as they proved in all the years afterwards.

'I was annoyed for about four days, but after that I began to accommodate myself to it. I was particularly disappointed that we hadn't beaten Kerry, because they had beaten us in 1955 and I've a great relationship with Kerry and its people. I always felt whenever I was in Kerry the only All-Ireland that was ever played was the one in 1955, and I wanted to change that. We didn't succeed in 1975, but we did beat Kerry the following year.

For the record, Dublin won by seven points in 1976, and Kevin Heffernan had finally realised a treasured ambition.

There was no history whatsover of hurling or football in the Heffernan family. His father had no interest in Gaelic games, and his outdoor pastimes were shooting, fishing, walking and pursuits of that nature.

'Location is extremely important, and we came to live in Marino very early on. I went to school in Scoil Mhuire, where football and hurling was next to religion. I never succeeded in getting on the hurling team at that stage, because I started late and a couple of years made a difference. When I went to secondary school in St Joseph's in Marino I succeeded in getting on the hurling team early on, because numbers were small. Strangely enough, in colleges I had more success in hurling, because the school was predominantly a hurling school. We won Leinster Colleges senior and junior, while our only success in football in Leinster was in junior football. I played a couple of years' interprovincial hurling for the Leinster Colleges and one year with the football team.'

> *'I was aware of the esteem in which I was held but I was also conscious that one is only as good as one's last match, whether manager, player or anything else. I was too long around to fall into that trap.'*

The guiding influence at St Joseph's was Brother Keane, affectionately known as the Goof. According to Kevin, he was a great scholar, a great Gaeilgeoir and a great hurling man.

'He was the man who imparted the *seanspiorad na scoile* that was to stay with us a lifetime. He was the biggest initial influence, and he was followed by Brother O'Donoghue, who was another tremendous Gaeilgeoir and hurling man. They were both people of outstanding character.'

I came on the Dublin senior team the year I was doing my Leaving and I got my jaw broken a few days before the examination, which was a matter of great concern at the time but it worked out okay.'

The Dublin football machine of 1955 was the talk of the country. They claimed the National League with a comprehensive twelve-points victory over Meath, and were even in more devastating form in the Leinster final, demolishing the same opposition by twenty points on a 5-12 to 0-7 scoreline. Thus they became raging favourites to win the All-Ireland crown. Both All-Ireland semi-finals went to replays; Dublin eventually saw off the challenge of Mayo, and Kerry defeated Cavan to set up the final everyone wanted to see. To add spice to the meeting, it was suggested that

Kerry's traditional catch-and-kick game was under threat from a hand-passing Dublin team, spearheaded by Ollie Freaney and roving full-forward Kevin Heffernan.

'The final was very disappointing from a Dublin point of view, as we had been a long time around, having lost narrowly to Meath on a good few occasions. One of the things I always regretted is that two of the physically strongest players we had in Marcus Wilson and Norman Allen were unable to play. Marcus was injured in the All-Ireland semi-final and Norman got appendicitis. As well as that Jim McGuinness did his knee the Thursday night before the final. We played Jim for half the game, which was very unfair to him, because he wasn't fully fit. He was one of our strongest fielders, and playing on John Dowling would have made a big difference if fully fit. That is not in any way detracting from the fact that Kerry beat us and beat us soundly on the day, but it was a pity we didn't have our full side to match against them. Whether we would have won or not is very debatable, but I'd have been more satisfied if there had been no extraneous consideration.

'We didn't play as well as we should and were tactically bad. I myself was tactically bad in the second half. I kept looking for a goal, whereas had I been a bit more mature and cooler football-wise I would probably have taken the points. As a manager I'd have "eaten" players if they had done the same thing.'

How did his role as a roving full-forward come about?

'The reason is very simple. It wasn't my usual position — I normally played in the corner — but the selectors decided to put me at full-forward against Paddy O'Brien of Meath in the League final of 1955. Paddy was an outstanding player, a big man with a wonderful pair of hands and I knew if I stood beside him and jumped for a high ball I wouldn't catch too many of them. The only tactic left for me was to get away from Paddy, so I had long talks with our outfield players to play the ball in low and I took off early. Once I got facing him I had the advantage, so that's how it came about. At the same time in England Don Revie was just starting to do the same thing in soccer, playing as a centre-forward. Centre-forwards traditionally stood in on the centre-half but Revie began developing this thing of roving out and turning to the centre-half and taking him on. Like all these things, you develop them and hone them until suddenly someone finds an answer and you have to start with something else.'

It all came right for Kevin Heffernan in 1958. He won his third League medal when Dublin beat Kildare in the final, and in September, Kevin collected the Sam Maguire Cup as Dublin defeated Jim McKeever's Derry in the All-Ireland final. Kevin remembers it took a lot of hard work.

'We had been beaten the previous year by Louth in the Leinster final and I remember coming off the field and it was the only time in my life that I felt ashamed. I thought the team had let everbody down. Louth went on to win the All-Ireland, so maybe I wasn't justified in thinking that, but I thought the team had played so badly and were spiritless. I thought it was a game that could have been won and we hadn't done the business, and I really was dreadfully disappointed and ashamed of our performance. Out of that I became very, very determined that we would right that some way or other. As a result we re-designed the team. My view was that we were playing far too much football in defence instead of having strong, hard, physical ball-winners. We changed all that and the following year we had a full-back line of Lar Foley, Mark Wilson and Joe Timmons and they were uncompromising players.

We were surrendering to the traditional in that sense but we had a marvellous footballing half-back line in front of them with Cathal O'Leary, Jim Crowley and Johnny Boyle. The team worked much better. We had John Timmons in the middle of the field with Yank Murray and we had virtually the forward line we always had. We were far more determined in '58, even though the final against Derry hung in the balance until late in the second half when Paddy Farnan scored a goal that changed everything.'

Kevin's overall feeling was of relief that finally the 'boys in blue' had done the business. He has fond memories of players who soldiered with him on the Dublin team for many years. 'Ollie Freaney, a fantastic footballer and a fantastic individual. Unique. There is no other Oliver. A supreme optimist and the supreme effort-maker when things were bad. I remember him saying to me once after we had lost yet another Leinster championship by a point or two, "wouldn't it be worse if Vincent's lost the championship!"

'Fellows like Des Ferguson and Jimmy Lavin were great players and great characters. And Jock Haughey, who got an injury that should have put him out of football for ever more and a year and a half later he won an All-Ireland with us.'

After the 1958 All-Ireland victory, Kevin and members of the team stayed up all night celebrating and there was a crowd in his house for breakfast, among them his good friend Paddy O'Flaherty, the goalkeeper. As a new day dawned, Paddy and Kevin began kicking the Sam Maguire Cup over and back to each other with comments like 'that's what all the blood, sweat and tears is about. There it is now'.

Kevin was at the helm again in 1983 when twelve-man Dublin defeated fourteen-man Galway. As manager of Ireland's compromise rules team he masterminded the defeat of Australia in their own back yard. That remains one of the high points of his sporting life.

Chosen at left-corner-forward on the 'Team of the Century', Kevin Heffernan won fifteen county football and six county hurling championship medals with St Vincent's. The club means everything to him.

'On return home after beating Australia in 1986 I said that going to Australia to play them was great, winning was better still, but having won and coming home was best of all. In a football sense Vincent's was always my home. That's how I view it. And like all homes and like all families, you have squabbles and arguments, but it's when some outside influence tries to upset things that you really see unity and purpose.

'I had so many satisfying things happen to me but in retrospect the thing about the game is the people you meet and the friendships you make. When you're finished with it they, more than anything else, are the things that stand out.'

Dermot O'BRIEN

Louth Captain 1957

SINCE LEADING Louth to their first All-Ireland success for forty-five years in 1957, Dermot O'Brien, an ace accordionist, has gone on to become one of the most popular music personalities in Irish show business, with a large following in a number of other countries.

But many people may not be aware that Dermot was not the captain when Louth began their Leinster Championship campaign in 1957. Another Ardee man, Patsy Coleman, was the captain but he suffered an injury and Dermot took over the role with great success. Even though Patsy recovered and played at right-half-back in the All-Ireland final, Dermot held on to the captaincy for Louth's victory over Cork by two points. It was the day the smallest county in Ireland beat the largest. Morever, Dermot was the last captain to receive the Sam Maguire Cup on the old Hogan Stand.

Dermot remembers how it came about that he was retained as captain.

'At the final training session, Patsy and I were called in to sort out the captaincy. I offered to step down as captain but the selectors suggested we toss for it and I won the toss.'

After all that, Dermot very nearly did not lead the team as he was locked out of Croke Park less than an hour before the game.

'I had injured my shoulder against Tyrone in the All-Ireland semi-final and it didn't respond too well to treatment until I went to see an orthopaedic surgeon in Navan, where I worked. He arranged to give me an injection on the morning of the match in Dublin, which he did. It deadened the shoulder for the game. But when I got to the ground the gates were closed. The Cusack side was closed so Pat Boyle, the driver, and myself went around the back alley to the Hogan Stand and after a lot of palaver at the gate this guy let us in. There's nothing tougher than to get past a gate-keeper at a Gaelic match, especially in Croke Park.

'The problem now was I had to get across the pitch to the dressing-rooms. You can

---

FACT FILE

HOME PLACE: Ardee, County Louth

BORN: 23 October 1932

CLUBS: St Mary's, Ardee; spent one year with Navan O'Mahony's in 1955

ACHIEVEMENTS IN CLUB COMPETITIONS: Three Louth Senior County Football Championship medals in 1951, 1956 and 1960; Louth Minor Football Championship medal in 1949; six O'Donnell Cups; three Old Gaels Cups; won two Meath Feis Cups with Navan O'Mahonys though only one year with club.

INTER-COUNTY ACHIEVEMENTS: One All-Ireland Senior Football Championship medal in 1957; two Leinster Senior Football Championship medals in 1953 and 1957; captain of Leinster in 1958 and captain of Ireland versus Universities in 1958.

imagine how tough it was to get onto that pitch. There was a little wicker gate almost behind the goals at the "Mick McQuaid" side but even though I explained my position the guy there said, "I have no instructions about this, I couldn't let you in". There's less than half an hour to go and I'm panicking. Just behind us banked up were hundreds of Louth supporters and among them a great friend of mine, a Roscommon man that I'd done several concerts with called Kevin Casey, "The Parody King". He was an unbelievable gentleman, a lovely fellow. And didn't he spot me! Banners and flags everywhere. Incredible noise, this is All-Ireland day! I made signals to Kevin indicating I couldn't get in and he started a chant, "let O'Brien through, let O'Brien through". I said to the guy, "look at this" and he opened the gate and just said "go on". I crossed the field and rushed into the dressing-room with the sweat dropping off me from pressure. I had the collar and tie and Sunday suit on me.

'There was bedlam in the dressing-room and the Louth chairman, Jimmy Mullen, a very placid man, was screaming, "We are not taking the field without him". And the loudspeakers blaring, "would the Louth captain please report to the dressing-room" as I'm crossing the field. It was awful. I washed my face, got the gear on and just said "up and at them, lads" then out and we were away. And an hour and a half later, I'm picking up the Sam Maguire Cup.'

Dermot feels Louth played their worst game of the year in that final as players who were expected to shine failed to make an impact. That they won in spite of this demonstrated that Louth had a team and not just a few star players.

'It was a hurly burly affair and not a great game. The scoring was close but we never really clicked. We knew we could play better football. The goal won it for us. Kevin Beahan took a sideline ball and put it in the angle of the crossbar and the upright. Dan Murray, the Cork left-corner-back, seemed to have it covered but Seán Cunningham came from nowhere and somehow got his hand to it and scored a goal. He said later that he hit the ball with his elbow. We were thrilled. That lifted us enormously but Cork made an unbelievable sortie down the field in the closing

Back, left to right: Jim McArdle, Dan O'Neill, Jackie Reynolds, Jim Judge, Tom Conlon, Ollie Reilly, Alf Monk, Barney McCoy, Mickey Flood, Seán Óg Flood, Aidan Guinness, Jim Quigley.
Front, left to right: Stephen White, Frank Lynch, Kevin Beahan, Séamie O'Donnell, Dermot O'Brien (Captain), Peadar Smith, Patsy Coleman, Jim McDonnell, Seán Cunningham, Jim Roe, Jim 'Red' Meehan.

minutes and a dangerous ball came right into the square and "Red" Meehan cleared it off our goal line. That was the winning of the game.'

After the final whistle had sounded Dermot began to make his way towards the dressing-room until someone grabbed him and told him to go to the Hogan Stand for the Cup. 'Now I'm turning the other way and must have gone about thirty yards away from the dressingroom towards the Hogan Stand when I felt a pull on my jersey. I turned around and who was it only my direct opponent, Paddy Driscoll. Instead of going to his own dressing-room he followed me to shake hands. It was the gesture of a real man.'

He has another memory of going up to collect the 'Sam Maguire'.

'It wasn't like today where there's pasageways and flowers, you had to fight your way. I'm sure I stepped on Christy Ring's toe. It was the first time I had ever met him and we became great friends afterwards. He was sitting on the Hogan Stand. He was very into football. He shook my hand and then I remember passing two priests from Ardee, Canon Harmon who knew me as a little boy and Fr Shane Cullen who was a great Louth footballer in his day. The President of the GAA was a lovely man called Séamus McFerran from Antrim. All through my speech in Irish he kept beaming at me and saying, "maith an fear". It was an unbelievable honour for me. In hindsight now I look at it and say, "of all the wonderful players that played for Louth why was I picked to collect the Cup"?' Dermot still retains his great love for the Irish language and speaks it whenever possible. His favourite radio station is Radio na Gaeltachta.

Dermot remembers the homecoming as an unbelievable experience. There were over forty thousand delirious supporters in the streets when the cavalacade reached Drogheda. Bonfires blazed and there was a welcome every yard of the way.

'We arrived in Ardee at three in the morning. We came up the Main Street in the back of a truck and thousands lined the route with flags, others leaned out their windows. The parochial hall was jammed to the rafters, nobody wanted to go to bed. I remember on the way up through the town I was standing in the truck beside Tom Conlon, our full-back who had a stormer in the final. It was agreed at the time that Tom's outstanding display had won the game for us. He just said to me, "isn't this something else?" And I said, "unbelievable, Tom". He then said, "you know it's good for you but I saw the two days and it's better for me".' Tom had been on the losing team against Mayo in 1950.

The memory of that All-Ireland victory and wonderful celebrations helped Dermot O'Brien through a very difficult phase of his life when he was forced to emigrate after the failure of a business venture. 'They can take what they like off you, but they can never take the All-Ireland captaincy or my music away.'

Dermot became interested in Gaelic football at the age of four or five when he

---

THE 1957 LOUTH TEAM

	Seán Óg Flood	
Ollie Reilly	Tom Conlon	Jim 'Red' Meehan
Patsy Coleman	Peadar Smith	Stephen White
Kevin Beahan		Dan O'Neill
Séamus O'Donnell	Dermot O'Brien (Captain)	Frank Lynch
Seán Cunningham	Jimmy McDonnell	Jim Roe

began playing the triangle in the local Brass and Reed Band of which his father Paddy was the leader. The band played at all the football games and Dermot took great interest in 'The Mary's' who in his younger days played in red jerseys with yellow collars. Nowadays, St Mary's line out in blue and white.

'When I got a little bit older, maybe nine or ten, I used to ramble on my own to the football pitch in Ardee which at that time was down near the river beside where we lived. We used to go down on Sundays to see the big games and if the ball went into the river it was our job to go and fish it out. I got into playing myself at the age of about twelve. We had a wonderful teacher in De La Salle College called Brother Patrick who came from Kilkenny. He used to make us feel great because he'd line out the teams on the blackboard and you'd look real important. It was just like the big games in the newspapers. We had little school leagues and it was there that I started to get into the game and find that I had a fair proficiency for playing it.'

He later played for two years with the Louth minor football team in 1949 and 1950 which he admits was a wonderful experience. Life in the County Louth town of the thirties and forties was very different from what it is today. 'I can still remember opening the windows of our house so that people gathered outside could listen to the match. Our big heroes here in Ardee were Paddy Markey, Seán Boyle, Jack Bell, Johnny Malone, Nicky Roe and "Gua" Mooney. Míchéal O'Hehir would say, "on the square for Louth today is Ray 'Gua' Mooney". And he's still known as the "Gua". They were the players we admired.

'We had a great kicker of the dead ball in Ardee called Seán Boyle and he was unique in his style of kicking the ball. He had a jab kick and never followed through. He just jabbed it and he could send the ball seventy or eighty yards. An extraordinary kick and I never saw it done before or since by anybody.

'It would be a great occasion when Seán Boyle would get a new pair of boots.

Cork v Louth. Action in the 1957 All-Ireland final.

There would be upwards of fifty or sixty people in the field watching. He would get three or four footballs and bring them out fifty or sixty yards and when he put one over, those watching would say, "boys, he's getting the feel of them now, he has it". The "boys" would be nodding their heads and smoking their pipes. Can you imagine that happening now? We'd come down from the field and tell everyone, "Seán Boyle has a new pair of boots and he's hitting the ball a mile".'

Dermot was a member of the St Mary's senior team that won the county championhip in 1951. He was only nineteen and the baby of the team.

'You went up to the field and the "boys" made me feel at home. It was great. You went into the dressing-room and you pulled on your jersey and you were so proud but you didn't open your mouth.

'I won my first Leinster senior medal in 1953 when we beat Wexford in the final and was selected at right-half-forward for the All-Ireland semi-final tilt with Kerry. I was marking Seán Murphy and wasn't doing so well, so after about twenty minutes I was switched into the corner on Jas Murphy. When I ran in he stuck out his hand and said, "How are you, you creátur"!

'They smacked three goals against us in a fifteen-minute spell during the first half and it could have been a cricket score only we brought on an unnumbered sub. He was a priest who wasn't supposed to be playing. His name was Fr Kevin Connolly, a wonderful man, famous in sporting circles in Louth. He played under his mother's name, McArdle, and he had an unbelievable game at centrefield. He caught everything and went on solo runs and being the 440 yards champion of Ireland they couldn't touch him. We ran Kerry to five points.'

It was because of the defeat by Kerry that Dermot came to understand what it would take to win an All-Ireland title. He realised it was big league stuff and he knew it would take a supreme effort to claim the Sam Maguire Cup. However, it was to be some time before he once again wore the red and white of Louth.

'I was badly injured towards the end of that game when I went for this high ball and fell over the shoulder of big John Cronin and landed on my back. I burst a blood vessel and was badly concussed with the result that I was out of work for a while and quit the inter-county scene. My mother was at the match and when she saw me falling and being carried off she became extremely ill and had to be taken to hospital. I stopped playing for the county team because I didn't want to bother her. I still played with the St Mary's seniors but I did not play for Louth from 1954 to 1956. Early in 1957 my mother said something like, "Your red socks are there, why don't you play for Louth? They say you won't play for them". So I said, "Maybe I will". She gave me the clearance and I was happy. That was early 1957 and some selector asked me "If we pick you, will you play? We don't want to be picking fellows who won't play". It was as blunt as that. And I said, "If I'm picked I'll play".'

His first game back was in the League against Dublin who had a very strong team at that time. He was chosen at centre-half-forward and scored two goals.

Louth beat Carlow in the first round of the 1957 Leinster Championship at Navan. A few days later in Ardee, Dermot met his teammate Stephen White who uttered the prophetic words: 'This team will win the All-Ireland this year'.

'That was in May and we hadn't won an All-Ireland since 1912 but here was a guy talking about it. All of a sudden the team took shape. Of the six forwards that played in Navan that day I was the only survivor in the Leinster final. Little by little it came together; Séamus O'Donnell was brought on; Jim Roe got his chance and took it; Jimmy McDonnell came back out of retirement and went to full-forward and had a brilliant year; Frank Lynch was taken on and he was only eighteen.'

Louth beat Wexford in the second round and then comfortably disposed of the Leinster Champions, Kildare, before facing Dublin in the Leinster final in a torrential downpour at Croke Park. 'Jimmy McDonnell scored two unbelievable goals for us and we beat them by five points. Here we were as Leinster Champions! We adjourned to the hotel and had a fabulous sing-song.'

Louth defeated Tyrone in the All-Ireland semi-final by six points with the help of terrific dead ball kicking by Kevin Beahan. 'When you have a centrefield man score four points as he did, two fifties, a fifty-five and a sixty-five yards free, that's a hell of a contribution to the team. We missed a penalty early in the first half but we came back and the forwards played great stuff. I had a very satisfying match. We were fairly cock-a-hoop for the final against Cork'.

Dermot O'Brien and his St Malachy's Céilí Band were resident in the Irish Club in Dublin in 1956. Before that the multi-talented singer-musician played with the Vincent Lowe Trio from 1953 to 1954.

'I cancelled all music in 1957 to devote my time to football. Why, I still don't know. There was something telling me we were going to do the business on the football field. Being the captain of an All-Ireland winning team was a great help and instant publicity. I travelled with the Louth team to America in May 1958 for two weeks but I got leave of absence from my job in Navan and went back from September 1958 to March 1959 and worked as a professional musician.'

As soon as television was operating in Ireland Dermot was in constant demand hosting his own programmes like 'Country Style', 'Jamboree' and later again 'The

Dermot O'Brien Show'. His recording of 'The Merry Ploughboy' in 1966 went straight in at number 1 in the charts. A very rare achievement.

'After I had recorded "The Merry Ploughboy" and we were playing it back a few times, my manager Jim Hand called me over to the open window of the Eamonn Andrews Studio in Henry Street in Dublin. It was a Saturday evening and down below on the street there was a whole cluster of people looking up at the window listening to the playbacks. Jim turned to me said, "that's a hit".'

Dermot O'Brien's musical education had begun twenty years earlier.

'When I was fourteen this inspector came into our classroom. He started writing a little musical test on the blackboard and it got progressively harder. He noticed that I was singing faster than anyone else of the forty boys. He stopped and said, "You, on your own, sing this". And I could sing it like reading the paper, I didn't think I had any special talent. I just sang it off.

'He continued to write tougher and tougher tests on the board. I sang them all and

'Some selector asked me "If we pick you, will you play? We don't want to be picking fellows who won't play". It was as blunt as that. And I said, "If I'm picked I'll play".'

I enjoyed showing off but I didn't think any more of it. When I went home my sister Aileen said, "we had the inspector today and I heard them telling the nun he discovered a genius in the school". "Begod" says I, "I didn't hear anything about that". I never related it to what I was doing.

'That very same evening around tea time I saw Brother Patrick going past the window and I got very worried in case I had done something wrong as Brother didn't come to your house unless it was serious trouble. My mother and father went into the front room with him and when he was gone my mother came in and said, "you never told us the inspector put you through singing tests today. Brother Patrick says you have to be taught music". The following day she lugged me up to the convent. It was November 1946 and we met this wonderful nun, Sr Malachy. She realised I was fourteen and time was running out and she grilled me in piano and ensured I did eight years' work in four years. My first stroke of luck was having Brother Patrick as a headmaster and my second stroke of luck was having Sr Malachy as a music teacher. I called my first céilí band after her.'

He later developed a keen interest in accordion music from listening to the likes of the Emerald Céilí Band. He loved the raspy sound of the accordion. Nothing would do him only to borrow one from his friend, Leo Farrell. He brought it home and learned to play it on his own. Dermot O'Brien later went on to became a major show business star and one of the greatest exponents of the accordion.

Jack MANGAN

Galway Captain 1956

JACK MANGAN became the first goalkeeper to raise the Sam Maguire Cup when he captained Galway to win the 1956 All-Ireland title. In a high-scoring and exciting game Jack's team defeated Cork by just three points, 2-13 to 3-7, and in the process bridged an eighteen-year gap to the last time Galway claimed the All-Ireland crown.

On that October day in 1956 at Croke Park those two 'Stars' from Tuam, Seán Purcell and Frank Stockwell, lived up to their reputations as 'The Terrible Twins' with truly outstanding performances. Stockwell accounted for 2-5 of the Galway total, the highest individual score in any sixty-minute final.

Jack recalls the build-up to the final as a special experience. There was a wonderful atmosphere and a great feeling of comradeship. The players shared a sense of anticipation and excitement and a quiet confidence following their comprehensive victory over Sligo in the Connacht final and a narrow win over Tyrone in the All-Ireland semi-final.

'We did not underestimate Cork in any way but we had a feeling that it was going to be our year. We arrived in Dublin the night before the game and everywhere we went the one topic of conversation was the match. After Mass on Sunday morning we had a kick-about on the strand and before we realised it we were in Croke Park. This was it! We were led around the pitch by the Artane Boys' Band and the atsmophere was electric. The feeling just cannot be described. I never thought I'd see the day. It was a different world. From the throw-in, it was obvious that this was going to be a cracking game. It was a typical traditional Gaelic football game; the exchanges were hard but never dirty. Seán Purcell and Frank Stockwell were brilliant. Frank was finishing everything Seán was giving him. Both teams deserve credit for the standard and spirit in which the game was played and the crowd showed their appreciation by their constant chanting and cheering. It was a pity any team had to lose.'

But what about the captain's famous speech, widely acclaimed as one of the best ever?

'After the match I thought, "God I have to go up on the Stand and get the Sam

---

FACT FILE

HOME PLACE: Bishop Street, Tuam, County Galway

BORN: 6 May 1927

CLUBS: Tuam Stars, Galway; Kickhams, Dublin; Clanna Gael, Dublin; College of Surgeons, Dublin.

ACHIEVEMENTS IN CLUB COMPETITIONS: Six County Senior Football Championships with Tuam Stars.

INTER-COUNTY ACHIEVEMENTS: One All-Ireland Senior Football Championship medal in 1956; four Connacht Senior Football Championship medals in 1954, 1956, 1957 and 1958; one National Football League medal in 1957; two Railway Cup football medals in 1951 and 1957.

Maguire Cup". What earlier in the morning had been a lovely thought, all of a sudden was terrifying. I had thought of what I would say if we did win, but then the match was so good and the sportsmanship so great that I thought I cannot let this day go without congratulating Cork because they were absolutely brilliant in defeat. I said something like "Any youngster who wants to play football should take the Cork team as an example." I only said what I meant'.

It is generally held that the Galway team of that era never fully realised their true potential, losing many important games. They lost by a point to Cork in the 1957 All-Ireland semi-final; lost at the same stage and by the same margin to Dublin the following year and then failed to Kerry in the All-Ireland final in 1959. By then Jack Mangan had retired from football.

Jack is one of the very few All-Ireland winning football captains now living outside Ireland. He has been residing with his wife and family in Bilston, Wolverhampton, for nearly thirty years.

> *'The match was so good and the sportsmanship so great that I thought I cannot let this day go without congratulating Cork because they were absolutely brilliant in defeat. I said something like "Any youngster who wants to play football should take the Cork team as an example." I only said what I meant.'*

Frank Stockwell came from the same town as Jack and says of him that it would be impossible to find a nicer person.

'He is meek, humble and wonderful company. He was a year ahead of Seán and myself and won a Connacht Colleges medal in 1945. The same year he was on the Connacht Colleges hurling team, although Tuam is not a hurling area. He was one of the best goalkeepers I ever saw. He had a tremendous leap off the ground and a wonderful pair of hands. If he was playing the game today I don't think anyone would ever score a goal on him because of the way goalkeepers are now protected. In those times you had forwards and backs all coming in on top of him and Jack would come out on top of everything and just up in the air right through them. He was totally fearless. And he had such tremendous anticipation that he could make a very hard save look easy. He was a very, very quiet man but at the same time everybody had great respect for him. He would never come the heavy on anyone. If a player made a mistake Jack would say: "don't worry about it, next time everything will be all right". His speech on the Hogan Stand after the All-Ireland will stay in the memory of everybody who was there that day. Old-timers still talk about it. It was an honour to play with Jack Mangan. He is one in a million.'

As Galway full-back for many years including All-Ireland final day 1956, Gerry Daly was well placed to assess the abilities of his captain.

'Jack was a brilliant keeper for about seventeen years. He won his first county championship with Tuam Stars when he was only sixteen, at a time when the standard of football in the county was very high. He was a fine schoolboy athlete, winning the Connacht Schools High Jump Championship. This of course stood him well as a keeper as he was a fine fielder of a ball with very safe hands.

'He broke his ankle rather badly at twelve and the medical opinion at the time was that he should quit football. Instead he had a special boot made and played on with the ankle heavily bandaged. Even today he still wears a surgical boot.

'He was an ideal captain and the popular choice of all the players in our build-up to 1956. Because he was able to survey the entire field his views on changes were always respected. In the 1957 National League final against Kerry he was sidelined with a broken collar bone. The match was extraordinary in that we played for twenty minutes of the second half without any score. Jack instigated the switching of Seán Purcell and Frank Stockwell which led to the winning goal.

'When in New York in 1957 with the Galway team he contracted pneumonia and was confined to bed for over a week. On our return he was still rather weak but we had to play the All-Ireland champions, Louth, within two weeks. He was unable to train and was advised not to play. But he did and was made "Sports Star of the Week" for his display. After our defeat by Dublin in 1958 Jack decided to call it a day despite the selectors wishing him to continue.'

Jack Mangan has no doubt who was the most difficult opponent he faced in inter-county football: Tom Langan of Mayo.

'He had a very deceptive and extraordinary type of shot. And it wasn't a chance. He used to practise it. He would half hit a ball but it wasn't a drop shot. He would drop it down and bend the ball. It never came straight at you, it was weaving. He used to hit the ball with the instep half down and it came in lurches towards you and was very deceptive. He was the first forward that I had seen who could do that. He was a tough opponent, thin and angular with elbows everywhere, but not at all dirty.

'That time you couldn't pick a ball off the ground. If you dived on a ball you had to get up and put your toe under it and lift it. There was some chance of that in a goalmouth. I always enjoyed being the goalkeeper. The actual thing of responsibility didn't bother me that much, because I thought "if you save it you save it, if you're beaten you're beaten." I would be very sorry for the team if I let in a soft goal but it certainly wouldn't put me off. There was a lot more body contact then and it was very exciting. If you lost possession, you couldn't drop on the ball so sometimes you had to give away a penalty.'

Jack says the Galway team of his time got quite used to being beaten. He played football for the fun of it and the pleasure of making friends. He regrets that Tom Sullivan never won an All-Ireland medal for Galway.

'He played in the 1945 All-Ireland semi-final and if I can remember correctly, the headline on one particular paper was "Tom Sullivan versus Cork". Tom was from Oughterard and went to America in the very late forties. He was an outstanding footballer and gave everything he had.'

Seán Purcell, the complete footballer, was the player Jack admired most. They

---

THE 1956 GALWAY TEAM

Jack Mangan (Captain)

Seán Keeley	Gerry Daly	Tom Dillon
Jack Kissane	Jack Mahon	Mick Greally
Frank Evers		Mattie McDonagh
Jackie Coyle	Seán Purcell	Billy O'Neill
Joe Young	Frank Stockwell	Gerry Kirwan

Substitute: Aidan Swords for Joe Young

Galway v. Cork, All-Ireland final 1956: *from left*, Seán Purcell, Frank Stockwell, Paddy Driscoll and Dan Murray

grew up together in Tuam. Jack remembers Seán as being very light when he was young but he always had a superb turn of speed and great ball control.

'He was a very polished footballer. As he developed he could play in any position. He was a natural footballer with a good temperament. He had everything including a brilliant shot. If we were behind, we could always depend on Seán to do something special. Frank Stockwell and Seán combined very well together. They didn't even have to look for each other on the field, they knew one another's play that well.'

Back, left to right: Joe Young, Jack Kissane, Gerry Kirwan, Mick Greally, Mattie McDonagh, Tom Dillon, Frank Evers, Seán Purcell.
Front, left to right: Billy O'Neill, Jack Mangan (captain), Gerry Daly, Frank Stockwell, Jack Mahon, Jackie Coyle, Seán Keeley.

243

Jack's father, Hugh Mangan, was born in Dublin but his work as a dentist took him to Tuam and there he met and married a local woman Katherine Keane.

As a youngster Jack and his friends played football non-stop in the 'Barleyfield' directly behind Seán Purcell's house.

Jack attended Tuam CBS where he thrived under the tutelage of Brother Murphy, a Kerryman who was an excellent coach and a great motivator.

'He treated us all like grown-ups. When we played football we could give him a crack and he could do likewise to us but there was nothing ever nasty. There was no such thing as pulling back just because it was Brother Murphy. We cycled to places like Ballinrobe and Roscommon to fulfil colleges fixtures. Brother Murphy was so full of enthusiasm for the game and spoke tactics, which we had never heard of before then.'

Jack, along with Seán Purcell and Frank Stockwell, played on the Connacht Colleges team which won the All-Ireland title in 1945. There was never any intention on his part to become a goalkeeper. It just worked out that way and he never regretted it. Later in his career he was chosen as captain of the Ireland team.

His older brother Henry remembers that Jack was often placed in goal in friendly games and street leagues as he was too young to play outfield.

'From a very early age he displayed an excellent eye and spring for an approaching ball. I remember my father often remarked on these assets.

'My father had a very good eye, he was a Connacht champion in billiards. He was an excellent shot. He was also a very good golfer, so Jack probably inherited his talent.'

Jack was just nineteen when in 1946 he was selected as goalkeeper for the Galway senior team against Wexford. Unfortunately, Galway football was at a very low ebb then and Jack had to wait until 1954 to win his first Connacht Senior Championship medal.

Jack was offered terms to play soccer with Drumcondra but he declined, opting instead to stay with Galway. Hopes were high that the Galway team of the mid-fifties was eminently capable of challenging for major honours. Consequently their first-round hammering at the hands of Mayo in the 1955 Connacht Championship was a bitter pill to swallow. However, that defeat proved to be a watershed.

'The players had a chat afterwards and came to the conclusion that the team had not been picked properly. Players had been placed in ridiculous positions. We expressed our dissatifaction to the County Board that no one was discussing anything with the players. After our discussions with the County Board it was agreed that Billy O'Neill should look after the training and physical end of things.

'I was elected captain after a vote. I didn't know what to do. At the time Seán Purcell had been captain and a very good captain.

'We were the best of friends and I was sorry for Seán losing the captaincy but he wasn't annoyed about it at all. I thought the main thing was to get the lads together and get a feeling of friendship. I felt if we could get the spirit in the team off the pitch it would automically follow us onto the pitch. After that whenever we played a match we'd meet afterwards and have a chat and talk about it whereas before we'd just play a match and everyone would go home.'

By September the following year Jack Mangan's leadership qualities had borne fruit and Galway were newly crowned All-Ireland champions.

John DOWLING

Kerry Captain 1955

JOHN DOWLING is a larger-than-life figure whose love of Gaelic football knows no bounds. An outstanding midfielder for Kerry in the fifties, John has a fund of stories of the great games and the great players that inspired a future generation and helped to shape the national game.

John was the inspirational captain of the Kerry team that unexpectedly defeated a Dublin team of all the talents in the 1955 All-Ireland final. It was the Kingdom's eighteenth All-Ireland.

John was nominated captain because his club, Kerins O'Rahillys, were reigning county senior champions. But Kerry had their lucky escapes, as in the Munster Final against Cork in Killarney.

'It was only the grace of God that we won by two points as Cork drove a number of close-in frees wide. We were very lucky. We met Cavan in the All-Ireland semi-final and a Tadhgie Lyne goal equalised it for us in the last minute. The semi-final between Dublin and Mayo also finished in a draw and both replays went ahead in Croke Park on the same day in front of a huge crowd. We beat Cavan by over four goals in the replay and I have always maintained that the extra game did us the world of good because of all the training.'

Kerry's traditional catch and kick game was under threat in the 1955 final from a Dublin team that had brought a new thinking to the game. It is still regarded as one of the most memorable, dramatic and emotional of the meetings between these two great footballing rivals. The Dublin machine, spearheaded by Ollie Freaney and roving full-forward Kevin Heffernan, were odds-on favourites to see off the Munster champions. Dublin had destroyed Meath in the Leinster final and Kerry were expected to be given similar treatment. But it did not work according to the script.

'Because of working in the shop I wasn't able to attend the day sessions but never missed one at night. Our trainer, Dr Éamonn O'Sullivan, continually emphasised the point that the Dublin forward line would have to be marked very, very closely all the time. They were called the 'Dublin Machine' and had great players like Kevin Heffernan, Ollie Freaney and Snitchie Ferguson. Most people outside of Kerry felt we weren't capable of beating Dublin. We were complete underdogs.

FACT FILE

HOME PLACE: The Kerries, Tralee, County Kerry

BORN: 21 October 1930

CLUB: Kerins O'Rahillys

ACHIEVEMENTS IN CLUB COMPETITIONS: Three County Senior Football Championship medals in 1953, 1954 and 1957.

INTER-COUNTY ACHIEVEMENTS: Two All-Ireland Senior Football medals in 1955 and 1959; seven Munster Senior Championship medals in 1951, 1954, 1955, 1958, 1959, 1960 and 1961; one All-Ireland Junior medal in 1949.

'I personally felt if my clubmate Dinny O'Shea and myself could do reasonably well at centrefield and keep the ball away from the Dublin forwards as much as possible, the Kerry backs would look after whatever passed us. As it turned out we did well at centrefield. Dinny never gets the credit but he really had a stormer in the second half. We were reasonably in command until the closing ten minutes when Dublin put it up to us but we held out to win by three points. I was very pleased with my own performance on the day. I always liked to play well and trained very hard. My display against Dublin that day was the highlight of my career. I remember scoring a point from a fifty and was very proud to see it go over. I felt in great shape and things went my way.'

John was mobbed after the match. He maintains that he got more clouts that day than during the whole span of his football career. 'Kerry people just lost their heads. They went wild and I as captain took the brunt of it. They meant well. They had me up on their shoulders and fellows came up beating me on the back and I pleading with them not to take it out on me! The man who ushered me up to the Hogan Stand had great difficulty doing so because of the Kerry supporters converging. In the end I had to climb a wire fence to get up for the cup. Séamus McFerran presented the cup to me but I didn't say too much. Short and sweet. The speeches at the time weren't like what they are today.'

John Dowling did not have the cup when he arrived back to a packed and deliriously happy Kerry dressing-room. Some of the Kerry supporters got hold of it along the way and it was delivered safe and sound a few minutes later.

Running on the pitch for the start of the game, John Dowling was astonished to find that none of his teammates were behind him.

'There was such an enormous crowd trying to get out on the field that they could only get me out and the rest of the team was held up for a while. I spotted a neighbour of mine, John Savage, sitting on the sideline and I went over and sat down alongside him and started talking to him for about a minute. I wasn't going to walk

Back, left to right: Ned Fitzgerald, Micksie Palmer, Seán Murphy, Ned Roche, Jerome O'Shea, John Cronin, Mick Murphy, Tom Moriarty, Bobby Buckley, Tadhgie Lyne, Jim Brosnan, John Joe Sheehan. Front, left to right: Gerald O'Sullivan, Colm Kennelly, Dinny O'Shea, Johnny Culloty, Paudie Sheehy, John Dowling (captain), Garry Mahony, Donal O'Neill, Tom Costello, Diarmuid Dillon, Dan McAuliffe, Tadhg Crowley (Sec. County Board)

out on the field by myself.' That incident illustrates the naturalness and friendliness of the man.

After the game John met Dinny Breen, a member of the 1904 All-Ireland winning Kerry team who insisted on buying him a drink. 'I said to Dinny: "I would love to have a drink with you but I don't think you'll be able to buy what I want which is a pint of milk!" Dinny smiled and said: "You're the first man I ever heard asking for a white pint"!'

There were big celebrations that Sunday night and the following evening the easy-going John sauntered in to the railway station for the journey home. Kerry trainer, Dr Éamonn O'Sullivan, and the team were already waiting for him with the Sam Maguire Cup. 'Dr Éamonn was a very precise man and he approached me and said: "You're supposed to have this cup". "No, doctor", I said, "the cup is in safe hands, you've got it and you look after it. The best man to look after it, is yourself".'

John Dowling's father was a farmer and he exercised a great influence on his football-mad son. Two families, the Kerins and the Dowlings, lived in the one yard. 'We would often play against each other in a game that could start around eight o'clock in the morning and wouldn't finish until eight or nine in the evening. That night a discussion would develop as to who won the game and sometimes we'd argue about a goal that was disallowed around dinner time that day. My family sold a goat so that they could buy me my first football. The second football I got was a present from the Kerries and Knockanish Coursing Club because we used to go out and beat the hares up to the slipper.

'My father was a great follower of O'Rahillys and Kerry through their highs and lows. There was little transport at the time but when I played for the Kerry minors against Cork in the Athletic Grounds in 1947, Mr Kerins, Mr Dillon and my father travelled to Cork to see me play. I got on very well with my father but we never talked about my football career. He was inclined to be overcritical of me. In his book every fellow was able to beat me. So we came to an agreement that we'd talk about everything, even games, but not about John Dowling. And it worked very well.'

John Dowling attended primary school in Edward Street in Tralee and then went to the 'Green' school. 'I always say I went to school to learn how to play football not to do my lessons and I think I qualified. While there I was greatly influenced by a fantastic man called Brother Croke. We enjoyed great success and I was captain of the team. In that team we had the likes of Paudie Sheehy, Seán O'Connor, Bobby Miller, Dinny Falvey, all of whom played at some time for Kerry in later years.'

Because of his displays at school level, John was selected on the Kerry minor team in 1947 and again the following year. He was on the Kerry junior team which won the

---

THE 1955 KERRY TEAM

Garry Mahony

Jerome O'Shea	Ned Roche	Micksie Palmer
Seán Murphy	John Cronin	Tom Moriarty

John Dowling (Captain)　　　　　　Dinny O'Shea

Paudie Sheehy	Tom Costello	Tadhgie Lyne
Johnny Culloty	Mick Murphy	Jim Brosnan

Substitute: John Joe Sheehan for Tom Moriarty

All-Ireland title in 1949. John has the distinction of having captained two Kerry teams in 1954. He led the junior team in the first round of the Munster Championship before being promoted to the senior ranks where he again took over the role of captain.

He has never forgotten the advice given to him in 1947 by Kerins O'Rahillys' team trainer Purty Landers, himself an outstanding footballer. 'When I started playing I was a bit of a wild character and he told me that if I didn't cool down a bit I'd never make the grade but that I had a great future in front of me if I learned to come to grips with my game and not be as wild as I was. I'll never forget that advice. At the time I saw one thing only and that was the ball, so by hook or by crook I had to get it and didn't always play the game.'

A natural storyteller, John Dowling loves talking about football. He has been involved in the game for over fifty years and is friendly with many of the past and present generations of footballers and hurlers. Nothing gives him more satisfaction than meeting people and talking about his favourite pastime.

John once travelled to America with the Jimmy Magee All-Stars along with many other well-known sport and music personalities. In one particular game in New York John was playing centrefield and the hurling maestro Christy Ring was right-half-back. 'We were playing badly so Christy came up to me and said: "Look, those musicians are good men at their game and you're supposed to be a good footballer but you're a disgrace out there today". Having said that he caught the ball around the half-back line, went the whole length of the Gaelic Grounds in New York and stuck the ball in the net. He then ran out waving his fist and said to me: "I want you to do that three times in a row". Christy just hated losing. Whenever he was in Tralee after that he would call to the shop and if I wasn't there he'd just say: "Tell him 'Ringey' was in" and then out the door without a second's delay.'

'My display against Dublin that day was the highlight of my career. I remember scoring a point from a fifty and was very proud to see it go over. I felt in great shape and things went my way.'

John Dowling always wanted to be a leader, so being captain of Kerry came very natural to him. Anyone who ever played with him agrees that he never gave less than total commitment and commanding leadership. Friendships mean everything to him. He was a very strong, determined player with plenty of skill. He was also a good fielder and could kick with both feet.

A most loyal club man, John never failed to answer the call from his beloved Kerins O'Rahillys.

'We were a family football team and the father of the family was Paddy Paul Fitzgerald, our chairman. The team trained in my father's farm two miles outside the town and walked in and out to training night after night. Actually the team that won the County Championship in 1953 was selected back in one of our out-houses. We had some of the finest footballers in that family team, men like Thomas Raymond, as good a player as ever caught a ball, John "Mull" O'Connor, Dinny and John Falvey, Joe and Michael Kerins, both of whom I played with from the time I was about six years of age, Pop and Michael Fitzgerald and many, many more great players. They were as fine a bunch of players as you'd ever meet. The late Paudie Sheehy of John Mitchels once remarked: "You'd meet these O'Rahillys fellows below in the church of a Sunday morning or a Wednesday night and the whole gang of them would be together. No wonder they were called a family team". We were known as the "Nari" pickers because the field we developed was once the dumping ground in Tralee so our opponents gave us that name. It has since become synonymous with the club.'

John Dowling missed the 1953 All-Ireland win over Armagh because he was serving a fifteen-month suspension at the time. He had played with a club in Cork and it came to the notice of the authorities who acted swiftly and very harshly. All that mattered to John was playing football, a case of 'have boots, will play'.

'Football was my life, so not being able to play competitively for such a long time was very, very hard. It was a new world for me trying to while away my Sundays. I bought a gun and took up shooting for the duration of the suspension. I went to very few games as it was very difficult not being able to take part. I was annoyed that I was never proved guilty. It was all based on hearsay. It was a fact though that I had played illegally.'

Another major disappointment for John was the 1960 All-Ireland final in which Kerry lost to Kevin Mussen's history-making Down team.

'In 1960 Dr Éamonn was not training the Kerry team owing to a dispute with the County Board. We trained under Gerald O'Sullivan from St Mary's in Cahersiveen who was a very good trainer. He was a dedicated man. Up to that time I had never ever taken time off for collective training with Kerry, although, of course, I trained diligently with my club and with the county. But in preparation for the 1960 final I decided to take time off and go to Killarney for the three weeks' training. We put a lot of hard work into it and we were playing an unknown Down team who turned out to be very good. Unfortunately, on the morning of the match I met with an accident.

'It all happened through a newspaper report that the Kerry full-back and full-forward lines were very slow. As a result we decided to find out for ourselves which was the slower of the two. I was chosen to represent the full-forward line and Jerome O'Shea the full-back line. We were staying in a hotel in Malahide and decided that the race would be a fifty or sixty yards' sprint across the lawn which meant going over the driveway. I was in front coming back, and passing the tarmacadam driveway I tripped myself by running in front of Jerome and the consequence was a "dead" and very badly burnt left leg. I also tore my togs and had to borrow a pair from one of the members of the Cork minors to play in the final as the ones that my mother had cleaned and ironed were in ribbons.

'Before the game there was a question about whether or not I would play. Gaffney Duggan and Rory O'Connor did the best they could picking tarmacadam out of my leg and my ribs. Unfortunately, I was badly burnt from the fall. People say that I was limping in the parade but having said that it was more of a burning than anything else and a "dead" leg. I wasn't able to give of my best. I was devastated.'

But he admits his biggest disappointment of all was losing the 1954 All-Ireland final to Meath. He recollects that Congress banned collective training that year and Kerry never once came together for training for the final. 'This is not an excuse for our defeat. I was captain and down the street was the 1953 captain Jas Murphy. People in Kerry felt it was only a matter of going up and collecting the cup and

Des Ferguson, Sean Murphy, Johnny Boyle and Jerome O'Shea with the ball. All-Ireland 1955, Kerry v. Dublin

bringing it down to my shop just ten yards from where Jas had it the previous year. I got no cup and I can tell you I was disappointed. Not taking away from Meath or anything: they beat us well on the day. Only Paudie Sheehy, John Cronin and to a lesser extent John Joe Sheehan played well. All the rest of us including myself had very bad games. I was bitterly disappointed and it was depressing in the dressing-room. Our minors were beaten the same day, so it was two heavy blows for Kerry to stomach.'

There was better luck five years later in the 1959 final, the seventy-fifth anniversary of the GAA, when John lined out at full-forward as Kerry, under the captaincy of Mick O'Connell defeated Seán Purcell's Galway.

John was on the mark early with two points in the first few minutes.

'John Flynn was behind the Canal End goal where I scored the points and when I got the first ball, he roared out "kick it over the bar, John" and it so happened I did. When I got the second ball, he said "repeat it". He met me some days later and he said: "did you hear me telling you kick the ball over the bar?", I said "of course, I did", and he replied: "you'd never have scored those two points only for me". Tralee is a wonderful town and full of great characters!'

Ned Roche who played full-back on the 1955 All-Ireland winning Kerry team remembers John as a most inspiring captain. 'John was strong and daring and could kick equally well with either foot. He was a marvellous fielder of the ball and gave of his best in every game. His love of all sport is unbounded. I first got to know John in the Munster Colleges Championship when playing with the rival college of St Brendan's, Killarney. Even then John was an outstanding footballer.'

John played against some wonderful players on the inter-county scene among them Paddy Driscoll, Cork, Jim Crowley, Dublin, Jim McKeever, Derry and Galway's Seán Purcell whom he rates the best he faced at county level.

'He had strength, agility and was a wonderful kicker of a ball with either foot. His pure physical strength made him a very hard man to stop.'

In more recent times he admired the wonderful skills of Jack O'Shea.

'Jacko had unlimited energy, great style, was a great fetcher and kicker and got wonderful scores. He did it over a period of fourteen or fifteen years at the highest level. He was really top class.'

John Dowling was more than just a wonderful player. He was an inspirational man in every sense of the word and to this day represents everything that is positive and enriching in Gaelic games.

Over the bar! All-Ireland final 1954, Kerry v. Meath

Peter McDERMOTT

Meath Captain 1954

Peter McDermott was one of the outstanding corner-forwards of his generation and also a distinguished referee. He will always be remembered as 'The Man in the Cap'. Or should that be 'The Man With the Cap'?

'"The Man in the Cap" thing was far from intentional on my part. Mícheál O'Hehir started calling me the "The Man With the Cap" and it began to stick. I didn't play up to it, or anything like that, it wasn't done for a gimmick, it was done for a purpose.

'I had a magnificent head of long black hair which was easy to sweep back and hold in place, so long as it was well plastered with Brylcreem. But when it came to playing football it was an infernal nuisance, because of its length. It was commonplace for caps to be worn then, there was nothing unusual about it. People used to say about Andy Merrigan of Wexford that everything was all right until Andy turned the cap backwards. Then you had to watch out for fireworks. When his dander was up and the peak of his cap went to the back, it was time to steer clear. I really got in on wearing a cap through Jimmy Brazil, who was working in Sheils of Thomas Street in Dublin. I used to deliver eggs to the shop. Mrs Sheils was an aunt of Ronnie Kavanagh, who played rugby for Ireland. Jimmy was a great fan of mine and likewise his brother, Peter. I had no more loyal supporters in Croke Park than the Brazils. Jimmy came to work one particular morning with this fantastic cap and I just happened to be there. I never saw one like it before. To me it was the "Rolls-Royce" of all caps. It was one of the modern "racing" style caps, with the crown stitched on to the peak. It wasn't at all like the big old-fashioned caps. I tried on this cap and was so taken with it that I offered to buy it. But Jimmy wouldn't have it any other way

---

FACT FILE

HOME PLACE: Cushenstown, Ashbourne, County Meath

BORN: 27 July 1918 in Pallastown, Belgooly, County Cork

CLUBS: Ardcath; Rathfeigh; Donaghmore; Young Irelands (combination of Bellewstown and Cushenstown in Duleek Parish) O'Mahonys, Navan; Ratoath; Oberstown.

CLUB ACHIEVEMENTS: Meath Minor Football Championship in 1936 with Rathfeigh; Intermediate Football Championship in 1938 and Senior Football Championship in 1942 with Donaghmore; Meath Junior Football Championship in 1947 with Young Irelands and Meath Senior Football Championship with O'Mahonys in 1953, 1957 and 1958.

INTER-COUNTY ACHIEVEMENTS: Two All-Ireland Senior Football Championship medals in 1949 and 1954; six Leinster Senior Football Championship medals, 1940, 1947, 1949, 1951, 1952 and 1954; two National Football League medals in 1945 and 1951; three Railway Cup medals; selected as sub on Ireland team of 1950.

'The Man in the Cap' Peter McDermot in the 1949 All-Ireland final

only make me a present of the cap. It was really lovely and not much in vogue at the time. It fitted like a glove, didn't come off too easily and didn't get into my eyes. I kept that cap for years and years and that was "the Cap". That cap lived with me, it fitted me well and was part of me. I'd be naked without my cap.'

The cap disappeared during a trip to the States in 1951. Meath won the National League Final in the Polo Grounds in New York in 1951 and from there, Peter and the team travelled to Boston to play a match. It was there that the cap vanished.

If one person, more than any other, helped shape the football career of Peter McDermott, it was local priest Fr Michael MacManus. 'He was very proud of his own accomplishments on the football field. He lined out with Meath against Kildare in Drogheda when priests were not allowed to play. He played under an assumed name. There was great rivalry between Meath and Kildare, as they played a whole string of matches against each other in the late twenties when Kildare football was at its peak. There was always the threat that Kildare would object to him playing, so some Meath officials went to the Bishop of Meath to ask permission for Fr Mac to play. The bishop could not grant the request, so Meath had to play without Fr Mac after that. But his reputation as an outstanding footballer lived on.'

In the early thirties, Fr Mac was transferred to Skryne parish as a curate which proved a godsend for the struggling junior club. It was the beginning of the Land Commission, which brought about a break-up of big ranches in Meath. Fr Mac was instrumental in securing a GAA pitch for Skryne from the Land Commission. He held the position of Chairman of Meath County Board from 1939 to 1945.

'I was seriously ill in 1942, so ill in fact with pleurisy and threatened TB that people came to my "wake". It was in the real bad years of the war and only for Fr Mac I wouldn't have lived to see the year out. He took me in hand and I eventually ended up in St Vincent's Hospital in Dublin. Because of his great ability as a footballer, he was an inspiration to me in every way.'

Peter McDermott is in no doubt that the most difficult opponent he came up against in inter-county football was Jack Bell of Louth.

'I think it is fair to say that Jack Bell made his name when playing on me in the marathon series of Louth versus Meath games in 1949. Jack now lives in Edmonton, Canada, and we've maintained correspondence. I went into the first of three games in 1949, full of belief, because I'd played on Jack previously and didn't find him that hard to cope with. But obviously Jack Bell had learned a lot in the meantime, or else I had deteriorated. I couldn't ask to be beaten by a fairer man than Jack. He always shook my hand and I shook his. There were no regrets after a match. That particular year, I was playing very well and getting rave notices. But the flag was lowered considerably when I met the one and only Jack Bell.'

Peter McDermott reckons the greatest disappointment he suffered on the football field was losing to Kerry in the 1947 All-Ireland semi-final. The winners qualified to play the final in the Polo Grounds in New York

'Young people today couldn't imagine how much we would have appreciated and valued a trip to New York in those times. It would have been the dream of all dreams. Meath had a good team in those years and we beat Laois in the Leinster Final. Then when it came to us playing Kerry, in the second semi-final, we were a complete flop. It wasn't that Kerry were so good, but that we were so extremely bad on that particular day.

Of course there were many good moments as well as bad ones, and Peter recalls with startling vividness what he considers was his best ever score, when he outjumped and outfoxed the 'Gunner' Brady to punch a goal against Cavan in the 1952 All-Ireland final.

'Even though I was small enough in stature, I had a long reach and I was able to use this to advantage all the time. I was good at flicking a ball to the net, which I don't see too many fellows doing nowadays. I'm disappointed, as a matter of fact, to see forwards going for the high catch when in close proximity to the square, as the smallest flick would stick the ball in the net every time. I hate to see fellows flailing at the ball with a big fist when all that is required is a little twist of the wrist, like turning the knob on the door. You get the ball on the knuckle part and give it that little turn at the correct moment, which gives it the deflection and even adds speed to the ball. I scored some very, very good goals in this manner in my time and remember getting great publicity for a goal that I scored in a Railway Cup match in

THE 1954 MEATH TEAM		
	Patsy McGearty	
Mícheál O'Brien	Paddy O'Brien	Kevin McConnell
Kevin Lenehan	Jimmy Reilly	Ned Durnin
Paddy Connell		Tom O'Brien
Mícheál Grace	Brian Smyth	Mattie McDonnell
Paddy Meegan	Tom Moriarty	Peter McDermott (Captain)

Croke Park. It went in from maybe twenty-one yards out, when I beat an opponent for a high one with a good flick. Another kind of flick I specialised in was a back-handed one where my policy was to jump a shade too far under the ball. Then when my opponent was sure I had outreached and that he had the ball in his hands, I'd give it a little nod and off it would go into the net.

'That particular day in 1952 against Cavan, the "Gunner" was reading the "Riot Act", telling players in no uncertain manner to do this, that and the other. I was playing on a very quiet player, Jim McCabe, a Colleges star, with a great reputation. McCabe was a pure footballer, and out-and-out Colleges type footballer, and that suited me down to the ground. I liked to think that I also played pure football. The "Gunner" had laid down the law for McCabe, telling him what he was to do and what not to allow happen.

'I had this thing, that if someone was taking a free for Meath, I'd retreat a distance and when the kicker would start his run up I'd start mine from a little bit further back, so as to give the ball time to arrive and then I had the perfect take-off. In this instance, I did a dummy run on McCabe, went in on the back-line and when I got him going for the back-line, I then switched inside him and outjumped the "Gunner" and McCabe in the square, beat them to the punch and got the ball into the corner of the net.

'I was charmed and had the winning of the game in the next minute, no names mentioned, but one our players elected to blast the ball himself, instead of passing it out to me and all I had to do was tap it over the bar. That was the famous day of the point that hit the top of the post.

'Meath were a point in front in the closing minute and ball appeared to be going wide, down into what is now the Nally Stand area and the strong wind brought it back into play. Edwin Carolan lobbed it back in towards the goal area and it went across and hit the top of the post at the far side and dropped over the bar — the equalising point and the game ended in a draw. Everybody said that the next day

Back, left to right: Paddy Brady, Ned Durnin, Richie Mee, Jimmy Farrell, Brian Smyth, Kevin McConnell, Mícheál Grace, Paddy Connell, Tom Moriarty, Bernard Flanagan, Frankie Byrne, Gerry Smith, Paddy O'Brien.
Front, left to right: Patsy Ratty, Jimmy Reilly, Kevin Lenehan, Tom O'Brien, Matty McDonnell, Peter McDermott (captain), Paddy Meegan, Patsy McGearty, Billy Rattigan, Larry O'Brien, John (Nobby) Clarke, Mícheál O'Brien.

couldn't be as wet as the first but, if anything, it was worse. In the replay, Mick Higgins scored all the frees for Cavan. I look back on this as an All-Ireland thrown away.'

A year later, in September 1953, Peter McDermott was back in Croke Park but this time as the referee of the All-Ireland Final in which Kerry defeated Armagh. Three years later, in 1956, Peter was again the man in charge as the Sean Purcell and Frank Stockwell powered Galway side triumphed over Cork, thus becoming the only man in the annals of the GAA to have refereed All-Ireland finals before and after winning an All-Ireland medal.'

Peter was asked to help in the preparation of the Down Junior football team in 1945 and was delighted when they won the All-Ireland title the following year. So began a very successful association with the Mourne County which led in 1960 to assisting with the coaching of the Down Senior Football team.

'The Down team was very popular, because of the attractive style of their play. I

Meath and Kerry parade in Croke Park, 1954

always like to think that I helped to introduce that particular fluent style into the team. Of course, it couldn't be developed if the players involved hadn't the flair. It was an honour to talk to a team of that calibre and all they needed was the freedom and encouragement to do their own thing. How could I ever pretend that I taught the 'Stars of the County Down' how to play football?'

In 1966, a motion was passed at the Meath County Convention which led to the appointment of a coach to assist Rev. Fr Tully with the training of the county senior football team. Peter beat Frankie Byrne and Brian Smyth in a close vote and that year Meath qualified for the All-Ireland final but lost to Galway. All came right the following year when Peter Darby captained Meath to victory over Cork.

In 1968, Meath toured Australia with Peter still acting as coach and that opened another chapter in his many-sided football career. When the Australian Rules players came to Ireland for a series of Test matches under compromise rules in centenary year, Peter was very involved in preparing the Ireland team. Mention of those games against those brawny men from Down Under puts Peter in mind of one of his all-time favourite footballers, a Meath man.

'I always had a great smack for the "Red" Collier. I hope he won't mind me saying this, but he had a great appearance with that tuft of red hair standing up, when things began to get rough. He was built like a little tank. They called him "Bluey" in

Australia, where he took the place by storm. There was something about the 'Red', he had that will to win and on top of all that, he was a good two-footed footballer with a great ability to place a ball well. He hit it low, sweet and hard. It was a joy for fellows up front to get a ball put to them like that, and it must have been great to be able to rely on that kind of service. This is where a good half-back can play such a leading role. Joe Lennon was a great example. He hit a brilliant ball upfield, all the time, never a ball wasted. A well-used ball, all the time, is a dream for a forward, who has made an opening and then has somebody to put it to his advantage.

The crowning glory of Peter McDermott's own football career was the 1954 All-Ireland Final. At the beginning of the Leinster Championship campaign, Peter considered himself semi-retired. At the time, he was County Secretary. His inter-county football career seemed at an end.

'Because I was secretary and sitting on the selection committee, I didn't deem myself in the running for a place on the team. Then we came to this famous match with Wicklow, which Bill Delaney was refereeing, and Wicklow were leading Meath, going into the final minutes. What the Meath selectors hoped to achieve in the last few minutes I'm not sure, but Paddy Meegan and myself were sent in from the substitutes and no sooner was I on the field than a Wicklow player nailed me from behind, a terrible bang to the back of my head. I'd have to admit to having made the most of it. This has since been referred to as the game of the long overtime. I deliberately stayed down for a long time and we talked on the ground about what to do. It was gamesmanship and as it happened Meath collected their wits and scored the two points that won the match, very much against the run of play. We then beat Kildare and I was severely injured during that game with a very heavy, late and dangerous foul.

> 'Even though I was small enough in stature, I had a long reach and I was able to use this to advantage all the time. I was good at flicking a ball to the net, which I don't see too many fellows doing nowadays.'

'I suffered badly broken ribs and I went off the field crying. It was the only time I ever went off in Croke Park, and there wasn't an awful lot of smpathy for me either. It brought home to me how lonely it can be for a fellow who is injured. He goes off and the game goes on and everybody is wrapped up in what's happening on the field. Nobody looked after me when the game was over. I had to get one of our employees to drive me home in my old Hillman car, because I wasn't able to drive the car myself such was the pain. We didn't seem to have much gumption in those years about these kind of things; you just got a wallop and you accepted it and hoped it would be better tomorrow. But tomorrow came and it wasn't better and my ribs were severely cracked. I was put in plaster and it was very painful.'

The injury kept Peter out of the next game, which was against Longford, but he was on the substitutes' bench when Meath defeated Offaly in the Leinster final. Midfielder Tom Duff fractured his leg during the game and Peter was called into the fray. Offaly were very much in the ascendancy at the time, but three goals, in each of which Peter played a part, helped clinch victory for Meath.

A team of no-hopers had proved everyone wrong and regained the Leinster crown after a one-year gap. So it was on to Croke Park and an All-Ireland semi-final victory over Cavan by a single point. Against all the odds, Meath were back in the All-Ireland Football Final. Peter McDermott thought to himself, 'miracles do happen'.

Peter recalls the build-up to the final as very low-key. Nearly every sports journalist dismissed Meath's chances. Interestingly, when Kerry won the All-Ireland the previous year, Peter was the referee. He was now facing them as captain of Meath. Kerry were regarded as a very good side. Peter recalls that two hard games against the 'Wee County' in the build-up to the final worked wonders: 'We played Louth on successive Sundays, prior to the final, and they beat us and beat us well. And it wasn't a question of us not trying, as we were all doing our best to keep our places. The wise fellows said afterwards that Meath pulled a fast one, but we didn't, Louth beat us fair and square.'

On the Sunday before the All-Ireland Final, Meath trained in Páirc Tailteann in Navan and from running and sprinting, Peter developed a pain from an old injury in his lower back. He was also County Secretary and had more than his share of hassle from people looking for tickets. To make matters worse, a severe toothache kept Peter awake all night on the eve of the All-Ireland. 'My dentist, the late Jimmy Connolly, was furious with me for not calling him to have a pain-killing injection during the night.

'Brian Smyth had a blinder for us. It was the kind of performance I would have loved to have had myself. Michael Grace also had a wonderful game. Paddy O'Brien went into that match with boils on the back of his neck, and played under a severe handicap with a bandage around his neck. While I only scored one point in the match, my main contribution was the fact that I played an important part in the goal scored by Tom Moriarty.

'I can remember particularly well going up to Brian Smyth a minute or two from the end and saying to him, "I want you to come up with me on the Hogan Stand to collect the Cup, because I went up with you in '49 and I'm asking you to come up with me on this occasion." One of the things I said when I collected the Sam Maguire was: "To beat Kerry in an All-Ireland Final is like winning two All-Ireland Finals". It was meant as a tribute, but was construed as gloating in certain quarters.'

The following Monday evening thousands welcomed home the victorious Meath team en route to the Market Square in Navan. 'I drove my old Hillman car with a sunshine roof, but it turned out a very wet evening. Patsy Ratty and myself brought the Cup home to Navan. Patsy stood up on the passenger seat of the car and held the Cup out through the roof and suffered a very severe wetting.'

There is about Peter McDermott a sense of contentment. He is happy with his life's achievements both at a professional and sporting level. And why not? His record in Gaelic games is indeed a proud one. An ambassador in every sense of the word.

Jas MURPHY

Kerry Captain 1953

JAS MURPHY was the surprise captain of the Kerry team that won their seventeenth All-Ireland senior title in 1953. Paudie Sheehy had filled the role when Louth were beaten in the semi-final but he was not chosen on the starting fifteen for the final against first-timers Armagh. It was cruel luck on Paudie whose father John Joe was a Kerry selector at the time. Consequently Paudie's club, John Mitchels, had to nominate a captain and they chose another Tralee man, Jas Murphy.

A similar situation had arisen in 1946 when Gus Cremins was dropped for the final and Paddy Kennedy was appointed captain. He went on to collect the Sam Maguire Cup after a replay against Roscommon. Interestingly, Jas and Paddy were both playing their club football outside Kerry and both were members of the Garda Síochána.

The 1953 All-Ireland championship took on even greater significance because of the fact that Kerry had failed to win the title since 1946. That represented Kerry's longest spell without a win since the first presentation of the Sam Maguire Cup a quarter of a century earlier in 1928. The victory of Jas Murphy's men marked the beginning of a new and very successful era for Kerry football. It was also the Golden Jubilee Year of the 'Kingdom's' first All-Ireland success. His contemporaries all agree that Jas Murphy was a natural footballer and a first-rate defender. He was a great fielder, had good anticipation, was very strong, and his long, well-directed clearances were delivered equally well with left or right foot.

It remains as much a mystery to Jas as to everyone else why he was selected to play only one more championship game. That was in 1954 when Kerry defeated Waterford. By general consent the Cork-based garda was then playing the best football of his career but the powers that be in Kerry chose to ignore him and never offered an explanation.

'I was getting married shortly after that game against Waterford but I told the selectors that I'd be ready for the Munster final. I never heard from them after that and nobody ever contacted me. I was not even on the panel. I never asked why I was

---

FACT FILE

HOME PLACE: Lower Bridge Street, Tralee, County Kerry

BORN: 30 May 1923

CLUBS: O'Rahillys; Geraldines, Dublin; St Nicholas, Cork; Garda in Cork.

ACHIEVEMENTS IN CLUB COMPETITIONS: One County Senior Football Championship in 1950 with Garda in Cork; one Kelleher Shield with St Nicholas.

INTER-COUNTY ACHIEVEMENTS: One All-Ireland Senior Football Championship medal in 1953; three Munster Senior Championship medals in 1950, 1951 and 1953; Munster Minor Championship medal in 1941; played right-full-back for Ireland versus Universities in 1951.

dropped but I was very upset for a long, long time afterwards. I stopped going to county matches for about three or four years although I continued to play with the Guards for a short time until I lost my appetite for the game. The lads in Tralee were very upset about the way I was treated but they got no answers from those in authority. I was forgotten about, which wasn't nice. It's my big regret and I'd still like to know why. The whole thing also upset my wife, Mary, very much. But as time went by I decided I was bigger than any of that and started going to matches again. In 1976, Mary and I went to the States with the Kerry team and it was a very enjoyable trip.'

The first Jas Murphy heard that he was to captain the Kerry team was on the Thursday before the All-Ireland final. The message came through to the hotel from Tralee to say that he had been selected by the John Mitchels club.

'It was a great honour but I wasn't sure how I'd fit into being captain because I was always a team man. I was very sorry for Paudie. Being Tralee men, we were friends all our life. For years we had travelled together from Cork to play with Kerry along with Jim and Mick Brosnan, Ned Roche, John Cronin and Bobby Buckley, so that made it even more difficult. I didn't canvass to be captain at all but there was canvassing going on for other players. I know that. But Tralee wouldn't let the captaincy leave the town. Goalkeeper Johnny Foley was another Kerins O'Rahillys man and if it wasn't me it would probably have been Johnny. I'm not sure what I said to Paudie. He was naturally disappointed but was glad that the club had nominated me as captain.'

Tralee CBS was where Jas Murphy's love of Gaelic football was nurtured. He recalls the many games played in the Urban District Council field at the Green, now the car park of the Brandon Hotel and home of the Dome for the Rose of Tralee Festival.

'The lads from Abbey Street and Mary Street all played football. There were many great games between Abbey Street, which was above the pump, and Mary Street, below the pump. The pump was a water tap which divided both streets. They were

Back, left to right: Donie Murphy, Tadhgie Lyne, Jackie Lyne, Ned Roche, John Cronin, Jerome O'Shea, Diarmuid Hannafin, John Joe Sheehan, Micksie Palmer, Mick Brosnan, Mick Murphy, Brendan O'Shea.
Front, left to right: Tom Ashe, Seán Kelly, Jim Brosnan, Seán Murphy, Jas Murphy (captain), Johnny Foley, Colm Kennelly, Bobby Buckley, Paudie Sheehy, Gerald O'Sullivan.

Jas Murphy with 'Sam Maguire' and friends

God's own people. You learned how to catch and kick as well as all the other basics of Gaelic football.

'There were two of us in the family but sadly my brother John died of meningitis. My dad was of a quiet disposition but my ma, who ran a pub, was very outgoing. She used love to see me out playing football. Every Friday evening there used to be big games in Tralee and when I was very young my mother would ask some of the older lads coming down from Strand Road to take me to the pitch. Often times I'd get in free by carrying in some of the players' boots. Those were great days.'

In secondary school Jas played on all the Tralee CBS teams and won two Munster Colleges championships. He also played two seasons with the Munster Colleges team. 'I loved Colleges football and played centrefield. Classy football was played in those games and they were a joy to watch. The ambition of every Kerry youth is to don the green-and-gold one day. Football is a second religion in Kerry.'

On completion of his training in the Garda Síochána, Jas was sent to Cork and soon afterwards he became the first member of the Gardaí to line out with St Nicholas. Three years later, in 1950, he was on the Garda team that defeated St Nicholas in the county final.

THE 1953 KERRY TEAM

Johnny Foley

Jas Murphy (Captain)   Ned Roche   Donie Murphy

Colm Kennelly   John Cronin   Micksie Palmer

Seán Murphy   Diarmuid Hannafin

Jim Brosnan   John Joe Sheehan   Tadhgie Lyne

Tom Ashe   Seán Kelly   Jackie Lyne

Substitute: Gerald O'Sullivan for Diarmuid Hannafin

'I played senior football with O'Rahillys first before I joined the Guards and I spent six months in the Depot in Phoenix Park. I was then transferred to Watercourse Road in Cork, which is the home of Glen Rovers. I played with "Nicks" until 1949 and we were beaten in the County final by Clonakilty. I was captain of the side that won the Kelleher Shield. Then in 1949 the Guards formed their own team and we won the Cork County Championship in 1950, beating "Nicks" in the final. We had some very good players like Phil "Gunner" Brady, Con McGrath, Paddy Driscoll, Dominic Murray and Pat Spillane.

Christy Ring played against us in the final. I knew him well and he was great fun. I played with him and I played against him and we also trained together in Blackpool. I had great time for Christy and I had many chats with him when he was driving the oil lorry. After training in the Glen at night we'd all come down for something to eat and all we'd have would be a glass of milk and some buns. Ring would nearly eat them all. He was some character. He was not as stylish a hurler as Jack Lynch but he was very, very strong. I would rate him the greatest ever. He had all the skills and was a marvellous man to get scores.'

'Every player has one lucky day. I had a great game. No matter where I went the ball came after me like magnet. Louth forwards would be coming in droves passing the ball and I'd go out and be able to take the ball off them.'

Jas Murphy spent two years of his football life, 1947 and 1948, in the Cork jersey. Why did such a loyal Kerryman decide to throw in his lot with the Kingdom's arch-rivals.

'I played minor with Kerry but lost track of county football for a while. When you're in the Guards life is different and with night duty and all that it wasn't easy. From 1946 onwards I was playing good club football with "Nicks" but Kerry didn't approach me so when Cork expressed an interest I decided to play. I was great friends with Weeshie Murphy and he probably had an influence on me. I played against Kerry in the 1947 Munster final, which we lost. I always gave of my best. It was a game of football. I was marking Frank O'Keeffe (father of John O'Keeffe) and we were great pals from our Tralee days.'

That was the year Kerry lost to Cavan in the historic All-Ireland final in the Polo Grounds in New York. Jas was a member of the Cork team that drew with Cavan in the 1948 League Final but lost the replay.

'I didn't play in the second game. Maybe the Cork selectors felt I wasn't giving of my best. I was injured for the Munster final in 1948 in which Kerry again beat Cork.'

The next year Kerry put out feelers. Jas was more than happy to declare for his native county for the 1949 championship. His friends John Cronin, Ned Roche and Tom Moriarty were also added to the panel, but things did not work out for Kerry, who went down to Clare in the Munster semi-final at Cusack Park. They made amends the following year, beating Cork in the final before losing to Louth in the All-Ireland semi-final. Jas was again in dominant form when Kerry came through Munster in 1951 but there was more disappointment when Mayo won the semi-final after a replay. Cork won the Munster final in 1952 and Jas was as far away as ever from that longed-for All-Ireland medal. A year later victory over Cork in the Munster

A dangerous ball. Kerry v. Armagh, All-Ireland 1953

final put Kerry into the All-Ireland semi-final against Louth. Jas Murphy had what he himself describes as 'the best game of his life'.

'Every player has one lucky day. I had a great game. No matter where I went the ball came after me like magnet. Louth forwards would be coming in droves passing the ball and I'd go out and be able to take the ball off them. All that season I was playing top-class football.'

He confesses that the burden of captaincy and the way it came about affected his own game in the All-Ireland final against Armagh. 'I was a free and easy footballer up to then and could concentrate on my own game but being captain brought added pressures. I had to do my best to look after the needs of fourteen other players and see that they were all right. I hadn't a great game and felt I wasn't fielding that well and was very nervous. I believe I would have had a repeat of my semi-final performance if I hadn't been captain. We had collective training back then and the team stayed in a hotel in Killarney. We were one big happy family and we had some good fun.'

Training was tough under Dr Éamonn O'Sullivan and a former Kerry footballer, Paul Russell. The team travelled on the mid-day train to Dublin on the Saturday before the game and stayed in a hotel in Malahide that night. 'On the day of the final, we came in by coach to Croke Park and made our way to the dressing-room by the back of the Cusack Stand. Micksie Palmer was a great character, always in great humour and very light-hearted. John Cronin was another happy-go-lucky fellow.'

There was drama shortly after Jas and his team arrived on the field. Over 86,000 spectators were already in Croke Park when thousands more forced their way in to the ground.

'It's said that up to 8,000 and probably more got in after breaking down the gates. Luckily enough they all sat down quietly on the sideline and in fairness no one ever came on to the field.

'I always felt we were going to win the game even though Armagh got an early goal. We knew then it wasn't going to be a pushover. We won it in the end by four points although Bill McCorry did miss a penalty for Armagh. I was relieved to hear the final whistle. It was a great feeling. The dressing-room was packed as people were climbing in everywhere.'

His lasting memory of the All-Ireland victory is a card received from a great football follower Jakes McDonald, a staunch John Mitchels man.

'I still remember what he wrote: "Congrats Jas for bringing home the jug". I went to all the schools and convents and one morning I was asleep when my mother came to my room and told me that Brian Sheehy [Paudie's brother] had called and wanted me to go to their school with the Cup so that they all could have a half day.'

A most courteous and friendly man, Jas Murphy made some wonderful friends in the course of his football career and enjoyed the game immensely.

'Winning was never a big part of the game and we never missed a night's sleep if we did lose. It was all part of the game. Paddy Bawn Brosnan was a great character and was a father-figure to the younger members. I remember one wet Sunday playing in the backs alongside Paddy Bawn in a league game against Clare and the pitch was waterlogged. A high ball came in and hit a pool of water as the Bawn went for the ball. As a result a splash of mud and dirty water struck Bawn in the face, "blinding" him. He immediately shouted for a towel. The baggage man Gaffney Duggan ran onto the pitch with a towel but Jackie Lyne, who was playing centre-half-back, took the towel from Gaffney, stuck it into the mud and gave it to Paddy Bawn. The towel was covered in mud and when the Bawn rubbed his face with the towel he made it worse. Sure the scene became a circus and we had great fun watching the Bawn going around "blinded" from mud and dirty rain water. The Bawn enjoyed it himself. It was innocent fun and something you wouldn't see nowadays. The game has become too serious.'

Mick HIGGINS

Cavan Captain 1952

IT WAS FITTING that a man born in New York should have been part of the winning team on that historic September Sunday in 1947 when Cavan defeated Kerry in the Polo Grounds to claim their third All-Ireland title. Anyone who knows him will attest to the fact that Mick Higgins is a modest man, not given to rambling on about his accomplishments on or off the football field. But he still takes great delight in recalling that memorable occasion forty-six years ago when a skilful Cavan side overcame an eight-points deficit to conquer the mighty Kerry in the first and only Final staged outside the country.

'Football at that time was more man-to-man marking and I remember the General Secretary, Paddy O'Keeffe coming into the dressing-room and telling us not to let down the good name of Gaelic Football and Ireland. It was a very sporting game, with Kerry's Joe Keohane claiming he couldn't hit our full-forward Peter Donohue, who got by him twice. He joked that Donohue wouldn't have got by him the second time, only for what Paddy O'Keeffe had said!'

That final is also remembered for Mícheál O'Hehir's magnificent commentary and his plea over the air to be allowed more time to describe the end of the match.

As Mick remembers, football matches were not that hyped up at the time, but the game in the Polo Grounds generated a great deal of publicity and had found a place in history, even before it started.

'It was a very warm day, a kind of pitiless heat, and I'd say the heat was an important factor in the game. We were younger than Kerry and I feel we were able to

---

FACT FILE

HOME PLACE: Kilnaleck, County Cavan.

BORN: 19 August 1922 in New York.

CLUBS: Minor: St Mary's College, Dundalk and Celbridge, County Kildare; Junior: Kilnaleck, County Cavan and Kill, County Cavan; Senior: Mount Nugent, County Cavan; St Magdalene's, Drogheda, and Bailieborough, County Cavan.

ACHIEVEMENTS IN CLUB COMPETITIONS: Two Cavan Senior Football Championship medals: one with Mount Nugent in 1946 and the other with Bailieborough in 1952; won Junior Football Championship medal with Mount Nugent in 1943; two Cavan Senior Football League medals with Mount Nugent and one with Bailieborough.

INTER-COUNTY ACHIEVEMENTS: Three All-Ireland Senior Football medals 1947, 1948 and 1952; seven Ulster Senior Football medals, 1943, 1944, 1945, 1947, 1948, 1949, 1952; two National Football League medals in 1948 and 1950 (won Home Final in 1950 but beaten by New York in Final); two Railway Cup Football medals in 1947 and 1950; five Dr McKenna Cup medals; played on Irish Team versus Universities in 1950, 1951 and 1952.

---

withstand the heat that much better. We were trailing by eight points after fifteen minutes and were backpedalling and not getting into the game at all, so at that stage it looked like a wasted journey for Cavan. But the first ball the Cavan forwards got, we scored a point, and in our second attack we also scored a point and I felt that the Kerry backs were a little jittery and that if we could get enough of the ball, we could still win. The turning point of the game was when the Kerry centrefield, Eddie Dowling went up for a high ball, overbalanced and came down on the hard ground and injured his back and had to go off. Eddie was having an outstanding game for Kerry and his loss, without question, was the turning point of the game. We won it well in the end by four points.'

When Mick Higgins was just five years old, his parents returned from America to Ireland, firstly to his mother's place in Kilnaleck, County Cavan, before moving to Kiltimagh, County Mayo, where his father was born, then back again to Kilnaleck. Mick first became interested in Gaelic football at St Mary's College in Dundalk and was a member of the team that won the McRory Cup in 1938. Although situated in Louth, St Mary's then played in the Ulster Colleges championship.

When in 1939 he moved to County Kildare to work with a relation, Phil Dobson, seventeen-year-old Mick played senior football with Celbridge and minor with the 'Lily Whites'. He was on the Kildare minor team beaten in the 1940 Leinster Final by Louth.

He returned to Cavan in 1942, where he played with local junior club, Kilnaleck and with the county in the Ulster Junior Championship. Less than a year later, he played his first game with the Cavan senior team and so began an inter-county career that saw him become one of the deadliest forwards in the game.

Cavan were a major force in that era and Mick garnered three All-Ireland Senior medals with the county, eventually leading them to their last All-Ireland success in 1952. That Cavan team was fortunate to qualify for the final, as it took a great comeback in the closing minutes of the semi-final to beat Cork.

Back, left to right: Paul Fitzsimons, Tony Tighe, Peter Donohue, Liam Maguire, Brian Gallagher, Victor Sherlock, Tom Hardy, Bartle McEnroe, Aidan Corrigan, Edwin Carolan, Simon Deignan, Vincent Clarke, James McCabe.
Front, left to right: John Sheridan, Terry Keoghan, Dessie Maguire Séamus Morris, Johnny Cusack, Séamus Hetherton, Phil 'Gunner' Brady, Mick Higgins (captain), Paddy Carolan, John Joe Cassidy, Brian O'Reilly.

'Cork were hot favourites and led by 1-3 to 0-2 at the interval. They were still in the lead with ten minutes left to play. Then we were awarded a penalty. The kick, while well taken by John Joe Cassidy, was brilliantly saved by the Cork goalkeeper. Encouraged by this "let-off", Cork swept upfield and Moriarty crashed the ball to the Cavan net and the game appeared over. But, although four points in arrears with six minutes of play remaining, we scored five points and just pipped Cork by a point. We scored seven points inside the last eight minutes. I'd say that was our best comeback, it was very exciting.'

The final against Meath went to a replay and Cavan won it by four points.

The dressing-room is always a tense place in the minutes before an All-Ireland final. It was no different in 1952. 'You'd have the same players that would be keyed up all the time. We had a lot of young lads. I remember Tom Hardy, Paddy Carolan and Brian O'Reilly were all tensed up and the more experienced players were doing their best to relax them, saying, "sure these Meath fellows aren't what they're blown up to be at all". I also tried to tell them, as best I could, to play their own game and keep at it.

'I think there was more tactics that time than now. We always had them worked out well before the match, because we always agreed we wouldn't say much when we'd get to the dressing-room. We thought it might upset the players. We always had our homework done in advance. Our goalkeeper, Séamus Morris, was the principal man in our defence, because he held it together. If any of the defenders started to ramble too far up the field, it was his job to call them back to give him cover. After four or five minutes kicking out a ball, Séamus would know which side of the field our opponents would be weakest. We always played on our opponents' weakest points. We knew each one's weaknesses, whether he had a good left foot or right foot. It was always easier to block down a shot from a left-footed player. We had plenty of time to work these things out and we never mentioned them on the morning of a match. We always believed in very quick frees and in fact played very open football. Tony Tighe, Edwin Carolan and myself were there from the 1947 team and we knew each other's play very well. If you were tackled, you could always let out the ball right or left and be sure that either Tighe or Carolan was running on to it.

'We played Tony Tighe at full-forward against Paddy O'Brien in the 1952 Final and got him to rove out. It was different from nowadays though, as Tighe stayed in the square until he saw the ball coming and he had such good anticipation that he could race out thirty yards and if he didn't get turning he would hand-pass the ball back out to Carolan or myself. It was all easy after practising it for a month.'

'We weren't into any dramatics and saved our energy for the game itself, instead

---

THE 1952 CAVAN TEAM

Séamus Morris

James McCabe Phil 'Gunner' Brady Dessie Maguire

Paddy Carolan Liam Maguire Brian O'Reilly

Victor Sherlock Tom Hardy

Séamus Hetherton Mick Higgins (Captain) Edwin Carolan

John Joe Cassidy Tony Tighe Johnny Cusack

Substitute: Paul Fitzsimons for John Joe Cassidy

of running up and down the field before the game. I still can't understand players doing six fifty-yards sprints before a match and then jumping around.

'Our trainer, Hughie Reilly, was very strict regarding the parade. We had to march properly in a line and there was no such thing as walking with your head down and a fellow on his right foot in front and you on your left. He was also very strict about the National Anthem and insisted we stand to attention with our hands by our side and not like some players nowadays with feet apart and hands behind their back. The whole thing was rehearsed in training.'

Edwin Carolan scored a last-minute point to bring the game to a replay. It was a disputed point with Meath players stating the ball was over the end line when Carolan collected it.

'He got the ball out at the corner flag and the Meath defence stood up, as they were under the impression that the ball was over the end-line, but the umpire didn't wave it wide and Carolan came in and kicked it over the bar from a very acute angle to draw the game. As soon as Edwin got the point, the referee blew the full-time whistle. The game was on 28 September, which was a very wet day.'

It was back to collective training for the replay, fixed for two weeks later and again a wet day. Mick was in bed with flu from the Monday to Thursday previous to the game, and was unable to train for that week.

'I got up on Thursday and was a bit weak, but every day I was getting a bit stronger and on the day of the final, I was ready to line out. Meath attacked first and Paddy Meegan got two short-in frees but missed them. Then we attacked and Tony Tighe was taken down and we were awarded a free about forty yards out. It was a wet ball and I thought to myself, "It's now or never". I got the first one over and from there on in, I never looked back. The game was described in daily newspapers as the difference between the two captains. Meegan missed the frees and I got them for Cavan. We were the better fielders on the day, though, and indeed two of the points that I got could have been goals, only that Tony Tighe was taken down. He looked like he could have scored a goal on each occasion. Cavan was the better team on the day and we won by nine points to five. I scored seven of the points, six from frees. I was lucky with the frees whereas Paddy Meegan, the Meath captain, was unlucky in missing three frees.'

There was keen rivalry between Cavan and Meath at that time and it was a sweet victory for the 'Breffni County', whose supporters swarmed onto the pitch as soon as the final whistle sounded. All the games against Meath were tough and hard hitting, so naturally enough the Cavan supporters were up in the air. Mick remembers it was nearly impossible to get from the Hogan Stand to their dressing-room at the Cusack Stand end.

'It was also very hard to get up to the Hogan Stand to collect the Sam Maguire Cup as people were continually shaking my hand. The speech was short, I hadn't much to say. I just thanked everyone, especially our supporters. It was harder to get from the Hogan Stand over across the pitch to the Cusack Stand than it was playing the game. I was so long playing, it did not mean much to be captain. I never thought of it, until I had to receive the cup and make the speech. We were a very united team and being captain did not mean a lot. The Cavan selectors always appointed the longest-serving team member to be captain. 'Big' Tom O'Reilly was captain from 1942 to 1945. In 1946, his brother John Joe was appointed captain and when he retired in 1950 I was the longest-serving member and I was appointed captain, until I retired in 1953. That is still the system in Cavan'.

Mick Higgins, the last man to captain an All-Ireland winning Cavan team, is better qualified than most to explain the decline in the county's football fortunes in the intervening years.

'You have to get at least thirteen good players, as you can afford to carry two weak players into an All-Ireland final and still win. What's been happening Cavan for the past number of years is that they have only about six to nine good players. People say that they're very inconsistent, but what they forget is that you can win if the whole nine are on song, but if you get into the second or third round you're going to be caught out, because some of those nine players are not going to function on the day.

'Not too many would have held out much hope for Donegal winning the 1992 All-Ireland title after their drawn match against Cavan in Breffni Park, but it just goes to show what proper training and the right attitude can achieve. I find it very hard to understand why Cavan aren't making a greater impact in the Ulster Championship, but it seems we just haven't enough good players at the moment. We haven't won an Ulster minor title since 1974 and St Patrick's College in Cavan hasn't won the McRory Cup since 1972. I was very lucky that in my playing days Cavan football was at its peak.

'It was a very warm day, a kind of pitiless heat, and I'd say the heat was an important factor in the game. We were younger than Kerry and I feel we were able to withstand the heat that much better.'

'There were outstanding footballers in the county at that particular time. Cavan had goalkeepers, Des Benson, Val Gannon and Séamus Morris; defenders, Billy Doonan, Paddy Smith, Brian O'Reilly and Big Tom O'Reilly; we had one of the best half-back lines in the country in P.J. Duke, John Joe O'Reilly and Simon Deignan; forwards, Tony Tighe, Peter Donohue, T.P. O'Reilly, Joe Stafford and Edwin Carolan. At centrefield, we had men of the calibre of Phil Brady, Victor Sherlock, Colm McDyer, John Wilson and Tom Hardy. In later years there were the likes of Liam and Dessie Maguire, James McCabe, Johnny Cusack, J.J. Cassidy, Paddy Carolan, Brian Gallagher, Séamus Hetherington and Paul Fitzsimons.'

After his playing days, Mick Higgins enjoyed significant sucess as a coach and manager. He trained Longford to win their first National League title in 1966 and was in charge again two years later when they won their first and only Leinster Championship title. Indeed, at one stage, during his time in charge of Longford, Mick, incredible as it may seem, also managed his native county and a conflict arose when Cavan and Longford qualifed to meet each other in the 1966 League semi-final, which was played at Carrick-on-Shannon.

'Even though I was managing Cavan at the time, Jimmy Flynn, the Longford Chairman, and Fr McGee asked me to give some coaching to Longford. This was later cleared by the Cavan Chairman, T.P. O'Reilly, and I began working with the Longford players in early 1966. Everything went smoothly until Cavan and Longford were drawn against each other in the National League semi-final. I made it clear that Cavan had first choice, so Seán Murray and Brendan Barden took charge of Longford for the semi-final. As it happened, Longford beat Cavan and I then trained Longford for the final in which we beat Galway.'

Mick was in charge of the Cavan senior team from 1962 to 1969 and, during that time, they won four Ulster titles in 1962, 1964, 1967 and 1969, the last time Cavan colours were seen in Croke Park in the All-Ireland Senior Championship. In 1972, Mick was asked by Colm McDyer, a former teammate, and Brian McEniff to train the Donegal senior team. He was with them through 1972 and 1973 and was highly praised when Donegal won their first Ulster title in 1972.

During the seventies, he was manager and selector of the Ulster Railway Cup team together with Paddy McFlynn of Down, Paddy O'Neill of Tyrone and Gerry Arthurs of Armagh.

Mick feels strongly that to make football more attractive to the youth, the authorities will have to clamp down on the dangerous high 'tackle' and, above all, the hitting of an opponent off the ball.

'This was unheard of in my time. Although football was more man-to-man, no opponent would resort to that type of conduct. There is too much emphasis on winning games. With County Boards accepting and looking for sponsorship and supporters' clubs supplying vast sums of money, the GAA are coming to the time that the players will be demanding payment. There is too much emphasis on training and getting fit, which means that trainers and coaches are not giving enough time to skills and ball control, with the result that the standard of football is falling.'

Had it not been for Gaelic football Mick Higgins, in all probability, would have returned to America to seek employment. But football opened many doors for him and gave him immense satisfaction. Most of all, Gaelic football gave him a reason to stay in Ireland and made him many great friends from all walks of life. In 1988, Mick was presented with the Bank of Ireland 'All-Time Greats' award and a year later was honoured with a 'Texaco Hall of Fame' award, due recognition for an outstanding sportsman.

Nowadays, an agile Mick enjoys attending games and the odd night out at 'the dogs', having trained a number of good winners over the years.

Mick was a member of the Garda Síochána all his life and spent the last twenty-nine years of his working life as a sergeant in the little village of Tullyvin. Where else, but in his beloved Cavan!

Seán FLANAGAN

Mayo Captain 1950 and 1951

A N INSPIRATIONAL CAPTAIN, Seán Flanagan is widely seen as one of the outstanding corner-backs of all time. Those who were lucky enough to see him perform attest to the fact that he gave new meaning to corner-back play. Never a man to shirk responsibility, Seán Flanagan thrived on the tense atmosphere of the big occasion. His leadership skills when captaining Mayo to two successive All-Ireland victories in 1950 and 1951 are talked about to this very day. He was named at left-corner-back on the 'Team of the Century'.

Seán Flanagan grew up in the townland of Coolnaha near Ballyhaunis in County Mayo. Both his parents were principal teachers at Crossard National School. Theirs was a musical household. His mother Annie, a native of Oranmore, County Galway, played the piano and his father Stanislaus, from near Kiltimagh, loved to play the violin.

Seán remembers travelling with his father to Galway at week-ends for violin lessons.

'We stayed with Mother's sister and dancing and singing were added to the activities there. Máire Ní Scolaíde was a constant visitor. Cousin Angela was a superb dancer. We later switched to Sister Patrick of St Louis Convent in Kiltimagh and won many prizes at the first revival of Feis Shligigh in 1930 and the Feis Cheoil. By then, we had broadened our musical interests to classical and jazz as well as trad.'

Schooldays were special, too, in the Mayo of the twenties. And Seán clearly remembers his first introduction to organised sport. There was no playground attached to Crossard National School and when he transferred to Toreen National

---

FACT FILE

HOME PLACE: Coolnaha, Ballyhaunis, County Mayo

BORN: 26 January, 1922 at 5 Mount St Crescent, Dublin. Died February 1993.

CLUBS: Ballaghadereen; Crossard; Sean McDermotts; UCD and East Mayo.

ACHIEVEMENTS IN CLUB COMPETITIONS: Two Sigerson Cup medals in 1944 and 1945 and one League medal with UCD. When the Mayo County Board decided to try amalgamated teams, I played centre-forward for East Mayo in 1957. The other lads did the work. I gave orders. We won, so I finally had a County medal. My Achilles tendon was in a bad way by then; Ballaghadereen won minor trophies like the Canon Henry Cup; formed own club, Crossard, in 1942; played one Senior match, defeating Ballyhaunis to our great glee. By 1943 most of the lads were in England.

INTER-COUNTY ACHIEVEMENTS: Two All-Ireland Senior Football medals in 1950 and 1951; two National Football League medals in 1949 and 1954; one Railway Cup medal in 1951; played from 1946 to 1956 — won only when I was captain. Member of first four Ireland teams 1950-1953. Captain in 1951 and 1952. Won all four.

School in 1929, there was no playground there either.

'The local farmers around Toreen chased us out of every field we tried. Around Easter 1934, Daddy organised a match between Aghamore boys and his own pupils and got the use of a field from Anthony Curley in Crossard, close to the old school. It was my first and only competitive game before I went to St Jarlath's later that year.'

There was no hurling around Seán's homeplace in those days. But during his time as Minister for Lands, Seán asked the Commissioners to convey to Tooreen CLG the field opposite his old school. They agreed and hurling is now well rooted in that area.

According to Seán, it was football that kept him in St Jarlath's College.

Back, left to right: Dr Jimmy Laffey (Chairman Co Board), Gerald Courell (co-trainer), John Forde, Henry Dixon, John McAndrew, Tom Langan, Joe Gilvarry, Tom Acton, Billy Durkan, Paddy Irwin, Seán Wynne, Mick Caulfield, Tommy Byrne, Seán Mulderrig, Éamonn Mongey, Paddy Prendergast.
Front, left to right: Jimmy Curran, Jackie Carney (co-trainer), Mick Flanagan, Peter Quinn, Seán Flanagan, Padraic Carney, Mick Mulderrig, Billy Kenny, Peter Solan, Mick Downey (masseur), Liam Hastings, Joe Staunton.

Back row, third from left: Paddy Jordan, Dr Michael Loftus, John Forde, Joe Gilvarry, Tom Langan, Paddy Irwin, John McAndrew, —, Henry Dixon, Liam Hastings, Michael Mulderrig, —, —.
Front, left to right: Willie Casey, Seán Wynne, Michael Flanagan, Éamonn Mongey, Seán Mulderrig, Fr Peter Quinn, Padraig Carney, Seán Flanagan, Paddy Prendergast, Jimmy Curran, Joe Staunton.

'I was one of the minor captains and Frank Kinlough was another. We were life-long friends. St Jarlath's College won eight successive championships. I played at centre-half-back on the last of these in 1939. I also captained the first ever junior championship side. This was for players under seventeen years. There was no cup for the winners, so I borrowed a golf cup from Dr J.G. McGarry, then professor of English. He later edited the *Furrow* from Maynooth. I also played for Connacht Colleges in 1939 at left-half-back. We were losing by 3 goals and 9 points to 3 points with a few minutes to go, so the referee gave us a penalty, which Máirtín Greaney converted. The manager, Fr Wyms, thought we had disgraced the province and refused to give us our jerseys. We revolted, "Didn't we do our best". Implacable logic. We at least won that argument, refusing to leave the hotel until we had his promise. Fr Wyms said "I gave you my word of honour as a priest". Tom Hogan of CBS, Tuam responded by saying: "We want your word of honour as a man, not as a priest". Courage 1939 style.'

Seán Flanagan entered Holy Cross College, Clonliffe in Dublin in 1939 and stayed there until he graduated in 1942 with first place in his degree. He played minor with Mayo in both 1939 and 1940. Roscommon won the All-Ireland Minor Final in 1939. The following year, Mayo had a powerful side, defeating Kerry by a big margin in the All-Ireland Semi-Final. But Mayo were forced to field without their entire half-back line in the final against Louth. Seán Mulhern was a first year student in Maynooth; Joe Carroll was a final year student in St Nathy's and Seán himself was a second year undergraduate in Clonliffe College. Incredibly, Seán was playing soccer in the field next to Croke Park when the minor teams came on to play. Later, he could see some of the action in Croke Park from his room positioned at the top of the college. Mayo conceded five goals that day and lost by seven points.

Seán is of the opinion that playing soccer greatly helped hone his skills and he later applied that knowledge in all his Gaelic games training.

THE 1950 MAYO TEAM

Billy Durkin

John Forde   Paddy Prendergast   Seán Flanagan (Captain)

Peter Quinn   Henry Dixon   John McAndrew

Pádraic Carney   Éamonn Mongey

Mick Flanagan   Billy Kenny   Joe Gilvarry

Mick Mulderrig   Tom Langan   Peter Solan

Substitutes: Seán Wynne for Billy Durkin; Mick Caulfield for Billy Kenny; Seán Mulderrig for Mick Caulfield.

THE 1951 TEAM

Seán Wynne

John Forde   Paddy Prendergast   Seán Flanagan (Captain)

Joe Staunton   Henry Dixon   Peter Quinn

Éamon Mongey   John McAndrew

Paddy Irwin   Pádraic Carney   Seán Mulderrig

Mick Flanagan   Tom Langan   Joe Gilvarry

Substitute: Liam Hastings for Henry Dixon

Because of his neighbours, the Robinsons, and some former school friends from his Tuam days, Seán chose to play for Dublin club, Seán McDermotts, during his holidays from Clonliffe. Mick Connaire, Eddie Boyle, Paddy McIntyre, the Robinsons, Tommy Banks, Jimmy Coyle and many other fine players were in the squad then. Seán continued to play with the club when he left Clonliffe College and, ironically, played against UCD — with whom he later lined out — in the 1943 Dublin Final.

'We were ahead coming up to full time, but let in a soft goal on the hour. The students then scored three points in extra time to deny us by a point. My immediate opponent was Dónal Keenan, who starred for Roscommon a few months later in the All-Ireland Final. Having held him scoreless from play, I felt I had done well. Some of our older players wilted in the last College assault. Watching Eddie Boyle's technique, both in training and in games, was a considerable help to me in the study of defensive strategy, especially in the full-back line.'

Seán teamed up with UCD for the following year, 1944, and there began his career in the full-back line on an outstanding team.

'We walked away with the Sigerson, walloping Cork in the Final at Croke Park. All they scored were two points, from fifties. I captained the 1945 side and we easily won the final in Belfast. Cork did give us some difficulty in the semi-final. We won the League without much problem, except in the final, when we were asleep for the first ten minutes and were down by 2 goals and 2 points to one point, or

> *'The performance of a team at its best is far greater than the sum of the individual abilities of fifteen players. I believe a captain can contribute. Some have certainly done so. Before the start of the 1950 championship season, I gathered the forwards together and told them that no team in Ireland would score more than ten points against us, giving them a target minimum. We achieved it.'*

thereabouts. I strolled up the field and said: "Right, lads, time to play a bit". We won it well in the end. Because the rule allowing students to play for College and home club was years in the future, local commitments destroyed us for the championship. We couldn't muster thirteen players to begin the second half and conceded a walk-over.'

When he was apprenticed to G.J. Quinn in February 1943, a new chapter in Seán's life began. G.J. was one of the famous Quinn brothers of Old Belvedere, who won the Leinster Senior Cup seven times in a row.

'He was a wonderful master, who made me work hard and saw to it that I had practical experience in every aspect of Civil Law. He had very little work on the criminal side and I was pleased with that. It became clear that office time was for work and I learned soon not to make any reference to sporting activities. A pattern developed. After another big win, Gerry would say to me on the Tuesday or Wednesday, "Tell the landlady you won't be home for lunch tomorrow". We would go to the Palace, a restaurant downstairs in Cathedral Street beside Tommy Moore's. The next hour was all about the match, incidents, personal or collective, then back to the grindstone.

'Of course, he was also an international cricketer, an attacking bat with Phoenix. He knew I was a cricket fanatic, who deeply resented the Ban. I had no interest in playing rugby, but would dearly have liked to try my hand at cricket at a serious level. Anyway, I developed an interest in rugby through G.J. Quinn and went to all the matches, including the war-time Irish XV games, where I first saw J.W. Kyle in action. Life would never be the same again. Here was a genius in action. I would go to Hell and back again to see him play. Money was the problem, of course, so I had to forgo foreign trips until the 1950s, except for one to Twickenham. Curiously, I was in digs with Jack Mattson, who was capped at full back versus England in the Triple Crown year.

'I met Jack Kyle via Gerry Quinn; he is a lively, modest man. He is the only sportsman I have ever asked for an autograph. One try scored at Lansdowne Road is my special gem. He deceived three opponents simultaneously with the ball. He did a shuffle of the feet, spun like a top and ran straight as a die to plant the ball by the Havelock Square End posts. My cousin, Joe Neary was with me. "How does he do it?", says Joe. I replied, "balance, timing, anticipation, instant acceleration, balance, balance, balance, guile". To use a cliché, he was something else. I later lost all interest in rugby. When the Ban went, I stopped going and wouldn't cross the road to look at a rugby match. Gerrry Quinn and I became very close friends; indeed my best friend of all. His untimely death at fifty-three years of age shattered me. I mourn him and always will, until we meet in Heaven.'

Seán Flanagan pursued his other sporting passion, cricket, all over the world.

'I saw every stroke of Denis Compton's 157 not out for Middlesex against Surrey at the Oval in 1947. Full of great strokes, graceful, impish. W.J. Edrich made 137 not out the same day.'

Over the years Seán watched most of the great cricketers at county and Test level, in places like Bombay, Jamaica, Lord's, Sydney, Hobart, Barbados and various county grounds in England.

Seán played Sigerson with UCD in 1946 when they lost to Cork in the Final. He moved to Dublin to a new job at the beginning of 1947 and stayed there, until he started his own practice in November 1948 in Ballaghaderreen. He played no club football during that period.

'We were robbed of victory in the 1946 Connacht Final at Ballinasloe. We had defeated Roscommon in the first round in 1945 at Sligo, but we put up a dismal performance at Ballina in the first round against Roscommon in 1947 and there was much disaffection among the players. I wrote resigning from the team. Finn Mongey wrote back to say he had placed my letter before the Board, who asked me to reconsider, and make myself available for the 1948 season. The League was starting in Tralee and I said I would not travel. Under fierce pressure from my friend Éamonn Mongey, I finally and reluctantly agreed to go. George, as we called him, was my closest friend in the squad. We left Dublin at noon and made the Grand Hotel at ten o'clock that night. In the bar, alone with a bottle of stout, I was addressed — or rather my back was — by a Kerryman, who crept in a few minutes later. "Are you playing in the match tomorrow? Is Roscommon a good team? I think they are the second best team in Ireland after Kerry" (Cavan were reigning champions at the time) I made no answer. He continued: "Where do you play?" and I said "full-back line."

'There was a long pause as he took a long drink from his pint and then said: "you're very small for a full-back. Kerry always had the best backs in Ireland, big, strong men." I turned and faced him and retorted: "I don't know who you are and I care less. Mayo came here in 1939 with 'Tot' McGowan, Tommy Regan, Tommy

Hoban and Jackie Carney and we beat the lard out of you. We propose to do the same to you tomorrow".

'It was the best tonic I ever had. We barely had fifteen the next day, but we played like demons. It was a draw, only because the referee gave a dubious free to Kerry in the last minute. A new Mayo team had been born. The names included Paddy Prendergast, Pat McAndrew, Billy Kenny, Peter Solan, Mick Flanagan and Seán Mulderrig'

Seán and the Kerryman he met in the bar later became lifelong friends. Mayo's defeat by Cavan in the 1948 All-Ireland Final was bitterly disappointing, but their gutsy performance on the day provided some consolation and gave great hope for the future. They won the 1949 National League final, but were comprehensively beaten by Meath in the All-Ireland semi-final of 1949. Meath, captained by Brian Smyth, went on to the win the title, beating Cavan in the Final.

'We made a nonsense of the semi-final. After our defeat, Fr Gibbons decided to canvass all members of the County Board and all delegates to the 1950 Convention to change the rule giving the captaincy of the senior team to the nominee of the county champions. He believed Mayo wouldn't win until I was captain.'

The change was made, Seán Flanagan from Ballaghadereen Junior Club was nominated captain of the Mayo senior team and things took a turn for the better. Immediately after he was notified of his elevation, Seán arranged a meeting with the Chairman of the County Board, Dr Jim Laffey.

'We were friends and I told him that he had only one duty to perform for us: "Apart from yourself and Finn Mongey, [the County Secretary] keep the County Board away from us until the day after we win the All-Ireland".

'In collective training for the Connacht final in July 1950, we were at lunch one day, when I saw the Reverend President approach the door. I jumped up and stopped him. He tried an unavailing sidestep, but I said: "Did you get a message from the Chairman". He muttered something about my attitude and I answered back saying: "Father, this is not easy for me either, but the Chairman's warning included you. Now get out and I'll see you when I have the Sam Maguire". Success makes enemies. There were others who resented my attitude and said things like "arrogant ... bully, who does he think he is?"

'Following the 1950 provincial final, I obliged six players to buy new Halliday boots and pledged the credit of the Board. I became the seventh, when Halliday's made a special pair for me two weeks before the Final.'

'In addition to the new blood of 1947 and 1948, we acquired some other great players, Seán Wynne, Mick Mulderrig and John McAndrew. We were coasting along in the final, leading by 1-3 to 0-1 when Billy Kenny was stretchered off. The rhythm of the forward line was disrupted, anyway we won.' The final score was Mayo 2-5 Louth 1-6.

Seán Flanagan again delivered the Sam Maguire Cup to his native county the following year, when his side beat Meath in the All-Ireland final by 2-8 to 0-9. He led Connacht to victory in the Railway Cup and also captained Ireland to a win against the Combined Universities. There was but one major disappointment that year when they lost the League Final to Meath.

Seán Flanagan won his second National League medal in 1954 when Mayo comprehensively defeated Carlow. Dr Pádraic Carney was brought home from

America for both the semi-final and the final and his appearance generated great publicity.

Seán Flanagan was a born leader and this manifested itself in many ways throughout his illustrious football career. Even when not holding down the position of captain, he would still endeavour to draw the best out of his colleagues.

'In the dressing-room in Sligo, before playing the All-Ireland champions, Roscommon, in 1945, I found myself on my feet making an impassioned speech. Being a mere member of the team, I had no right to take it on myself to say anything. Whether this was effective, or some other alchemy worked, we played like demons. Henry Kenny scored a goal from an unlikely place. We beat Roscommon, only to lose the Connacht final to Galway. When Henry Kenny

decided to play one more year — and very well too — I was asked and agreed to relinquish the captaincy to him. The 1946 Connacht final at Ballinasloe was decided on the scoreboard by a totally illegal goal. Roscommon were attacking close to our goalposts, many bodies, but little room. A forward got a toe to the ball, which went wide, striking the legs of the umpire Seán Mullarkey. The whistle sounded and the Mayo backs moved away for the kick-out. Jimmy Murray rushed in from the 40 and kicked the ball unopposed into the net. When there was no reaction from the other umpire, Jimmy grabbed the green flag and raised it aloft, swinging it back and over. The referee then awarded the goal. We were beaten by a point, but after an objection the Council ordered a replay and we were badly beaten. Had we played that year at All-Ireland level we would hardly have won, but the experience might have changed the course of Mayo history.'

Over the next eighteen months, following that disappointment against arch-rivals Roscommon, a number of new and gifted players arrived on the county scene in Mayo. This influx of talent convinced Seán Flanagan that Mayo now had a team capable of winning that elusive All-Ireland title.

'Under J.P. (Tot) McGowan, the 1946 team had done collective training in Castlebar. He was a deep thinker, especially on defensive play. Paddy Prendergast was the key element here when he arrived in 1947. He was a superb athlete. Though we lost in 1948, we were now invited everywhere. When in London, I invited the forwards to White Hart Lane and the backs to Highbury. I asked the players to study Joe Mercer in particular. Pint-sized and frail-looking, his shadowing and timing of the tackle were an object lesson. Scott and Barnes were superb full-backs. We discussed all aspects of the play later, and adapted them to Gaelic. One of Arsenal's great strengths was the counter-attack. Having absorbed a lot of pressure, the forward strike depends on the first pass out of defence. Make it long, fast and accurate. The space is there. The forwards did likewise after watching Eddie Baily and company.'

When Seán was chosen as captain, it made him even more determined than ever that player power would prevail. 'Éamon Mongey was a tower of strength throughout. He was a great player, a thinker, fiercely determined and a very close friend. Unfortunately, Pádraic Carney and I never got close. For all his genius and unrivalled natural ability, he insisted on going his own way. He did star in the 1951 All-Ireland final and in the 1954 League semi-final, when the Board brought him back from the US. During training for the All-Ireland semi-final in Carney's home town in 1949, Mongey, Prender and I pleaded with him to adapt his play to suit a small full-forward, Peter Solan. He insisted we needed Tom Langan at full-forward. We agreed that Langan would be ideal, but he was going to be placed at centre-half-forward. Carney got an inordinate amount of possession in the first half that day. He kicked them all high into the square to be gobbled up by Paddy O'Brien. It was to be seven years before Seán Purcell, with far less possession, showed how a small full-forward could be used. Two goals and five points was a handy haul for Frank Stockwell. We wanted Pádraic Carney to use possession in the same way. We should have won in 1949.'

Cleary Seán Flanagan had strong views on the role of a captain:

'The performance of a team at its best is far greater than the sum of the individual abilities of fifteen players. I believe a captain can contribute. Some have certainly done so. Before the start of the 1950 championship season, I gathered the forwards together and told them that no team in Ireland would score more than ten points against us, giving them a scoring target minimum. We achieved it.'

His advice to those entrusted with the task of promoting Gaelic games was:

'Catch 'em young, treat them gently. No player to play any other grade while still a minor. Under-21s not allowed to play senior. Not enough care is taken with young talent. For one Dermot Earley, thousands have been murdered by too early promotion. The games are physically tough, so bones need to be mature. It is too early to break a young person's heart. Mayo has a sad history here.'

(Interviewed in November 1992. Seán Flanagan died in February 1993.)

278

Brian SMYTH

Meath Captain 1949

VERY FEW have contributed as much to Gaelic games both on and off the field as Brian Smyth of Meath. He won practically every honour as a player, including two All-Ireland senior football medals and went on to become a highly respected inter-county referee, before eventually taking over as chairman of the Meath County Board, for over seven years. During that time, Brian brought the same level of commitment and enthusiasm to the office as he had done so proudly, years earlier, on the playing fields while wearing the green and gold of Meath.

In 1949 Brian scored four of his side's points in a 1-10 to 1-6 final victory over a highly fancied Cavan side, thus becoming the first Meathman to captain an All-Ireland winning team.

He was a reluctant captain for the first match in the championship. The system in Meath at the time meant that the senior champions had the right to nominate the county captain for the following year. As Skryne had won the championship in 1948, it was their prerogative to name the captain for 1949. However, the club did not

---

FACT FILE

HOME PLACE: Batterstown, County Meath   BORN: 23 March 1924

CLUBS: Batterstown Junior Football Club; Flathouse, Dunboyne Junior Football Club; Skryne Senior Football Club; St Peter's, Dunboyne Intermediate Football Club. Played hurling with Flathouse; Batterstown; Rathoath; Oberstown in Skryne and St Peter's, Dunboyne.

ACHIEVEMENTS IN CLUB COMPETITIONS: Won Junior Hurling Championship medal with Flathouse in 1941/42. (It was the first championship winning team. Although only a townland, it became famous in later years as the place where the popular television programme, 'The Riordans' was filmed on the farm of the late Willie Connolly. Remains as picturesque as ever.); won Junior Hurling Championship medal with Batterstown in 1948/49; one County Senior Hurling Championship medal with St Patrick's in 1953; one Intermediate Championship medal with St Peter's, Dunboyne in 1962; won Feis Cup hurling competitions with St Patrick's in 1954, 1955 and 1956; won Meath Senior Football Championships with Skryne in 1947, 1948 and 1954; won Feis Cup football competitions with Skryne in 1946, 1947, 1948, 1949 and 1958.

INTER-COUNTY ACHIEVEMENTS: Two All-Ireland Senior Football Championship medals with Meath in 1949 and 1954; one National Football League medal in 1951; five Leinster Senior Championship medals in 1947, 1949, 1951, 1952 and 1954; captained All-Ireland team versus Combined Universities in 1950 and played in same competition in 1951; won an All-Ireland Junior Hurling medal in 1948; one Leinster Junior Hurling medal in 1948 and a Division 2 National Hurling League medal in 1948/49.

nominate a captain.

'As we were leaving the dressing-room on the day of the first championship match in 1949, no decision regarding a captain had been arrived at. Myself and Mícheál O'Brien, the other Skryne representative playing that day, were left to make the decision ourselves. Eventually, I reluctantly accepted the captaincy and the subsequent honour that the decision brought.'

On their way through the Leinster championship that year in which they easily accounted for Westmeath in the final, Meath had to overcome Kildare, Wexford and Louth, who provided far and away the stiffest test. Indeed, it took two replays before Meath finally saw off the challenge of the 'Wee County'. Victory over Connacht champions, Mayo in the All-Ireland semi-final ensured that the Meath 'Forty-niners' had booked themselves into Croke Park for final day, a day Brian Smyth will never forget.

'On our way to Croke Park we called in to Austin Marry's farm at Rathfeigh where there was a cup of tea waiting for us. It was only then the occasion was really brought home to us, as cars bedecked in Meath colours wended their way to Dublin. As we continued our journey, spellbound by the astonishing numbers on the road, we began to wonder was anybody at all staying at home. There was bedlam when we reached the gates of Croke Park and were besieged by our own supporters.'

Because of all the hysteria, the Meath players arrived in the dressing-room much later than had been planned. 'This, I believe, helped to ease the tension and while some of our players needed a strengthening bandage, there certainly was none of the massaging and bandaging that is part and parcel of today's set-up.'

Brian recalls that when it was almost time to leave the shelter of the dressing-room, Fr Tully and the selectors spoke individually to each player. Then they finished up by impressing upon the team as a whole what was required of them to give the vast Meath following an occasion to savour and make 1949 a year to remember.

'As we left for the pre-match parade, each in turn was handed a bowl, which was

Back, left to right: Paddy O'Brien, Matty McDonnell, Charlie Smyth, Larry McGuinness, Paddy Dixon, Kevin Smyth, Des Taaffe, Tommy Farrelly, Bill Halfpenny, Jim Meehan, Johnny Bashford.
Front, left to right: Jim Kearney, Paddy Connell, Mícheál O'Brien, Frankie Byrne, Kevin McConnell, Séamus Heary, Brian Smyth, Christo Hand, John Meehan, Peter McDermott, Pat Carolan, Paddy Meegan.

filled with holy water to dip a finger in and make the Sign of the Cross. I suppose it was Fr Tully's way of saying, 'I have done my bit and hope God can do the rest'. Arriving on the pitch, my first reaction was to do the usual: give the ball a hefty lash and follow up and catch it, before getting the other players involved. However, I was so flabbergasted, first by the immense roar and then by the enormous crowd packed everywhere, that I just stood and gazed, as if in a trance. Then, that great warrior, Peter McDermott, came over and said, "most of these people are from Meath, let's do them proud".'

It was not until Brian had recovered from the initial shock that he realised the extent of the green-and-gold colours scattered all over the ground. He also recognised neighbours and friends sitting on the sideline. It was only then he came to understand what the whole occasion meant to the people of Meath.

'Nerves soon disappeared and before long the final notes of the National Anthem heralded the start of the contest and I shook hands with my direct opponent on the day, that great gentleman and Cavan captain, the late John Joe O'Reilly.'

Reports of the match indicate that Brian Smyth played a captain's part at centre-half-forward, scoring four points and creating many other vital scores. When the final whistle blew and Meath had annexed their first All-Ireland title, there was an amazing sight as both Meath and Cavan supporters poured on to the pitch.

'Eventually, I was landed at the steps of the Hogan Stand to receive the Sam Maguire Cup and having being presented with it, I just took it and said nothing. I often wondered what the supporters thought of me for not thanking them for their support but then, like me perhaps, they were in a world of their own, not fully realising the enormity of the occasion. However, Fr Tully and his selectors were as much to blame as me for not having prepared a speech, for the day before the game I asked them what I was supposed to say after the final whistle and they told me: "don't count your chickens before they're hatched".'

The journey through a sea of people across the field to the dressing-room was hazardous and Brian remembers being tossed to and fro with everyone trying to touch the cup.

'Were it not for some of the selectors retrieving the cup, I dread to think what would have occurred. If the dressing-room was quiet beforehand, it certainly was bedlam afterwards, as everyone began to realise that all the years of endeavour had finally paid off. I think the players suddenly realised that they were heroes of a never-to-be-forgotten occasion.' Eventually, Croke Park emptied and the celebrations continued on the streets into the early hours of the next morning. Players, selectors and officials were hosts of the Royal Meath Association in Brú an Airm, Parnell

---

THE 1949 MEATH TEAM

Kevin Smyth

Mícheál O'Brien	Paddy O'Brien	Kevin McConnell
Séamus Heery	Paddy Dixon	Christo Hand

Paddy O'Connell · Jim Kearney

Frankie Byrne	Brian Smyth (Captain)	Mattie McDonnell
Paddy Meegan	Bill Halfpenny	Peter McDermott

Substitute: Pat Carolan for Frankie Byrne

Street, Dublin that evening.

Next day, Brian and his team, still somewhat dazed (perhaps for different reasons), were astounded by the good will of their many supporters. Huge crowds lined the route on the way to Navan via Clonee, Dunboyne and Dunshaughlin. There were many torchlight processions at various locations, and bonfires, lit the previous night, were re-kindled as the people of Meath honoured their history-making team.

'Celebrations continued throughout the weeks that followed with all the towns and villages being visited to mark the occasion. I am sure many a cow was left unmilked as its owner joined in the festivities. It was a wonderful occasion and it is my sincere hope that the "powers that be" will never forget the part played by people such as those in keeping Gaelic games alive at grass-roots level.'

In his playing days, Brian was never too proud to accept well-intentioned advice and criticism, particularly if it meant advancing his own game. He believes that criticism during a training session in the forties made him determined to become an even better footballer.

'We were training one night in Navan and our trainer at the time, Fr McManus, came to me and said: "Smyth, you're a great man to get a ball, but I'm damned if you know what to do with it". I was playing junior football at the time and those words set me thinking, so I decided to change my whole approach to the game. From then on I concentrated on using brain instead of brawn.'

His contemporaries agree that one of Brian's greatest qualities as a player was his anticipation and the fact that he used the ball well and could kick with both feet. But, above all else, he prided himself on being a team player and, as such, earned the respect and admiration of teammates and opponents alike.

'My contribution both as a player and administrator was prompted first of all by my initial introduction at club level by men who moulded my career from the start and secondly for the love of all things the GAA stands for. I often wonder why, with very few exceptions, players are not prepared to put something back when they have finished their playing careers. Adminstration, like playing, can be frustrating at times, but in the overall context it can be a very enjoyable way of spending some of our leisure time. There is nothing to compare with a good healthy argument and debate at Board level, when one can voice his or her opinion on any particular subject and at the end accept decisions without acrimony.'

His job as driver with CIE in the early days meant Brian had to work on Sundays, which was a major drawback to a man determined to keep his place on the Meath team. However, following intercessions by the Meath County Board on his behalf, an agreement was reached whereby Brian would be facilitated to pursue his footballing career.

Then in 1952, Brian secured employment with Meath County Council and continued to work there, until he accepted early retirement in 1986.

'I intend to spend the remainder of my years working on my farm, while still maintaining my involvement with the GAA. It is my sincere hope that the Hall of Fame award I received from the County Board doesn't mean making way for younger people.'

Brian pays tribute to the mentors in charge of Batterstown GFC, who spotted his talent and encouraged him in every way. Coaching was unheard of back then, so training methods had to be devised.

'Every evening a different aspect of the game was studied, as to how best it could be perfected, with the result that when I reached my teens I had a vast knowledge of the game stowed away which stood to me in later years. One thing on which a lot of emphasis was placed was the art of taking scores from various angles, both off the ground and out of the hands. Players would stand on the end line and try and score from that area on both sides of the goalposts. I have no doubt that this practice trained me in the use of both feet, as I was equally adept with either foot. While the way of life then was far different from the present day and the game was that bit tougher than now, the enjoyment of playing the game, win or lose, has not changed and let's hope it never does.'

What are his final thoughts on the greatest day of his sporting life? He feels that not enough credit has been given to the men in charge at the time. Rev. Fr Tully, in Brian's estimation, assumed the coaching role with the same attitude and commitment as Seán Boylan has done. He believes that both had a really fine rapport with players under their care and the players in turn reciprocated by giving their all.

> *'I was so flabbergasted, first by the immense roar and then by the enormous crowd packed everywhere, that I just stood and gazed, as if in a trance. Then, that great warrior, Peter McDermott, came over and said, "Most of these people are from Meath, let's do them proud".'*

'Fr Tully's selectors at the time, Jack Fitzgerald, Ted Meade, Paul Russell (a Kerryman), Billy Egleston, Joe Loughran and Matty Gilsenan were men of established ability, both on and off the field, and played a major part in the 1949 success. It should be noted that the system of five selectors plus chairman and secretary lasted until 1985 when it was changed to the coach appointing two selectors. However, no matter what system of selecting is in place, it is my opinion, the ability of players on the day is the main ingredient for success. Training and coaching in 1949 were far different from the present day. One of the main differences was that collective training was permitted and Meath finalised their training at Gibbstown, where we were away from the pressure of the many supporters. This had a two-way effect. Nobody realised the hysterical atmosphere throughout the county, which only came to us as we made our way to Croke Park.'

The GAA played a major part in moulding Brian Smyth's life-style, providing an outlet for his wide ranging skills and taking up the vast bulk of his spare time. He has no regrets, only fond memories of games played and wonderful lasting friendships.

'It can be summed up in comments to me by an adversary of my chairman days who said: "you enjoy a profile that many politicians would envy; you are known the length and breadth of Ireland and your popularity will never wane". This remark brought home to me what my involvement with the GAA means and I began to realise that as long as the Association maintains the ideals on which it was founded in 1884 and the grass roots of club commitment continues to be recognised, it will remain the life blood and hope for a struggling country'.

John Joe O'REILLY

Cavan Captain 1947 & 1948

JOHN JOE O'REILLY was unquestionably one of the finest captains and centre-half-backs Gaelic football has known. Although his fame grew posthumously, he had already attained legendary status before his untimely death at the age of thirty-four in 1952. His sudden death shocked the nation as only five years earlier, he had captained Cavan to victory over Kerry in the historic All-Ireland Football final in the Polo Grounds in New York. The inspirational John Joe collected the Sam Maguire Cup for a second time in 1948 when Cavan beat Mayo by a point.

His name is indelibly linked with Cavan's greatest era when the county contested eight All-Ireland Finals between 1933 and 1949. John Joe himself arrived on the Cavan senior team in 1937 when he lined out at right-half-back in the All-Ireland semi-final against Mayo. It marked the beginning of an exceptional football career, during which he played in six All-Ireland Senior Finals. The first three in 1937, 1943 and 1945 were under the captaincy of his brother, 'Big Tom' and John Joe himself was at the helm in 1947 and 1948 and again in 1949 when Cavan lost to Meath by four points.

John Joe O'Reilly was born on a farm surrounded by lakes and the River Erne in the Derries, Killeshandra, County Cavan. It was part of the lands of the Trinity Abbey, a famous seat of learning in the tenth century. Down the lake was Cloughorter Castle where Eoghan Rua Ó Néill died in 1649. From a very early age, John Joe showed great promise as an athlete, winning numerous prizes at school sports. His older brother, Tom, remembers fair-haired John Joe as someone very special even from his very earliest days.

'One had only to mention that something had to be done and he would slide off without a word to complete the task. No trying to put it onto someone else like the rest of us. Even in later times when he'd come home on holidays, he loved to go out to the field and work at whatever had to be done. He had a great attitude and was very sincere. If he had lived, he would have retired early out of the army to get a farm. That was always his ambition.'

John Joe attended Corliss National School and later went on scholarship to St Patrick's College, the famed football nursery in Cavan town, which he captained to two McRory Cup victories. Even at that early stage, he showed signs of his immense

---

FACT FILE

HOME PLACE: Derries, Killeshandra, County Cavan

BORN: 3 August 1918   CLUBS: Cornafean; Army Team, Curragh.

ACHIEVEMENTS IN CLUB COMPETITIONS: Two County Senior Championship titles with Cornafean in 1937 and 1938.

INTER-COUNTY ACHIEVEMENTS: Two All-Ireland Senior Football medals in 1947 and 1948; two National Football League medals in 1948 and 1950; four Railway Cup Football medals with Ulster in 1942, 1943, 1947 and 1950.

talent and leadership qualities which led to him being chosen as captain of the Colleges provincial team. He joined the army Cadet School at the Curragh in 1937 and two years later received his commission. He was one of a number of officers selected to train and carry out manoeuvres with the American and British armies in the North of Ireland in 1942. By 1945, John Joe had attained the rank of commandant. He played for the army football team in the Kildare Championship and also displayed considerable talents as a basketball player and athlete, winning army 100 and 220 yards titles.

'Big Tom' believes that one of his brother's greatest attributes as a player was that he could mark a man and still play the ball. 'He was very fast, fit and intelligent. Kevin Armstrong, to my mind, was as good a footballer as ever played and yet John Joe could always mark him. He always played his position. I liked to be galloping around the whole field and couldn't be bothered staying in the one place. He played at left-half-back with Cavan in the early days and he never liked the position, preferring to play in a central role. I played centre-half-back at that time and often swapped positions with him.'

> 'He was a born leader and an outstanding centre-half-back.
> I would say he was one of the greatest centre-half-backs of all time. His judgement, speed to the ball and safe hands were truly wonderful.'

In the centenary year of 1984 John Joe was chosen as centre-half-back on the 'Team of the Century'.

Mick Higgins, who captained Cavan to All-Ireland success in 1952, knew John Joe better than most and admired him greatly. 'He was a born leader and an outstanding centre-half-back. I would say he was one of the greatest centre-half-backs of all time. His judgement, speed to the ball and safe hands were truly wonderful. He was very quiet-spoken and always had words of advice and encouragement to all new players coming on to the county team. He was a sportsman supreme, never resorting to foul play. His positional play made football look easy and his distribution was excellent with long accurate clearances. As a sportsman and footballer, he stood above all others as a truly great man. He earned the respect and admiration of all the players. He was known as the most popular officer in the Curragh. John Joe's early death was a great loss to Cavan and the GAA as he was a truly outstanding gentleman.'

Simon Deignan, another member of the Cavan team and fellow officer in the Curragh, remembers John Joe as a kind and considerate man. 'When I first made my debut in Croke Park, winning an All-Ireland minor medal in 1938, John Joe was one of Cavan's brightest stars on the senior team. "Big Tom" O'Reilly was the captain at the time. Then in the mid-forties the change of captaincy passed down to John Joe whose influence proved particularly important to later successes. He was a friend to each member of the team, a person with a charisma that drew upon all the resources of people around him. To put this quality in its true perpective, his fellow team members were prepared to give of their all on the field of play. He was a career soldier, an officer of the highest qualifications and I had the pleasure of serving in the same barracks with him.

'In 1943 or thereabouts there was a Dr McKenna Cup fixture in Cavan town and during those days of the national emergency travelling by bus or otherwise was always difficult. The bus connection to Cavan did not suit my requirements. At the time I was an apprentice officer stationed in the Curragh. Naturally, I was very reluctant to miss the opportunity to play for my county and relied upon my captain and superior officer to solve the problem. This he did, by making a bicycle available to me. I hit off on the one-hundred mile trip after duty on the Saturday and when I arrived in Cavan at ten o'clock that night I was greeted by my captain and warmly congratulated. No doubt other members of his team could recount a similar type of incident as proof of John Joe's consideration and special leadership qualities.

'His contribution on the field of play was outstanding and will be recounted for many years to come. Players such as Peter Donohue, Joe Stafford, Tony Tighe, Mick Higgins, John Wilson, Paddy Smith and myself along with many more are proud to have been associated with a Cavan team under the captaincy of John Joe O'Reilly. He led us to many famous victories but none more memorable than the All-Ireland crown in the Polo Grounds in New York. His untimely passing at the age of thirty-four brought Cavan's dominance in Ulster football to an abrupt end.'

John Joe paid a visit to 'Big' Tom's office in Dublin a day or two before he entered hospital to undergo an operation for a kidney complaint.

'He was laughing and joking the same as ever. He was always full of fun and life. Somebody in my office asked him how he was and he joked that it must be "debauchery" or something like that. He never drank in his life and it would be impossible to find anyone as fit.'

Sadly, Comdt John Joe O'Reilly never recovered from the operation and he died in the Curragh General Hospital.

He was laid to rest in the little cemetery of Brigid in Killeshandra with military honours. The coffin, draped in the Tricolour with his officer's cap and sword on top, was brought the long journey from the Curragh on a gun carriage for burial close by to where he had kicked football as a young boy.

THE 1947 CAVAN TEAM

Val Gannon

Bill Doonan		Brian O'Reilly		Paddy Smith
John Wilson		John Joe O'Reilly (Captain)		Simon Deignan
	P.J. Duke		Phil Brady	
Tony Tighe		Mick Higgins		Colm McDyer
Joe Stafford		Peter Donohue		T.P. O'Reilly

THE 1948 TEAM

Des Benson

Bill Doonan		Brian O'Reilly		Paddy Smith
P.J. Duke		John Joe O'Reilly (Captain)		Simon Deignan
	Phil Brady		Victor Sherlock	
Tony Tighe		Mick Higgins		J.J. Cassidy
Joe Stafford		Peter Donohue		Edwin Carolan

Substitute: Owen Roe McGovern for John Joe O'Reilly

The *Curragh Bulletin*, a weekly magazine circulated to all army personnel, paid tribute to the dead officer in a front page article headed, 'A Last Salute to John Joe'.

'Published tersely in Camp Routine Orders, splashed in newspapers both at home and abroad, all of which seemed to regard it as something of national importance, was the news which has left his acquaintances sorrowing ...

'His brief illness was accompanied by painful and trying treatments which were borne with a resolute resignation, and a constant cheerfulness which inspired the open admiration of those who tended him and those who visited him.

'It is saddening to think that never again shall we see his frank goodnatured grin, nor hear the distinctive broad Cavan accent of his voice in greeting. Would that we

Back, left to right: John Wilson, Colm McDyer, Edwin Carolan, Tony Tighe, Peter Donohue, Terry Sheridan, Eunan Tiernan, Brendan Deignan, Phil Brady, Brian O'Reilly, Hugh Smith (Secretary, County Board).
Front, left to right: Joe Stafford, Bill Doonan, Simon Deignan, John Joe O'Reilly (captain), T.P. O'Reilly, Mick Higgins, Val Gannon, Owen Roe McGovern, Dan Denneher, Paddy Smith. Absent P.J. Duke (injured).

Back left to right: Tony Tighe, Brian O'Reilly, Victor Sherlock, Des Benson, T. P. O'Reilly, Peter Donohue, J.J. Cassidy, Mick Higgins, P. Lynch (Chairman Co. Board).
Front, left to right: P.J. Duke, Bill Doonan, Edwin Carolan, John Joe O'Reilly (captain), Simon Deignan, Phil Brady Paddy Smith, Joe Stafford.

Above: John Joe O'Reilly with the cup.
Left: Taken after the Polo Grounds Final in New York, 1947. The setting was the courthouse, cavan. Back, left to right: Eunan Tiernan, T.P. O'Reilly, Tom O'Reilly, Peter Donohue, Tony Tighe, John Wilson, Phil Brady. Centre, left to right: Mr McGeough, Bill Doonan, Terry Sheridan, Val Gannon, Simon Deignan, Colm McDyer, P.J. Duke, H. O'Reilly (Trainer). Front, left to right: H.L. Smyth, Joe Stafford, Owen Roe McGovern, John Joe O'Reilly, Edwin Carolan, Paddy Smith, P. Lynch P.J. Duke, absent from the team photo on p.287, is second from right in the centre row.

could see him, just once again, rallying a seemingly beaten team to victory by sheer magnetism of personality and redoubling of his already phenomenal physical exertions!

'The large gathering which attended the removal of his remains to the Garrison Church and the colossal crowd which followed his funeral to his lonely resting place amongst his people in distant Killeshandra churchyard, the little knots of women telling Rosaries by country cross-roads, bore eloquent testimony of the high regard in which he was held. Safely, we may say that there was not one who attended the obsequies but did so out of genuine high esteem and affection for him ...'

John Joe O'Reilly was later immortalised in the song, 'The Gallant John Joe' and it has since been recorded by many stars of Irish music.

On the third anniversary of his death, the then President of the GAA, Séamus McFerran, unveiled a memorial to the memory of the gentle sportsman.

Big Tom still retains happy memories of the days he walked the two miles from home to Corliss National School with John Joe. The family lived a mile off the main road and the two boys spent much of the time on their way to and from school kicking stones.

Paddy KENNEDY

Kerry Captain 1946

PADDY KENNEDY, acknowledged as one of the most outstanding footballers of his generation, was captain in 1946 when Kerry defeated Roscommon in a replay to claim their sixteenth All-Ireland. Gus Cremin had been captain in the drawn game but he was surprisingly dropped for the replay, and Paddy Kennedy, now switched from centre-half-forward to midfield, was chosen to lead out the Kerry team against a Roscommon side that had allowed the Munster champions to come back and force a draw in the first game.

Six minutes from time in the first game, Jimmy Murray's team led by six points and Kerry looked a beaten side. Then a goal by full-forward Paddy Burke and another soon after by Tom 'Gega' O'Connor allowed Kerry survive to fight another day.

Kerry won the replay by four points on the scoreline Kerry 2-8, Roscommon 0-10, and even though Gus Cremin came on as a substitute during the game and scored a vital point, it was Paddy Kennedy who collected the Sam Maguire Cup, thus becoming the first Annascaul man to achieve that honour.

As a matter of fact, Kerry used three captains in 1946: Gus had replaced Eddie Dowling, who led the county to a comprehensive Munster final victory over Waterford but was not on the team for the All-Ireland final.

Ballydonoghue-born Gus Cremin was naturally disappointed to lose the captaincy, and to this day feels he should not have been left out of the starting fifteen for the replay, a view shared by many of his contemporaries. As modest and unassuming a man as you could wish to meet, Gus admits that none of the Kerry team showed their true potential the first day, but reckons he played considerably better than others who held their place. A report of the match in the *Independent* would seem to bear this out. 'Keenan's two points from frees seemed to give

---

FACT FILE

HOME PLACE: Annascaul, County Kerry

BORN: 25 September 1916, Died 19 May 1979

CLUBS: Kerins O'Rahilly's; Geraldines, Dublin; Garda, Dublin

ACHIEVEMENTS IN CLUB COMPETITIONS: One County Senior Football Championship medal with Kerins O'Rahillys in 1939; three County Senior Football Championship medals with Geraldines in Dublin in 1940, 1941 and 1942; one County Senior Football Championship medal with Garda, Dublin, in 1948.

INTER-COUNTY ACHIEVEMENTS: Five All-Ireland Senior Football medals in 1937, 1939, 1940, 1941 and 1946; ten Munster Senior Football Championship medals in 1936, 1937, 1938, 1939, 1940, 1941, 1942, 1944, 1946 and 1947; two Railway Cup Football medals in 1941 and 1946; one All-Ireland Minor Football medal in 1933.

Roscommon a winning advantage but the pace was beginning to tell and with young Cremin playing a captain's rallying part consistent Kerry pressure brought the scores that earned a replay.'

And what about the famous point he scored after being sprung from the substitutes' bench in the replay? 'The sides were level when Kerry were awarded a free in the middle of the field and I dropped it in around the fourteen-yards line. Bill Carlos caught it, tore through and kicked it out into the middle of the field again. I fielded the ball, and as Éamonn Boland came towards me I just side-stepped him. Although I saw Gega O'Connor waving at me over in the corner looking for the ball, I decided to let fly and it went over the bar. It was a great moment, but it was something I had done regularly in practice.'

Gus points out that it was the selectors' decision to drop him, and he never had any animosity towards Paddy Kennedy, whom he greatly admired as a footballer.

'Paddy had a powerful kick with either left or right foot and had great anticipation. He was an outstanding fielder of a high ball with a safe pair of hands. He was also a very clean player and very seldom a foul was given against him. He was the perfect example of what a Gaelic footballer should be and was a pleasure to watch.'

The next time Kerry won the Sam Maguire Cup, in 1953, Paudie Sheehy, the captain, was relegated to the substitutes for the final and Jas Murphy was appointed to captain the side that beat first-timers Armagh by four points. Like Paddy Kennedy, Jas played club football at the time in Kerry and both were then members of the Garda Síochána. Tralee-man Jas rates Paddy the classiest footballer of them all.

'I saw him playing with my old club, Kerins O'Rahillys, and also with Kerry, and would you believe it I even played against him in 1947 during my time on the Cork team. He had everything. He was a good team footballer and had all the skills. He could also field a ball magnificently, had a great sidestep and could kick with both

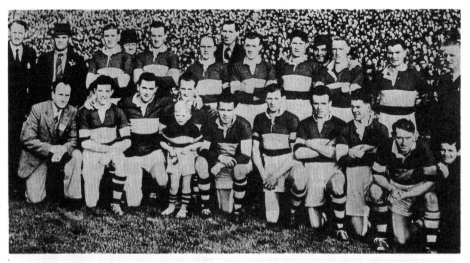

Back, left to right: Jim Whitty, Joe Merriman, Jackie Lyne, Jerry Myles (Joint Hon. Sec. Co. Board), Bill Casey, Frank O'Keeffe, Michael O'Ruairc (Joint Hon. Sec. Co. Board), Dan Kavanagh, Paddy Burke, J. Curran, Dan O'Keeffe, Paddy 'Bawn' Brosnan, Dr Éamonn O'Sullivan (Trainer).
Front, left to right: Eugene Powell, Teddy O'Connor, Joe Keohane, Paddy Kennedy (captain) (with mascot Donal O'Keeffe), Tom 'Gega' O'Connor, Eddie Walsh, Batt Garvey, Jackie Falvey, Dinny Lyne.

left and right foot. Paddy Kennedy could kick the ball over the bar from the middle of the field. He was able to use the shoulders and was an inspirational player. Kennedy was a lovely fellow and in my opinion he was *the* class footballer.'

Paddy Kennedy joined the Garda Síochána in the late thirties and was stationed for a time at Rathmines in Dublin. He left the force some years later to take up a position as a mineral water company representative. He was also manager of the Crystal Ballroom in Dublin up until the mid-seventies.

Paddy had been ill for a number of years prior to his death and fought the bravest battle of all, against cancer, in the last months of his life. His untimely death a few months short of his sixty-third birthday on Friday 19 May 1979 brought grief to his county and his country. There was no more ideal a role model for aspiring footballers than Paddy Kennedy, who epitomised everything that is positive and enriching in the game. His name is still revered around his native place, where the Paddy Kennedy Memorial Park bears testimony to the gentle giant. It was there in that little Kerry village of Anascaul on the shores of the Dingle Peninsula that he first learned to play the game in which he was to become such a master.

Kerry-born Tom Woulfe, who initiated the movement against the ban on foreign games was a lifelong friend of Paddy Kennedy. Both Tom and Paddy were members of the Tralee CBS which won two Munster Senior Colleges football titles.

'As a footballer Paddy was a legend in his native Kerry even as a teenager, and footballing legends of any age are extremely rare in those parts. For over a dozen years up to his retirement in the late forties he epitomised the grandeur and the gracefulness of the game. It can be said with confidence that Paddy never made an enemy on the football field. He was clean, competitive and courageous; modest in victory and magnaminous in defeat. When the media had elevated him to the status of national folk hero a quarter of a century after his retirement from football, he would explain away the phenomenon with childlike charm by saying, "Sure only for Mick O'Connell and the comparisons that they are making between us, I'd be forgotten long ago". Pretension was foreign to a man of his integrity. He never lost his appreciation of the simple things in life and here his talent for generating laughter comes to mind. He had been in poor health on and off for upwards of seven years. His courage and resignation throughout was inspiring. His total acceptance of God's will as the end approached will be an abiding and cherished memory for those of us close to him. It was good to have known him.'

Shortly before he died, Paddy had an unexpected visitor, someone he had not seen for many years. Tom Woulfe was at Paddy's bedside and witnessed this meeting, which made a lasting impression on him.

THE 1946 KERRY TEAM

Dan O'Keeffe

Dinny Lyne	Joe Keohane	Paddy Bawn Brosnan
Jackie Lyne	Bill Casey	Eddie Walsh
Teddy O'Connor		Paddy Kennedy (Captain)
Jackie Falvey	Tom 'Gega' O'Connor	Batt Garvey
Frank O'Keeffe	Paddy Burke	Dan Kavanagh

Substitutes: Gus Cremin for Jackie Falvey

'Paddy was very low at that point, idir bás is beatha, when Phelim Murray, the former Roscommon footballer, appeared at his bedside. Paddy and Phelim marked each other in the replayed All-Ireland final in 1946.

'Small wonder that they should have fashioned a bond of friendship, because both were footballers to their fingertips and the only injuries that either caused to an opponent was a broken heart. It was a deeply emotional encounter and a prime example of the depth and durability of the bonds of friendship on the field of play.'

Phelim Murray himself regarded Paddy Kennedy as the cleanest and best footballer he ever played on. 'He had a wonderful facility to drop-kick a ball with either foot, and it was virtually impossible to block it. He was an absolute gentleman with never a trace of a dirty trick. I remember in the drawn All-Ireland in 1946 he came up to me near the end of the game and said, "Phelim, I think it's your All-Ireland", and I said, "You never know, anything can happen, there's still over five minutes to go". And it did happen, because Kerry got two goals to level the game and then went on to win the replay.'

Knocknagoshel-born Moss Walsh first met Paddy Kennedy when he attended CBS Secondary School in Tralee. Even at that early age Paddy's remarkable talents as a footballer were very much in evidence, and he was looked up to by his classmates as someone very special on the football field. Moss later played alongside Paddy during the forties when they were both members of Dublin club Geraldines.

> 'God rest you,
> Paddy Kennedy,
> Your reward you've
> surely won, When duty
> called, you gave your all
> Both off the field and on.'
>
> **Inscription on Headstone**

'Paddy was a very personal friend of mine from our days in the CBS until his death. He was an outstanding footballer, and no finer sportsman graced the Gaelic field than this fine athlete. His manners on the field were impeccable, his play clean and skilful and his captaincy a model for all to copy. I have seen many great centrefield players during fifty years watching Gaelic football and I have to say that in my opinion, Paddy Kennedy excelled them all. The inscription on his headstone in Bohernabreena Cemetery in County Dublin is aptly written:

'God rest you, Paddy Kennedy,
Your reward you've surely won,
When duty called, you gave your all
Both off the field and on.'

It would be forty years after Kerry's defeat of Roscommon before another Annascaul man, Tommy Doyle, took possession of the Sam Maguire Cup.

By then Paddy Kennedy had gone to his eternal reward and had left behind a legend that will continue to be an inspiration to future generations of Gaelic footballers.

Tadhgo CROWLEY

Cork Captain 1945

THE TEAM Tadhgo Crowley guided to All-Ireland success over Cavan in 1945 bridged a gap of thirty-four years since Cork had previously won the title. It would be a further twenty-eight years before Cork, under the captaincy of Billy Morgan, again laid claim on the Sam Maguire Cup in 1973. But by then, Tadhgo Crowley had passed on to his eternal reward at the early age of forty-two in 1963.

Tadhgo Crowley first came to prominence on the inter-county scene in 1939 when he played both minor football and hurling for Cork. He lined out at midfield alongside Éamonn Young when Cork defeated Kilkenny in the 1939 All-Ireland Minor Hurling decider and the same year he was a member of the Cork team that beat Kerry in the Munster Minor Football Final — the county's first championship victory over Kerry at minor grade.

As a member of a family steeped in Gaelic games, Tadhgo began playing with his home-club Clonakilty at a very young age. His older brother John had lost an eye in an accident, but that did not deter him from playing club football for many years. John usually played at full-forward and was known as 'Shutter' because of the patch on his eye.

In those years, Clonakilty ruled the roost in Cork football and were well served by the likes of Mick Finn, Jack Cahalane, Shommy O'Donovan, Fachtna O'Donovan, Con and Humphrey O'Neill, Jim Ahern and Thady Regan. From 1939 to 1952 the club won seven County Senior Football Championship titles. Remarkably, immediately before that great run of success, Clonakilty had lost in six successive finals.

The great Éamonn Young, who played at midfield in the 1945 All-Ireland Final, remembers Tadhg, or 'Tadhgo' as he prefers to call him, as a man who enjoyed life to the full.

'Tadhgo was selected for the Cork senior football team shortly after he had finished playing minor. He was an excellent player, very big, very fast and very clever. His best position was centre-half-back and he often played there for Munster. I remember the day we beat Ulster in the Railway Cup Final and we stopped off on

---

FACT FILE

HOME PLACE: Clonakilty, County Cork

BORN: 24 April 1921. Died December 1963   CLUB: Clonakilty

ACHIEVEMENTS IN CLUB COMPETITIONS: Seven Cork County Senior Football Championship medals and seven West Cork Junior Hurling medals.

INTER-COUNTY ACHIEVEMENTS: One All-Ireland Senior Football Championship medal in 1945; three Munster Senior Football Championship medals in 1943, 1945 and 1949; two Railway Cup medals in 1946 and 1948; one Minor All-Ireland Hurling medal in 1939; Munster Minor Championship football and hurling medal in 1939.

our way home as we often did in the Horse and Jockey pub outside Thurles. We were sitting around the fire chatting with Mrs. O'Keeffe when Tadhgo said: "Well mam, were you listening to the Railway Cup match between Munster and Ulster on the radio?" Mrs. O'Keeffe said she was and Tadgho then said: "Did you hear much of that fellow Mick Higgins?" "No I didn't Tadhgo," Mrs O'Keeffe said. Quick as a flash Tadhgo answered: "Hard for you mam because I was on him". That's the kind of fellow Tadhgo was. He hadn't a swelled head or anything, it was just that he was great fun. Mick Higgins in my opinion was the best centre-half-forward in Ireland in his time.'

Tadhgo Crowley was over six feet in height with broad shoulders and weighed over fourteen stone. He was very well built, intelligent and exceedingly fast. According to Éamonn, Tadhgo was the second fastest man on the Cork football team of 1945. The fastest was Mick Tubridy who was an accomplished athlete.

Éamonn Young tells of an occasion when Clonakilty were playing Saint Nicholas in a Kelleher Shield match in Bandon. It was during the winter and the river adjacent to the pitch was flooded.

'There was only one football and a great friend of mine, Fachtna O'Donovan, passed the ball to Tadhgo and he in turn shoved it to Mick Finn who belted it into the river. Mick did this intentionally as Clonakilty were losing at the time. The ball floated down the river so it looked as if the match would have to be abandoned and the Saint Nicholas team would be deprived of the victory. But unfortunately for "poor old" Clonakilty, Tadhgo and the rest, a man jumped into the river, swam after the ball and brought it back. The game was finished and Clonakilty were beaten. The man who retrieved the ball was the future Taoiseach Jack Lynch!'

Éamonn Young recalls playing for the Army team, Collins Barracks, against Tadhgo Crowley's Clonakilty in the 1952 County football final.

'The rivalry between the two teams was something fierce. Clonakilty had been involved in three replays before they reached the Final. Then they drew with us in the Final but beat us in a replay. When Tadhgo was accepting the Cup from the Cork County Board he very, very seriously and very solemnly thanked the County Board and also thanked all those who had attended Clonakilty's victory and cheered them on. He also thanked the four teams that Clonakilty had beaten and said they were great people. Then he added: "there's one thing about Clonakilty anyway, nobody can deny the fact that we gave everyone of them a second chance". He got great fun out of saying that.'

Later, Tadhgo established a reputation as an excellent referee and was much in demand for inter-county games and county finals.

Tom Lyons, a national schoolteacher in Darrara outside Clonakilty and author of two books, *Fifty Years of Clonakilty Senior Football, 1932-1981*, and *Clonakilty GAA Story, 1887-1987*,' tells yet another story which illustrates the mischievious and fun-loving nature of Tadhgo Crowley.

'One of the greatest sporting challenges in Cork is to lift a 28 oz road bowl over the viaduct railway bridge which spans the main Cork-Bandon Road. It has never been accomplished. When Tadhgo was in his prime, a big sum of money was offered by a certain newspaper to anybody who could do it and it aroused great interest. One Sunday on their way to a match in Cork, Tadhgo and his friends stopped their car under the viaduct. Tadhgo took off his coat, rolled up his sleeves and started doing exercises on the road. Soon a huge crowd had gathered and all traffic stopped to see this fine strapping man, well known to many, attempting the lift. He ran up and down the road under the bridge, took a few practice swings to the mighty cheers of the crowd and then when everyone was worked up with anticipation, Tadhgo and his companions, fast as lightning, hopped back into the car and took off towards the city leaving the huge crowd perplexed and cursing after them!'

From 1941 to 1946, Cork won six All-Ireland titles, five hurling and the one football. It was the greatest period ever in the county's sporting history, Jack Lynch, who played at right corner forward in the 1945 Football Final shared in all the hurling victories and became the only player in the history of gaelic games to win six All-Ireland senior medals in a row.

Eamonn Young recalls President Sean T. O'Kelly visiting the dressing-rooms shortly before the teams were due to take the field for the 1945 Final. 'He was there saying a few words to us all and he was a man whom we all revered because he was in the G.P.O. in 1916. He went over to Tadhgo, shook his hand and wished him the best of luck. I can still remember Tadhgo, a huge, heavy shouldered, black-haired man, bending over in a benign kind of fashion talking to the small white-haired President of Ireland. He dwarfed poor Sean T. who was already very small.'

And what are Eamonn Young's memories of Tadhgo as a captain.

'He was a very good footballer and was an excellent centre half back. He had speed, height, strength and football ability because he played both football and hurling from the time he was twelve years of age and most important he was very, very fast. Now after that, you get to the mental aspect of the thing without which of course a man couldn't get anywhere. He was terribly clever at centre-half-back and had a great sense of anticipation which was most important for such a pivotal position. He was a tough, hard man and also had a great sense of humour.'

Éamonn believes Cork were lucky Mick Higgins was not playing for Cavan in the 1945 Final and also that Cavan switched Tony Tighe from his midfield position.

'We were in terrible trouble at midfield because Tony Tighe was having a great game, but then he was changed from centrefield and went in on Tadhgo for a while. We were lucky Tighe went in centreforward because Tadhgo was able to break even with him. Tighe was in wonderful form on the same day and only for Tadhgo holding on to him, I'd say we'd have been beaten. When Cavan were pressing us very much at the end, Tadhgo, Caleb Crone, Weesh Murphy and Dave Magnier held the thing together. We won the game by four points, 2-5 to 0-7. It was a great period for Cork hurling and football and the prestige of players generally was very, very high. Our victory meant that football which was always the poor relation became

---

THE 1945 CORK TEAM

Moll O'Driscoll

| Dave Magnier | 'Weesh' Murphy | Caleb Crone |
| Paddy Cronin | Tadgho Crowley (Captain) | Din O'Connor |

Éamonn Young · · · · Fachtna O'Donovan

| Tocher Casey | Humphrey O'Neill | Mick Tubridy |
| Jack Lynch | Jim Cronin | Derry Beckett |

Substitute: Jim Ahern for Tocher Casey

Tadhgo Crowley charges in from the left to cut off two Cavan forwards. Beside him is Dave Magnier and at the back Paddy Cronin.

important after that.'

On the night of the All-Ireland Final the victorious Cork team was staying in Barry's Hotel in Dublin and Éamonn recalls having his sleep disturbed by two hungry teammates. 'Tadhgo and Fachtna O'Donovan went downstairs and raided the kitchen in the hotel and brought food up to the rooms. I remember Fachtna wakening me up and I looked over and saw Tadhgo with a big knife carving a beautiful ham. Fachtna then said to me: "is it beef or ham you'll have?"'

Tadhgo Crowley is still fondly remembered by those who were privileged to know him as a great footballer and a great character.

Back, left to right: Jim Barry (Trainer), Tocher Casey, Moll O'Driscoll, Lar O'Shea (Selector), Dave Magnier, Fachtna O'Donovan, Jack Lynch, Caleb Crone, Din O'Connor, Dan Harrington (Selector), Mick Sheehan (Lord Mayor, Cork) Front, left to right: Paddy Cronin, Derry Beckett, Weesh Murphy, Jim Cronin, Mick Tubridy, Tadhgo Crowley, Humphrey O'Neill, Éamonn Young, Andy Scannell (Selector), Jack Young (Father of Éamonn Young).

Jimmy MURRAY

Roscommon Captain 1943 & 1944

'I AM CONVINCED *my parents had a greater influence on my football career than anybody else. They must have realised at a very early age that I was football mad, which indeed I was. My first letter to Santa Claus was for a football, which he duly delivered. That ball was kicked for hours on Christmas Day by the Murray brothers and our pals. We had a session again on St Stephen's Day, and that evening I greased the ball with neat's foot oil, an oil used by farmers to soften leather boots. When I had it well greased, in my childhood innocence I left it before a huge open fire to dry, as I thought. Of course, after a few minutes, there was an explosion and my ball was in bits. However, Santa Claus came again to me two nights after with a new and better football! It was only in later years I realised the sacrifices my parents made in order to ensure that I was free to go training five nights a week for three or four months each summer, when Roscommon were going well. My family ran a country business, bar, grocery, hardware and drapery in the village of Knockcroghery. Ninety per cent of our customers were and still are farmers, and during the summer months the shop never got busy until after tea-time. Many evenings, when I felt I should stay at home, my parents would not hear of it and forced me to go to the training sessions. My mother never saw Phelim or myself play. In 1943, my parents were at home and one of my most treasured possessions is the telegram of congratulations from my parents, which was delivered as we sat for our celebration meal on Sunday night.' (There was a Sunday telegram service in 1943.)*

WHENEVER ALL-TIME GREATS of Gaelic games are being discussed, the name Jimmy Murray never fails to command special mention. And not without ample justification.

As the man who captained his native Roscommon to two successive All-Ireland final victories in 1943 and 1944, Jimmy is one of an elite band of footballers. Since the Sam Maguire Cup was first presented, only four other players have captained

---

FACT FILE

HOME PLACE: Knockcroghery, County Roscommon

BORN: 5 May 1917

CLUBS: St Patrick's, Knockcroghery; Roscommon Gaels.

ACHIEVEMENTS IN CLUB COMPETITIONS: Six County Senior Football Championships in 1942, 1943, 1945, 1946, 1948 and 1949; two County Junior Football Championships in 1936 and 1938; one County Senior Hurling Championship with Roscommon Gaels in 1938 and one County Junior Hurling Championship with St Patrick's in 1945.

INTER-COUNTY ACHIEVEMENTS: Two All-Ireland Senior Football Championship medals in 1943 and 1944; one Junior All-Ireland Football medal in 1940; four Connacht Senior Football medals in 1943, 1944, 1946 and 1947; two Connacht Junior Football medals in 1939 and 1940; Oireachtas Football medal in 1943 plus a number of tournament medals.

---

back-to-back All-Ireland-winning football teams: John Joe O'Reilly of Cavan in 1947 and 1948; Seán Flanagan of Mayo in 1950 and 1951; Enda Colleran of Galway in 1965 and 1966 and Dublin's Tony Hanahoe in 1976 and 1977. The only other player to captain two Sam Maguire Cup winning teams was Kerry's Joe Barrett in 1929 and 1932.

However, no one has yet bettered Jimmy's record of having led his county team on five occasions in the All-Ireland final parade. This happened twice in 1943 - Roscommon beat Cavan in a replay to bring the Sam Maguire Cup to the county for the first time — once in 1944 and twice again in 1946 after Kerry forced a replay by scoring two goals in the closing six minutes.

It was a heartbreaking end to a game Roscommon looked certain to win and all the more distressing for Jimmy Murray who was lying on the sideline, nursing a broken nose.

'I had lost a fair amount of blood and I imagine I looked a messy sight. One of the St John's Ambulance men got to work cleaning the blood from my face. He said he wanted "to make me presentable when I received the Cup". Indeed, thousands of other people, including myself, thought Roscommon had won. What happened is history. Kerry scored two late goals to draw the match and went on to win the replay. The extraordinary thing is that I came back into the game after Kerry scored the second goal. I can't remember exactly how it happened, but I definitely got back on the field and even got one chance of scoring a point, which I missed. It would have made history for me and for Roscommon if I had scored

'Of course, that was my greatest disappointment in football and the thought of that day still hurts. We felt terrible. I knew coming off Croke Park that day that we should have won the game and when you feel like that it's very hard to win a replay. I don't like making excuses for losing, but I think we were a very tired team in the replay. Collective training was permissible at that time and in 1946 Roscommon had seven spells of training, nearly two weeks each time, and it was just too much. The hunger was gone.'

Jimmy consoles himself with the thought that the Kerry-Roscommon replay of 1946 is still regarded as one of the greatest finals of all time. He believes the 1946 Roscommon team to be the best he played on.

'To me, they were the perfect machine that season and it was a joy to be part of it. We played great football to reach the All-Ireland final and even if Laois gave us a fright in the semi-final, we still finished with great confidence.'

Before their meeting with the Leinster champions, it had taken two games to decide the outcome of the Connacht final. Controversy raged after the first game, Mayo objecting to a late Roscommon goal, which had given Jimmy Murray's men victory by one point. The Connacht Council ordered a replay, which Roscommon won. Jimmy Murray has a different version of events to that of Mayo's Seán Flanagan.

'I scored a goal in the first game and I don't know why they wanted to disallow it. I wasn't inside the square, I was out a fair bit when I kicked the ball. The umpires and referee were discussing what to do and on the spur of the moment, I ran in and put up the flag. As a boy, I had seen my folk-hero, Brendan Nestor, doing the very same thing in the Connacht final against Mayo. Years afterwards, Brendan and I discussed both incidents and I remember him saying: "God, they made an awful lot about those things, sure there was nothing to it!" And there wasn't much to it either, just a spur of the moment reaction.'

The 1946 All-Ireland defeat by Kerry more or less signalled the end of the most successful of all Roscommon teams. And what a team! Graded junior in 1938, Roscommon lost to Galway in the very first round of that championship that year. Yet five years later, they were crowned All-Ireland senior champions.

It all began when they won the 1940 All-Ireland Junior final against Westmeath by a comfortable margin. The match was played in Longford and Jimmy recalls that Hugh Gibbons had an outstanding game for Roscommon. Around that period, Roscommon also won two All-Ireland minor titles, with victory against Monaghan in 1939 and, two years later, against Louth.

Back in the senior ranks in 1941, Roscommon were beaten by Galway in two successive Connacht finals, each time by a single point, so it was a case of third time lucky in 1943 when they claimed their first provincial senior title for twenty-nine years, with a four-points win over Galway at St Coman's Park in Roscommon.

'We had an all-Pioneer pipers' band in Knockcroghery at that time and they always played the teams around the field before our games. It was an added bonus for me to be marching behind friends from my home place and they used to look back at me and smile. When the break-up came to go to our positions, they shouted words of encouragement and gave me a clap on the back.

'Once the final whistle blew, the scenes of excitement were terrific. I remember the band lined up outside Coman's Park after the game and they marched through the town playing music, with all the youngsters running after them clapping and cheering.'

To win an All-Ireland title demands a tremendous amount of dedication and commitment from everyone involved, not just the panel of players but also from the backroom team.

'I have said it before that without Dan O'Rourke and John Joe Fahy, I believe Roscommon would not have won in 1943. Dan O'Rourke played a major part in the

---

THE 1943 ROSCOMMON TEAM (Replay)

Frank Glynn

Larry Cummins	J. P. O'Callaghan	Bill Jackson
Brendan Lynch	Bill Carlos	Ownsie Hoare

Éamon Boland   Liam Gilmartin

Phelim Murray	Jimmy Murray (Captain)	Dónal Keenan
Derry McDermott	Jack McQuillan	Frank Kinlough

THE 1944 TEAM

Ownsie Hoare

Bill Jackson	J.P. O'Callaghan	John Casserly
Brendan Lynch	Bill Carlos	Phelim Murray

Éamon Boland   Liam Gilmartin

Frank Kinlough	Jimmy Murray (Captain)	Dónal Keenan
Hugh Gibbons	Jack McQuillan	John Joe Nerney

Substitute: Derry McDermott for John Joe Nerney

---

success of the team. When we started training we stayed in Dan's house in Tarmon near Castlerea and his own family fed us for weeks and weeks on end. It was much later that we came back to Roscommon town to train. Dan O'Rourke arranged for Tom Molloy from Galway to train the team and also got a masseur by the name of Toddy Ryan, another Galway man.'

Roscommon had defeated Leitrim in the first round of the Connacht championship in 1943 but what Jimmy Murray remembers most about that day was what John Joe Fahy said to him before the game.

'He handed me the list of names in the dressing-room and said: "I hope I'll be doing the same thing on the last Sunday in September". I took it with a grain of salt

Back, left to right: Ownsie Hoare, Jimmy Murray, Phelim Murray, Jack McQuillan, Frank Glynn, Larry Cummins, Frank Kinlough, Liam Gilmartin.
Front, left to right: J.P. O'Callaghan, Brendan Lynch, Donal Keenan, Derry McDermott, Bill Jackson, Bill Carlos, Éamon Boland.

Front, left to right: John J. Fahey (Co. Sec.), Brendan Lynch, Jimmy Murray, Bill Carlos, Jack McQuillan, John P. O'Callaghan, John Joe Nerney, Ownsie Hoare, Derry McDermott.
Back, left to right: Billy Keogh (trainer), Phelim Murray, Éamon Boland, Jack Casserly, Bill Jackson, Hugh Gibbons, Dan O'Rourke (Co. Chairman), Frank Kinlough, Donal Keenan, Liam Gilmartin.

and thought to myself: "That's a bit farfetched, to win a Connacht final would be enough for me."

'John Joe was a terrific organiser. He was always praying for the team and the lads used to joke about him having the Rosary beads with him while we were playing.'

The build up to the All-Ireland semi-final against Louth was something new for the Roscommon players, who were not accustomed to such close scrutiny and fan-worship.

'A lot of older people still say to me that the game against Louth was the best they ever saw. Louth had a great side at the time and were very confident of victory. It was a very high-scoring game between two young teams and we won it by four points. The game was played in a downpour and the scenes in the dressing-room after the match were something special. There was a certain fulfilment in the achievement and I found it hard to believe we had qualified for the All-Ireland final.'

Everything about his first All-Ireland remains etched in Jimmy Murray's memory. 'It was no different then than it is now and every man, woman and child was talking football and breathing football for weeks beforehand. Huge crowds turned up to our training sessions in Roscommon town.

'We stayed in the old hospital and trained in St Coman's Park. Every young fellow in the town wanted to carry our boots down to the field. The young girls in the convent used to lean out the windows and shout at the players. We were heroes with all those youngsters and received letters from all over Ireland.'

The night before the final, Jimmy and some of the team went along to the Theatre Royal to see Jack Doyle and Movita. Before the final curtain, Jimmy and 'Big' Tom O'Reilly, the Cavan captain, were brought out on stage and introduced to the capacity crowd: 'Tom often said to me since: "Weren't we an awful pair of eejits!" '

That Sunday in September 1943 when he took the field as captain was the proudest moment of Jimmy's life. It was the first time a Roscommon senior team had appeared in an All-Ireland final and Croke Park welcomed the newcomers with a mass of blue-and-gold flags.

There was tension in the dressing-room before the game and Jimmy admits he was just as nervous as the next. The minutes waiting seemed like hours as the team prepared for their greatest challenge.

'Even players who had been cracking jokes all morning now looked as if they were due for the torture chamber. There were white faces all around me, although some fellows were more relaxed than others. We used often remark that Liam Gilmartin was so relaxed before a game that he could lie down and sleep in the dressing-room and then go out and play a blinder. But most of the team would be on edge, even if it wasn't such an important game. And it was so much worse on All-Ireland day.'

His first impression when he stepped onto Croke Park was that he never saw grass look so green. Nor was he prepared for the deafening noise that greeted his team.

'The reception we got was something terrific and it brought us back to earth. I looked at the crowd and felt very lonesome. Then I checked to see if the rest of the team were behind me and was glad to see their familiar faces. There was no such thing as running around the field, kicking the ball, we just huddled together waiting for the band to form in front of us. We chatted away but everyone was jittery, although letting on to be relaxed.'

Once the parade got under way, nerves calmed a little. This was it. All the long, hard nights of training seemed worthwhile. And Jimmy Murray was where he always wanted to be, marching behind the band on All-Ireland final day.

'As a young fellow, I had imagined leading this parade in my own back yard and in my own bedroom. I loved looking at the newspapers on a Monday morning after the final, just to see a photograph of the parade. I always thought it would be wonderful to march behind the band in Croke Park. Now I was doing it and better still, I was captain of the Roscommon team in their first ever All-Ireland. It was a great feeling. Then other thoughts crossed my mind and I wished I was away from the pitch and sitting in the stand. I looked up at Mícheál O'Hehir in the commentary box and I imagined he was saying something like: "Here comes Roscommon led by the fair-haired Jimmy Murray". It sent a tingle up my spine. It brought my mind back to my native village, Knockcroghery, and I tried to envisage what my father and mother were doing. I knew my mother would be praying and I could imagine all the crowd in the kitchen listening to the radio and I said to myself: "We have to do something for those people". It made me feel good, and fierce determined to do or die for the sake of Knockcroghery, more than anything else. I had a great village feeling. They told me afterwards that they had to go out to the yard because the kitchen couldn't hold all the people.

> 'The reception we got was something terrific and it brought us back to earth. I looked at the crowd and felt very lonesome. Then I checked to see if the rest of the team were behind me and was glad to see their familiar faces.'

'We reached the middle of the field and I met the Cavan captain and my immediate opponent, Big Tom O'Reilly, who had a big smile on his face. He had been there a few times before and looked very relaxed. He was a great character and a very nice fellow.'

Cavan dominated the early exchanges as Roscommon struggled to find their true form.

'We played like a bunch of kids for the first twenty minutes and Cavan were running around us. We settled a little when Liam Gilmartin scored a point and then Phelim added two more which meant we were just four points down at half-time.'

A few minutes into the second half, Jimmy scored the goal that he cherishes more than any other in his career.

'I remember distinctly, we got a free in our right-half-back position and Brendan Lynch hit a very long ball. He was very, very strong, a huge man and he had a terrific long kick. The ball came in very high and I remember thinking: "I can't get this ball, it's too high for me". So I faced the backs and forwards, who were all jumping for the ball and hoped for the break. It just came down and I snapped it and kicked it like lightning into the back of the net. It was just one of those things, my brain just happened to click. Somebody was praying for me, it must have been my mother at home. Anyhow, the ball just broke into my hands and I let fly.'

Considering Roscommon's mediocre first-half performance, Jimmy Murray was more than pleased to come away with a draw. The team was a little calmer for the replay which Roscommon won by five points. It turned out to be a dogged game, during which Cavan were reduced to fourteen men when Joe Stafford was sent to the line.

Jimmy Murray has fond memories, too, of the homecoming with the Sam Maguire Cup on that never-to-be-forgotten Monday evening in 1943.

'The Roscommon Association in Dublin put on a great reception for us on Sunday night and the whiskey flowed like buttermilk. Hundreds of Roscommon people living in Dublin came to the railway station on Monday evening to see us on our way home. The train was bedecked with Roscommon colours and even the driver and guards had Roscommon caps. We got a great reception at every station on the way and when we finally arrived in Athlone, we heard loud explosions, which turned out to be fog signals. The place was packed with people and I had to get out on the platform to say a few words. It was a fine September evening and all the way from Athlone to Roscommon, bonfires blazed. They had a torchlight procession on the platform at Knockcroghery and a big bonfire blazed at the railway gate. That was very special. On the approach to Roscommon, the train had to slow down for fear of people wandering onto the track. We were given an official reception by the County Council, followed by an all-night dance in the Harrison Hall.'

Jimmy Murray was again at the helm when Roscommon retained their crown the following year, with a two-points win over Kerry.

'To beat Kerry in the final was a wonderful feeling. I have always maintained that no team can be regarded as champions until they beat Kerry. They took the lead about ten minutes from time and soon after it started to rain. I remember a man saying to me afterwards that as soon as he heard Mícheál O'Hehir saying it was raining, he knew Roscommon would win. He always maintained we played better in the rain. It was a great game of football.'

Brendan Lynch, his teammate for many years, acknowledges Jimmy Murray's great contribution both as a player and captain.

'Jimmy commanded respect and obedience, not by demands he made on players but by his own example and dedication. You felt that for some reason you owed it to him to be prepared physically and mentally for a match. When he said "we must win our next game", you took this as a command to train harder and give of your best, because you knew that was what Jimmy would be doing and you felt it would be disloyal if you did not prepare properly. He was tough, both physically and mentally, in his approach to football, a great judge of a new player and totally ruthless in his criticism of players who didn't meet his standards of conduct, on and off the field. His abiding criticism was "That shagger isn't worth a damn" or "He'd make a good dancer". He was marvellous to rally a team when things looked bleak and his cry from the forty yards mark, "Come on Roscommon" really spurred us to greater and greater effort. He was as gracious in defeat as in victory to the opposing team. On the other hand, he could be as tough as iron when a hatchet man on the opposing team tried to do the dirt on him or on a teammate on the field of play.'

Typically, Jimmy himself feels it important to acknowledge the contribution of the great Rocommon players who inspired him as a youngster. They provided the platform for future generations. Names like Andy Madden, Pat Shallow, Paddy Brennan, the Quigley brothers, Harry Hession, Tom Haig, Luke O'Connor, Tom

1944 teams parade before the final

Barlow, Jimmy Oates, Tom Brady, Dan O'Rourke, Mike O'Rourke, Jack Cummins and many more.

'I was often told about the great deeds of those men by the old "Gaels", I met around the village. I remember being enthralled by the stories and have no trouble recalling their names. In my youth, I had the pleasure of watching Tom Shevlin, Tommy Moran, Jimmy Creighton, Edwin Dooley and Peter O'Gara play for Roscommon and longed for the day I could prove myself good enough to wear the blue-and-gold. When I first made the county panel, the two players I admired most were Paddy Kenny and Harry O'Connor. Kevin Winston from Ballinlough made his debut for Roscommon the same day as myself. He was one of the most complete footballers I ever saw playing. Had Kevin remained in the county he would of course have been part of our set-up.'

Naturally enough, Jimmy Murray would love to see Roscommon win the Sam Maguire Cup again.

'Even after all these years, people still bring youngsters up to me for an autograph. It never wears off and will be there until I die. Tradition is very important and I believe it is the greatest contribution from the 1943 and 1944 teams to the present generation. I would say to young people of our county: "Have the urge and determination to win an All-Ireland. It is worth all the sacrifices. Memories live for ever".'

Joe FITZGERALD

Dublin Captain 1942

A KERRY MAN, Joe Fitzgerald, had the distinction of captaining the Dublin team that brought the Sam Maguire Cup to the capital city for the first time.

Strangely, three of the midfielders in action on the day came from the Dingle area. Mick Falvey partnered Joe at centrefield while one of their direct opponents on the Galway team was another neighbour, Dan Kavanagh, from the parish of Dún Chaoin. And the green-and-gold connection did not end at that. Kerry-born Jack Flavin, who won an All-Ireland medal with his native county in 1937 and figured on the Galway team that beat Kerry in 1938, was again in the Galway forward line in 1942.

Except for a few short years while a member of the Garda Síochána, Joe Fitzgerald has lived all his life in the county of his birth. Yet ask him who he would support if Dublin were playing Kerry in the morning and he will leave you in no doubt of his allegiance. He won an All-Ireland medal with Dublin and has continued to cheer for them ever since. Even in 1985 when his near neighbour, Páidí Ó Sé, captained Kerry to victory over Dublin in the All-Ireland final, the amiable Joe saw no reason to row in behind the Kingdom. No disrespect intended on his part, it is just that the happiest memories of his football days were with the 'Dubs'.

'During the time I was playing here in Kerry the selectors never noticed me at all. I don't know why but that was the case. They had a junior team in Kerry at the time and I wasn't even considered for that. No one ever approached me at any stage to play for Kerry. I was playing great football then with the Gaeltacht, probably better than the days I played with Dublin.

'I still support Dublin. I would never have won an All-Ireland medal much less be an All-Ireland winning captain only for them. I had great times with Dublin and they still treat me very well and have never forgotten me. I would love to have played for Kerry but I have no regrets. I am very happy with what I have achieved. Maybe if I had been picked by Kerry I might never have won an All-Ireland medal.'

Joe Fitzgerald first came to the notice of the Dublin selectors as a result of outstanding displays with the Geraldines club. On leaving CBS Secondary School in

---

FACT FILE

HOME PLACE: Ballydavid in the parish of Kill, County Kerry

BORN: 18 August 1915

CLUBS: An Ghaeltacht, Kerry; Geraldines, Dublin; West Kerry; Dingle.

ACHIEVEMENTS IN CLUB COMPETITIONS: One Senior Football Championship medal with Dingle in 1948; three County Senior Football Championship medals with Geraldines in 1940, 1941 and 1942; two Oireachtas medals with Geraldines.

INTER-COUNTY ACHIEVEMENTS: One All-Ireland Senior Football medal in 1942; two Leinster Senior Football Championship medals in 1941 and 1942.

Dingle, Joe had worked on the family farm for a few years before being called for training to the Garda Depot in the Phoenix Park.

'I was stationed in Rathmines after coming out of the Depot and went out a few evenings kicking the ball with a pal of mine in the Guards called Charlie O'Sullivan. Charlie was then playing with Geraldines and it was he who encouraged me to join the club. We had some great times.'

Joe began playing for Geraldines in 1940 and was home in Kerry on a short holiday later that year when he received a letter from the secretary of the Dublin County Board, Harry Conlon, informing him of his selection at midfield on the Dublin team the following Sunday.

'I never expected it. Harry was the secretary of the Geraldines team and had watched me playing on numerous occasions and was confident I could do a good job for Dublin. I went back for the game and they kept me on. I didn't always play at centrefield and played on a few occasions for Dublin at left-half-back. In fact I played the first half of the All-Ireland semi-final in 1942 against Cavan at left-half-back but was moved to centrefield after half time. I was midfield for the final against Galway.'

> *'I didn't realise*
> *I was playing in*
> *an All-Ireland at all*
> *as I was so used to playing*
> *in Croke Park with the Geraldines.*
> *I suppose that was the reason*
> *I wasn't in the least excited.*
> *It was like playing a club match.'*

Joe Fitzgerald has no idea why he was chosen as captain of Dublin. He was never informed by anyone and he never bothered to ask why. Joe was captain when Dublin easily defeated Carlow in the 1941 Leinster final before losing to Kerry in the All-Ireland semi-final after a replay.

'I can't understand why I was chosen as captain. I wasn't the captain of Geraldines either. In fact there were two other Geraldines players, Paddy Henry of Sligo and Jimmy Joy from Killorglin, on the Dublin team in 1942. I was captain of the county team from 1940 to 1942.

'There was a fellow on the Dublin team when I started playing with them first called Con Martin. He also played soccer, even though it was against the GAA rules then to do so. I often saw his name afterwards on the Aston Villa team. He was a great player. He would come up to take a fifty and wouldn't care whether it was from right or left, he would hit it like a shot out of a gun right over the bar. Oh, God, yes, he was good!'

Dublin had a much tougher task in the 1942 Leinster final when for the second successive year they were opposed by Carlow. This time Dublin prevailed by a very narrow margin to set up a semi-final meeting with Cavan. 'We just beat them by about three points. It wasn't easy, I can tell you. Our trainer was Peter O'Reilly and he was a great player as well.'

Unlike what we have become accustomed to in recent times, there was very little hype in the run-up the All-Ireland final. Dublin were given little chance of beating Galway who had lost the two previous finals to Kerry.

'We trained in Parnell Park every evening and then had a cup of tea or maybe a raw egg afterwards. There was no fuss at all on the day. I said nothing to the players in the dressing-room. I left it to the selectors to say what needed to be said. I wasn't a bit nervous. I didn't realise I was playing in an All-Ireland at all as I was so used to playing in Croke Park with the Geraldines. I suppose that was the reason I wasn't in the least excited. It was like playing a club match. Most of the Dublin county championship matches were played in Croke Park, and we were there so often with Geraldines that we didn't take any notice of it. It would be different if you went up from Dingle for the day to play in an All-Ireland final in Croke Park, but that was not the case with the Dublin players. It certainly made a difference to have played in Croke Park so often. As far as I was concerned the fact that it was an All-Ireland final made no difference whatsoever. I led the team out on the field, but that was no big deal. I wasn't a man for too much fuss. I just liked to get on with the game and give of my best. It had no effect at all on me.

'People thought we weren't good enough to win an All-Ireland. Galway had a great team at that time with the likes of Charlie Connolly, Joe Duggan and the two Kerry men, Jack Flavin and Dan Kavanagh.'

And what of the final itself? 'It was a good game and a nice day for the match. Galway were leading by four or five points at half time so that made people think we would be well beaten. But we came back well in the second half and I remember on one occasion the ball coming down and I was within ten or fifteen yards of the Dublin goal, defending. I went up for the ball with one of the Galway players and it fell between us. I had to stoop very low to pick it up and I then kicked it full force into the hands of Jimmy Joy who was on his own up in the forward line. He shot it over the bar to level the game. We then scored two more points without reply. Tommy Banks got the last point for us.

'I was lifted shoulder high over towards the Hogan Stand to collect the cup. It was a great honour to be getting something that the whole of Ireland had been fighting for tooth and nail. The few sentences I said were all in Irish, every word of them.'

The incident in which Joe set up an important point led to some controversy afterwards. 'There was a letter in the *Evening Press* implying that I had picked the ball "perhaps unintentionally" off the ground near the end of the game. It also stated that if Galway had got their free they would surely have scored a point instead of a point being scored against them.'

Joe is adamant that he did not lift the ball off the ground. It was dropping very low when he stooped to lift it but he is in no doubt whatsoever that what he did was perfectly legitimate. He was also pleased with his own performance on the day.

Those I have spoken to say that Joe's attributes as a player were his high-fielding, the fact that he could kick equally well with left or right foot and his great power. He also had very strong hands and was difficult to dispossess.

THE 1942 DUBLIN TEAM

Charlie Kelly

Bobby Beggs	Paddy 'Beefy' Kennedy	Caleb Crone
Paddy Henry	Peter O'Reilly	Brendan Quinn
Mick Falvey		Joe Fitzgerald (Captain)
Jimmy Joy	Paddy Bermingham	Gerry Fitzgerald
Mattie Fletcher	Paddy O'Connor	Tommy Banks

Many of his neighbours and friends from Kerry were in Croke Park that day to cheer on the local man. They were all delighted to see Joe playing for Dublin. It was also a great honour for the Gaeltacht.

He admits it never crossed his mind to bring the Sam Maguire Cup to his home-place. 'I don't know why I never thought of it. I suppose I didn't want to be lugging it around. No one asked me about bringing it to Kerry. It was different times. The cup was in the Garda barracks in Rathmines for a long time. There were numerous photographs taken of the cup with plenty of guards around it.'

An Irish-speaker, Joe Fitzgerald liked nothing better than playing against Kerry and beating them. 'We beat Kerry in a challenge game about three weeks after winning the All-Ireland final and it was a great thrill. I played much better than I did in the All-Ireland final. I always raised my game when playing against Kerry and was determined to beat them.

'At half-time that day a few of the Kerry players came over to ask me to declare for Kerry but I said no. When I was in Kerry they wouldn't give me my place. I was annoyed at the time that the Kerry selectors ignored me. I was playing good enough foootball to be on the Kerry team. I didn't improve that much by just going to Dublin.'

Joe also captained the Leinster team that beat a Munster selection boasting fourteen Kerry men in the Railway Cup semi-final of 1943. That too gave him great satisfaction. Leinster lost to Ulster in the final.

Dublin were beaten by Louth in the first round of the Leinster Championship in 1943. According to Joe the team was much changed from the one which had fashioned an All-Ireland victory the previous year.

'There were a lot of players from other counties who declared for Dublin right away after we won the All-Ireland final. Many of them were picked for the Dublin side and a good deal of the players who were part of the All-Ireland winning team were left out. They broke up a winning combination which was a very strange thing

Back, left to right: Paddy 'Beefy' Kennedy, Paddy O'Connor, Charlie Kelly, Mick Falvey, Caleb Crone, Tommy Banks, Paddy Bermingham, Bobby Beggs.
Front, left to right: Mattie Fletcher, Peter O'Reilly, Brendan Quinn, Joe Fitzgerald, Gerry Fitzgerald, Paddy Henry, Jimmy Joy.

to do. We lost out badly. I played a few League matches after that but I never again played in the championship for Dublin.

'I came back to Kerry about two years later and played with the Gaeltacht. Football was a great pastime and I loved playing it. There was nothing much else to do at the time, no radio or television. Football was everything. They love football in all parts of Kerry.'

There are six parishes in the Gaeltacht: Cuas, Marhin, Ballyferriter, Dunquin, Ventry and Kill which was Joe's native place.

He looks back fondly on his early days playing for his native parish.

'There used to be a football competition organised every year between the six parishes. There were plenty of strapping young men around back then. Every team had to have players from their own parish as no outsider was allowed play. There was fierce rivalry between the parishes and it was a great introduction to football. I started playing from the time I was about fifteen.

'My God, they were good days, surely. Very good days. There used to be big crowds at the games as there was a great population around here back then. We won the competition in our time and got a cup and a set of medals. It was the next best thing to an All-Ireland.'

Joe Fitgerald attended CBS Secondary School in Dingle where he came under the influence of Brother Ryan, who was a great source of encouragement.

'He was all out for football. You wouldn't have to do much lessons for him so long as you played football. He would bring us up to the sports field to kick ball. That's what we wanted, anything to get hours off from school. During my time, Dingle CBS won the Dunlo Cup which was a competition between all the schools and colleges in Kerry. We had a very good team with the likes of Paddy Bawn Brosnan, his brother Tim, Bill Casey and Johnny Moriarty.

Joe is in no doubt that the game was better in his time. He considers there to be not enough high fielding in the present game.

'As well as that if you shoulder a man now you're whistled up. There are too many frees altogether for nothing at all. And I dislike this thing of players staying on the ground after a hard shoulder until they get a free.'

The 'Boy Wonder' Tommy Murphy, a Laois player of renown, was in Joe's opinion the best player of his era.

Nowadays, Joe Fitzgerald resides about three miles from Dingle on the high road to Ventry. His house is surrounded by mountains, among them Mount Eagle and Brandon Mountain, the second highest mountain in Ireland. His house is less than three miles from where Páidí Ó Sé, another All-Ireland winning captain, now runs a very successful pub.

Joe Fitzgerald is a proud Kerryman with more than a little touch of blue.

Bill DILLON

Kerry Captain 1941

WIDELY ACCLAIMED AS ONE OF THE GREATEST half-backs of his generation, Bill Dillon was captain of the 1941 three-in-a-row Kerry team, the first to win fifteen All-Ireland titles.

Kerry defeated Galway in the final by four points with a team comprising fourteen of the players that beat the same opposition the previous year.

After the game Bill was quoted as saying: 'I am particularly glad that the big crowd that came to see the final under difficult circumstances was not disappointed. We got the close game we had expected from Galway, but few can deny we deserved our fifteenth title and new record. There was not a weak spot in the team who brought off once again that famous Kerry rally.'

Bill Dillon was born in the family home at Cooleen in Dingle. The house was situated at the water's edge and was on two levels, the lower one being a boathouse, which flooded with every high tide. Bill's grandfather, William Kennedy, had retired from the British Navy and Coastguard to this residence.

When Bill was just nine years old the family moved to Green Street, as the residence was proving inaccessible for the doctor attending to Bill's grandmother during her final illness.

Bill Dillon's love of beagling is legendary and seemingly developed at a very young age. According to his sister Eileen, who died in 1992, Bill was scampering around the mountainside from the time he was in short trousers. In fact his schoolmaster often said: 'We'll continue when Billy Dillon comes back from the mountain'. His knowledge of the West Kerry mountains was unrivalled. At his funeral the talk was as much about his love of beagling as of any of the great games he played for Kerry and Dingle.

His introduction to football was through the Christian Brothers in his home town. Among his classmates were such future Kerry stalwarts as Seán Brosnan, Bill Casey and Paddy Bawn Brosnan. In fact Bill and Seán Brosnan were midfield partners on the Kerry minor team that beat Mayo in the 1933 All-Ireland final.

Bill came onto the Kerry senior team in 1937 and the same year was centre-half-back when the Kingdom won the All-Ireland final, defeating Cavan in a replay. 'Green Flag' in the *Irish Press* was highly impressed with young Bill's

---

FACT FILE

HOME PLACE: Green Street, Dingle, County Kerry

BORN: 1 June 1915. Died 19 May, 1979.   CLUB: Dingle

ACHIEVEMENTS IN CLUB COMPETITIONS: Six County Senior Football Championships medals in 1938, 1940, 1941, 1943, 1944 and 1948.

INTER-COUNTY ACHIEVEMENTS: Four All-Ireland Senior Football medals in 1937, 1939, 1940 and 1941; seven Munster Championship medals in 1937, 1938, 1939, 1940, 1941, 1942 and 1944; one All-Ireland Minor medal in 1933.

---

performance: 'Bill Dillon was a wonderful success at centre half-back, and in the early stages when Cavan were in a dangerous mood the Dingle boy rose to great heights.'

P.F., writing in the *Kerryman*, agreed: 'Dillon was a pronounced success at centre-half. His great fielding was early apparent. He was fortunate in being marked by a clean player, another high ball specialist. When all is said and done Dillon was the big man in the Kerry defence.'

'Carbery' was also loud in his praise in the *Cork Examiner*: 'Devlin found Dillon as nimble and lissome as a hare on Connor Hill. Again the Daingean boy played glorious football. It was a treat to watch this pair of 'D's' — watchful as the deities of Olympia.'

According to 'Green Flag' in the *Irish Press* he was also in magnificent form in the drawn game. 'Bill Dillon, the Dingle firebrand, was the hero of the Kerry half-back line in the drawn game and has now been promoted to the centre-half-back berth. Dillon certainly starred last Sunday fortnight and with Myers and Keohane has played even better in the trial games.'

But Bill's prowess as a footballer had its drawbacks. In those days football was only played on Sunday, and that too was the day for hunting. He often made his way down from the mountains just in time to play an important club game. On one occasion a Tralee team was travelling back to play Dingle in a county championship match. Bill was observed on a mountainside with his dogs many miles from Dingle. There was joy in the Tralee camp, as they felt Bill would not be in a fit state for the match, if he got there at all. As the teams warmed up, Bill's figure was noticed over the top of Greenmount, and a runner was quickly despatched to Green Street to get his boots. Bill played in his stockinged feet until the boots arrived and had an outstanding game.

Because of his forays around the mountains Bill was an exceptionally fit man. At

Back, left to right: John Joe Sheehy (Selector), Denis Reidy, Jerry Myles (Joint Hon. Sec. Co. Board), Gerry Fox (Selector), John Hickey (Selector), Jack McCarthy, M. Wade (Selector), Paddy Curran (Selector), Con Brosnan (Selector and Trainer), Inset: Joe Keohane, Charlie O'Sullivan, Michael Lyne.
Centre, left to right: D.J. Baily (Chairman, Co. Board), Tim Landers, Seán Brosnan, Billy Casey, Billy Myers, Jimmy O'Gorman, Ger Teahan, Paddy Kennedy, Murt Kelly, J. Pierce, Mícheál O'Rourke Joint Hon. Sec. Co. Board).
Front, left to right: Johnny Walsh, Eddie Walsh, Dan O'Keefe, Tadhg Healy, Bill Dillon, Paddy 'Bawn' Brosnan, J.J. Falvey, Tom 'Gega' O'Connor.

twenty-two years of age he weighed ten-and-a-half stone. He was 5 feet 10 inches in height. His lack of weight was no disadvantage whatsoever, even in the era of catch and kick. Former colleagues and others who remember him playing testify to him resembling 'a coiled spring' or 'a roll of wire'. He was teak-tough and an exceptional high fielder. He was also one of the few exponents of the one-handed catch. It was the era of full-time training, but Kerry trainer Dr Éamonn O'Sullivan often sent Bill home as he considered him to be super-fit.

Much to his annoyance, his promotion to the Kerry team greatly interfered with his beagling activities. While preparing for the trip to Dublin on the eve of an All-Ireland final Bill would be unapproachable. He found it difficult to conceal his regret at missing out on a day's hunting.

His feelings prior to the Kerry football team's departure to the United States in 1939 compared to those of an emigrant leaving the country for ever.

At the core of it all were his worries over the welfare of his beloved beagles.

One Sunday morning on the steps of St Patrick's Cathedral, Tadhgeen Galvin, a friend of Bill's, wondered where both would be at that hour if they were at home in Dingle. Bill estimated somewhere at the back of Conor Hill, whereupon the two men became very emotional.

Paddy Bawn Brosnan, a teammate on the Kerry team for many years, rated Bill an oustanding half-back.

'He was a great fielder and could kick a ball sixty or seventy yards. I rated him very highly. Bill was a great man for the beagles and spent most of his time outdoors up in the hills, which meant he was very fit. He had to be one of the fittest playing football at the time. We played a lot of football together and I'd say he was one of the first attacking defenders. At that time if you were playing as a half-back you wouldn't be going up the field, as there was no hand to toe, but he was inclined to move up in attack at every opportunity. A grand footballer.'

Although Bill retired from inter-county football following Kerry's defeat by Roscommon in the 1944 All-Ireland final, he continued to line out with Dingle until the early fifties.

Bill Dillon's immense contribution as a footballer is sometimes overlooked when the great names of the thirties and forties are recalled. Yet newspaper reports spanning well over a decade suggest he was unquestionably one of the outstanding defenders of his generation.

Fr Jack McKenna was a lifelong friend of Bill Dillon's and played alongside him on most of Dingle's county championship winning sides. He remembers Bill as a special person and the mainstay of the club team in the golden age of Dingle football. 'He

---

THE 1941 KERRY TEAM

Dan O'Keeffe

Billy Myers	Joe Keohane	Tadhg Healy
Bill Dillon (Captain)	Bill Casey	Eddie Walsh

Seán Brosnan — Paddy Kennedy

Johnny Walsh	Tom 'Gega' O'Connor	Paddy Bawn Brosnan
Jimmy O'Gorman	Murt Kelly	Charlie O'Sullivan

Substitutes: Tim Landers for Billy Myers; Michael Lyne for Johnny Walsh

was a brilliant half-back, and a feature of his play was his athletic spring for a ball, enabling him to land well clear of his opponent with the ball securely in his possession. His long drives down the field to his forwards always put the opposition under pressure.

'Bill was tall and spare, with absolutely no excess weight. He loved the outdoor life — the hills and the valleys of the Dingle Peninsula were his playgrounds and he traversed them regularly with the pack of Dingle beagles. It was a common sight in those days to see Bill on a Sunday morning after early Mass sounding the horn to summon the beagles from all over the town for a day's hunting and then moving off for Conor Hill or Mount Brandon.

'He was one of the most cheerful men on any team he graced. He was a great home bird, his attitude being get to the pitch, play the match and then home. In the county final in 1939, when Dingle were defending their title against Tralee O'Rahillys, Bill scored a remarkable point. There was a gale-force wind blowing and Dingle were battling against it in the second half as the Rahillys were whittling down their half-time lead. Mid way through the half Dingle were awarded a free kick a full sixty yards from the posts. Bill took it and drove the ball into the wind. It never swerved or deviated in any way until it dropped over the bar for a truly memorable point. The match ended in a draw, and sadly Dingle lost the replay.'

As the teams warmed up, Bill's figure was noticed over the top of Greenmount, and a runner was quickly despatched to Green Street to get his boots. Bill played in his stockinged feet until the boots arrived and had an outstanding game.

On Saturday, 19 May 1979 Bill Dillon, while waiting for the morning bus for his weekly outing to Tralee, collapsed and died. He was just two weeks short of his sixty-fourth birthday. By an extraordinary coincidence his death came just hours after Paddy Kennedy's and a matter of weeks after that of another All-Ireland winning Kerryman, Seán Brosnan.

Seán Brosnan, Bill Casey, Bill Dillon with cup, Paddy 'Bawn' Brosnan, Paddy Kennedy, Charlie O'Sullivan and Murt Kelly.

Dan SPRING

Kerry Captain 1940

ONE OF THE most loved and respected of all Kerry men, Dan Spring was full-forward and captain when the Kingdom beat Galway to win the 1940 All-Ireland Football final by one point on the scoreline Kerry 0-7, Galway 1-3. It was the Kingdom's fourteenth All-Ireland and it equalled Dublin's long-standing record that had stood since 1923.

Reports indicate that it was a dogged game played on a slippery pitch in which the defending champions snatched victory in the closing seconds with a point from play by corner-forward Charlie O'Sullivan.

The Kerryman reported the homecoming under the heading, 'Tralee Welcomes Kerry Team' and 'Rejoicing in Strand Street'.

'A large crowd gathered at the Tralee Railway Station on Monday night to welcome the victorious Kerry team and County Board officials on their return with the All-Ireland football title and Sam Maguire Cup.

'Loud cheers were raised as the train steamed in and there were individual ovations for the different players as they emerged from their carriage. The cup was prominently displayed and was carried in triumph from the station to the head of a procession. An escort of torch-bearers fell in after the cup and to the strains of the Strand Street Fife and Drum Band, the cheering crowd marched to Strand Street, the home of O'Rahillys, whose club had the honour for the first time in its history of nominating the captain of a champion Kerry team.

'A huge bonfire blazed at the railway gates in Upper Strand Street and there was much rejoicing. Dan Spring, the Kerry captain who has the custody of the Cup was congratulated on all sides by his neighbours and friends in bringing home the laurels.'

Dan Spring's name was synonymous with political and sporting life in Kerry for over sixty years and his three sons all made their mark at a high level in sport. Dick, the Tánaiste and Minister for Foreign Affairs, won three rugby caps for Ireland as well as playing both football and hurling for Kerry. Dónal, too, was an all-round sportsman and was capped at rugby on seven occasions. Arthur concentrated on

---

FACT FILE

HOME PLACE: Strand Road, Tralee, County Kerry

BORN: 22 July 1910

CLUB: O'Rahilly's, Tralee

CLUB ACHIEVEMENTS: Two County Senior Football Championship medals in 1933 and 1939.

INTER-COUNTY ACHIEVEMENTS: Three All-Ireland Senior Football medals in 1939, 1940. (Won medal as substitute in 1937.) Four Munster Senior Championship medals in 1936, 1937, 1939, 1940. One Railway Cup Football medal

---

Gaelic football in his young days, winning an All-Ireland minor medal with Kerry in 1963. He went on to become a prominent figure in golf, firstly as a player and more recently as a course designer.

The Tánaiste has fond memories of his father who was, he says, 'a big influence in all our lives. He is often described by many of his colleagues both from the football and political point of view as a big man, a big man on the landscape but he was also a big gentleman. I have to say I don't know very much about his football career even though I have often tried to get information from some of his colleagues but I think as time goes by their memories are fading. There are some good stories about trips to America in 1932 when they played in the Polo Grounds in New York. It took them something like six days to cross the Atlantic on the SS *Hamburg* from Cobh and he said that there were fellows trying to jump out the portholes, sick as dogs after a day or two at sea. It was the time of the Depression in America and there wasn't much out there. I suppose there was less in Tralee.

'He enjoyed his football immensely. I know that he was very proud to have played for Kerins O'Rahillys, our famous Tralee team, and of course particularly to be their first captain of an All-Ireland winning Kerry team. There is a sort of a gap in his football career and I often used to query him about that but he never actually answered the question. He had been on the Kerry team in the early thirties and then there was a gap. He never actually told us what happened. Did he fight with the selectors? Did he go out of favour or whatever?

'But he certainly came back in great style in 1939 and 1940. In my Trinity days I used to go down to the basement of the college, pull out the old newspapers and read the accounts of those matches. One man I made a point of meeting one time when I was up in Navan was the 'Boiler' McGuinness with whom he had some great tussles. In fact the 'Boiler' broke two of his ribs in one final. I enjoyed reading those reports.

'My father was quite proud once we played some game. We still played championship football at home and I played for Kerry in hurling and football. Once

Back, left to right: Joe Keohane, Tadhgeen Drummond, Bill Dillon, Bill Myers, Jimmy O'Gorman, Bill Casey, Tadhg Healy, Charlie O'Sullivan, Seán Brosnan, Jerry Beckett, 'Doc' Reidy.
Front, left to right: Eddie Walsh, Dan Spring (captain) (with mascot Harry McCarthy), Danno Keefe, Murt Kelly, Tom 'Gega' O'Connor, Paddy Kennedy, Johnny Walsh.

when someone said, "Bad news your sons playing rugby", he retorted by saying, "Look, if it was good enough for de Valera it's good enough for any of mine. Nobody can say anything, Fianna Fáil or otherwise". He was very proud and he came to all the matches. He was just very pleased that we were involved in sport.

'He had a great influence on my career. I suppose he didn't have to push me towards politics because from very early on I was out on platforms or doing posters with him. He was an amazingly patient man because in those days he used to do all his correspondence in longhand. He would sit at the kitchen table at night time and would write volumes of letters, twenty or thirty, and then it used to be a question of whose turn was it to go out to the local shop to find threepenny stamps. I couldn't sit at a table with three or four children trying to do lessons and at the same time concentrate on my work. But he could do it oblivious of what was around him, yet there in a strong paternal manner. He was quiet but industrious.

My father would have gone to a lot of the club matches, certainly all the Kerins O'Rahillys games. He had a very old friend, Jim Daughton, from the north Kerry area who used to help him at elections, and also in the bog saving turf. Jim had one request and that was for my father to go with him to the Munster hurling final. It was an annual pilgrimage. On one occasion during the war they went to Thurles in John O'Donnell's car as my father didn't own one. Two priests, along with my father and mother set off for Thurles and before they returned had seventeen punctures. They never got to the game and had to listen to the match on a radio in a pub or a house a few miles from Thurles. But they pretended on their return to have been at the game.

'He got particular satisfaction during the GAA's Centenary celebrations when the All-Ireland captains were introduced on the field. He possibly would have liked if we had continued to play Gaelic but at the same time there was never a remark made or otherwise that he was disappointed in that respect.

'There was a corner-forward for Kerry in my father's time, Charlie O'Sullivan, and in later years when he joined the Garda Síochána he used to be on point duty outside Trinity College. I remember any time my father came to Dublin he would roll down the window and exchange greetings with his old friend of many years. It was heartwarming. His form of relaxation on vacation was going out saving turf which was a big thing in his life to get away from it all.'

Dan Spring was a Labour TD from 1943 until 1981 when Dick took over his seat. It was always inevitable that one of the family was going to enter politics because the feeling always was that if a Spring did not stand the seat would be lost. Dónal remembers his father as a physically very strong man who 'always had time to kick a ball around with us. One way he had an influence on all of us was that you never

---

THE 1940 KERRY TEAM		
	Dan O'Keeffe	
Bill Myers	Joe Keohane	Tadhg Healy
Bill Dillon	Bill Casey	Eddie Walsh
Seán Brosnan		Johnny Walsh
Jimmy O'Gorman	Tom 'Gega' O'Connor	Paddy Kennedy
Murt Kelly	Dan Spring (Captain)	Charlie O'Sullivan
Substitute: Paddy Bawn Brosnan for Dan Spring		

dared to show fear whether you were playing a game of football or were just kicking the ball around in the back yard. He hated to see guys "funking" the ball. That was the word he used. It's a real Kerry word. He believed you should never hide from anything. One thing he couldn't bear was to see guys who were cowardly on the pitch. In life there were always guys of different shades and he was never a man to have any prejudice whatsoever but on the football pitch he couldn't stand cowardly players. He wasn't a great lover of fancy players either. I remember a particular Kerry footballer one day wore white football boots in Austin Stack Park and my dad didn't stop talking about those boots for a week.

'He was tremendously popular with all his friends. The abiding memory for me in an ironic way was his funeral. I could not believe the effect he had on people.

'He always loved going to the football matches and in his later days had an even greater passion for hurling. The last match I was at with him was when Dublin beat Kerry in the National League final at Croke Park some time in April 1987.'

The few times Dónal succeeded in getting his father to talk about the good old days he would concentrate mainly on some funny incidents that had happened. He also liked to reflect on the days when forwards could charge the goalkeeper. He himself was a big man and got particular pleasure out of that part of the game.

> 'He hated to see guys "funking" the ball. That was the word he used. It's a real Kerry word. He believed you should never hide from anything.'

'I think he felt football was getting soft compared to when he played. He used to love having a go off us when the three of us came home from playing for Kerins O'Rahillys. I remember one time we played against Lispole in the West Kerry final and they beat us and all we heard from him during tea was, "there was a time when one Spring could beat Lispole, now three Springs are getting hammered by Lispole". He got great pleasure out of saying that and that was the end of the conversation. He had huge affection for the Dingle area and a lot of that had to do with the people he played football against. He loved going back to see Bill Dillon, Paddy Bawn and people like that. It used to be part of the constituency until it was taken away at one stage, it was believed in an effort to try to get his seat, but that didn't work.

'He stood for thirteen general elections and defended the seat, sometimes with very small margins against all sorts of onslaughts. Every election I remember as a kid, Dan Spring's seat was marked down as a possible loss. It became a standing joke and of course he was delighted once they kept saying that.

'I suppose deep down he must have been a little bit disappointed that none of us really stuck to the football as much as we might have but he never complained about it. I think he got a certain pride out of the fact that in the other sports that we played we had a certain amount of success and he enjoyed going to Lansdowne Road.'

Dan Spring never got involved in the GAA after he quit playing. According to Dónal he had a cold attitude towards some of the people running the organisation. He felt too many of the people involved at high level were professional committee men rather than sportsmen.

Dan Spring had to retire injured in the 1940 All-Ireland final and was replaced by Paddy Bawn Brosnan who has fond memories of his captain.

'I played on many occasions against Dan in the Kerry county championships and we had some great tussles. He was a hard man to mark. He used to play at full-forward for Kerins O'Rahillys and I was full-back with my club, Dingle. I also played a good few games with him on the Kerry team. He was a very good player and then of course you'd have your work cut because he was such a big strong man, about six foot three. He was also a great man to kick a score.

'Dan got hurt in the All-Ireland final and I came on in his place in the second half. I had hurt my leg before the 1939 All-Ireland semi-final so Dan took over my place and won an All-Ireland medal. He was older than us and was coming near the end of his career in 1940 so he didn't play much for the county after that although he continued to play for his club.

'Dan was a gentleman, a very nice man and we were great friends. I enjoyed his company and we had some great times.'